Families at Work

Families at Work
Expanding the Boundaries

Edited by: *Naomi Gerstel*
Dan Clawson
Robert Zussman

Vanderbilt University Press
Nashville

© 2002 Vanderbilt University Press

First Edition 2002

This book is printed on acid-free paper.
Manufactured in the United States of America

Library of Congress Cataloging-in-Publication Data

Families at work : expanding the boundaries / edited by : Naomi
Gerstel, Dan Clawson, Robert Zussman.— 1st ed.
    p. cm.
    ISBN 0-8265-1397-2 (cloth : alk. paper)
    ISBN 0-8265-1398-0 (paper : alk. paper)
    1. Work and family. 2. Husbands—Employment. 3. Husbands
Attitudes. 4. Fathers—Employment. 5. Fathers—Attitudes.
I. Gerstel, Naomi. II. Clawson, Dan. III. Zussman, Robert.
HD4904.25 .F359 2001
306.3'6—dc21
                                           2002001702

Contents

Preface

Naomi Gerstel, Dan Clawson, and Robert Zussman

Not so long ago, it all seemed very obvious. The dissolution of the household economy—of family farms, "mom and pop" stores, family businesses—separated much work from families. This separation was both spatial and normative. Home became what many came to see as homelike ("home sweet home") because it appeared to specialize in love, between wife and husband, parent and child. Work became work precisely to the degree that it involved the grubby calculations and relentless rationalization of the factory and office. In this understanding, which took hold in the middle of the nineteenth century and held sway in much of the twentieth, connections between family and work were merely external, a series of exchanges in which the family provided labor to a market economy which, in turn, provided income to the family. A good relationship between work and family was taken to be one in which each remained as separate from the other as possible.

For a long century, the separation of work and family, in practice and in belief, seemed both natural and inevitable. Moreover, the separation of work and family was accompanied by a number of assumptions, assumptions celebrated in popular culture and without challenge from the social sciences. One of these assumptions was that the separation between paid work and family would be accompanied by a differentiation between women and men. Men, working for pay, would be specialists in rationality, in instrumentality. Women, staying at home, would be specialists in emotion and nurturance. A second assumption was that the relationship between work and family could and would be free of conflict, that a basic function of the family was to manage any tension, that power relations between employer and employed husband, between husbands and wives, between parents and their children would not create serious frictions, resentment, or exploitation. A third assumption was that the only kind of family that mattered—the kind everyone aspired to, the only one that would be viable in the modern world—was the nuclear family. Other family forms—single parent or extended kin, for example—appeared either as pathology or as relics of some quickly disappearing past. A fourth assumption was that only paid work, only work absorbed into market relations, counted as work. Unpaid work within the family—making meals, taking care of children, calling, writing, inviting relatives, cleaning toilets, fixing leaky faucets, taking out the trash—became invisible.

Today, it no longer seems so obvious. The separation of work and family seems neither natural nor inevitable. Most important, women have joined the paid labor force in unprecedented numbers. Over the last 30 years alone, the rate of labor force participation among all married women has grown from 43% to 62%; among married mothers with children 17 or younger it has gone from under 40% to over 70%. Under these conditions, the old assumptions simply do not hold. The differences between men and women—in the kind of work they do, in the kinds of skills they possess, in the kinds of emotions they express—seem to be in steady retreat. We have come to see that employment creates endless tensions for families, and families create endless tensions for the workplace. The nuclear family no longer enjoys the prominence, numerical or ideological, that it enjoyed even a few decades ago. And social scientists–along with uncounted women and men overwhelmed by their responsibilities at home and at work, have taken to calculating the economic (and moral) value of housework of all sorts.

This book is an attempt to make sense of the new relationship between work and family occasioned by, above all else, the rise of women's employment (especially white middle-class married women's employment). Let there be no mistake about it: Work and family have always been connected, even at those moments when they appeared most separate. What has changed is the character and conception of that connection.

The title of this book, *Families at Work*, needs some explanation. First, this book is about "families," not "family." Family, in the singular, is an ideological formulation, implying a unity of experience that no longer exists and probably never existed. Families, in the plural, recognizes variations among families—over time, among groups, among individual families, and for individuals within families. Second, this book is about "families at work," not "families and work." "Families and work" implies that work and family are separate, that they occupy different places and different times. "Families at work" is meant to convey a more intimate connection between family and work, that a great deal of work (much of it unpaid) goes on within the household and has the family itself as its object. The phrase "families at work" is also meant to suggest that families are themselves under construction, that they are involved in a more or less constant process of creating and re-creating themselves.

The first section of this book examines the construction and reconstruction of gender for women and men called on to combine families with work in historically new ways. The second section turns to child care. The third section looks at the ways that families and work, both paid and unpaid, are embedded within and shaped by a community context. And the fourth section looks at working families in the still broader context of politics and policies.

This book began with Gerstel's and Clawson's participation in the national conference on "Work and Family: Expanding the Horizons" in San Francisco in spring, 2000. Zussman invited Gerstel and Clawson to solicit what they thought to be interesting articles from that conference for a special issue of *Qualitative Sociology*, which Zussman edits. That special issue, which appeared in December 2000, included the articles by Cooper, Lareau, Kurz, Oliker, Gerstel, DeVault, and Klatch that are reprinted here. The other articles and chapters—Yodanis and Carrington in part one; Deutsch, Hondagneu-Sotelo and Avila, and Uttal in part two; Pattillo-McCoy and Nelson in part three; and Scott, London and Meyers as well as Gerstel and Clawson in part four—that appear in this collection were selected to develop the framework and agenda of *Families at Work*.

The editors would like to thank Michael Ames, Anita Garey, Mary Ann Clawson, Laura Clawson, and an anonymous reviewer for their helpful comments, as well as Kate Zussman Gerstel for her patience.

Part One
Family Labor and the Construction of Gender

To think about the relationship of work and family is to think about gender. Until recently, studying work within families seemed to mean studying women (just as studying paid employment seemed to mean studying men). The massive increase in women's employment has changed all that. By the end of the twentieth century, 65% of all women, 70% of married women, and 72% of unmarried mothers with children under 18 were employed at some point during the year. Less than 20% of married couples were "traditional" in the sense that only the husband was employed.

As women, especially married women with children, participate in the labor force in numbers almost equal to men, there has been a parallel pressure for men to increase their share of work within the family. Not only liberal feminists but also men-only social movements directed toward family, like the Promise Keepers, the Million Man March on Washington, the Mythopoetic movement, and various fathers' rights groups, have urged men to accept new responsibilities. So far, however, most evidence suggests that changes in the rhetoric of masculinity have outstripped changes in its practice. Have increases in women's paid work outside the home led to changes in the division of labor inside the home? So far, the answer is that they have, but only a very little.

Although employed women do less than they used to, women, regardless of their employment, continue to do most of the work in the home. Attitudes toward this division of labor are clearly more egalitarian now than they were in previous decades. Nonetheless, neither men's fathering nor men's housework has kept pace with attitudinal changes.

There is little agreement about how to explain such intransigence in the allocation of family work. A few, mostly much cited near classics, explain the division of labor by the continuing force of early socialization. Others explain it by men's and women's divergent positions in adulthood.[1] Most important, paid work reinforces gendered expectations about who should do what kind of work. In the context of labor markets that remain segregated by gender, different kinds of jobs allow men and women more or less time, energy, and flexibility for domestic work. Moreover, while nearly as many women as men are now holding jobs, women continue to earn less than men. As a result, women and men may enter into an implicit contract wherein a woman exchanges household labor for economic support from a man, who, if no longer the *only* breadwinner, remains the *primary* breadwinner.

Yet another set of explanations for the tenacity of the division of labor within the family can be grouped around the concept of gender construction. Men and women are not equally involved in family work because their different efforts—men on the job, women in the home—affirm and reproduce gendered selves. These different efforts help create and reinforce a sense of masculinity or femininity. Thus, by performing different work, men and women actively "do gender" (West and Fenstermaker, 1993).

Of course, neither socialization nor gender contracts nor gender construction operates independently. The gender construction approach, for example, posits active agents making choices but acknowledges the limitations imposed on those choices by social structure and imbalances of power (Ferree, 1991; Coltrane, 2001). All the articles in this section analyze the ways in which ongoing job demands and the reproduction of gender operate simultaneously.

Part of a rapidly growing literature on fatherhood (Marsiglio et al., 2001), the first two papers in this section focus primarily on men. Both contribute to our understanding of the processes underlying the allocation of domestic labor in which mothers do more family work. Both ask not only how much fathers do but why they do not do more. Both emphasize the ongoing construction, and reconstruction, of masculinity as a means to resist demands for labor at home.

In "Being the 'Go-To Guy,'" Marianne Cooper analyzes an emergent Silicon Valley high-tech masculinity, hegemonic at least within the glamour industries of northern California. As one respondent told her, "Guys constantly try to out-macho each other, but in engineering it's really perverted because out-machoing someone means being more of a nerd than the other person." It is a masculinity bolstered not only by job demands on time and energy but also by a nascent workplace ideology of gender. Nerd-macho depends in part on a willingness to work extraordinarily long hours, on the "amazing effort" of "a real man" who works 90 hour a week, not "a slacker" who works only 50 hours a week. This new masculinity, like the self and fatherhood it helps construct, functions as a mechanism of control in, and for the benefit of, the technology industry. And it requires a commitment that excludes family responsibilities for all but a very small number of exhausted superdads.

Examining northeastern workers in a range of jobs, Annette Lareau discovers still other ways that fathers avoid family responsibilities. Lareau, however, focuses not only on what fathers don't do but also on what they actually do. In particular, fathers do help make the family a center of entertainment and play.

Lareau demonstrates that fathers are not a good source of information about behavior within families. Their lack of involvement limits their knowledge. They are, however, an indispensable source of information about the ideology of parenthood, particularly fatherhood. The fathers Lareau interviewed could have responded to her questions about their children by saying, "I don't know," "Ask my wife," or "I'm not involved in that." They don't. Men, Lareau argues, are ideologically committed at least to appearing involved in nurturing activity. They make up stuff; they appropriate their wives' and kids' knowledge as their own; they appropriate their wives' work as their own. It is a powerful statement that men no longer believe it enough to be a good provider, even if they (and their wives) have not figured out what it is they should be. Lareau's work shows that fathers continue to dominate, but this is not old-fashioned domination—the father brought in to discipline the kids, the ultimate source of authority, made all the stronger by his absence—but a much modernized form of domination that involves teasing, the delegation of authority, and presence. These new forms of domination still generate privilege, even if it is not privilege of exactly the same sort as before.

Fathers find themselves curiously silent on matters of family life. Lareau had trouble getting her fathers to give details of family life, even though they spoke expansively about other aspects of their lives. Cooper found that the fathers she interviewed kept quiet about family responsibilities, silenced by a logic of the market that reinstates the priorities of paid work over family as the center of a new masculinity.

Just as Cooper and Lareau try to understand why men do not do family work, Carrie Yodanis tries to understand why women do not do certain kinds of paid work. In her article, "Constructing Gender and Occupational Segregation: Women and Work in Fishing Communities," Yodanis focuses on a rural community, a fishing village on a peninsula in the northern Atlantic Ocean, a type of community and family business rarely represented in studies of families and work. In this village, most fishing is done by men who are owner-operators. Their wives serve as "shore captains." Fishing, then, is a good example of the "two-person career," which sociologists developed as a concept to explain the labor of the housewife who preceded the superwomen. As Yodanis suggests, the work of the supportive wife may even have expanded with the advent of new technologies, especially cell phones, as their fishermen husbands call wives to perform a host of work-related tasks. Relying on a gender construction approach, Yodanis argues that women's exclusion from fishing, the most lucrative employment in the area, is not the result of overt discrimination. "Not being a fisherman is at the core of what it is to be a woman in a fishing community. Women, by separating themselves from fishing, are defining themselves as women."

In "Domesticity and the Political Economy of Lesbigay Families," Christopher Carrington examines the division of family work among gay and lesbian couples. His discussion of the effect of employment on the household division of labor in lesbian and gay families addresses issues of gender construction and caring labor outside the usual framework of heterosexual couples; it thus allows us to see clearly the role of structural factors in the issue of "who does what." At the same time, by focusing on lesbian and gay families, Carrington's article helps to destigmatize the discussion of these couples *as families.*

Carrington finds that the families he studied often present (and perhaps perceive) themselves as egalitarian. Few, however, meet that ideal. Processes very similar to those operating in straight families operate in lesbigay families: Job demands shape the division of domestic labor. The partner who does more paid work does less of the unpaid family work. Given the association of domesticity with femininity and paid jobs with masculinity, some of the women (dedicated to their careers) and some of the men (dedicated to their homes) find they must compensate for the choices they make. Often, with the help of their partners, they make jokes, express guilt, or conceal the inequality they enjoy or deploy.

The small number of families who do manage to become egalitarian either downsize or are affluent enough to purchase domestic services in the market. The affluent gay and lesbian couples that Carrington describes buy domestic labor (from the equivalents of the poor women whom Hondagneu-Sotelo and Avila discuss in the next section of this book). This dependence on domestic service is remarkably similar to the situation of women in the emerging middle class of the nineteenth century. In short, Carrington's analysis shows how what we think of as "family" is made possible by affluence, especially for those on the margins of social life.

Note

1. For reviews, see Lorber, 1994; Risman, 1998; and Connell, 1995. For classics see Chodorow, 1978; and Gilligan, 1982.

References

Chodorow, N. (1978). *The reproduction of mothering.* Berkeley: University of California Press.

Coltrane, S. (2001). Research on household labor: Modeling and measuring the social embeddedness of routine family work. *Journal of Marriage and the Family, 62,* 1208-1233.

Connell, R. W. (1995). *Masculinities.* Berkeley: University of California Press.

Ferree, M. M. (1991). The gender division of labor in two earner marriages. *Journal of Family Issues, 12,* 158-179.

Gilligan, C. (1982). *In a different voice.* Cambridge: Harvard University Press.

Lorber, J. (1994). *Paradoxes of gender.* New Haven: Yale University Press.

Marsiglio, W., Amato, P., Day, R., & Lamb, M. E. (2001). Scholarship on fatherhood in the 1990s and beyond. *Journal of Marriage and the Family, 62,* 1173-1191.

Risman, B. (1998). *Gender vertigo.* New Haven: Yale University Press.

West, C., & Fenstermaker, S. (1993). Power and the accomplishment of gender. In Paula England (Ed.), *Theory on gender/feminism on theory.* New York: A. de Gruyter.

1
Being the "Go-To Guy"

Fatherhood, Masculinity, and the Organization of Work in Silicon Valley

Marianne Cooper

Driving down a busy freeway into the heart of Silicon Valley, one sees billboards everywhere heralding the arrival of the new economy. Ads for e-mailing, high-speed Internet connections, and dot.com job openings permeate the skyline. Even a sign for *Forbes* magazine announces, "High octane capitalism ahead." While it is undeniable that the new economy is here, it is also undeniable that this is largely a male endeavor. A recent report by the American Association of University Women (2000) found that women make up only about 20 percent of information technology professionals and that they receive less than 28 percent of the bachelor's degrees in computer science. In fact, Silicon Valley itself is often referred to as the "Valley of the Boys," an appropriate adage now that San Jose boasts the highest number of available single men in the country, surpassing Alaska (Conlin, 2000).

It is within this male-dominated, turbo-capitalism environment that the fathers I interviewed negotiate their work and family lives. The intent of my study was to explore the mostly ignored experiences of working fathers. What I discovered through my examination of these men's work and family lives was the emergence of a newly constituted masculinity that coincides with the new way work is organized in the new economy. Two questions addressing both sides of the work-family equation flowed from this discovery: How does this new masculinity articulate with processes of labor control? And how does it articulate with processes of family life, particularly fathering? Thus my findings are twofold. First, they show that as a gendered construct, this new masculinity functions as a key mechanism of control in high-tech workplaces that rely on identity-based forms of control. Second, they show that the successful enactment of this new masculinity shapes how these fathers both think about and manage their work and family lives.

Methods

Many researchers report difficulty in recruiting men to participate in studies of this kind (Daly, 1992). However, men eagerly responded to my interview request. I obtained a sample of 20 fathers through various methods. Through friends and acquaintances I sent out an E-mail message requesting one-hour interviews with fathers working in high-tech companies to discuss how they balance work and family life. I also sent the same E-mail message to the parents' list server at one large company and a university. I received more than 30 E-mail responses. I ruled out those who were self-employed, since I wanted to get information about workplace culture, interactions with coworkers, etc. I ruled in knowledge workers who seemed to have significant industry experience in a variety of companies as well as those who worked for well-known companies in Silicon Valley. I conducted semistructured open-ended interviews with the 20 participants. The interviews took place at cafés, homes, and workplaces and lasted between 1 and 2 hours. All interviews were tape-recorded and fully transcribed.

The interviewees work in all different types and sizes of high-tech companies. While some work for large companies that make millions of dollars a year, others work for small start-ups. Thirteen interviewees are software engineers, one is a service engineer, one is an engineering project manager, three are in sales/business development/management, and two are computer researchers.

My informants ranged in age from 30 to 44; the average age was 37. Though incomes ranged from $60,000 to $200,000, most were concentrated in the $80,000 to $150,000 range. Except for one informant who was MexicanAmerican and did not have a bachelor's degree, the rest were white and held college degrees. Three participants had Ph.D.s, two had MBAs, three had master's degrees in computer science, and one had a master's degree in math. All fathers are currently married. Seven of their spouses work full-time, four work part-time, three are students, and six are stay-at-home mothers.

A New Masculinity for the New Economy

In recent years, there has been a growing interest in the definition and practice of masculinity reflected by the emergence of the "New Men's Studies" (Carrigan, Connell, & Lee, 1985; Brod & Kaufman, 1994; Connell, 1995). Much of this scholarship draws upon R. W. Connell's theory of hegemonic masculinity. For Connell, hegemonic masculinity "is the configuration of gender practices which embodies the currently accepted answer to the problem of legitimacy of patriarchy, which guarantees (or is taken to guarantee) the dominant position of men and the subordination of women" (1995, p. 77). While there is a hegemonic form of masculinity, which in the United States could be seen as a rich, good-looking, popular, athletic, white, heterosexual man, masculinity is not unitary or homogeneous. Rather, there are "multiple masculinities," some subordinate and some dominant, which are created by differences in ethnicity, race, class, sexual orientation, age, and occupation (Connell, 1987).[1] Even hegemonic forms of masculinity are historically and locally contingent. As Connell points out, hegemonic masculinity "is not a fixed character type, always and everywhere the same. It is, rather, the masculinity that occupies the hegemonic position in a given pattern of gender relations, a position always contestable" (1995, p. 76).

Given that the form and content of hegemonic masculinity is dependent upon the social and historical context in which it operates, it follows that the Silicon Valley context should shape the particular type of masculinity found in the high-tech world of the new economy. Indeed, scholars have already established that technical knowledge and expertise are socially defined as masculine (Cockburn, 1988; Turkle, 1984, 1988; Hacker, 1990) and that within these male domains computing cultures possess a specific masculinity (Wright, 1996; Kendall, 1999, 2000). For example, Wright found that the masculinity characteristic of engineering and computer cultures is one "requiring aggressive displays of technical self-confidence and hands-on ability for success, defining professional competence in hegemonically masculine terms and devaluing the gender characteristics of women" (p. 86); Kendall (2000) found that the masculinity enacted by young male participants in an online interactive text–based forum was constructed around a "nerd" identity, characterized by qualities like fascination with technology and real or perceived social ineptitude.

This nerd masculinity, common in the high-tech world, is glorified in depictions of Silicon Valley life. Even the success story of the founders of Silicon Valley is a phenomenon often referred to as "The Revenge of the Nerds." Men who in their youth were marginalized for being geeks and nerds came back as adults to get the last laugh. Using their intellect, they launched a technological revolution and in the process of changing the world became very rich and very powerful.

The consequence of the facts that technology is the foundation of the new economy and that those who participate in it enact a masculinity which diverges from traditional masculinity is the emergence of a newly constituted masculinity in the Valley. Here, technical skill and brilliance are more important than looks and athletic ability. In the Valley, competition isn't waged on the basketball court or by getting girls. Here men compete in cubicles to see who can work more hours, who can cut the best code, and who can be most creative and innovative. As one interviewee put it:

> Guys constantly try to out-macho each other, but in engineering it's really perverted because out-machoing someone means being more of a nerd than the other person. It's really geeky. It's really sad. It's not like being a brave firefighter and going up one more flight than your friend. There's a lot of see how many hours I can work whether or not you have a kid. That's part of the thing, how many hours you work. He's a real man; he works 90-hour weeks. He's a slacker; he works 50 hours a week. (Scott Webster)

Moreover, high-tech companies are organized in ways that deviate from traditional masculinity. Because it is believed that bureaucratically organized companies stifle creativity and out-of-the-box thinking, typical high-tech companies have a flat hierarchy and a less rigid and austere workplace culture (Kunda, 1992; Burris, 1998). Furthermore, these companies embrace managerial discourses that champion teamwork, adaptability, open communication, and creativity. These qualities run counter to traditionally masculine practices. Alvesson (1998) makes this point, noting that in knowledge-intensive jobs,

> there may be limited space for employment of many of the traditionally used sources of male power and male identity associated with bureaucracy and rationality. New discourses advocated by management theorists as well as by corporate practitioners instead con-

struct work and organizations in terms of creativity, intuition, flexibility, flattened hierarchy, social interaction, and team building, etc. (p. 2)

Thus, the Valley is based upon a masculinity that corresponds with what the technology industry needs to satiate and expand its markets.

Ideological reasons, and in some cases biographical ones as well, also underpin this new masculinity. All of the high-tech workers I spoke with profess an egalitarian gender ideology in regard to women in the workforce. They feel it is important for more women to go into the high-tech industry, and many of the fathers I interviewed wished they worked with more women. In fact, in an effort to diversify their teams, several said that they go out of their way to recruit women, extending searches longer than necessary to try to find qualified women candidates.

To be sure, the majority of my sample perceive themselves to be qualitatively different from other men in terms of their more enlightened personal attitudes toward and relationships with women. This self-perception is evident through comparisons the interviewees make between themselves and men who they feel are sexist or stereotypically macho.

> I don't drive a pick-up truck and wear tattoos. I'm very modern. I believe in sharing the household work and believe that my wife's career is important. (Rich Kavelin)

> Communication is something that is important to us. So when something goes wrong, when we have a disagreement or a misunderstanding, my wife feels doubly hurt. Because she thinks, well, we put such a value on trying to communicate and it failed. I think it makes it worse than if she were married to Joe Six-Pack. (Jay Masterson)

Many interviewees also separated themselves from frat boys and locker room guys, men who they think are sexist and hostile toward women; that's not what kind of men they are. Unlike stereotypical working-class men who openly degrade women and put them down, these men actually feel virtuous for not being sexist like them or completely ignorant about emotions and relationships like most men. These interviewees think of themselves as "modern," not frat boys; progressive, not stupid jocks.

Biography may also underpin this new masculinity. Though not a focal point of my study, my perception is that as nerds, approximately two thirds of my sample were victims of traditional hegemonic masculinity in their earlier lives. Accordingly, they may also have personal as well as ideological reasons to oppose a traditionally macho masculinity.

Taken together, type of work, ideology, and, in some cases, biography work against the form of masculinity that remains dominant in much of society. Nonetheless, there is still a hegemonic masculinity in the new economy, but one that takes on somewhat different characteristics. Though the essence of this masculinity is rooted in technical expertise, its other characteristics involve working a lot of hours and working with a small team of *great* people to get things done. James McNichol and Scott Webster, both software engineers, describe the team dynamic:

> James: It's like a sports team, not in the sense of locker room, but in the sense that there is just a natural order, and everybody gets their place and you work together. There are lots of models that boys grow up with for how that kind of team works and what you do and don't do, like not questioning the coach. And there's a lot of doing and thinking about it afterwards instead of considering the options beforehand. It's not an articulate culture.

> Scott: The key element of this whole environment is the team mentality. It's an idea derived from male tradition probably. Even as a contractor you have to live with it, too. You have to be part of the team. You can't fall out. If you get injured, you come back as fast as you can or you play with your injury whether it's emotional or physical.

The successful enactment of this masculinity involves displaying one's exhaustion, physically and verbally, in order to convey the depth of one's commitment, stamina, and virility.

> Engineers have this idea that you are out there and you are building something, and these small companies are going to do huge things, and lots of people are going to get rich, and it's gonna happen because we are great. Even under normal circumstances, when there are no extraordinary demands, you see people working 36 hours straight just because they are going to meet the deadline. They are going to get it done, and everybody walks around proud of how exhausted they were last week and conspicuously putting in wild hours. It's a status thing to have pizza delivered to the office. So I don't know why it happens, but I really feel like it is kind of a machismo thing: I'm tough. I can do this thing. Yeah, I'm tired, but I'm on top of it. You guys don't worry about me. I can get my thing done. . . . The people who conspicuously overwork are guys, and I think it's usually for the benefit of other guys. (Kirk Sinclair)

Theoretically, the knowledge work these men do is gender-neutral. As opposed to manual work that requires physical strength, knowledge work requires only mental ability. Therefore, either men or women can perform knowledge work. Yet, as Leidner (1993) found and the above quotations illustrate, most jobs can be constructed as either masculine or feminine by emphasizing certain aspects of the job and de-emphasizing and reinterpreting other dimensions. The gendering of jobs that are potentially gender-neutral illustrates how gender is constructed through work and how gendered subjectivities are formed. In this case, masculinity is constructed by imbuing knowledge work with a masculine sensibility that isn't intrinsic to the work. Willis (1977) found a similar trend among working-class men.

> Manual labour is suffused with masculine qualities. . . . The toughness and awkwardness of physical work and effort—for itself and in the division of labour and for its strictly capitalist logic quite without intrinsic heroism and grandeur—takes on masculine lights and depths and assumes a significance beyond itself. Whatever the specific problems, so to speak, of the difficult task, they are always essentially masculine problems. It takes masculine capacities to deal with them. . . . The brutality of the working situation is partially reinterpreted into a heroic exercise of manly confrontation with *the task*. Difficult, uncomfortable or dangerous conditions are seen, not for themselves, but for their appropriateness to a masculine readiness and hardiness. (p. 150)

The same male "readiness and hardiness" is both needed and glorified in high-tech knowledge work as well.

> There's a certain glamour to heroic efforts. If you look at a well-managed company that delivers a reliable product on time with no fuss, there's no talk of it. But the release of an important product becomes lore when the engineering team worked for a week solid to get it done. Those kind of amazing efforts are talked about. (Kirk Sinclair)

Remarkably, poor planning is reinterpreted as a test of will, a test of manhood for a team of engineers (men). Sheer determination and strength of character achieve the task, releasing a product on time. Presented with an overwhelming challenge, it takes masculine capabilities to complete the mission, to overcome the odds.

A "masculine mystique" permeates descriptions of what the interviewees do at work (Collinson & Hearn, 1996a). It's as if these men are digital warriors, out conquering enemies, surmounting insurmountable odds in their quest to win. The interpretation of this work in such masculine terms points to the "doing of gender" in everyday social interactions (West & Zimmerman, 1987). Here, masculinity is performed and achieved by infusing the work with masculine meanings that convey to others one's internal strength, competitive spirit, and ability to get the job done.

Gender and the Labor Process

Not surprisingly, the new masculinity and the workplace practices associated with the achievement of this gendered subjectivity benefit the technology industry. Technical brilliance, innovation, creativity, independent work ethics, long hours, and complete dedication to projects are the main requirements for companies trying to position themselves on the cutting edge. This link between gendered subjectivity and labor process conditions suggests that masculinity may then be a way to control worker's participation in the labor process. Despite the likely link between gender and strategies of control, scholars have noted the absence of research about gender in organizations and about how gender works in the dynamic processes of consent and control (Kanter, 1977; Acker, 1990; Collinson, 1992; Collinson & Hearn, 1996b; Pierce, 1996; Alvesson & Billing, 1997; Lee, 1998).

Ignoring gender, most labor process theorists have instead focused on class-based forms of worker control (Braverman, 1974; Edwards, 1979; Burawoy, 1979, 1985). Lee (1998) addresses this lack of gender analysis and develops a feminist theory of production politics that takes account of the role gender plays in the development of control strategies. Lee's theory argues that "factory regimes are gendered institutions in which gender is a central and primary organizing principle of production politics" (p. 165).[2] Lee draws upon Acker's (1992) definition, which states that a gendered institution is one in which "gender is present in the processes, practices, images and ideologies, and distributions of power in the various sectors of social life" (p. 567). In applying feminist theory to the shop floor, Lee argues that "production relations rely on gender ideology, organization, and identity, factors that also shape the terms and forms of production politics" (p. 165). Lee's addition of a gendered analysis to a literature focused on class challenges the primacy given to class in labor process accounts. In doing so, she refutes Burawoy's claim that labor process activities are "independent of the particular people who come to work, of the particular agents of production" (1979, p. 202).[3]

With labor process scholars looking at how gender works on the shop floor (Collinson 1992; Lee 1998), it would make sense for scholars concerned with identity-based forms of control to pay attention also to gender, a key aspect of an individual's identity. Identity-based forms of control, or what Etzioni (1961) termed normative control, is control that works by laying claim to the workers' sense of self, engendering in them a deep personal commitment to the goals and values of the company. As stated by Kunda (1992):

> [U]nder normative control, membership is founded not only on the behavioral or economic transaction traditionally associated with work organizations, but, more crucially, on an experiential transaction, one in which symbolic rewards are exchanged for a moral orientation to the organization. In this transaction a member role is fashioned and imposed that includes not only behavioral rules but articulated guidelines for experience. In short, under normative control it is the employee's self—that ineffable source of subjective experience—that is claimed in the name of the corporate interest. (p. 11)

Thus this type of control is a self-surveilling one which monitors work behavior by eliciting thoughts, feelings, and emotions that correspond with the interests of the company. However, research on normative control has not looked through a gendered lens (Edwards, 1979; O'Reilly & Chatman, 1986; Kunda, 1992). Instead, it has focused on mechanisms through which organizations attain identity-based consent, like strong workplace cultures, and on the characteristics of the organizational identity without discussing what the gender, racial, or class dimensions of this identity might be.

Kunda (1992) is particularly guilty of this omission in his ethnography of normative control in the engineering division of a high-tech company. Though Kunda convincingly illustrates how the company engineered its culture so as to create a member role that was internalized by employees, his analysis omits the way in which gender intersects with corporate culture, giving rise to a particular type of normative control operating in this firm. In fact, there is no mention that men overwhelmingly dominate engineering divisions. Therefore, Kunda makes the same mistake many other labor theorists do. His argument rests on the assumption that a workplace comprised mostly of men is actually gender-neutral.

Even though Kunda's ethnography is ostensibly not about gender in organizations, it could be read as such. Mumbly (1998) provides this alternative reading, arguing that Kunda unwittingly offers an analysis of the social construction of white-collar masculinity. Through a comparison with Collinson's (1992) ethnography of working-class masculinity, Mumbly highlights the gendered dynamics that Kunda disregards. Mumbly notes that the self-identity of these engineers is so embedded in their work that there is almost no distinction between their private and public selves. Indeed, he illustrates how the acceptance and enactment of organizational membership can lead to a devaluation of family life and can, in its extreme, cause burnout. The type of masculinity constructed among these engineers is rooted in technical expertise, mental ability, and mental, emotional, and physical endurance, not physical prowess. Ultimately, Mumbly illuminates what Kunda doesn't see—that masculine subjectivities are created and constructed through participation in the labor process itself, that normative control is gendered.

Both Mumbly and Lee offer correctives to the literature on the labor process by asserting that gendered discourses, practices, and ideologies are of primary importance in the organization of work. Moreover, they point out that conceptions of masculinity and femininity are reflected in the way work is organized. As workers enter "gendered institutions," they come into contact with specific understandings of femininity and masculinity. They must then negotiate their own gendered subjectivity within the context of an institutional setting.

Masculinity: The Invisible Control Strategy

High-tech companies rely on normative control to manage the white-collar, or knowledge, workers they employ for three reasons. First, with such a tight labor market, workers are not dependent on any one company for the reproduction of their labor power. Consequently, more coercive tactics, already thought to be incompatible with managing educated and highly skilled workers, are untenable because employees would just leave oppressive work environments. Second, normative control is seen to be well-suited to companies that want to encourage creativity and innovation, characteristics which aren't associated with coercive, technical, or bureaucratic styles of control (Kunda & Van Maanen, 1999). Third, at this point in the technological revolution, the member role and work behaviors that high-tech companies seek are so pervasive and diffuse throughout Silicon Valley itself that little articulation of these practices is needed in order to guide workers' thoughts and actions. Dylan Fitzgerald describes this collective consciousness:

> My sense is that being in Silicon Valley that [the culture] is already so much around that [description of it] isn't needed. I mean, you almost just have to refer to it and everyone goes yeah. They know what you're talking about. And everyone here knew that. They knew they were signing up for a start-up company in Silicon Valley and that was part of the expectation. It was going to involve a commitment to a small group of people who are all counting on each other to make the thing work, and there was a potentially big financial pay-off if the whole thing worked out.

These workplace practices are so entrenched that interviewees often used the term *Silicon Valley* as shorthand for what is to them a clearly defined way of being and of doing. Companies can then rely on the internalization of these shared understandings to regulate workers. This is particularly beneficial for smaller companies with limited resources because they don't have to invest a lot of time or money into codifying and perpetuating the culture.

The culture of Silicon Valley is dominated by the logic of the market. A "masculine ethic" (Kanter 1977, p. 22), or the assumption that a worker doesn't have any outside obligations that conflict with their ability to put work first, makes 10-hour days the norm. Yet this market logic is made palatable because it is cloaked in a youthful playfulness that pervades the Valley. Indeed, young people (mostly men) with technical skills flock here in search of stimulating work and opportunities to strike it rich. But behind the flextime and casual dress is a culture in which the view-point of the shareholder reigns supreme. Beneath the playfulness a serious adult game is being played, a game in which large amounts of money can be won or lost. In order to win in this world, you have to be inventive and brilliant, you have to squash your competitors by cornering the market, and you have to do it all quickly. The pace is intense. If you stop to take a breath, you might miss out.

The fast pace, frenzied lifestyle, and devotion to work are norms clearly internalized by my interviewees. This internalization process is evident when my interviewees report feeling pressure to work, but view the pressure as emanating from an internal rather than an external source. Accordingly, the interviewees more often attribute intense work ethics to individual personality traits than to management and coworker expectations.

For example, Dylan Fitzgerald's daughter had health problems when she was born. As a principal founder of the start-up in which he currently works, he feels he was given a lot of flexibility to take care of family matters. He said that he took five months off for paternity leave and felt no pressure from his coworkers to return. Yet, as we continued the interview, it became clear that he in fact had worked during this time and that he was under pressure, but in his view it was his own.

> [After my daughter was born] I didn't come back to work at all for about two months and was part-time for about six months and I was just extremely fortunate to have the flexibil-ity. I'm sure my coworkers would rather have had me back, but I didn't get any pressure. I tried to keep up with E-mail. I tried to keep up with what was going on. I probably came in once or twice a week for particular meetings. But it wasn't that people were pressuring me but my own sense of things that needed to happen, that I knew people were counting on getting done. So there was kind of a self-generating pressure.
>
> I think what really happened was that I worked a couple hours a day, maybe even half-time toward the end. But because I was not actually meeting any of the deadlines that I had planned for myself, I kept feeling like I wasn't doing what I was supposed to be doing.

In reality, Dylan did not take time off from work. Instead, he worked less than the amount he expected of himself as a member of a start-up. This pattern of actually working when an interviewee stated that he had taken time off for paternity leave occurred several times.

> When I was on paternity leave with my first child, I actually did a fair amount of work. At the time I was writing programs that really ran on a standard PC, so while Brad was sleeping, I wrote. Basically I built an entire product, so I had no compunction about work because I was actually working. (Alan Payne)

The desire to work all the time is seen by James McNichol as arising out of an addiction to work as well as workplace expectations:

> So I think there are a couple things going on. First, if you are talking about software guys, most of these guys are just addicts. It's one of the most addictive professions that I know. And it attracts addicts so they are just strung out. They just can't withdraw from working. They can't withdraw from programming especially. Second, the level of management in high-tech companies is just for shit. I mean you've got these nerd addict engineers managing other nerd addict engineers. The managers are giving the engineers the message all the time that you've got to work and most of them don't know how to delegate. It's just pitiful; it's just awful. My god, I mean, talk about sweatshops. I mean, they are oblivious. The managers have no idea what an altered state they are in all the time while they are managing these guys. So I think engineers are getting constant messages that if they are not working all the time then they will be replaced. I mean their entire self-esteem is based on the code they are cutting. It's really sad. But give an addict any free time at all, and they will work.

Interestingly, though James thinks that managers pressure people to work, he believes that he works so much because of his own individual desire to work, his own addiction.

> I work way more than anyone gives me the message to work. I give myself the message that I have to work all the time. I struggle with that all the time. I'm just as much an addict as the rest of these guys, but it's just intrinsic to personality types. . . . I'm getting better, though. It used to be just because I was an addict. I was just anxious as hell unless I was working. This sense of mastery that you have over this piece of computer software is just astounding. It's just unrivalable [*sic*] in the real world. The real world looks like a series of terrible mishaps that you have very little control over. So, you know, the lure of spending your time in front of a machine where you just have complete control over is pretty extraordinary.
>
> I think lately I've gotten much better. I'm working a lot right now because we are very close to bringing out a new product, but I've gotten much better. Hey, when you got here I was fixing my bike. I mean, I'm not working right now. It took me a long time to realize that just because I wasn't working nine-to-five doesn't mean I have to work all the time. I just learned that I had to take time for myself, take time away from work when things weren't busy. And I think that's taken just years and 12-step programs literally just to learn not to fall into those traps.

Despite James's belief that he works a lot because of his own individual desire to work, it is clear that internal and external pressures go hand in hand. Internal pressure is generated through an implicit comparison to some external Silicon Valley standard of the amount of work that is necessary or required. It seems that the interviewees compare themselves to some real or mythic person (male) who works when they are asleep, who cuts code that doesn't have bugs, who scores the deal that they just lost, who takes his company public while they struggle to get theirs off the ground. The pressure they experience is internal, but it is created through a comparison to an external standard to which they feel they don't quite measure up. Thus, the force causing them to work both surrounds them and is internalized by them, creating normative patterns, understandings, and definitions about work. These normative beliefs are so shared and internalized that the control strategy has no obvious or definite point of origin. Eerily, it is coming from everywhere and nowhere at the same time. This is precisely the self-enforcing type of discipline characteristic of normative control. As Kunda points out, under normative control, "discipline is not based on explicit supervision and reward, but rather on peer pressure and more crucially, internalized standards of performance" (p. 90).

High-tech companies rely on normative control, control that depends on the knowledge worker's identity. However, these identities, rooted in work and internalized by the interviewees, are not gender-neutral; rather, they are suffused with masculine qualities. Therefore, behaving in accordance with them achieves a specific gendered subjectivity. In other words, the interviewees work in order to become "real men," and they become "real men" by working. The masculinity created and constructed by the labor process borrows from, but is not identical to, traditional masculinity. It emphasizes not physical strength but mental toughness. It does not require hazing women but does require a willingness to be absorbed in one's work that, by effect if not design, excludes both women and family responsibilities. Kunda (1992) misses this step in his examination of high-tech engineers. His analysis of the member role created by the culture of the company overlooks the gendered aspects of this identity. Hence, he misses the point that enactment of this membership role is equivalent to enactment of a particular kind of masculinity, that being a member is tantamount to being a man.

So where do these identifications with work come from? How are they created? Do organizations produce them, and/or are there wider structural causes? Though my data cannot offer definitive answers because I did not study any one organization in depth, I can posit some preliminary explanations that future research should more thoroughly examine. As discussed earlier, the culture of Silicon Valley is diffuse, not organizationally bound. Consequently, organizations may not have to actively or consciously engender identities in employees by manufacturing their culture. This culture may already exist a priori, so to speak. In addition, the focus on casual and flexible workplaces eliminates bureaucratic elements. Although this can't, on its own, produce identifications with work, it does get rid of the formal apparatuses, which could otherwise cause the organizational identity to appear external and therefore distinct from one's own identity. Finally, in the new economy, lifetime, even long-term, employment is a thing of the past. For most workers, and particularly for high-tech workers, short-term employment and job-hopping among firms is common practice. In this new type of career structure, one's career is one's own possession, independent of any particular firm. Thus, concern over employability may serve as a powerful tool for creating identities rooted in work.

Fatherhood in the New Economy

This new masculinity is primarily constructed in the public sphere, for it is only by living up to the expectations at work that these men can become *genius warriors, tough guys* who get the job done no matter what. It is only in the public arena that they become *heroes* and *go-to guys* by delivering on the projects they *sign up for.* However, as fathers, these men have private lives and personal responsibilities that conflict with these public requirements. Moreover, as "progressive" men, most interviewees are ideologically, if not always practically, committed to fatherhood and a fairer domestic division of labor between themselves and their wives. Though most of my interviewees did less around the house and less with their children than did their wives, the majority of them expressed a sincere interest in being active fathers. Most displayed negative feelings toward the lack of care they received from their own fathers and were consciously trying not to reproduce these distant relationships with their own children. Thus, the new masculinity contains an internal contradiction: How can anyone simultaneously be the go-to guy at work and at home?

Superdads

Three ways of resolving this contradiction emerged among my interviewees. Seven of them attempt to meet all work and family obligations without sacrificing anything in either sphere. The result is that these Superdads sacrifice themselves. Superdads invest heavily in both career and family. These fathers tend to have a more egalitarian gender ideology, regardless of whether or not their wives stay home. They also possess a care orientation that engenders a strong emotional connection between them and their families.

This care orientation has two components. First, these fathers talk about being attentive to the emotional, physical, and spiritual needs of those around them. Second, this attentiveness coincides with a broader definition of care that includes emotion work and care work, as well as paid work. Superdads seem to notice when caring work like laundry or shopping needs to be done, and they don't appear to resent doing it. This attentiveness and broader definition of care enables them to anticipate the needs of their family and to empathize with their wives. Rich Kavelin, a Superdad who works in business development, illustrates this caring orientation when he describes a typical evening at home with his 3-month-old son and his wife, Joan, a social worker on an 8-month maternity leave:

> When I get home at 6:30 P.M., the baby is essentially my child for the rest of the evening. My wife very often goes out and just hands me the baby and says, "Here he is. He loves you. Here's your daddy." She grabs the car keys and splits because she's with the child nonstop for 10 to 12 hours during the day and she needs a little personal time. So she will go out, and generally she's out for about an hour or so and I'll hang out with the baby. I'll feed him, play with him, talk to him. When she gets home, it alternates. About half the time I'll make dinner, and half the time she makes dinner. If there are chores to be done like dishes or laundry, I'll pitch in and help with that. So I don't expect her to do everything.

Rich's acknowledgment that his wife both needs and is entitled to "personal time" reflects his ability to empathize with her, to recognize the actual work involved in taking care of a child. In addition, his more egalitarian philosophy is made clear through his desire to share in taking care of their son and through his desire to share in the domestic division of labor. The possession of such a care orientation is stressful and overwhelming for Superdads because, in addition to demands at work, these fathers feel responsible for demands at home as well.

Traditionals

Three participants resolved the new masculinity contradiction by approaching work and family through a traditional male model. Despite these interviewees' ideological belief in egalitarianism, especially in the workplace, they didn't seem to practice what they preached at home. In contrast to Superdads, Traditionals[4] divide the domestic division of labor along traditionally gendered lines. They speak about their families in emotionally disconnected ways and talk about caring for their family in a limited fashion, placing more emphasis on work and the income it provides. This curtailed definition of care coincides with an inattention to the needs of those around them. They either don't notice or overlook the work required for family life, leaving it instead for their wives. Unlike Superdads, these fathers appear to lack the ability to sympathize with their wives. They also appear to be less stressed than Superdads because their energy and emotions are less divided between work and home. Interestingly, Traditionals took the least amount of time off for paternity leave.

Unlike Superdad Rich, Edward Vicker, a traditionalist, does relinquish all the caring work to his wife. Edward, an engineering project manager, is married to Jessica, a full-time homemaker who cares for their two young sons. Edward describes their domestic division of labor:

> My wife does most of the home care. Occasionally I'll do some vacuuming and I gotta make sure I pick up my own clothes and keep the closet clean or else she gets on me about that a little bit. She does the general cleaning and I do all the outside stuff, cutting the lawn, and maintenance or repairs. I do usually end up loading the dishwasher after dinner cause I normally get done first. See, my wife has it timed perfectly. I go over and I load my dishes in the dishwasher. And by that time the kids are starting to finish a little bit, so she starts handing stuff over to the counter to me. So by the time I get out of there, everybody is done and I've got all the dishes to do, so that's really the only inside task that I do on a regular basis.

In contrast to Rich, who doesn't expect his wife to do everything around the house and wants to do his part, Edward not only expects his wife to do everything but feels manipulated by her when he does a single domestic task.

Fathers who relinquish their part of the caring work and expect their wives to be responsible for all domestic chores sometimes encounter resistance. In Edward's case, he and his wife have fights about who does more work for the family.

> We fight occasionally. She feels like she's doing more and I feel like I'm doing more. Like in the fall when football season starts, I'll sit down and watch two football games in a row, six hours worth. She isn't very happy about that. She's running around chasing the kids all day and feeding them and then she's like, "You don't do anything around here."

> And I'll say, "I go to work for 40, 50 hours a week." And then she's like, "Don't you think I'm working around here?" So it goes back and forth like that.

Ironically, Edward recognizes the work his wife does while he is relaxing on the couch. Yet he detaches himself from any obligation to share in this type of family work because he feels he has already done his part by working at the office.

Transitionals

Between the Superdads and the Traditionals sits the largest group, the Transitionals. Similar to the Traditionals, the Transitionals partially resolve the new masculinity contradiction by reneging on their egalitarian ideology somewhat and instead leaving a lot of the family work to their wives. Yet, like Superdads, the Transitionals want to be involved fathers and are responsible for at least some of the family work. Consequently, Transitionals have a harder time balancing work and family than the Traditionals. However, they are not as conflicted as the Superdads because they hold onto the care orientation more loosely, frequently handing off duties, obligations, and emotion work to their wives. While some Transitionals lean toward being a Superdad, others lean toward being a Traditional.

Like Edward Vicker, Chris Baxter, a Transitional father in business development, also has clashes with his wife when he "backslides into assuming that because she's home full-time she has all this extra time to clean the bathrooms and cook dinner." Chris and his wife, Emma, have a 7-year-old daughter and a 4-year-old son. It seems that ideally Chris would like Emma to be a traditional stay-at-home mom. Yet Emma sees motherhood in more professional terms. She is at home to raise the children, not to be a homemaker or a maid. A recent clash over decorating illustrates this tension:

> I think in terms of motherhood, one of the things that I see her having a greater responsibility for than I is home decorating, and sometimes she accepts it and other times she really pushes back. A part of it is that we are both terrible at it. But I think she's better than I am, so I kind of push that on her. So I'll say, "You're staying here at home and part of staying at home is making it a wonderful home, right?" And she's like, "I'll sign up for leading the brainstorming on that, but I'm not signing up for doing that as well as deciding what to put here and there and finding the contractor, while you just sign up for writing the check because you are the one working." So although at times it would be nice if she did that, in the end I think it's better if we do it together because then we are both doing it.

Chris is caught between his wish for his wife to be traditional and his knowledge that a more egalitarian partnership is fairer and more rewarding in the long run.

Comparing Superdad Rich, Traditional Edward, and Transitional Chris, it is easy to see the degree to which each possesses a caring orientation. At one end of the spectrum we have Rich. He embraces a caring logic. He sympathizes with his wife, he wants her to have personal time off, and he wants to do a part of the caring work by cooking dinner and helping out with domestic chores. At the other end of the spectrum we have Edward. Edward is unsympathetic toward his wife. He feels no responsibility or obligation to help with the housework. Instead, he feels that he is entitled to leisure. Chris stands in the middle. He holds onto the care logic loosely, willing to take part in the caring work only after his wife commands him to. At her prompting, he is reminded of how busy she is at home and is then willing to help.

Being the Go-To Guy

Scholars have found that a father's masculinity is called into question when his family obligations encroach upon his work obligations (Pleck, 1993; Hochschild, 1997; Levine & Pittinsky, 1997). These findings suggest that ideas, norms, and expectations about what is and is not masculine have a regulating effect on the thoughts, choices, and actions of fathers. Indeed, an examination of the work-family practices my interviewees engage in shows that the strategies they employ to manage their work and family lives reflect a desire to personify and embody the public aspects of the new masculinity. To maintain the image and the reality that they are go-to guys, these fathers rely on a combination of the following practices: self-sacrifice, silencing work-family conflict, disguising the care they do perform, and turning to women, both at work and at home, to help them mediate between their public and private responsibilities. Moreover, even the way these fathers think about and conceptualize care reflects a desire to make family fit within the demands of the high-tech world, to make family fit within the narrow boundaries of this gendered subjectivity. Thus, the internalization of the Silicon Valley member role not only impacts how these fathers work but also spills over into how they think about and participate in family life.

Self-Sacrifice

To reconcile their desire to be involved in family life with their desire to be a serious player at work, Superdads and some Transitionals pay a tremendous personal cost. By trying to live up to expectations both in the workplace and at home, these fathers sacrifice all personal time. Rich Kavelin articulates the stress this causes in his life:

> The most difficult thing about having a kid has been letting go of personal time. I don't mind the work. It doesn't bother me. . . . But now and then I'd like to be able to go play golf with my friends. My wife still has some personal life because we make an extra effort. She goes to girls' night, to ladies' night. She has a mothers' group and support groups. It's actually more important to me that she has a social life because if you think about it I'm here all day. I have people that I interact with at work, adult conversation, and I'm using my mind, whereas she's at home with somebody who is drooling and spitting up and going "ahhh." So her need for human contact is much higher, and I'm okay with that. But every now and then I get a bit grumpy and think, "Why the hell can't I just go get a beer with Neil tonight. I miss my friend Neil."

Like Rich, Dylan Fitzgerald, also a Superdad, is overwhelmed with work and being there for his 2-year-old daughter, Anna. Dylan feels torn every day between the demands of his job and his desire to be at home with his child. This tension leaves him feeling as if he's underperforming in both realms.

I'm continually feeling like I'm not quite doing what I want to be doing in either place, and I'm doing absolutely nothing else that isn't one of those two things. I mean, the concept of free time or hobbies, well, it seems kind of laughable at this point.

Not only do the Superdads sacrifice personal time. They also survive on minimal amounts of sleep in order to meet conflicting obligations. Often they work during the day, come home to help with dinner and put the kids to bed, then work more after their kids and their spouses fall asleep. Alan Payne, a software engineer, conceptualizes his workday in two shifts.

In engineering there just isn't a sharp divide between work and family. I've finally been able to turn that to my advantage, but it has cost me a lot of sleep because what I do is I work two shifts. I work a shift in the day at the company starting at around 10 A.M. and ending at 6 P.M. Then I come home and spend time with my family. When the kids go to bed, I log on and work another shift from about 10 P.M. to 2 A.M.

By forfeiting sleep and personal time, Superdads constantly scramble to meet competing commitments, which leaves them feeling exhausted and overwhelmed. Rich Kavelin expresses this fatigue:

I signed up for this life, right, . . . and you pay a price if you have a high-paying job or a career that you are really fulfilled by. So my price is that I'm exhausted. I hardly get any sleep.

Superdads attribute their exhaustion to career demands. Yet what really seems to be causing their fatigue is that they possess a caring orientation within a social world so dominated by the market that there is little space, time, or energy left for care. So within this context, their attentiveness to the emotional and care needs of their families makes their work load triple that of other fathers who aren't as attentive to the needs of those around them. The Superdads' unwillingness to cut back either at work or at home, and their willingness to live a completely insane lifestyle, signify how central both home and work are to their identities. Not wanting to give up either part of their identity, Superdads completely embrace both the public and private requirements of the new masculinity. Accordingly, Superdads lead lives much bigger than a typical Silicon Valley day can hold.

Silencing Conflict and Care

A prerequisite to being a committed team player is a devotion to work that borders on addiction. Therefore, the intrusion of private sphere issues into the public sphere shatters the image that one is an addict, that one is always ready, willing, and able to work. Addiction means you bring work home—you don't bring home to work. This devaluing of private needs and overvaluing of public needs is quite evident in the hesitancy many fathers feel about bringing up work-family conflicts at the workplace. Instead of openly discussing conflicts, most fathers I interviewed keep problems to themselves, thereby conveying the impression that work comes first.

Rich Kavelin managed a recent work-family conflict with silence. His boss wanted him to leave on a business trip the same day that he and his wife needed to meet with their priest to discuss their son's christening. It was the only available day the priest had in months. Here is Rich's description of the incident:

> So here I am talking to the VP on the phone and he's like, "We need to do this now, we need to hook up with these guys from X, we need to set this up, here are my contacts, we are going on the 29th," and I looked at my calendar and literally I started to sweat. I'm going, "Umm . . . that day is difficult for me; is there any other day we can go?" and he's like, "I don't think so, Rich. My calendar is pretty full, but check with my secretary tomorrow." So I called up the secretary the next day, and I was sweating like a horse. I said, "Hey, you gotta get me out of this because my baby is getting christened and if I don't meet with the priest it's not going to happen and my family is going to kill me and my wife will divorce me and I won't have any kids, and life will be terrible." So she looked, and the only day I could replace that with was four weeks away, so I said, "What is he doing in between?" She said, "He's going to Germany for a week, then Mexico, then to England, then to Boston, then California, and then he can meet with you in New York." And the guy lives in Pennsylvania, and he has two kids and a wife, and I'm going he doesn't have two kids and a wife, he has people that live in his house, that's basically what he has.

Though Rich is willing to express that the day is difficult, he's not willing to explain the real reason he cannot leave, that he has a family conflict. He told me that he didn't want to tell his boss about the christening because right now he's the VP's "go-to guy." The VP depends on him, gives him interesting assignments, and is clearly impressed with Rich's work. Despite Rich's disdain for the way his boss puts work before family, he does not want to jeopardize his position by identifying himself as someone who prioritizes both work and family. It's as if any connection with the private sphere will be a mark against him. Thus, Rich consents to the logic of the market, to the requirements of the new masculinity. He does whatever it takes to convey that he does not have other needs, that he is autonomous and independent and always ready to go when the boss calls.

Like Rich, other fathers dealt with work-family conflict with silence.

> I can remember various times when I had to leave in the middle of the day to drop my son off at baseball practice. I might not have been real forthcoming about that because that may seem a little less important to somebody, particularly if they are not a parent. It would be a lot easier for them to understand if I said my son is at his school and the school is going to close in half an hour and I've got to pick him up before it closes. That's like an emergency. But when it sounds like something that is more optional, I might not be so quick to volunteer it. (Stan Espe)

The hesitancy and silence about work-family conflict maintains the idea that these fathers do not have any obligations outside of work. The above quotation also points out that the most legitimate way in which the family can come into the workplace is through an emergency. In emergency situations it is clear that family comes before work. But when things are functioning smoothly in normal, everyday life, family is less of a priority than work.

> When personal things come up in people's lives, like losing a parent or something like that, there is absolutely no question that people would get time to go take care of that. Of course, there is also the expectation that when just day-to-day stuff comes up, you will be willing to rearrange your family life to put in extra hours that week or spend a Saturday doing work so we get things done on time. So in real crisis situations there would be no question that family life would get taken care of, but there might be week-to-week conflict that's just kind of unavoidable given the way the company has set its goals. (Dylan Fitzgerald)

But how often do real crises come up in family life as opposed to the fairly constant crises of the high-tech industry? Though presented as such, this is not an even and fair trade. Instead, workplace demands are met at the expense of care.

In addition to the silence surrounding work-family conflict, there is also silence about paternity leave. A curious discovery is that 10 fathers in my sample were given paid time off, ranging from 2 to 3 weeks. This paid leave was not an explicit policy or benefit. Rather, these leaves were secretly arranged through managers who granted the leave but didn't inform the human resources department. The other 10 took vacation time and unpaid leave. The desire by some managers to give their employees paternity leave could, if discussed openly, be mobilized to institutionalize men's parenting. Regrettably, however, this countervailing force remains shrouded and untouched, a sign of just how inhospitable the high-tech world is to matters of the heart. To be sure, the silence about work-family conflict and about paid paternity leave disguises the care performed by fathers. The secrecy also devalues care by making it a taboo issue, marking it as something that is not worthy of discussion. Taken together, the silencing and disguising of care is a strategy that allows fathers to parent while preserving the idea that their parental duties do not come before their workplace obligations.

Turning to Women in Order to Care

Through Rich's incident with the VP about his son's christening, we can see the way in which women help men mediate between home and work without being detected. Rich feels comfortable telling the secretary the real reason he cannot leave on that date because he has no fear that she will think he is less committed to work or less of a player. He assumes that as a woman, she will understand his predicament. The secretary solves Rich's problem by finding an alternative date, which enables him to keep his commitments to his job and to his family. Not only do most fathers rely on the women in their lives, namely their wives, to do much of the actual work involved in family life, but they also rely on their wives for help in negotiating the details of work and family life. A common theme that emerged was that wives often set times at which their husbands had to be home. The wives enforce these times by telling their husbands the time they need to leave work in order to get home on schedule and by calling or paging to remind them. These reminders can also serve as "excuses" for fathers to go home, since it conveys to others that it is the wife, not the husband, who is responsible for the father leaving work. Thus, women become symbols, interpreters, and mediators of care in a world where "real" men are not allowed, or at least are not supposed, to care.

Market Language

The degree to which the new masculinity is internalized and embodied by my interviewees can be seen in the way some fathers draw upon market language and market concepts to make sense of their intimate relationships and personal lives. In describing his relationship with his wife, Chris Baxter said:

> Our pediatrician tells us that we are supposed to go out on a date once a month, but we get busy, so we go out about once a quarter. We know mentally what we are supposed to do, but whether we execute on that, well, it depends.

This statement "once a quarter" reveals a temporal order dominated by the fiscal year. It also reduces an intimate aspect of personal life to a task that if "executed" can be scratched off the "to do" list, analogous to something being moved from the in box to the out box. Sadly, one gets the sense that this task is a low priority, like a nonurgent memo that becomes covered with more important papers on a desk.

Several fathers portrayed their personal lives in contractual terms. In the same way they "sign up" for projects at work, they "signed up" for a particular family life, too. Dylan Fitzgerald used this contractual talk:

> I'm very conscious of the fact that if I had an extra two to three hours a day to do work I could be getting more done here, improving the company's odds of succeeding. I'm also very conscious that I'm not spending as much time around the house with my daughter as I committed to when we planned the whole thing out.

It appears that Dylan and his wife carefully planned out caring for their child, in the same way that projects are planned out at work. Like transactions in the market, the care for their child is arranged on the basis of a contract with each party agreeing to perform different parts. Now Dylan is caught in the "time bind" (Hochschild, 1997), unable to "deliver" in the way he would like in either part of his life.

In a recent article about Silicon Valley life entitled "Running on Valley Time" (Plotnikoff, 1999), Scott Epstein, a high-tech marketing executive, uses market language to explain the impact his absence has had on his two young sons. Though he is uncertain about whether or not his long working hours have hurt his children, he is certain that his absence means he has less of an influence over how they are raised.

> I think if you asked my kids, "Do you see your daddy very much?" they would say no and that they want to see him more. Because I'm home less, I have less of a say on how my kids are raised. It's harder to push through my thoughts and see them put into action.

His response indicates that he views his influence upon his children in the same way that he views his influence on marketing campaigns. One imagines him sitting down with his wife and presenting her with a meeting agenda that outlines his ideas in bulleted format. He then "pushes through [his] thoughts" and sways her to his viewpoint. The end result of this meeting is that a parenting "strategy," informed by his know-how, is "put into action." Yet Scott is keenly aware from his own work experience that the only way this family project will be kept on track is through persistent monitoring and reinforcement. Such supervision is very time-consuming, so he concedes the project to his wife and instead focuses his influence on pushing through his ideas at work.

The embodiment of the new masculinity can also be seen in the way some fathers shape and curtail their beliefs about care in order that family life does not interfere with the demands of the market. By reshaping and redefining care, family life is made compatible with the bottom line. Eric Salazar expressed this sentiment when he discussed his paternity leave. His supervisor gave him a paid two-week leave when his daughter was born:

> On the one hand I was very grateful that I was being paid for the leave and that I wasn't taking it out of vacation or sick time. But at the same time I honestly felt that it was something I deserved. So I was thankful, but I wasn't overwhelmed by the gift from my boss. I think that it's something that really should be the norm. It's never enough, but realistically I think two weeks would be capitalistically fair for the company to offer that.

Eric assesses the needs for his family within the constraints of capitalism. In doing so, we can see how the market creates the terms within which family policies are negotiated. Ultimately, what is fair for capitalism is by default both fair for the family and a suitable practice for a man who is both a father and a serious high-tech worker.

Chris Baxter also reveals the priority given to market needs, at the expense of familial needs, when he discussed which employees are entitled to flexibility in their job:

> As a manager I have a much easier time giving extra flexibility to folks I know will get the job done and come in on the weekend because Thursday afternoon they took off to go to their child's check-up or whatever. Somebody missing deadlines, who is always over their budget, they are not going to get that flexibility. I hate to sound like a capitalist, but at the end of the day, the company shareholders aren't holding shares so that we have flexible lives. They are holding the shares because they are expecting a return on them. So if you can generate some return and balance your life, then it's great. But job one is the return.

For Chris, not only do market demands come before family concerns but a worker must also earn the privilege to meet family demands by first meeting all market requirements. Interestingly, though he is obviously a free market supporter, Chris tries to distance himself from sounding like a capitalist. Sensing the coldness of his outlook, he points to real world constraints, not his own belief system, to justify his opinion about flexibility. However, it is very clear that his belief system does not stand outside of the market. His thoughts, feelings, and emotions are overlaid with a market sensibility that shapes his understanding of care and its importance relative to the market. By characterizing care needs in a way that is congruent and acceptable to capitalism, these fathers construct family life in a way that is compatible with the workplace expectations of the new masculinity. In this way, care never infringes on the market, but the market continually intrudes upon care.

Given that these fathers work in a "high octane capitalism" environment, it isn't surprising that they try to shape and curtail care practices so they fit within the capitalist paradigm. Yet what is somewhat astonishing is how deeply the ideology and practices associated with the new masculinity infiltrate the interviewees' lives. Indeed, the use of market language and market concepts to explain one's personal life makes clear the depth to which the new masculinity penetrates. Not only does it influence work and family practice. It also acts upon the interviewees' hearts, minds, psyches, and souls. Thus, the new masculinity is an all-encompassing gendered subjectivity that impacts every part of the interviewees' existence, from work to family to everything in between.

Resistance

The extent to which individual fathers will go to achieve and enact this gendered subjectivity varies. There do seem to be limits as to how far some men will go for their job. Several fathers told cautionary tales about absentee fathers whom they refused to be like. Rich Kavelin will not be like his boss, the senior VP who travels all the time. He also will not be like his former boss at a start-up he used to work for:

> The CEO of this start-up company had three kids—4, 7, 10—nice kids but he never ever ever sees them because he's at work 7 days a week. He does triple sevens. He works from 7:00 in the morning until 7:00 in the evening seven days a week. He thought he was a good father because once a year he'd go camping for a week with his kids or one day on a weekend he would take them out to ice cream for two hours and he'd say it's not the quantity of time, it's the quality of time. And I'm just thinking, his kids aren't going to have any idea who he is. He doesn't think these little moments matter, but they do. I mean, the guy was a real shit when it came to his kids. I'm sorry. He's 40, and he's bound and determined that he's going to make his multimillions, and he thinks he is doing the right thing for his kids, because he thinks he's doing all this for them, since one day they will be rich. They will be rich with money but poor as people.

Rich recognizes that his former boss led an "emotionally downsized" life and refuses to buy into "a reduction of needs" ideology (Hochschild, 1997). Yet it remains unclear how Rich will maintain his line in the sand when he wouldn't even tell his current boss about his son's christening.

Not only are there variations among fathers. Individual fathers themselves embrace and resist this gendered subjectivity at different stages in their life course. For example, Kirk Sinclair is a defector from the triple seven world. He currently works from home and is in charge of sales for a small software company, but formerly he worked as an engineer who wanted to be known in his field. After spending a year as a vice president of engineering in a struggling firm, working so much that he never saw his children, he decided to change his quality of life. Kirk has changed his priorities.

> I still want to be successful financially. I still want to be respected in my field. But I'm not out for fame and glory any longer. And I think I've got a much more reasonable balance of life.

An in-depth look at the process Kirk went through in order to change his life highlights the contours of the new masculinity and its relationship to work and family life.

Kirk's reputation was made through his involvement in a start-up called Innovate that was very successful. At that point in his life he personified the Silicon Valley warrior:

> I worked hard at my start-up because I was Ali; that was my log-in name. I was famous at the company, and I was infamous. Salespeople and marketing people would come and talk to me. They wanted me to meet with customers, and really decisions didn't get made unless I got to play, and I just liked it. I liked being in charge. I never had that in my life, and it was just a lot of fun. I got to make decisions that were worth huge amounts of money, and I had never done that before.

When his second child, Andi, was born, he took only a couple of days off from work. This was and continues to be a "sore point" with his wife, who wanted him to take more time off. Kirk's quick return to work stemmed from his desire to get back to the office, not from management expectations.

> I had a very supportive management structure above me. The woman whom I reported to was a strong family supporter. And it would have been absolutely okay for me not to be there, which is to say, clock out. . . . So I can't say that I was under any pressure from the office. I was under a fair bit of pressure from myself. Then I was mostly doing engineering work. There's this kind of machismo culture among young male engineers that you just don't sleep. So Andi was born, and I went back to the office, and I didn't have a lot of people saying to me, "Jesus, what are you doing here?" My boss was saying, "Hey, what are you doing here?" but none of my colleagues were surprised that I was there.

Even though Kirk wasn't pressured by his boss to return to work, it seems he was pressured by the cultural expectations of his peer group about the importance of work and its priority over other parts of one's life. Kirk so identified with the cultural expectations about work that he experienced the pressure to return to work as emanating from inside him, not from the environment that surrounded him. For Kirk to be Ali he had to work all the time; he had to be around so that he could participate in all aspects of the company. In his mind, the company could not succeed without him.

When his start-up went public, it was bought by a larger competitor. Unhappy with the management changes that resulted, Kirk left and went to work as the vice president of engineering at a small biotech start-up.

The company was far away, and for family reasons we were not going to move. So the commute was 90 minutes each way every day. It was stupid to think that I could pull it off. If the job had been absolutely great, I would have probably toughed it out. But the job just wasn't that great. It was a little company. We weren't doing very well. It was called GS, it was a small biotech company, a very interesting market, exciting field, but we were not set up to succeed.

So the job sucked and the commute was driving me nuts. I would get up at 4 A.M. and be at the office by 6:00 so that I could beat the commute rush down. I didn't see the kids in the morning, and then there would be a board meeting or something, so I would stay until 9:00 or 10:00 at night, get in the car and drive home and I wouldn't see them when I got home. So really I went for a year seeing them almost not at all, and it was a very, very tough year for my wife. I mean, every time the phone rang, it was me on my cell phone saying I wouldn't be home. She was supportive of me taking the job. It was clear she hated me having that job, and I just was not having any fun. It took me a long time to give myself permission to quit that job, to admit that I had made a mistake. So I resigned in October of last year, 9 months after I took the job, and was talked into a fairly extended transition that saw me there basically until the end of May. And at that point I was exhausted, emotionally and intellectually. I didn't have anything left, so I took all of the next summer off and we traveled a bunch and just hung out with the kids.

I started looking around for other jobs. There is a lot of hiring going on. I have a good track record and know a lot of people. So lots of other vice president jobs were available at companies that was [*sic*] venture-backed, and you know it was a chance to get on the Innovate rocketship again and make a lot of money. But the problem is that with those jobs you need to be at the office early, [and] they need you to stay late. They need the job to come first, and I had spent a year letting a real crappy job come first. The family really suffered. The kids didn't see me. And frankly I didn't want to do that again.

The reason it was so difficult for Kirk to walk away from his job was because he had "signed up" to do the job and in doing so his name and his capabilities became responsible for making it work. Thus, he committed himself mentally and emotionally to getting the job done.

> We all knew walking into it that this was something that needed to be turned around. It was broken. I don't know if it's machismo or not. I mean, I was committed to make this thing work. And it was very, very hard to quit 'cause I had convinced myself that I would do that job and so I had to convince myself that it was okay to fail.

In order for Kirk to allow himself to quit, he had to renegotiate aspects of his identity. He had to come to terms with the fact that he was not the person (man) to accomplish "the task" (Willis, 1977). The price of success was too high, too costly. Poignantly, he derides himself for even thinking that he could rise to this insane challenge and feels that he set himself up for failure. It is interesting that Kirk's desire to quit is seen and experienced by him as acceptance of failure. In Kirk's mind, then, you either win or lose, you deliver or you don't. What has changed for him now is that his identity is no longer solely based on the paid work he performs, what his colleagues think of him, and whether or not he's the go-to guy.

> Until not too long ago, a huge part of my identity was wrapped up in what I did for a living and was I famous in my field. Did people call me to solicit my opinion on developments in the industry. And now I don't care about that so much. I don't need to see my name in print. I don't need to see my papers cited in other people's papers.

Now his identity is built more around his family and less around his work.

> With the job I have now, I'm working with people whom I intellectually respect; the product is outstanding; it's very easy to sell. I'm getting to do some stuff that is professionally very important, and I get to see my kids every morning and be here in the afternoon when they get home. I chose this job not because it's the one that is going to make us rich. It probably won't. On the other hand, it's a good living. I'm having a fun time, and I get to be around the kids all the time.

In order for Kirk to resist the organization of work in the Valley, he had to reconstruct his identity, particularly his gendered subjectivity. He had to let go of the desire to outperform others, win battles, and be the best. In essence, Kirk had to let go of the public requirements of the new masculinity in order to embrace its private dimensions. He had to let go of being the go-to guy at work in order to be the go-to guy at home. In reordering his life, he revalued care and recognized that he and his family had needs.

Conclusion

The examination of the work-family phenomenon requires a bridging and reworking of different domains of theorizing so that instead of sitting in either the public or the private, analysis can move back and forth between the public and the private, the market and the home. Approached from this viewpoint, my study of fathers employed as knowledge workers in Silicon Valley sought to draw connections among gender, work, and family. Thus, my discovery of a new masculinity led me to question how it articulates with processes of labor control and with processes of family life.

What I found is that fathers internalize the characteristics of the new masculinity, which shapes both how they work and how they parent. To achieve this gendered subjectivity, men must be technically brilliant and devoted to work. They must be tough guys who get the job done no matter what. Fathers so identify with these qualities that their desire to work all the time is experienced by them as emanating from their own personality traits rather than from coworker or management expectations. Consequently, the type of control these fathers experience is an identity-based one. However, this identity is not gender-neutral. Rather, because workplace practices are suffused with masculine qualities, performance of them achieves a masculinized subjectivity. To maintain this masculine subjectivity, fathers employ work-family practices, such as remaining silent in the face of work and family conflict, which serve to give the impression, if not the reality, that work comes first. Moreover, the embodiment of the go-to guy image impacts how these fathers conceptualize and experience their private lives as evidenced by their use of market language to make sense of their personal relationships as well as their desire to fit family needs within a capitalist paradigm.

These findings have important implications for labor process and work-family scholars. For labor process scholars, my findings highlight the centrality of gender in the organization of work. Therefore, research about processes of control, particularly research on identity-based forms of control, must analyze the gendered dimensions of the phenomenon they describe in order to gain an accurate and complete understanding. For work-family scholars, my findings highlight the need to think about the ways in which gendered subjectivities explain work and family practices. For example, when taken into consideration, gendered subjectivities may account for the failure of people to make use of family-friendly policies even in ostensibly open organizations. In sum, my study illustrates the importance of studying work and family issues in a holistic manner that more accurately reflects the holistic nature of our everyday lives.

Notes

1. Though some scholars take a more essentialized view of masculinity (and femininity), believing that certain practices indicate that a person is a man or woman (Collinson & Hearn, 1994), I take a less embodied viewpoint. I agree with Alvesson and Billing (1997), who see masculinity and femininity as "traits or forms of subjectivities (orientations in thinking, feeling, and valuing) that are present in all persons, men as well as women" (p. 85).

2. Lee is working from Burawoy's (1985) theory of factory regimes, which entails two components: the labor process, meaning the technical and social organization of production, and the production apparatuses, meaning the institutions that regulate and shape the workplace politics (p. 19).

3. Other scholars have critiqued Burawoy's disregard of the gendered dynamics on the shop floor. See Davies (1990) and Knights (1990).

4. I am invoking the typology Hochschild (1989) used as it conveys and describes the three distinct positions held by the interviewees. The terms *Traditional* and *Transitional* come directly from Hochschild (p. 16).

References

Acker, J. (1990). Hierarchies, jobs, bodies: A theory of gendered organizations. *Gender and Society, 4,* 139–158.

Acker, J. (1992). Gendered institutions: From sex roles to gendered institutions. *Contemporary Sociology, 21,* 565–569.

Alvesson, M. (1998). Gender relations and identity at work: A case study of masculinities and femininities in an advertising agency. *Human Relations, 51,* 969–1006.

Alvesson, M., & Billing, Y. D. (1997). *Understanding gender and organizations.* London: Sage.

American Association of University Women. (2000). Tech-savvy: Educating girls in the new computer age. Washington, DC: American Association of University Women. Retrieved May 28, 2000 (http://www.aauw.org/2000/techsavvybd.html).

Braverman, H. (1974). *Labor and monopoly capital.* New York: Monthly Review Press.

Brod, H., & Kaufman, M. (1994). *Theorizing masculinities.* Thousand Oaks, CA: Sage.

Burawoy, M. (1979). *Manufacturing consent.* Chicago: University of Chicago Press.

Burawoy, M. (1985). *The politics of production.* London: Verso.

Burris, B. (1998). Computerization of the workplace. *Annual Review of Sociology, 24,* 141–157.

Carrigan, T., Connell, R. W., & Lee, J. (1985). Towards a new sociology of masculinity. *Theory and Society, 14,* 551–604.

Cockburn, C. (1988). *Machinery of dominance: Women, men, and technical know-how.* Boston: Northeastern University Press.

Collinson, D. L. (1992). *Managing the shopfloor.* New York: W. de Gruyter.

Collinson, D. L., & Hearn, J. (1994). Naming men as men: Implications for work, organization, and management. *Gender, Work and Organization, 1,* 2–22.

Collinson, D. L., & Hearn, J. (Eds.) (1996a). *Men as managers, managers as men.* London: Sage.

Collinson, D. L., & Hearn, J. (1996b). Breaking the silence: On men, masculinities, and managements. In D. L. Collinson & J. Hearn (Eds.), *Men as managers, managers as men* (pp. 1–24). London: Sage.

Conlin, M. (2000, March 6). Valley of no dolls. *Business Week,* 126–129

Connell, R. W. (1987). *Gender and power.* Cambridge: Polity Press.

Connell, R.W. (1995). *Masculinities.* Berkeley: University of California Press.

Daly, K. J. (1992). The fit between qualitative research and the characteristics of families. In J. Gilgun, K. Daly, & G. Handel (Eds.), *Qualitative methods in family research* (pp. 3–11). Newbury Park, CA: Sage.

Daly, K. J. (1998). Reshaping fatherhood. In S. Ferguson (Ed.), *Shifting the center* (pp. 384–399). Mountain View, CA: Mayfield

Davies, S. (1990). Inserting gender into Burawoy's theory of the labour process. *Work, Employment, and Society, 4,* 391–406.

Edwards, R. (1979). *Contested terrain.* New York: Basic Books.

Etzioni, A. (1961). *A comparative analysis of complex organizations.* New York: Free Press.

Faludi, S. (1999). *Stiffed.* New York: Morrow

Hacker, S. (1990). *Doing it the hard way: Investigations of gender and technology.* Boston: Unwin Hyman.

Hochschild, A. (1989). *The second shift.* New York: Avon Books.

Hochschild, A. (1997). *The time bind.* New York: Metropolitan Books.

Kanter, R. M. (1977). *Men and women of the corporation.* New York: Basic Books.

Kendall, L. (1999). "The nerd within": Mass media and the negotiation of identity among computer-using men. *Journal of Men's Studies, 7,* 353.

Kendall, L. (2000). "Oh no! I'm a nerd!" Hegemonic masculinity on an online forum. *Gender and Society, 14,* 256–275.

Knights, D. (1990). Subjectivity, power, and the labour process. In D. Knights & W. Willmott (Eds.), *Labour process theory* (pp. 297–335). London: Macmillan.

Kunda, G. (1992). *Engineering culture.* Philadelphia: Temple University Press.

Kunda, G., & Van Maanen, J. (1999). Changing scripts at work: Managers and professionals. *Annals of the American Academy of Political and Social Science, 561,* 64–80.

Lee, C. K. (1998). *Gender and the South China miracle.* Berkeley: University of California Press.

Leidner, R. (1993). *Fast food, fast talk.* Berkeley: University of California Press.

Levine, J. A., & Pittinsky, T. L. (1997). *Working fathers.* San Diego: Harcourt Brace.

Mumbly, D. K. (1998). Organizing men: Power, discourse, and the social construction of masculinity(s) in the workplace. *Communication Theory, 8,* 164–179.

O'Reilly, C., & Chatman, J. (1986). Organizational commitment and psychological attachment: The effects of compliance, identification, and internalization on prosocial behavior. *Journal of Applied Psychology, 71,* 492–499.

Perlow, L. (1995). Putting the work back into work/family. *Group and Organization Management, 20,* 227–239

Pierce, J. L. (1996). Reproducing gender relations in large law firms: The role of emotional labor in paralegal work. In C. Macdonald & C. Sirianni (Eds.), *Working in the service society* (pp. 184–219). Philadelphia: Temple University Press.

Pleck, J. (1993). Are "family-supportive" employer policies relevant to men? In J. C. Hood (Ed.), *Men, work, and family* (pp. 217–237). Newbury Park, CA: Sage.

Plotnikoff, D. (1999, October 31). Running on valley time. *SV Magazine,* 6.

Turkle, S. (1984). *The second self: Computers and the human spirit.* New York: Simon and Schuster.

Turkle, S. (1988). Computational reticence: Why women fear the intimate machine. In C. Kramarae (Ed.), *Technology and women's voices: Keeping in touch* (pp. 41–61). New York: Routledge & Kegan Paul.

West, C., & Zimmerman, D. (1987). Doing gender. *Gender and Society,* 1, 125–151.

Willis, P. (1977). *Learning to labour: How working-class kids get working-class jobs.* New York: Columbia University Press.

Wright, R. (1996). The occupational masculinity of computing. In C. Cheng (Ed.), *Masculinities in organizations* (pp. 77–96). Thousand Oaks, CA: Sage.

2
My Wife Can Tell Me Who I Know

Methodological and Conceptual Problems in Studying Fathers

Annette Lareau

Social scientists repeatedly have stressed the importance of interviewing fathers in studies that examine family life. This is seen as particularly important in efforts to understand work-family conflicts, a topic that has gained more attention in recent decades (Hays, 1996; A. Hochschild, 1997; Hoffman & Youngblade, 1999). Yet many studies of families target only mothers (but see Coltrane, 1995; Hood, 1993; Marsiglio, 1995). In addition, a large number of studies have suggested that many fathers continue to have a limited "helper" role in important aspects of family life, including child rearing (A. Hochschild, 1989; Hood, 1993; Press & Townsley, 1998; Walzer, 1996). Our study used in-depth interviews and intensive observations to examine the roles fathers and mothers played in their children's daily lives. We focused on white and black families with children in third and/or fourth grade.

Our findings address two related points. First, in terms of research methodology, the study raises important questions about the usefulness of fathers as sources for some types of information and about the validity of the answers they provide. We found that most fathers did not know very much about the details of their children's lives because, relative to mothers, they did not provide very much day-to-day care. This lack of involvement in daily family affairs did not make fathers unimportant, however. The children in our study appeared to be strongly connected to their fathers.[1] They seemed to value their fathers highly as a source of entertainment, a center of conversation, and teachers of certain life skills. But for social scientists seeking a source of useful information about children's behavior, fathers proved inadequate. The answers they supplied during interviews frequently were vague, and when pressed for specifics, fathers tended to retreat into generalities.

Significantly, neither vagueness nor the use of generalities was typical of the fathers we interviewed when talking about their work or about topics of personal interest, such as their leisure activities. Clearly, our interviewees were not reticent by temperament. Had we been seeking information about fishing or basketball, for example, interviewing fathers would have been a richly rewarding undertaking. Unlike questions about children's activities, queries on these topics would have netted us many long, detail-laden quotes. If relying on fathers as a source of insight into children's daily lives carried no greater risk than that of reducing the quantity of usable data, pursuing fathers might arguably be worth the effort involved. However, more than the quantity of data is at stake. Many (although not all) fathers appeared to believe that they *should be* active in their children's lives. Their adherence to this belief affected their responses to the questions we posed in the interviews. At best, embracing an ideology of involvement complicated fathers' answers; at worst, it seriously compromised their validity.

Fathers often reported they were drawing on what their wives had told them; they did not see a clear distinction between what they had learned from their own interactions and what they had learned from their wives. Moreover, fathers who seemed unfamiliar with the details of their children's daily lives nevertheless suggested that they were intensively involved in the children's lives; some even suggested an egalitarian division of labor. Finally, few fathers seemed comfortable offering a "don't know" response, even when such a response would have been the most truthful. Vague generalities appeared to be preferable to absolute accuracy. To be sure, fathers were a valuable source for understanding the ideology of parenthood. It was our examination of behavior, which is a very common focus in social science research, which proved so problematic.

If interviews exposed fathers as a poor source of information about children's daily lives, observations showed them as a focal point of family life. Thus, in addition to a methodological concern, this paper has a second, more conceptual goal. We believe that the way family life is studied should be revised. In our study, what fathers did do emerged as being as important as what they did not do. The fathers we observed were a powerful presence in the household. They provided affection, humor, and advice to their children. These important contributions of fathers often have been downplayed by sociologists. Instead, there has been a preoccupation in the literature with the (unequal) division of labor in households (A. Hochschild, 1989). Studies of family life have not sufficiently stressed the contributions of fathers (e.g., creating laughter, promoting athletic development and masculinity, or providing a "gravitational center" for conversations) (but see Coltrane, 1995; Townsend, 1999). These patterns suggest fathers hold a position of power and privilege in the family as they dominate family life. Still, this domination appears to have a different and subtler form than in earlier decades.

Methodology

Our study of the contours of childhood focused on third- and fourth-graders and their families. The purpose of the study was to understand the ways in which parents manage their children's lives outside as well as inside the home. In particular, we were interested in detailing variations in how much work it was for parents to get children through their daily lives, and we wanted to examine the ways in which parents managed competing pressures, for example, between children's organized activities and work.[2] Most of the data collection took place in a northeastern metropolis.[3] We met with families who lived in a white suburban community and with urban-based families living in two neighborhoods, one mainly white and working-class and the other (nearby) mainly black and poor. We conducted separate interviews of the mothers and fathers of 88 children. The author, with the assistance of research assistants, carried out separate two-hour interviews of all of the mothers and most of the fathers (or the guardians, when appropriate).[4] To protect the confidentiality of participants, all names used in this article are pseudonyms.

The study compares boys and girls in middle-class, working-class, and poor families (see Table 2.1). We recruited study participants from public school classrooms.[5] Half of the children are white, and half are black. In some instances, especially for black, middle-class families and white, poor families, the classrooms did not provide a sufficient number of students. To help fill out the sample, we recruited additional students from other classrooms in the school and from informal social networks.[6]

Mirroring national trends, in this study, middle-class families, both black and white, are much more likely to be two-parent households than are poor families. Working-class families lie in between. In general, the fathers we interviewed were regularly present in the home, but we did interview some divorced fathers and mothers who shared custody. We also interviewed some fathers who did not live in their children's homes but who were nevertheless active in their children's lives. Still, among families below the poverty level, both black and white, the lack of daily, coresidential, paternal involvement was striking (but see Steir & Tienda, 1993 for a discussion of informal and sporadic involvement). As a result, almost all of the evidence here comes from the working-class and middle-class rather than the poor families. We interviewed 51 men.[7]

We sought to go beyond parents' descriptions of family patterns by conducting

---

Table 2.1: Distribution of Children in the Study by Social Class and Race[a]

Social Class	White	Black	Total
Middle class[b]	18	18	36
Working class[c]	13	12	24
Families in poverty[d]	13	14	28
Total	44	44	88

a. For the intensive study, we followed one black boy, one white boy, one black girl, and one white girl from each of the three social class categories.

b. Middle-class children are those whose households have at least one parent who is employed in a position with a significant amount of occupational autonomy, usually in a professional or managerial position, and who has a college degree.

c. Working-class children are those whose households have at least one parent who is employed in a position with limited occupational autonomy, usually in a skilled or semi-skilled position. Parents' educational level may be high school drop-out or high school graduate, or may include some college courses, often at a community college. This category includes lower-level white-collar workers.

d. Poor children are those whose households have parents who are on public assistance and do not have steady participation in the labor force. Most of these parents are high school drop-outs or high school graduates.

---

repeated observations of family behavior. After completing the interviews, we followed 12 children and their families more intensively. Nine of the 12 children came from the pool of families drawn from the public school classrooms; three families, including both middle-class black families, were recruited from other networks. Usually, we visited daily, for a total of about 20 times in each family's home, often in the space of a month. In most cases the families were paid $350 for their participation in the study. The observations were not limited to activities inside the home; we also followed children and parents as they took part in school and church activities, organized play, kin visits, and medical appointments.

The composition of the observation teams varied according to the race of the family. Two white graduate students and I (a middle-aged white woman) observed the white families. One white graduate student, one black graduate student, and I observed the black families. A white male fieldworker observed the boy in the white family who was poor; all of the other white fieldworkers were female. All of the black families with boys had a black male fieldworker as part of the research team. Each field visit was written up in detailed field notes. We often carried tape recorders with us (especially after the family adjusted to us) and then used our recordings for assistance in writing up field notes.

Unquestionably, our presence altered family dynamics, especially at first. Over time, however, we saw signs of adjustment (e.g., yelling and cursing increased on the 3rd day of observation and again on the 10th). It was difficult for family members to sustain dramatic changes in their behavior for prolonged periods. In addition, the ways in which families sought to impress fieldworkers differed. For example, the mother in one of the poor families sprayed roach spray everywhere the day of an overnight visit; a middle-class mother engaged in elaborate conversations, even when she was tired. The working-class boys and the poor black boys clearly were more comfortable with the black male fieldworkers than with the white female fieldworkers, especially at first. In general, however, children and other family members did not appear to alter their behavior from one fieldworker to the next. Overall, children seemed to find participating in the project particularly enjoyable. They expressed pleasure when the fieldworker arrived and asked her/him to stay longer and not to leave.

Feeling Involved but Knowing Little

We encountered methodological and conceptual problems in our effort to interview fathers to understand the behavior of children and adults in routine areas of family life. Fathers *felt* they were involved in their children's lives. As a result, they reported high levels of activity. When pressed for details, however, it became clear that often these men were relying on their wives as a source of information. Fathers also discussed children's activities in much more general terms than their wives did. Yet, during the same interviews, fathers were able to provide details about other subjects such as work or leisure activities. Although not as central to the objectives of the study, the study of beliefs was easier. Here, fathers were often clearer. They often (but not always) expressed a vision of fatherhood as being active in their children's lives. We concluded that this ideological commitment appeared to shape interview responses (a pattern noted, using quantitative data, by Press and Townsley, 1998). Put differently, fathers' objective lack of knowledge about children's behavior was not, at least in our interviews, accompanied by an honest statement of ignorance. Rather, in keeping with a view of themselves as heavily engaged in their children's lives, fathers appeared to exaggerate their involvement. Intensive probing, however, revealed that fathers had limited knowledge. For example, it was common for fathers to describe a pattern of "50-50" involvement in many aspects of their children's lives. Mr. Johnson, a white man who was a dentist and an Army reservist, considered himself an involved father. He attended the spring parent-teacher conference (held one weekday afternoon in his son's third-grade classroom). He reported reminding the children 50% of the time to practice piano; and he indicated that he took his son to Cub Scout meetings. From Mr. Johnson's perspective, these actions qualified as heavy involvement in child care.

Our interview data and field observations, on the other hand, show that fathers such as Mr. Johnson, who saw themselves as heavily involved, had far less knowledge about their children's daily lives than their wives did. These men's wives knew the names of their children's good friends, for example, and they had detailed information about their children's lives outside the home. Mr. Johnson's wife, Harriet, a former teacher who is now a homemaker, is a good example. She provided very detailed information about her son's friendship patterns, likes and dislikes, school situation, and troubles with piano. The intense nature of her involvement is clear in the following excerpt from an interview during which Mrs. Johnson described, with great agitation, how several years earlier, when her son was a kindergartner in a private Christian school, the teacher had recommended that the child repeat the grade. The parents refused. Instead, Mrs. Johnson switched the boy to a public school and surreptitiously initiated a tutoring program:

> I truthfully lied to the child. I told him we were going to a reading and math "fun class." No one ever told him he was being tutored. I took the standard work to [the tutor]. She went through it. . . . They had a little party when his class was done. They went to the pool to swim, and I had something [for them] to eat.

Her concern and direct involvement are reflected in her description of this period as "the worst summer I had ever had in my life." Her distress made it difficult for her to sleep at night. Fortunately, her son's academic problems were not long-lasting; now a third-grader, he was near the top of his class. Mrs. Johnson continued to follow her son's schooling very closely, however, visiting the school regularly to collect additional information.

Mr. Johnson was much more general and distant. Nevertheless, he perceived himself to be intimately involved. Consider Mr. Johnson's response to the interviewer's questions concerning the strengths and weaknesses of his son's teachers. Not only did he focus his answer on the general problem of overcrowding in the classroom, but also—even at that level of abstraction—Mr. Johnson cites his wife, Harriet, as the source of his insights:

Now I talked to his mother, and they were all concerned about so many in the class. Teachers can't do a whole lot. ... You can't teach the five troublemakers. They get left out. And we always emphasize teaching the bright ones, but you don't have to teach the bright ones. They teach themselves. It's the five troublemakers that aren't getting attention, except negative attention.

He does not know details about the composition of his son's third-grade class:

Interviewer:	Do you know who those troublemakers are in Joey's class?
Mr. Johnson:	I couldn't name them. He tells us stuff, but I don't know, and I've never observed.

Providing Mr. Johnson with a list of the names of the children in the classroom did not help him summon any further details: ·

Interviewer:	I'm going to show you this list again of the children in his class. Can you tell me any of the parents that you would recognize if you ran into them in the grocery store [or] if they came into your office?
Mr. Johnson:	Well, I'm not sure. Some of the names sound familiar, but I can't place them. [Respondent appears to feel bad that he doesn't know the names.]

It was common for the men we interviewed to speak in generalities, even to pontificate about the nature of children's lives, but then to be unable to provide concrete details. This tendency resulted in many uncomfortable moments in interviews as fathers, when pressed for details by the interviewer, visibly struggled to supply answers.

Interviewer:	That's okay. I'm just wondering if anyone pops into your head.
Mr. Johnson:	Hank, because I know his dad. I'm not sure. Harriet could tell me the ones I know.

There was not the slightest trace of irony in Mr. Johnson's voice when he explained to the interviewer that his wife could tell him "the ones I know." He viewed himself as "knowing" these other families, but he saw his knowledge as interdependent with his wife's knowledge.

Similarly heavy interdependence surfaced in other interviews, including in many families where both the mothers and the fathers worked full-time. Mr. Imes is a white middle-class banker; his wife is employed full-time as a paralegal. Both work 40-45 hours per week. When asked how often would "you" meet parents of other children in his daughter's class, he asked for clarification of what was meant by "you":

Interviewer:	On average, how often would you run into them in the grocery store or would you run into one of them?
Mr. Imes:	Me, personally, or Susan [his wife]?
Interviewer:	You.
Mr. Imes:	Not that much.

A moment later, he referred the interviewer to his wife:

> Interviewer: We're just trying to get an idea about how much parents share information.
>
> Mr. Imes: Susan does more of that than I do, with the mother of one of Joanne's friends. They talk about school stuff all of the time. She's also involved with the Girl Scouts with Joanne.

In his last comment, Mr. Imes glossed over his relative lack of participation. By phrasing his reply that his wife "does more of that than I do," he implied that he did talk to other parents about his daughter's activities; he simply did this less than his wife. This was a different claim than his earlier, more direct statement, that he did not do "that much."

In addition to relying on their wives, fathers were much more general than mothers in their interviews. One mark of a good interview is the production of detailed, vivid quotes. Yet, as a group, fathers' answers were distinctly less detailed than the answers their wives provided. A white working-class father, Mr. Faringer, for example, when asked about his son Joseph's music lessons, was more general in his comments than was his wife:

> Interviewer: And when did he start taking guitar lessons?
>
> Mr. Faringer: Oh, about two months ago.
>
> Interviewer: And how did that happen?
>
> Mr. Faringer: Just from watching TV, I think. He just wanted to start to play. We signed him up and got a guitar. He always wants to play. We'll see how it goes.

Mrs. Faringer's answers covered the same material but in a more specific and informative fashion, both in terms of when her son's lessons started and why he was interested, and regarding problems that were developing over the issue of practicing:

> Interviewer: I wanted to ask you a little bit about Joseph's activities. You said he plays the guitar. When did he start playing the guitar?
>
> Mrs. Faringer: In May.
>
> Interviewer: And did he ask you to play the guitar?
>
> Mrs. Faringer: Well, it was MTV. He saw one of them on there, the guitar players. My husband would occasionally sit down, and they'd say which guitar this was. And then he decided he wanted to play. But when he was little, we had those little ones with the strings, the regular acoustic guitar for a child. He would play with that. It was funny because Roy Orbison was on [TV]. There was an hour show of him. He'd stand there in front of the TV and we taped it, the Roy Orbison special. He would play his guitar like he was him. It was funny. But I know he said he wants to play. He's not practicing as much as he should. And I told him that once that goes, the practicing, then he's not gonna be able to play. Because, to me, it would be a waste—unless he takes a break and starts up when he's a little bit older.

We found a similar pattern among the Connors, a white working-class family. The interviewer began with the prompt, "These are just some things that kids do, and if you could tell me if Debbie's ever done any of these."

Interviewer:	What about music lessons?
Mrs. Connor:	No. She wanted to take the violin last year really bad, and we said no.
Interviewer:	Did she press for that? Was that something she really wanted to do?
Mrs. Connor:	Yeah. She begged. And . . . she's not responsible. The flyer came home from school, and it said that if anything happened to the violin it was $200. Well, [the dog] loves chewing wood. . . . And she doesn't put anything away, and she's not old enough to be responsible for something that big. Now if it was something I had to buy myself, or something he couldn't eat, I may have had second thoughts. But no way would a violin that's gonna cost two hundred dollars if she doesn't put it away and he's gonna chew it up.

Mr. Connor's response was short and completely nonverbal:

Interviewer:	Music lessons or piano lessons?
Mr. Connor:	[Shakes his head, no.]

Fathers also often started with the term "we," as in "we signed him up," but then, when probed for more information, reduced their own role. For instance, in the black middle-class Murray family, where both parents worked full-time, Mr. Murray said:

Interviewer:	How did he get involved in those [soccer, bowling, karate] ?
Mr. Murray:	We signed him up for it, and if he didn't like it, we wouldn't have continued it. But he seemed to like everything he was doing, so he kept going.
Interviewer:	Who signed him up?
Mr. Murray:	Umm . . . his mother. [Both laugh.]

Some might suggest, following the research on gendered speech patterns (Tanner, 1990), that the lower levels of verbal participation by fathers in interviews is part of a general pattern of fathers talking less than mothers in private spheres. Yet we found that fathers' patterns of speech were *uneven*. Fathers discussed items of interest to them, such as fishing and work, with vivid details and often at length. The following quote from a white working-class father, Lester Jennings, demonstrates this pattern. For example, Mr. Jennings and his wife have three children: a 20-month-old son, a 4-year-old daughter, and a 9-year-old daughter, Holly, a third-grader who participated in our study. Mr. Jennings is a plumber. Mrs. Jennings runs a small, in-home child care business. In the quotes below, Mr. Jennings is recounting regular fishing trips he takes with his brother and the children from both families. Note the details he provided:

Interviewer:	Do the kids have their own fishing poles?
Mr. Jennings:	Well, I have them. Usually what we do is, we'll throw all the poles out.

We'll bait them and throw them out and then when the fish hits, we'll set
the hook and they will take turns landing them. They can't cast them up
and all that. If they did all that, that would get somebody hurt. So it's a lot
safer to just let them reel them in and take them off and throw them back
in.

Taking small children fishing was not without frustration; again Mr. Jennings painted
a vivid picture:

> Interviewer: They don't scare the fish?
> Mr. Jennings: Well, that's what you get for taking them. I come back every time I go and
> then I ask myself—I don't know why I take them out there. They'll fish
> for a minute and then they'll want to throw rocks and chase each other
> around. [Shakes head, with a slight, wry smile.] But I still think it's
> important to take them. But it's real easy to take the kids and do some-
> thing and then give up on them because they don't pay attention. But I
> think they'll eventually like it.

At other points in the interview when discussing items of interest to him (e.g., camp-
ing), Mr. Jennings's description was also similarly detailed.

In contrast, this father's responses to questions about his daughter's regular weekly
activities were decidedly more general. Below, he is discussing Holly's involvement
in Brownies:

> Interviewer: Have you had any complaints about it—even little things that bugged you
> a little bit?
> Mr. Jennings: Not really. Not with the Girl Scouts. Like I say, I've gone and picked her
> up some, and all the ladies seemed real nice. And I don't have any
> problem with it at all, really.

Mr. Jennings's broad-stroked answer not only contrasted with the detail he offered
when discussing fishing. It also differed markedly from his wife's response:

> Interviewer: When she goes to Brownies, has there been anything that you've felt
> uncomfortable about, even little things that sort of bothered you?
> Mrs. Jennings: Oh, there was a little problem that was with the leader this year. The
> leader [was] having a little problem communicating—whatever. It wasn't
> her fault. She just was diagnosed with MS a couple years ago, and so she
> legally couldn't . . . she was legally blind and she couldn't drive. But she
> was just great with the kids. And then there was a communication
> problem between her and the other leader, because of her not being able to
> write certain notes and things to the kids. Then the other leader started her
> student teaching this semester. So they just started this problem about not
> having one leader. But they asked for volunteers, and so they had one [or]
> another parent or adult at each meeting like from that March on. I could
> go. . . . So as long as we all filled in they could keep the troop; otherwise,
> they were gonna have to disband it, because they didn't have the required

> supervisor. But, no, I've been real happy, you know. Other than just normal . . . miscommunication.

While stressing how happy she was with Holly's Brownie membership, Mrs. Jennings also highlighted formidable problems (none of which Mr. Jennings noted or seemed aware of). This pattern of Mr. Jennings speaking in generalities and Mrs. Jennings providing vivid details also appeared in other activities, including homework and softball (where Mr. Jennings was a coach). Mr. Jennings, even in the details he provided about the children and fishing, seemed preoccupied with *his* point of view (i.e., how the children are disrupting the fishing). He seems less engaged with the kind of experience his children were having and *their* perceptions of the experience. We found this pattern with other fathers. It was easy to have them talk at length about their beliefs about child rearing as well as work and leisure experiences in their lives. The interviews were less fruitful, however, when focused on the daily behavior and labor involved in shepherding children through the day.

Family observations confirmed the pattern that fathers were far less involved than mothers in the organization of children's daily lives, although, as we show below, there were other important contributions fathers made to the collective good of family life. As many other studies have suggested, fathers were helpers of mothers, recruited, directed, and monitored by mothers. Although the topic of mothers' "invisible labor" (A. Hochschild, 1989; Hays, 1996; DeVault, 1991; Walzer, 1996) is beyond the scope of this article, we note that the fathers' role in the planning and coordination that inevitably accompany household labor is so small as to be nonexistent. This lack of participation on the fathers' part was particularly prominent in areas that involved family members' activities in settings outside the home (e.g., children's leisure activities) (Berhau & Lareau, 2000; Smith & Griffith, 1990). Even when fathers were coaches or had other prominent roles in organizations, we found that mothers provided "hidden" assistance (e.g., calling team members to reschedule rained-out practices), a pattern that was not generally reciprocated when women had leadership roles.

Still, from observations, it was clear that fathers did play a powerful symbolic role in the family, although they were not engaged in the details of their children's lives. For example, among the Williamses, a black middle-class family with only one child, Aaron Williams, a trial lawyer, played a very important role. He set the tone for the household and stressed the importance of homework. In a car ride home from school, he discussed homework with his son, Alexander. The following field note describes the exchange:

Mr. Williams: Alexander, did you bring your spelling words home today? [Either Alexander did not hear him, or he was ignoring his father. I could not tell which was the case. Aaron glanced at me and repeated the question, verbatim, in a louder voice. Alexander responded this time.]

Alexander: Yeah, they're in my book bag in my spelling folder. The test is not until Friday. I did well on the last one. I do well on all of them. I never get below a 93.

In addition, the father directed his son to begin the homework as soon as they got home:

> As we pull into the driveway, Aaron tells his son, "As soon as you get into the house, I want you to start your homework." [Alexander does not turn around, but he does respond.] "Okay." As we walk into the house, Clara [Alexander's mother] tells her son, "I want you to go to your desk and start your homework. I'll be up there to help you in a minute. I have to get dinner started."

Despite the father's important public role, it was Alexander's mother, who also worked full-time (as a very high level manager in a major corporation), who actually closely supervised the process of getting homework completed that afternoon. She checked on Alexander regularly (while she made dinner) and gave him specific directions including the sequence he should follow in completing the tasks. At one point Alexander came and directly asked his father for help with homework:

> After working for about 15 minutes and finishing his math, Alexander needs to work on riddles. He doesn't know what to write. He says to me, "My dad is good with riddles." He goes and asks his father for help. Alexander walks out of the room to his father's bedroom. Aaron is lying on the bed, reading the paper. His shoes are off, and both feet are on the bed. Alexander leans on the bed beside him. "Dad, are you good with riddles? I have to write a riddle on joints." Aaron does not take his attention off the paper for very long. He glances at Alex. Responding in a distracted/disinterested tone of voice, he says, "Go ask your mother. She is good with riddles."

Thus, Mr. Williams had a powerful, active presence in all of Alexander's sporting events and in promoting the importance of schoolwork. In terms of the (considerable) labor of organizing and running the activities of daily life, however, Mrs. Williams was in charge.

There was tension between Mr. and Mrs. Williams about their relative contribution to Alexander's care and to household labor. They differed in their assessment of their contributions. Mr. Williams reported it as 50-50; Mrs. Williams reported it as 60(her)-40 (him).[8] In separate interviews, each alluded to this tension. Mrs. Williams asserted that she "needed more time for myself," that her load was "too much." Mr. Williams felt his wife did not sufficiently appreciate his many contributions:

> My thought is that I want to . . . do as much of that kind of thing for him as humanly possible. . . . His uniform is just miraculously clean and ready to get, and . . . neither she nor he thought about the fact that that had to get washed. . . . I'm sure she doesn't remember that. [Laughter.] I know my wife.

He saw his schedule as being very different when he had a trial and when he didn't:

> Keep in mind that when I'm on trial I can't do the things that I would love to do through the day. But on Saturdays I still transport him. . . . I take him to the tennis center religiously on Saturdays. I take him to all of his sporting events religiously on the weekend,

and when I can through the week. Typically, he has had at least one or two weeknights that he's played something.

Two weeks of almost every month, Mr. Williams was engaged in a trial, often working from 5:30 A.M. until midnight. But, as we have shown, there were also important gender differences in the amount of direct engagement with Alexander even when Mr. Williams's professional obligations were less burdensome.

Thus, one major methodological problem with including fathers in interviews about household, childcare, and other routine aspects of family life is that many fathers simply do not know very much about the details of family routines (but see Deutsch, 1999, for portraits of equally sharing fathers and mothers). The lack of information supplied by fathers did not appear to be tied to gendered differences in speech patterns, since there were variations in the level of detail within a single interview. Nor, as we will show, do the differences suggest that fathers were simply uninvolved in family life. Fathers were indeed part of family life, but especially compared to mothers, they were uninformed about the details of their children's daily activities. Thus, in terms of collecting the best possible data for answering our research questions, we found that conducting interviews with mothers was significantly more useful than conducting interviews with fathers.[9]

Beliefs and Behavior

While it was hard to extract detailed information from fathers on the behavior of family members, it was easier for fathers to talk about their beliefs. Fathers were especially likely to have clear beliefs about their importance in their children's lives. Here, for example, Mr. Williams, the black trial lawyer, states his commitment to take a meaningful part in his son's life:

> I know that I want for Alexander to have the advantage of a father. A meaningful father in his life was something I didn't have. I didn't have a relationship with my stepfather either. I certainly think that a child is substantially better off if he has sort of the advantage of two parents in his household. And I am convinced that Alexander is a better person because he has a mother and a father. That doesn't mean that people who don't have that advantage will not live rich lives. I certainly was not going to father a child and not be a part of his life. That's very important to me. I feel . . . I have very strong views about that. I have exceptionally strong views about that.

In other interviews, fathers' beliefs about the importance of children having proper guidance from adults also readily surfaced. As a result, our research difficulties appeared to be tied to our focus on fathers' behavior in routine daily family activities. Our methodology would have had a better fit with the research question if we sought to measure their beliefs rather than their behavior. Yet this finding is not simply methodological. It has an important conceptual dimension because many fathers appear to be ideologically committed to the *idea* that they should play an active role in their children's lives. In other words, fathers embraced the vision that they were engaged parents. They did not, for example, casually dismiss our questions with the statements "I don't know" or "I'm not involved in that." Instead, they stressed what they did do (as with Mr. Williams doing the laundry), appropriated their wives' knowledge as their own (as with Mr. Johnson and the list of children in the classroom), and amplified their involvement (as when Mr. Murray stated that "we" signed him up). They followed in the path of Mr. Imes, who said his wife "does more of that than I do" rather than admit outright that he does not take an active role. This "fudging" of data appears to be linked to a powerful shift in dominant ideology of the ideal role of fathers in family life (Marsiglio, 1995). Fathers are no longer simply the good "provider" but are expected to play, at least at the symbolic level, a more active role in children's lives than in earlier decades (Bernard, 1991). Yet this very commitment to beliefs confounds data collection. Without field observations inside families, it is difficult to know how much fathers' (and mothers') answers in interviews are ideologically driven and how much their answers reflect actual practices. Fathers are, however, an excellent and possibly indispensable source of information about the *ideology* of parenthood. This is an important area of research. But there is danger when the ideology of fathers overwhelms their reports of behavior, particularly without the researcher being aware of the shift.[10]

Variations

By exploiting a relatively small, purposeful sample, our study seeks to help illuminate broader methodological and conceptual issues in the literature (Burawoy, 1992). We now discuss social class and race differences we observed in what fathers did do. In terms of fathers' ignorance of details or tendency to obscure their lack of knowledge, however, we found no striking patterns by social class and/or race, with one prominent exception. Fathers who were single parents, and especially the two fathers whose wives had died in recent years, provided quite explicit answers about their children's lives. For example, Mr. Tyson, a black middle-class lawyer whose wife had died of a sudden illness, gave many details of the rhythm of his son's life. He described running back and forth between various activities (e.g., taking his son to Cub Scouts while his younger daughter got her hair braided by their next-door neighbor), and he provided many details regarding his children's schooling. He looked back on his former role in the family with new realizations:

> I usually cooked on Sunday when [my wife] was living. But I didn't have to cook the whole meal. I mean, I realize that now. [Laughs.] I always felt like I was cooking on Sunday. . . . You know, the stuff that went with the meat—I didn't have to make those things. I made meat. Those other little things I never had to deal with. So now I have to make the whole thing. It's more of a production.

Similarly, Mr. Tyson also laughed at how he had naively counseled his wife to "relax" about homework:

> [My wife] always did the homework with them. And she would call me at work sometimes. I would give her a really hard time. I'd say, "Relax!" . . . You know, "It's first grade. How hard can this be?" [laughs] . . . until I started doing it.

Fathers were not the only ones whose claims of pervasive involvement in their children's lives emerged as questionable. One white mother who was on public assistance was not generally present in her daughter's life. Her mother (the child's grandmother) cared for her daughter. The grandmother provided clear details in response to the interviewer's questions; the girl's mother provided general answers that were at times inconsistent, particularly regarding her (the mother's) involvement in the child's homework. Thus, it was not a matter of the respondent's gender per se but, rather, the effect of the twin factors of the respondent feeling as if he or she *should be* involved in a child's life and the limited actual contact that appeared to offer the greatest opportunities for distortion of data.[11] This pattern raises profound questions about the validity of data in studies of fathers who believe that they should have a relatively egalitarian role in child rearing. Fathers (and absent mothers) did not appear able to support their claims with detailed information. Yet this detailed information is one important sign of data quality and veracity.

In sum, fathers' tendency to stress their contributions, limited though they were, rather than openly admit a minor role, may reflect their internalization of new social expectations linked to fatherhood. In a carefully done study comparing time-diary data and reports from nationally representative surveys, Press and Townsley (1998) conclude that "widespread changes in social expectations about husbands' domestic roles are affecting how husbands report their housework behavior" (p. 214). They find husbands "overreport" household labor much more than wives do (i.e., 149% compared to 68%).[12] This pattern of exaggeration takes a different shape by gender, with egalitarian beliefs for husbands linked to higher levels of overreporting. Most important, they conclude that this overreporting bias could account for the claims that men's housework has increased in recent years.[13] Our study provides further support for Press and Townsley's conclusion that fathers may be exaggerating their involvement in their children's lives.

Because of the inequality in the amount of respondents' knowledge, the possible distortion linked to the provenance of that knowledge, and the potential for social expectations to shape perceptions of involvement, we find it to be a reasonable strategy to interview mothers only if the research question focuses on details of routine family life. At the very least, researchers need to identify and much more clearly distinguish among gender differences in symbolic roles, parenting roles involving direct contact, and the invisible labor of planning for these roles.

The Role of Fathers in Families

In addition to the methodological concerns discussed above, our findings lead us to reconsider some important conceptual issues. A large number of studies have detailed the relatively limited contribution of fathers to household and child care labor. As a result, social scientists have become preoccupied with what fathers do not do. We need to change, and broaden, our research questions to examine what fathers *do* contribute.

The third- and fourth-grade children in our study displayed warmth and pleasure toward their fathers; they looked forward to seeing them. As we will show, fathers made many important contributions to families, particularly in initiating laughter, shaping the flow of conversation, and imparting life skills to their children. In *these* daily routines of family life, fathers were important.[14] Put differently, we found that fathers did dominate family life. This domination was not in the earlier cultural form that stressed overt authority, discipline, and men's role as economic provider. Instead, through teasing, the creation of a powerful presence, and a transfer of responsibilities to their wives, fathers had privileged status in family life.

Laughter, Fun, and Affection

Although fathers talked to children less than mothers did and provided less daily custodial care of children, their presence was important. Fathers added color, fun, informality, and "accent" to family life. Mothers were likely to worry, chastise, and punish. Fathers were playful. In our family observations we were repeatedly struck by the ways in which the fathers who participated in our study enlivened and lightened the tone of family life. Fathers often made other members of the family laugh. On the day described in the excerpt below, the black middle-class Marshall family had driven out of state to see an exhibition of art by a close friend. Tommy Marshall first creates laughter over a purchase his wife was planning and then gently teases his daughter Sarah:

> Tommy came over to join us. He said, "Mom says she likes number 22." We found the painting [a nice, abstract pastel] and the price. Tommy said, matter-of-factly, "Well, hot dogs and beans next week." We all laughed at that. Sarah said, with her mouth partially full, "That's $290!" Tommy said, "Oh, that's no problem, Sarah. We'll just sell some of your stuff!" Sarah said, "What do I have? All I have is clothes." Her father said, "That's all you have, huh, Sarah? No television, no Walkman, no tape recorders?" She giggled. "Well, you're the one who paid for all that."

Much of the laughter introduced by fathers was light playfulness interwoven with the humdrum of family routines. Mothers also had fun with children, listening to jokes, hitting a tennis ball around, baking cookies, or watching television. But in the families we observed, a larger proportion of interactional time between children and fathers was spent in play or leisure activities compared with interactions between mothers and children. In the latter cases, there was more stress on duties (e.g., taking a shower, doing homework, getting ready for bed).

There are methodological issues in studying, for example through interview data, the role of fathers or others in initiating laughter. Laughter often passes quickly. It is also heavily embedded in interactional patterns in family life. Children also often prompted interludes of laughter. Regardless of who initiated it, however, when family members came together and laughed over a child's actions, the moment was short-lived. For example, the Irwins are an interracial family composed of a black father (who worked as a lower-level technician), a white mother (who baby-sat children in the home part-time), and their two daughters. In this example, in early evening the family is getting ready to go out for dinner. Constance, a fourth-grader, has a case of "pink eye" that requires having drops put in her eye. In the space of just a few minutes, a tussle breaks out between the sisters, which in turn prompts a disciplinary action during which Mrs. Irwin raises her voice and loudly scolds Constance, which is then followed by a show of irritation by Mr. Irwin. The episode ends with a flash of family laughter:

> Everyone [continues to] watch Constance get her drops. Victoria comes over to the sofa but is instructed not to stand so close by Mrs. Irwin: "Please don't stand right here, honey." Everyone laughs during the eye drop event, enjoying Constance's performance, who makes a cute face when a drop doesn't make it into her eye [and instead goes down the side of her face].

These interactional moments were hard to elicit in interviews. Yet one of the most prominent roles of fathers was to promote laughter. Compared with mothers, they spent less time with children but still, in a limited but nonetheless powerful way, had an important impact on family life.

In addition, the children in our observations often displayed high levels of adoration for their fathers. Fathers had special ways of interacting. Mr. Williams often called his son "Handsome," in a gentle, affectionate fashion. Mr. Talinger queried Garrett in the car on the way back from a soccer game, asking him, "Who was the ball hog?" Mr. Yanelli called his son "Pook" and rubbed the top of the boy's head for a few seconds, in a clearly affectionate manner. Mr. Handlon, recently home from work, let his daughter Melanie, age 10, playfully punch his large belly as she stood on the stairs talking with him about her day. Thus, as other studies have shown, fathers are often specialists in play and laughter with their children (LaRossa and LaRossa, 1981).

Fathers as a Gravitational Center

Fathers often dominated the conversational space in families. Among the white, middle-class Handlons, for instance, interaction rituals shifted when Mr. Handlon came home from work. Mrs. Handlon worked 30 hours per week as a church secretary, but she finished work by the time school let out each day. Thus, mother and children typically were together in the afternoon after school. Mr. Handlon was a credit manager in a large business, and he generally did not get home until after 6 P.M. Soon after arriving home, Mr. Handlon frequently became the gravitational center of conversation. On Christmas Eve, for example, he dominated the family dinner hour by recounting his annual practice of playing golf on Christmas Eve, no matter what kind of northeast winter weather prevailed.

Allowing fathers to be the center of attention, however, did not necessarily mean they were always treated with respect. For example, as the family sat around eating pizza, Mr. Handlon and the two older boys (Keith, 14, and Robby, 12) discussed baseball players. Mrs. Handlon and Melanie listened quietly, as these field notes show:

> There is a discussion of who else might be traded. Robby is confused and asks again about [a catcher] being traded. His dad (quietly and calmly—but authoritatively) lectures

him about trading and says [the catcher] won't be [traded]. He then says, "[A famous pitcher] was traded." Both boys react to this statement as if even an idiot would know this piece of information. They both say, "Duhhhhh." [They are mocking their dad's effort to inform them.]

Similarly, in the black middle-class Marshall family, it was Mr. Marshall who often controlled topics of conversation. He had a special interest in sports and in the current standing of many sports teams, information of less intrinsic interest to his wife.

When fathers did not want to talk, the conversational space would often simply close and silence would prevail, as when the Williams family was riding home early one evening. Mr. Williams was reading papers in the backseat while Mrs. Williams drove. Alexander asked questions from time to time, but his father's desire for a lack of conversation appeared to set the tone, making for a mostly quiet ride home. This relative silence differed from other occasions when the family rode in the car together and Mr. Williams was talkative.

Fathers also showed their central position by having others in the household walk over to them, rather than the fathers going to speak to the others. For example, Mr. Irwin showed his power in many nonverbal ways, including his preoccupation with his choir work and with playing computer games while Mrs. Irwin prepared dinner and minded the girls. In this example, it was late afternoon on a warm spring day. Mr. Irwin was playing a computer game; Mrs. Irwin was making dinner. The girls were watching a Fox cartoon movie. Constance was simultaneously reading a *Humpty Dumpty* magazine, especially during the commercials:

> The apartment is warm. At one point, when the windows are steamed up, Mr. Irwin decides to open a window. He calls to his wife in the kitchen, "I am going to open a window." Despite the small size of the apartment, she can't hear him clearly. She says, "What?" He repeats his statement. She comes out of the kitchen saying, "I can't hear you." [He doesn't move but stands with his hand on the bottom of the window.] He says, "I am going to open a window." She says, "Fine."

There were times, of course, when fathers did get up and go to others. But as an overall pattern, fathers were more likely to stand or sit and have mothers and children come to them. We saw this pattern as a sign of fathers' privilege.

Fathers' presence was felt even when they were not physically present. For example, in the white working-class Fallon family, the children's stepfather worked every other weekend. Mrs. Fallon did not drive. The routine of all family members changed radically, depending on Mr. Fallon's work schedule. The family went out shopping together at the local mall on the weekends Mr. Fallon was free; they stayed home on weekends he worked—even though the family lived within walking distance of a large shopping area and close to major bus routes. Mealtimes, too, were designed around Mr. Fallon's work schedule. In other families where fathers traveled for work, dinners were more elaborate when fathers were home than when they were on the road (DeVault, 1991).

Similarly, fathers were protected from interruptions in a way mothers were not. Events one Saturday morning in the Handlon family are illustrative. By 9:00 A.M., the household is filled with activity. Mrs. Handlon is up and dressed. She has already prepared pancakes for Keith, Robby, and Melanie. She supervises the children as they squeeze fresh orange juice, and she repeatedly prods them to get ready to go to church for a pageant rehearsal. Her efforts to get the children through the morning explicitly excluded Mr. Handloom's involvement. The fieldworker summarized the last segment of the morning's events this way:

> Mrs. Handlon then quickly said, "You need to get your stuff together. We need to get going." Robby puts down his glass and leaves the room. Mrs. Handlon stands up and heads to the counter/sink area. Seconds later, someone begins to adeptly play a quick melody on the piano and she sighs, "Gee, on the one day when Mark gets to sleep in. All he needs is to hear that." She rushes into the dining room area and I hear her say, "Robby, stop that. Your father is sleeping." She returns to the kitchen and says, "Yes, Mark is not a morning person, and he likes to sleep in on Saturdays."

Some fathers did take an active role in sharing responsibilities for child rearing or took an active role in specific tasks, such as children's athletic activities. In general, however, the responsibility for the labor of child rearing had been transferred to mothers. Many studies of family life have shown a labor gap in the time mothers and fathers spend on childcare and household labor (Hoschchild, 1989). Our data, however, makes a somewhat different point. In addition to the shift in labor away from fathers to mothers, mothers had the additional labor of getting children to protect fathers' time and space. Thus Mrs. Handlon stopped what she was doing to hurry in to hush her son. Fathers' tranquility was protected in a way we did not observe for mothers.

Life Skills

Fathers, along with mothers, taught children important life skills. This key role of fathers, including middle-class fathers, in stressing physical prowess has not been sufficiently emphasized in studies of what fathers do. Observational data suggests that, particularly with boys, fathers stressed masculinity, especially physical prowess, and that mothers typically did not. For example, white working-class Mrs. Yanelli described her "no-no-my-baby" reaction when her husband and his brother taught 9-year-old Billy how to fight expressly so that he could take on a classmate who had been bothering him. Mrs. Yanelli proudly reported that her son went to school and "got the job done." Fighting, as the Yanellis knew, is in direct violation of school rules. Their son was suspended, but the suspension appeared to be an acceptable cost, given the importance of the boy's being able to successfully defend himself on the playground. In the white working-class Fallon family, the 12-year-old boy often wrestled with his stepfather on the living room floor in the evening. His mother, 9-year-old sister, and baby sister watched. The wrestling, in which each bout lasted a few minutes, was usually done in silence (except for grunts). It was a routine family event.

Mothers and fathers sometimes held different opinions regarding life skills. Mr. Murray, a black college-educated father, described the situation in his household in regard to what he taught his 9-year-old stepson:

> My wife doesn't really want him involved in extremely physical activities—being a mother, I guess, not wanting to see [laughing] her baby hurt. But me being a male, I realize that's just a part of, I mean, that's a part of growing up. It's gonna happen. You know, he's gonna knock his head against something. He's gonna come home bloody one day. It's just a part of life. So I don't shy away from the physical sports, basketball, football, soccer . . . even boxing . . . organized, not street fights. [They laugh.] Not a street fight. But organized, organized boxing.

He and his wife disagreed. She wanted tennis; he wanted football:

> She loves tennis because there's no physical contact there. The most he can do is, like, twist his ankle or something. But me, I like football. It's very physical, but, you know, I don't think it's anything that he can't handle. I mean they're not…no one's gonna kill him. He may get bruised up, but he won't be dead. So those are our biggest disagreements—discipline and maybe physical aspects of any activity that he's involved in.

At that point, the mother had "won" the argument. The boy was playing tennis. His stepfather hoped, however, that changes would occur in the future. Generally, of all of the aspects of children's lives in third and fourth grade, including school, homework, physical care, food, friendship networks, and other elements, we found fathers particularly interested and active in children's athletic development. If fathers were active in coaching, it was likely to be a softball team rather than Brownies. Even with girls, fathers took an interest in formally and informally cultivating involvement in basketball, softball, soccer, and other athletic activities.

In addition to lessons about physical strength and fighting, fathers also taught children, especially boys, life skills about fixing objects. One Saturday afternoon, for example, white working-class Mr. Fallon taught his 12-year-old stepson how to fix a bicycle by having the boy hold his younger sister's bike while Mr. Fallon demonstrated how to put the chain back on the spokes. The younger sister was in the kitchen at the time, but in a gendered lesson of life skill, all instruction went to her brother, not to her.

There were variations among the parents in the types of life skills they sought to teach children. In addition to differences in how and what they taught boys and girls, black parents were sensitive to the special dilemmas of raising black boys in American society. Mothers, but especially fathers, spoke of these issues in interviews. Such concerns also surfaced in observations. Black middle-class fathers reported experiencing racial insults in daily life (e.g., watching white women clutch their purses to their chests and look fearful as they walked down the street at night, concerns about racial discrimination in housing purchases, difficulties in employment). There were variations among parents as to when children should be taught about the looming racial problems that they would likely face in their lives. Some parents reported in interviews that they felt they needed to wait until their children were older than in fourth grade to talk to them about these issues. For example, Mr. Tyson, a lawyer and a single father, had introduced the ideas generally but was deliberately waiting until his son was older before providing him with information about other realities that the father believed his son would inevitably have to confront:

> When he was younger, we had conversations about different races and getting along with all different types of people. You know, there're good and bad people morally. Race isn't so important. . . . I'm starting to try to explain to him different historical type things. I mean, we've read books on slavery and things like that. [But there are] a lot of the hard lessons that he's gonna learn in life about discrimination. I haven't presented them to him as blatantly yet.

Black fathers and mothers also monitored children's schooling carefully for signs of racial inequity (Lareau & Horvat, 1999). As in studies by others (J. Hochschild, 1995), we found concerns about discrimination especially prevalent among the middle-class black families in our sample. The white families we studied lived in predominantly white worlds. Compared with the black families, the white families did not report, and we did not observe, the transmission of special life skills designed to help children negotiate race relations, either as children or as adults.

Overall, across race and class, fathers played an important role in the transmission of life skills, especially in the areas of physical prowess and masculinity. Moreover, fathers shaped the conversational space in families and introduced humor and playfulness on a regular basis. Thus, we believe it essential that social science research redirect attention from a focus on fathers' deficiencies (e.g., their failure to do much housework or child care) to isolating and analyzing the contributions fathers do make.

Discussion

This article has identified important methodological and conceptual difficulties in the study of fathers and their roles in family life. In conducting our study of aspects of family life, we invested extensive resources to interview fathers about children's daily routines. We asked detailed questions about children's participation in sports, including who enrolled the child, who wrote the check, when the activity began, when it ended, who provided the transportation of the child to and from the activity site, who prepared the refreshments, what the parent hoped the child would get out of the activity, and what complaints the parent had about the activity. Most fathers did not know the answers to most of these questions. They were best at discussing their beliefs, such as answering general questions about broader life goals for children. They excelled at discussions of their own work experiences, their leisure activities, and masculinity. We found it extremely uncomfortable (and discouraging) to spend so much time pressing fathers for answers they could not provide. We did sometimes gain interesting insights from these interviews, but, overall, we question whether, for our purposes, the considerable energy and resources devoted to interviews with fathers were worth it. We found that despite its large volume, the data from our interviews with fathers, once transcribed and analyzed, yielded overly general findings and lacked vivid quotes.

It is entirely possible, of course, that more skilled interviewers, particularly male interviewers, might have elicited richer answers from the fathers in our sample. But the fact that most of the interviews with fathers *did* have rich moments—just not ones that addressed topics of interest to us—undermines this explanation. In addition, many other studies have noted the lack of fathers' involvement in children's lives, particularly fathers' limited participation in child rearing (Deutsch, 1999; Hood, 1993; Lareau, 1989; Marsiglio, 1995; Townsend, 1999; Walzer, 1996). There is even less contact between fathers and children after divorce; the majority of children in divorced families do not see their fathers on a weekly basis (Arendell, 1986; Maccoby & Mnookin, 1992).

Obviously, fathers' degree of involvement depends on the aspect of family life under investigation. We were interested in the detailed, day-to-day labor of parents in getting children through the day. Before we started the study, it had seemed important to allocate almost half of our resources to interviewing fathers. As it turned out, our focus on this kind of behavior (e.g., who does what) was a key problem because, at least in our families, most fathers did not do that much (but see Deutsch, 1999). If our research question had been different, interviewing fathers would have yielded more useful data. It would be a serious mistake, for instance, to omit fathers in a study of the transmission of masculinity. Similarly, if our primary focus had been on the ideologies of motherhood and fatherhood, it also would have been crucial to conduct interviews with both parents equally.

Based on our experience with mothers and fathers as unequally viable sources of information on family life, we conclude that researchers who are interested in family behavior and who have limited resources should focus on plumbing the *best* source(s) of information for answering their particular research question, even when that means excluding one parent.

Families as Interactional Groups

Emile Durkheim (1933), in his discussion of social collectives, made an important point often overlooked in studies of family life. He argued that the collectives have a reality in and of themselves (i.e., *sui generis*) or, put differently, that the whole is more than the sum of its parts. This insight is crucial in the construction of more sophisticated models of family life. Families are groups with members interacting in a fluid and dynamic fashion. Recall the Irwin family's experiences with eye drops. In the space of a few minutes, they moved through the girls tussling, the mother yelling at the older daughter, a reconciliation, the father admonishing the same daughter, and then a moment of social connection as the entire family came together to laugh at Constance's deliberately funny facial contortions when an errant drop trickled down her cheek. We found this kind of dynamic common: Moments of social connection tended to be brief, even fleeting. Highlighting the nature of social connections in family life, recognizing them as fluid and ever-changing, is crucial to a more elaborate notion of the elements of family life. Analyses of families must necessarily, then, incorporate the different vantage points and experiences of various members of the group. Such analyses also must be attuned to interactional processes, embedded in a broader context, rather than discrete actions studied in isolation.

Of course, a focus on the dynamic nature of social interaction *and* the importance of various vantage points means that researchers need to attend to the input of all group members. Interviews, especially interviews of only one parent, are insufficient to capture group dynamics. In our own case, it was repeated field observations inside families that brought to our attention the many positive contributions fathers make. Without the observational part of our study, we might have added to the number of studies portraying fathers as deficient in key areas of family life. Family observations are extremely difficult to carry out. It is difficult to gain access. The visits are intrusive. One needs repeated observations so the family can regain a routine. The visits also are extremely labor intensive and, we found, emotionally exhausting. Still, we discovered the field observations were crucial to capturing dynamic relationships of family life. In the case of fathers, at least, researchers are likely to miss a significant part of their role in the family unless studies are designed to capture fluid and fleeting exchanges in the routines of daily life. However, partly because of the formidable barriers to drawing such a complex interactional portrait, family sociologists often look only at the parts, and then imply a vision of the whole. We have countless studies of work hours, wage gaps, hours spent in child care, time spent in various household chores, and other easily quantifiable aspects of home life and work-family relationships. The proliferation of such studies has shaped the field, suggesting that household labor is deservedly the key to understanding family life. Yet, as we have shown, focusing on household and child care labor tends to obscure other important aspects of family life, notably "hanging out" together, laughter, transmission of life skills, and conversational rhythms.

Other factors also contribute to a misunderstanding of the roles family members play. Fathers sometimes take on prominent roles as, for example, Mr. Williams did when he instructed his son to do his homework. But these symbolic and public roles need to be distinguished from the more "hands-on" character of tasks that involve actually directing a child in the details of a given activity, such as completing a homework assignment. It is simply inaccurate to say that fathers such as Mr. Williams do not have a role in homework. But current measures of the time spent helping children with homework, or self-reports of the level of involvement, do not sufficiently capture the real-life dynamic.

Thus, when fathers report a role in homework, talking with children about school, or talking to other parents, they are indeed telling the truth; they see themselves—and others see them—as being involved fathers. The difficulty, at least in analytical terms, is that the quality of that involvement differs significantly by gender. Studies of household division of labor, child care, and other family routines do not allow us to capture sufficiently the unequal differences in the power and sense of responsibility that mothers and fathers have in the enactment of family events.[15]

This data is suggestive of both a pattern of continuity and change in the fathers' role in families over time. In terms of continuity, there are signs that fathers remain a powerful, indeed dominant, force in family life. As we have shown, in observations we saw fathers claim the conversational floor, set the tone for a talkative or quiet family life in a given moment, and transmit socially desirable life skills, especially to their sons. Yet the forms of domination we observed contrast with a more traditional role of men as "good providers" with a stress on fathers' more overt authority in the home or fathers as the threatened source of discipline if children misbehave (Bernard, 1991). As Naomi Gerstel suggests, the focus on fathers' presence, their role in teasing family members, and the transfer of household responsibilities to their wives is a "modernized form of domination" that, nonetheless, generates privilege.[16]

Moreover, in studying family life, sociologists have not been random in their approach. Instead, they are particularly likely to take up the (considerable) difficulties of women's roles in juggling the competing and complex demands of home, child rearing, and work life (but see Farrell, 1999, and Skolnick,1991, for broader overviews of family studies). However, this stress on the perspective of *mothers* privileges one set of family members over others, notably fathers and children (but see Galinsky, 1999; Thorne, 1987, 1992). Our study found that children were not particularly aware of the amount of labor mothers provided; from the children's perspective, food simply appeared, clothes became clean, and parents automatically supplied transportation. The background labor involved was not a central concern in their lives.[17] Of course, mothers (as we have shown) are core family members. Where limited resources constrain a study to only one family member, mothers are a good choice. Ideally, however, there should be an effort to expand the boundaries of sociological research to include the perspectives of others as well, notably fathers. If we seek out and measure fathers according to their contributions to household labor, we are likely to find them wanting. The task is to reframe our questions to take seriously how fathers see themselves. Here, we stress that fathers are important members of families, but their importance centers on their *presence* and on the meaning that they have for children (and wives).[18] The social role of fathers in teasing, talking to, and teaching children needs to be carefully assessed. Studies of divorce, in particular, might profit from a more systematic investigation of the loss of these elements when fathers are no longer present in the home.

Thus, in addition to methodological concerns, we see important conceptual concerns of imbalance, especially in the study of fathers. We find the study of family life to be disproportionately skewed to selected, usually easily quantifiable, topics and to privilege the views of mothers. Merely calling social scientists' attention to these overlooked areas is not likely to result in any significant change in the field, however. Interactional family dynamics are less easy to quantify than hours spent in household labor. They require more time to observe, more time to analyze, and more time to shape into publishable articles. Creating more sophisticated models of family life will require a concomitant change in priorities among researchers, the institutions that employ and promote them, and the agencies that fund them. We hope that a greater recognition of the importance of broadening and deepening the focus of family research will help bring about these necessary, sweeping changes.

Acknowledgments

Earlier versions of this essay were presented at the Sloan Work-Family Conference, San Francisco, March 2000 and at the Center for Working Families, University of California at Berkeley, October 1999. I appreciate the comments provided by these audiences. Barrie Thorne, Arlie Hochschild, and Anita Garey also provided useful suggestions; the paper benefited from the comments provided by Patricia Berhau, Katherine Mooney, Julie Press, Karen Shirley, Dan Clawson, and Naomi Gerstel. I am grateful to the Spencer Foundation, the Sloan Foundation, ASA/NSF Grants for the Discipline, Temple Grant-in-Aid, and Southern Illinois University for funding the research. I also wish to thank the Center for Working Families for providing office space and intellectual support. Finally, I am indebted to the research assistants who worked on the project, particularly Wendi Starr Brown, Gillian Johns, Greg Seaton, Mary Woods, and Jennifer Murphy, whose field notes or tables appear in this article. All errors, of course, are my responsibility.

Notes

1. Most of the children who participated in the study lived in families where fathers were present in the home. Those children whose fathers did not live with them also appeared to have strong attachments, provided that they saw their fathers regularly (i.e., weekly). Because we limited the interviews to fathers who had a regular presence in their children's lives, our analysis does not address children's relationships with fathers they rarely or never saw.

2. Following Pierre Bourdieu's lead, we were also interested in the advantages parents and children gained by using particular strategies for interacting with educators, medical personnel, and other adults in children's lives (Lareau, 2000).

3. Additional interviews were carried out in a small midwestern community.

4. Multisite research projects often rely primarily on research assistants. As principal investigator, I chose to be heavily involved in all phases of data collection. Overall, I did most of the classroom observations, about half of the in-depth interviews, and an average of one quarter of the direct observation of family life (this proportion varied across families), including three overnight visits. One consequence of this pattern was that while a number of the families we observed had one male researcher, all of the interviewers were women.

5. I carried out classroom observations for 2 months in each of the public school classrooms from which I drew the students. After observing in classrooms, I sent a letter requesting interviews with parents (specifying my interest in interviewing mothers and fathers separately).

6. Seven families declined to be in the intensive study, including one poor white family, two poor black families, one working-class white family, and three middle-class black families. Thus, the response rate was 63% (i.e., 12/19). Among the sample of 88 children, only a few mothers refused to be interviewed. Nine fathers refused—or agreed but then were never available for interviewing.

7. This figure includes single fathers, stepfathers, one live-in boyfriend, and one grandfather.

8. Our own assessment of the division of labor in the Williams household differed from both figures. We rated the division as closer to 73, with Clara doing the greater share. Part of the problem of assessment, of course, centers on whether one focuses on general statements— "As soon as we get in the house, I want you to do your homework"—or on direct engage-

ment—"What do we need to do here?" See A. Hochschild (1989), however, for a discussion of family myths.

9. Single-father households or divorced fathers with regular overnight custodial care were an important exception. These fathers' grasp of the details of their children's daily lives was similar to that of the typical mother in a dual-parent household.

10. Of course, all interviews (and field observations) are constructions. We do not mean to imply here that other interviews or observations are not subject to the same processes. The problem, however, is one of degree. In our interviews fathers simply could not support a number of the claims they made moments earlier. We did not find this pattern with single fathers or mothers.

11. Clearly, men and women have been socialized to have very different relationships to parenting and are judged differentially as well. These gender factors also are heavily intertwined with the relationships to family life. Our point here, however, is that both mothers and fathers did engage in dramatic claims that did not seem to be supported by detailed probes.

12. For comparability, the authors compared only four housework tasks traditionally defined as female: cooking, washing dishes, cleaning, and laundry. Thus, strictly speaking, it is not a study of child care and fathers' involvement in children's lives. The point here is conceptual, however, rather than empirical.

13. Mothers probably exaggerate their involvement in children's lives as well, claiming symbolic motherhood particularly when full-time work conflicts with other motherhood obligations (see Garey, 1999). But when pressed for details, we found mothers could supply them on children's activities, with the exception of mothers who were not living in the home in a sustained fashion. Moreover, important parts of children's labor are difficult to avoid, even with the effort to "out-source" or commodify aspects of family life (A. Hochschild, 1997). For children who are 9 and 10, the labor demands are considerable.

14. Our point here is not to weigh the relative contributions of fathers. Rather, we simply highlight areas that have received insufficient attention.

15. One possibility is to diversify the sample of fathers, dramatically increasing the number of fathers who typically possess detailed information, particularly single fathers and divorced fathers who have regular, overnight visitation with children. The problem, however, is that these men are rare. They are difficult to pick up in many samples. In addition, there is a pressing need to diversify samples to include variation by racial and ethnic background, family structure, and social class. Another possibility is to use a nested design, with 90-minute face-to-face interviews with mothers and shorter (e.g., 20-minute) telephone interviews with fathers.

16. Naomi Gerstel, personal communication, June 1, 2000.

17. Also, as Deutsch (1999) has shown, children's attachment to parents is not strikingly sensitive to parents' contributions to child care and household labor.

18. There are signs of this from other studies. Studies of divorce also suggest great distress, at least in the short term, from the dissolution of the family unit (Furstenberg & Cherlin, 1991). There is considerable evidence of economic decline (Kurz, 1996) as well as a decline in contact between children and fathers (Maccoby & Mnookin, 1992). However, since we lack a great deal of data on what fathers do in families aside from their economic contributions, it is hard to understand (aside from the economic drop) why family members are distressed by the absence of fathers.

References

Arendell, T. (1986). *Mothers and divorce*. Berkeley: University of California Press.

Berhau, P., & Lareau, A. (2000). *Beyond the walls of the home: The importance of gender.* Unpublished paper. Temple University, Philadelphia.

Bernard, J. (1991). The good-provider role: Its rise and fall. In M. Hutter (Ed.), *The family experience* (pp. 467–485). New York: Macmillan.

Burawoy, M. (Ed.) (1992). *Ethnography unbound*. Berkeley: University of California Press.

Coltrane, S. (1995). The future of fatherhood. In W. Marsiglio (Ed.), *Fatherhood* (pp. 255–274). Thousand Oaks, CA: Sage.

Deutsch, F. M. (1999). *Halving it all: How equally shared parenting works*. Cambridge: Harvard University Press.

DeVault, M. (1991). *Feeding the family*. Chicago: University of Chicago Press.

Durkheim, E. (1933). *The division of labor in society*. Translated by George Simpson. New York: Free Press.

Farrell, B. G. (1999). *Family: The making of an idea, an institution, and a controversy in American culture*. Boulder, CO: Westview Press.

Furstenberg, F., Jr., & Cherlin, A. (1991). *Divided families: What happens to children when parents part*. Cambridge: Harvard University Press.

Galinsky, E. (1999). *Ask the children: What America's children really think about working parents*. New York: Morrow.

Garey, A. I. (1999). *Weaving work and motherhood*. Philadelphia: Temple University Press.

Hays, S. (1996). *The cultural contradictions of motherhood*. New Haven: Yale University Press.

Hochschild, A. R. (1989). *The second shift: Working parents and the revolution at home*. New York: Viking.

Hochschild, A. R. (1997). *The time bind*. New York: Metropolitan Books.

Hochschild, J. (1995). *Facing up to the American dream: Race, class, and the soul of the nation*. Princeton: Princeton University Press.

Hoffman, L., & Youngblade, L. (1999). *Mothers at work: Effects on children's well-being*. Cambridge: Cambridge University Press.

Hood, J. (Ed.) (1993). *Men, work, and family*. Thousand Oaks, CA: Sage.

Kurz, D. (1996). *For richer for poorer*. New Brunswick: Rutgers University Press.

Lareau, A. (1989). *Home advantage: Social class and parental intervention in elementary education*. Philadelphia: Falmer Press.

Lareau, A. (2000). Contours of childhood (Working Paper). Berkeley: Center for Working Families, University of California.

Lareau, A., & McNamara Horvat, E. (1999). Moments of social exclusion and inclusion: Race, class, and cultural capital in family-school relationships. *Sociology of Education, 72*, 37–53

LaRossa, R., & LaRossa, L. (1981). *Transition to parenthood*. Beverly Hills, CA: Sage.

Maccoby, E. E., & Mnookin, R. H. (1992). *Dividing the child: Social and legal dilemmas of custody*. Cambridge: Harvard University Press.

Marsiglio, W. (Ed.) (1995). *Fatherhood*. Thousand Oaks, CA: Sage.

Press, J., & Townsley, E. (1998). Wives' and husbands' housework reporting: Gender, class, and social desirability. *Gender & Society, 12*, 188–218.

Skolnick, A. (1991). *Embattled paradise: The American family in an age of uncertainty*. New York: Basic Books.

Smith, D. E., & Griffith, A. (1990). Coordinating the uncoordinated: Mothering, schooling, and the family wage. In G. Miller & J. Holstein (Eds.), *Perspective on social problems* (vol. 2). Greenwich, CT: JAI Press

Steir, H., & Tienda, M. (1993). Are men marginal to the family? Insights from Chicago's inner city. In J. Hood, *Men, work, and family* (pp. 23–44). Thousand Oaks, CA: Sage.

Tanner, D. (1990). *You just don't understand: Women and men in conversation*. New York: Morrow.

Thorne, B. (1987). Re-visioning women and social change: Where are the children? *Gender & Society, 1,* 85–109.

Thorne, B. (1992). *Gender play*. Rutgers, NJ: Rutgers University Press.

Townsend, N. (1999). *The package deal: Marriage, work, and fatherhood in men's lives*. Paper presented to the Center for Working Families. University of California, Berkeley.

Walzer, S. (1996). Thinking about the baby: Gender and divisions of infant care. *Social Problems, 43,* 219–234.

3
Constructing Gender and Occupational Segregation

A Study of Women and Work in Fishing Communities

Carrie L. Yodanis

Women throughout the world play a vital role in the fishing industry (Nadel-Klein & Davis, 1988). They process and sell fish (Davis, 1986; Krabacher, 1988; Giasson, 1992). They manage fishing households and finances (Sinclair & Felt, 1991; Felt, Murphy, & Sinclair, 1995). They knit heads and repair nets (Thiessen, Davis, & Jentoft, 1992). They assist on boats, filling bait bags, cleaning fish, or cooking for the crew (Allison, 1988; Porter, 1989). In Scotland, wives of fishermen even carried their husbands through the water to their boats (Nadel-Klein, 1988).

Nevertheless, while women are unquestionably essential to fishing industries, they do not fish. Study after study, from country to country, has confirmed that throughout the world, fishing is dominated by men. It is men who catch fish, whether as the owners and operators of boats or as crew members on fishing fleets (Nadel-Klein & Davis, 1988). Data from both the 1990 U.S. Census and a 1998 survey conducted by *National Fisherman* show that approximately 95% of fishermen are men (U.S. Census Bureau, 1999; Fraser, 1998). It is men who enjoy the potential to earn a high income, be their own boss, and work in the environment of the open ocean that fishing can provide. Some women catch fish on their own or from someone else's boat (Allison, 1988; Kaplan, 1988), but these women are the exception.

Studies of women and fishing often aim to show that while women do not fish, the work they do related to fishing is essential to the success of the industry. Nadel-Klein and Davis (1988, p. 21) write that "the 'fishery' itself entails far more than the capture of fish." But all work related to the fishery does not result in the same pay, status, and power. Women participate in lower-status and less lucrative jobs and fisheries (Allison, 1988) and are usually considered only assistants to their husbands (Nowack, 1988; Thiessen et al., 1992). It is men who catch fish—the work which provides the best rewards (Shreenan, 1992).

By not fishing, women living in fishing-dependent communities miss out on the most available, and often the most lucrative, source of income throughout their lives. Girls baby-sit or work in restaurants, making only a percentage of what boys their age make by working as the crew on their fathers' or other fishermen's boats. As one fisherman's wife living in a remote fishing community explains, "[Fishing] is only

© 2000 by Human Sciences Press, Inc. Reprinted from *Qualitative Sociology* Vol. 23, No. 3, pp. 267-290.

work for boys. . . . This is a boy's world up here." By not fishing, women give up as much as $100,000 a year from lobster fishing and the possibility of making $1,000 a day diving for sea urchins or $20,000 from catching one tuna.

Why don't women fish? The most readily given and widely studied answers for occupational segregation start from the assumption that women do not do certain jobs because they are women. Whether as a result of gender role socialization, established traditions, or discrimination and exclusion by men, women can be viewed as blocked from fishing because of their gender. In this article, I discuss how these factors do indeed work to block women from fishing. However, women's lack of fishing can also be viewed from a different angle—that of gender construction: Women are women because they do not fish. After listening to women and men talk about their lives, work, and families during in-depth interviews and field research in fishing communities on the North Atlantic coast of the United States, I found that gender in fishing villages is defined in relation to fishing. "Man" is defined as one who fishes and "woman" is defined in opposition to that which is a fisherman. To be a woman is to not be a fisher(man). Fishing serves as the basis for gender boundaries. Relations to fishing construct people as men and women in a fishing community; therefore, women do, and define the work they do as, nonfishing work. The result is a strong, unequal, and persistent gender division of labor in fishing communities.

Explanations of Occupational Sex Segregation

Occupational sex segregation is generally explained as an outcome of employers' preferences and practices (constraints) or workers' preferences and actions (choices) (England and Brown, 1992; Reskin, 1993). Workers' "choice" theories examine the extent to which women come to the market with different qualifications (i.e., human capital) and preferences than men and thus obtain or select different jobs. These differences in qualifications and preferences largely result from women's and men's different socialization, training, and roles in families and schools (Polachek & Siebert, 1993). Employer and structural "constraint" theories explain occupational segregation between women and men as a result of differing experiences in the workplace. Women and men, it is argued, have different work as a result of "tastes" for discrimination, statistical discrimination, and other institutionalized discriminatory policies and practices which favor men over women for certain jobs and positions (Bielby & Baron, 1986; Reskin & Ross, 1992).

West and Zimmerman (1987) provide a theoretical framework from which to understand the reciprocal relationship between choices and constraints in the construction of occupational sex segregation. They argue that gender is not a thing or a characteristic of an individual. It is more than a role or an occasional public display. Gender is an ongoing accomplishment of interaction. Every social interaction is accompanied by behaviors deemed appropriate for women and men, as categorized by a socially defined biological sex. Although most of these rules for behavior are unconscious, individuals are held accountable for acting according to the behaviors appropriate to someone of their sex. Through this process of sex-appropriate interaction, gender is continually created and re-created. The production of gender during interaction is so pervasive and unquestioned that gender differences, although a social creation, appear as inherent, natural distinctions between men and women.

Work, one of the most important means through which identities are constructed, is also a key setting in which gender is constructed. Through the work that they do and the way that they do their work, women are constructed as women, men are constructed as men, and women are constructed as inferior to men (West & Fenstermaker, 1993). In this way, gender construction is closely tied with occupational sex segregation and gender inequality. Within the constraints of narrowly defined gendered rules for behavior, women choose "women's work" or to do their work in "woman-appropriate" ways. These "choices," in turn, reinforce and maintain the constraints and result in women holding jobs with less pay, status, and power than men.

Evidence for this comes from numerous studies. Through studies of flight attendants, insurance salespersons, shop workers, managers, McDonald's drive-thru servers, table servers, lawyers, paralegals, and unpaid domestic work, researchers have consistently found that women, in their work, become "women" through actions such as flirting, deferring, and caring for others (Hochschild, 1983; Berk & Berk, 1987; Hall, 1993a; Pierce, 1995). Men, in their work, become "men" by being tough, strong, and aggressive when joking, taking risks, and performing tasks (Halle, 1984; Collinson, 1992; Pierce, 1995; Collinson & Hearn, 1996). These gendered behaviors are the result of organizational policies and practices which define work as gendered and therefore give women and men different titles and positions and require them to act and dress differently. The result is unequal occupational status, authority, and income for women and men (Martin, 1992). These gendered approaches to work persist when women and men perform different work or similar work or hold nontraditional jobs. Even when women and men perform similar routinized interactive service work or when women work as marines and men work as nurses, behaviors and approaches to work continue to construct women as women, men as men, and men as superior to women (Leidner, 1991; Hall, 1993b; Williams, 1989, 1995). As a result, gender differences and inequality, although constructed through workplace interactions, appear natural and innate.

Clearly, the process of gender construction affects how women and men do the work they do. What we know about gender construction and its relation to occupational segregation is based on the work that men and women do and on the organizations within which they work. We know less about how women and men construct gender by distancing themselves from work that is not typical for their gender and thereby maintain the distinct division between "women's" and "men's" work. For example, Williams (1989) argues that there are few men in nursing because men do not want to lose their manliness through becoming a nurse. She also argues that women who serve in the U.S. Marine Corps are less concerned about gender identity than men. (It is men's desire to maintain masculinity, rather than women's desire to maintain femininity, that limits women's positions in the military.) However, she does not talk to "typical" men or women to investigate why they decide not to do nontraditional work. Similar to the studies of women who fish, her research focuses on the exceptions.

In this article, I present results from a community study in which I focus on the perspective of women who do *not* do men's work. I describe the interactive process through which the majority of women distance themselves from "men's work" of fishing and select and carefully define themselves as doing other work as they construct themselves as "good" women, based on a heterosexual, feminine definition of good wife and mother. By looking at the case of women in a fishing community, I demonstrate the power of gender construction in reproducing work segregation, and thus inequality, between women and men. The segregation continues over time, through substantial community and industry changes, among both traditional and progressive women, and even when women work on fishing boats. This persistence is likely a result of the ideological inequality or gender status beliefs that form along with economic inequality as women construct gender in fishing communities.

Research Setting and Method

Rocky Haven is a town resting on the end of a small peninsula in the Atlantic Ocean. There are no stores, theaters, or restaurants in the town—only small wood-sided houses, a lobstermen's co-op, a boat building company, a church, and a post office. It is about a 15-minute drive to a convenience store or restaurant and nearly an hour's drive to a well-stocked grocery store or movie theater. Fishing, mostly for lobster but also for tuna, sea urchins, and scallops, is the main local industry. Most fishermen own and operate their own boats. About 40 lobster boats sit in the harbor, and thousands of lobster traps and buoys are stacked on wharves. Remote and peaceful, Rocky Haven is breathtakingly beautiful.

This article is based on my research in Rocky Haven and neighboring communities located in the eastern coastal region of the United States. My research was part of a larger comparative study on the effects of changes in the fishing industry on the families and communities. During my research, I lived and worked in a town neighboring Rocky Haven for two summers and one autumn—a total of nearly a year of fieldwork. I talked with and got to know fishermen, their wives, partners, and children both formally and informally. We talked at a local diner and coffee shop and met at town plays, town meetings, and public suppers. I went out fishing one day with the only woman "fisherman" in the area.

In addition, I conducted in-depth interviews with 54 women and men from fishing families. I interviewed people whom I met by living in the town, whom I purposely targeted because of a particular characteristic, such as work or reputation, or who were recommended to me by other participants. The final sample of participants ranged in age from 18 to 78, and all were white. In contrast to descriptions of fishing communities as closed to outsiders, I was very much welcomed (Ellis, 1986; Acheson, 1988). With a few exceptions, mostly when I first arrived in town, both men and women were very willing to be interviewed.

In such a small setting with a very strong information (i.e., gossip) network, it was impossible to conceal who had been interviewed. Instead, the tight network served to increase interest in the study. Those who had not been interviewed expected to be and seemed eager to tell me their side of the story. In fact, whom I had and had not interviewed was the topic of radio conversation among the fishermen on the day I went fishing.

This situation did affect, to some extent, the content of the interviews. Most notably, what were considered by fishing families to be very personal questions, particularly direct questions regarding income and marital relationships, resulted in resistance or false information. Therefore I addressed these in subtle ways, allowing people to provide as much information as they were comfortable with. For example, rather than asking, "How much did you earn from fishing last year?" I asked, "How does fishing as a living today compare with when your father was fishing?" People then sometimes told me how much they earned, while others would merely describe, without precise figures, the increase or decrease in income and standard of living that fishing provides. In both cases, I had the information I needed.

With few exceptions, the interviews were easy and immensely enjoyable to conduct. Fishermen and their wives were fascinating, entertaining storytellers, freely sharing detailed stories of hard times and hilarious accounts of life in the community. The interviews normally lasted an hour, and some lasted many hours. Usually they were conducted in the homes of the fishermen and their wives, but a few people preferred to be interviewed in the local diner. The interviews were tape-recorded and transcribed. Data analysis was conducted using grounded theory with the assistance of Lotus Notes, a data management software adapted for qualitative analysis (Glaser & Strauss, 1967).

During the years I studied the fishing industry, I also learned from other numerous and varied sources of information. Some of this information—from newspapers, magazines, novels, and data from previous studies and reports is used in this article.

Why Women Don't Fish

Most discussions about why women do not do certain types of work are based on the assumption that something about being a woman blocks them from doing the work. These factors vary and include notions of biological differences, socially learned differences, women's choices, or men's resistance. In this section, I address various choice and constraint explanations of how being a woman blocks women from fishing.

Biology

Work in the fishing industry is often described biologically. Fishermen are said to have "fishing in their blood," "saltwater in [their] veins," or "been born that way" and "can't do anything else." Women, likewise, give biologically based reasons for not fishing:

> I get seasick. The smells bother me, the bait and the diesel.
> I don't know if I could physically handle it. I'm not strong. I'd probably get sick.
> It's too early in the day for me. That's the big thing. If he would start at 6:00, I would be fine, but he gets up at 4:15. . . . I can't come home and take a nap.
> I can't nap. It's either eight hours or nothing.

> It comes down to more, well, strength issues.
> I think it's only a physical kind of thing. It's pretty hard work.

Women say that they simply are not physically able to fish as a result of weak stomachs or weak arms. But seasickness, smelly bait bags, and early work hours are not enough to deter everyone from practically the only, and most profitable, job in these isolated communities. These are women, as shown later, who overcome these problems to work in fishing boats under "acceptable" circumstances. And while fishing is a physically demanding job, new technology, such as hydraulic haulers for fishing gear, has greatly reduced the brute strength needed to do the job. As one fisherman and his wife observed, "You don't even really have to be [that strong to fish] with the equipment that is on the boats nowadays. . . . No, you don't. It's more of a stamina type thing than it is strength."

In Rocky Haven and wider American society, occupational sex segregation is commonly explained as a natural result of inherent, unalterable biological differences between women and men. Yet as many studies have shown, the true explanations for why women do not fish are more complex. This study also supports the conclusion that looking to social processes provides more accurate explanations of both why occupational segregation exists and why biological explanations are so common.

Gender Role Socialization

The differences between women's and men's orientations toward fishing are socially learned. There are significant differences in the way parents introduce male and female children from a very early age to fishing. When asked, "Would you like to see your kids fish?" one fisherman answered:

> I think my little boy, he loves rope. He's always pulling it and playing with it, tying things up. I took him fishing last week. He caught his first fish. He went right crazy. He's 4^1/2. He caught a mackerel about that big on a little Snoopy fishing pole. . . . I would encourage him, and I wouldn't try to sway him either way, but if he wanted to do it, I would see that he could.

I then asked him about his 9-year-old daughter.

> She won't have anything to do with bait or fish or anything like that. I'll come home and she won't give me a hug until my sweatshirt is off.

When I asked his daughter if she would like to fish, her response was similar: "I don't think so. . . . It's really stinky out on the boat."

From a very early age, boys are both subtly and overtly encouraged to fish; girls are not. Boys are said to love fishing from the time they are toddlers. Parents interpret even the smallest actions, such as playing with rope or a toy fishing pole, to indicate an orientation toward fishing. Fathers, uncles, and grandfathers take boys fishing and give them old traps and small skiff boats so that they can set up their own small fishing business. This time is viewed as an apprenticeship period in which boys learn the skills and social norms needed to be fishermen in the harbor. As they learn more, they build up their gear and enter the inner circle of fishermen.

Parents view girls' relationship to fishing quite differently. While a girl may go out on her father's boat or receive traps, these efforts are not seen as part of an apprenticeship or as serious steps toward the start of a fishing career. One wife of a fisherman describes her 12-year-old daughter's experience with fishing: "She has been out with her father, but she doesn't go on a regular basis. It was really cute, because when she was little, she would say that she was going to be a fishergirl, but that has kind of gone by the wayside now." Her daughter's interest in fishing was considered "cute," not something to be taken seriously and encouraged. Another woman explains that her husband has not taken their 9-year-old daughter out on the boat, although she wants to go. He will, she says, when she is older. She explains what he has done for her:

> He has a few traps around the shore for her, she doesn't know about yet. She will get her chance to go out. Right out here where you can practically walk ashore. It will be a big deal to her.

Girls' early experiences with fishing are viewed as a game rather than a training period. Going out on the boat is seen as fun rather than as an educational experience. Girls are given traps more as toys than as tools. When given traps, girls are often not even expected to fish them themselves. Their fathers will fish them instead.

After a childhood of such different gender role socialization, adult women and men are likely to make different choices about fishing. Men have been taught to love fishing and therefore fish. Women have not been encouraged to fish and therefore prefer not to. However, as I will demonstrate, women's opposition to fishing is more than simply a result of lessons learned in early childhood and more than merely a distaste. Women, every day throughout their lives, continually act to distance themselves from the act of fishing, even when they work on fishing boats.

Cultural Traditions

Many women and men say, as did one fisherman's wife, "It is just tradition more than anything" that explains why women do not fish. It is a part of culture, a custom. And indeed there are many, almost universal, cultural traditions of fishing communities that contribute to women's not fishing. There are strong superstitions, such as the belief that having a woman on a boat, and even near the water, is bad luck. These superstitions can push women away from boats and access to fishing. Allison (1988, p. 256) shares the following story of a woman who now fishes:

> Joan did not go fishing on her father's boat when she was young, as women were considered bad luck. She recalled that when she was about 12 years old, she was on her father's boat when he was taking it through the locks in Seattle. There was an accident; it was blamed on her because she was the only woman on board.

Cultural products have reflected and reinforced these beliefs and practices, romanticizing the gender-based division of labor in fishing families. The image of the man out at sea and the woman working, waiting, and worrying for her man's safe return is a pervasive theme in art and literature. In the 1880s, Winslow Homer painted pictures of fishermen's wives working and waiting for the fishermen's return on the beaches. Travel and regional magazines perpetuate this image through articles such as "Married to the Sea" and "Fisherman's Wife," which are written to celebrate the continued existence of the supportive, traditional, on-land role of women in the fisheries. Novels also emphasize the supportive role of women in the fisheries. In *The Perfect Storm,* Sebastian Junger (1997, p. 12) in his tale of the deaths of six fishermen in a 1991 hurricane, reconstructs the following scene:

> So in early August 1991, Bobby left on the first swordfishing trip of his life. When they left the dock his eyes swept the parking lot, but Chris had already gone. It was bad luck, they'd decided, to watch your lover steam out to sea. Chris had no way of knowing when Bobby was due in, so after several weeks she started spending a lot of time down at Rose's wharf, where the *Andrea Gail* takes out, waiting for her to come into view. There are houses in Gloucester where grooves have been worn into the floorboards by women pacing past an upstairs window, looking out to sea. Chris didn't wear down any floorboards, but day after day she filled up the ashtray in her car.

There is a clear message in art regarding the idealized roles for men and women in fishing families and communities.

Today, however, most men and women in fishing families and communities do not live according to these superstitions or these idealized images. Men often take women—wives, daughters, friends—out on their boats for pleasure trips on the weekends or for the opportunity to experience a day of fishing. And although a romanticized image of the dedicated, waiting, and worrying fishermen's wives persists in literature and art, women's actual lives often contradict these cultural images. For example, a woman living in a remote fishing community wrote a newspaper column entitled "Day in the Life of a Fisherman's Wife." In this series of articles, she gave wives advice on how to support and "really appreciate our men of the sea" as they suffer from sore feet during fishing season or cabin fever during the off-season winter months. Ironically, this woman stopped writing the column because she was too busy operating the new bowling alley she had recently opened in her town. While she reinforced the image of traditional women in her articles, she leads a life outside of that image—a life in which she had her own career goals. Strong cultural images of fishing families persist over time, yet the actual behavior of women and men can and often do violate these customs.

Discrimination

Gender-based discrimination is often the driving force barring women from certain workplaces and positions. Male employers or employees can act to make a work environment unappealing, hostile, or completely inaccessible to women (Bielby & Baron, 1986; MacKinnon, 1987; Jacobs, 1995).

Fishing in Rocky Haven and the surrounding areas is primarily done through owner-operator means, with fishermen each fishing from their own boats. While working as an apprentice or assistant is a common first step in fishing, being hired by an employer is not how one establishes oneself in the fishing industry. Rather, one buys and fishes from one's own boat. Although employers do not exist to control entry into the business, fishermen maintain formal and informal mechanisms that limit the number of new, competing boats in a harbor. For example, in lobstering harbors, there are often fishermen's co-ops, whose membership is controlled by the harbor fishermen. Acceptance into the co-op is often required for fishermen in a harbor and essential for successfully selling one's catch. Fishermen have also been known to use rejection, threats, and destruction of equipment (cutting gear loose or sinking boats) to discourage entry to new fishermen (Acheson, 1988).

Blatant gender-based discrimination, or efforts to keep women out of fishing, is not particularly pervasive in the fishing industry. While the small number of women in fishing makes the extent of discrimination difficult to determine, the only woman independent boat owner and operator in Rocky Haven is an important case to consider. She is unquestionably different in many aspects from women in Rocky Haven—she is unmarried, is childless, moved to Rocky Haven later in life, and teaches women's studies at a local university. While these characteristics may make her more willing to resist heteronormative rules and gender discrimination, being an outsider should make her more prone to negative reactions from fishermen, and her academic background should make her more aware of the existence of discrimination. Yet she reports that it was not hard to fish in Rocky Haven as a woman. No one damaged her gear or boat; no one was rude or hostile toward her; no efforts were made to keep her from working out of the harbor; and she was welcomed as a member of the fishermen's co-op. Instead of experiencing hostility and rejection, she built strong, long-lasting, trusting relationships with the fishermen in the harbor. She tells the following story:

> I was on the board of directors. Got elected to the board of directors at the co-op and served on that for 3 years. I helped with decisions, went to all the meetings, and never thought that the men thought anything about the fact that I was a woman—until I went to the state lobster association meeting. There were other members of the board from this co-op there. All of a sudden, everybody was introducing me and saying, "Now, we're the only co-op that has a woman on its board of directors." I thought, "Ah-ha, they're proud of themselves," that, number one, they let me get into the co-op, and secondly, they elected me to the board. I had not thought about that because here, nothing ever gets said.

However, subtle, rather than blatant, forms of discrimination are used by men to let women know that they are not welcome and to create working conditions that are intolerable for women (Benokraitis & Feagin, 1995). There are examples of subtle discriminatory behavior in the fishing industry. Sexual discriminatory language can promote an unwelcoming climate for women (Menzies, 1991). For example, sea urchins, which comprise a relatively new and highly lucrative fishing industry in the United States, are called "whore eggs" (Lauer, 1999). There is a strong preference for the term *fishermen,* often even among the rare women who fish (Allison, 1988; James, 1994). One woman made the following public statement:

> I am a licensed commercial fisherman. I am a wife, mother, and grandmother. If anyone there calls me, mistakenly, a "fisher," please refrain. I do not eat mice, porcupines, or other things that "fishers" find attractive.

There is also public disrespect shown toward women by fishermen. The VHF radio, used throughout the day for communication between fishermen, is the medium for "jokes," criticism, and sexual exploitation of women—sometimes local women and wives. This radio network serves to alienate women from work on the water.

The on-land social networks and activities among fishermen also exclude women. Like corporate leaders playing golf in the country club, talking on the wharf or spending a stormy day together playing cards provides an opportunity for people to learn about fishing and build friendships and trust. Women are often not welcome in these social settings. One wife explains simply that women are not welcome on the wharves. The woman cited previously, the only woman fishing in Rocky Haven describes an old hangout for fishermen in town:

> They used to go to what was called Bub's Fish House over here. They would stay there all day on bad days. There'd always be smoke coming out of the chimney, and they'd be in there chewing the fat or talking or what have you.

But she never went:

> I was never comfortable. A couple times I had to go get somebody because somebody would call the store and say, "Is my old man down there? Could you go get him?" But I didn't much like going over. It was that male-female thing.

There are unquestionably subtle forms of discrimination that work to deter women from fishing. This subtle discrimination not withstanding, fishermen do not seem to create a highly hostile work setting for women. The few women who fish as helpers or on their own describe a supportive and friendly work environment on the water. Kaplan (1988, p. 502) describes the situation for commercial fishing women she studied:

> Women fishers who worked on the same boat for a few years with a stable crew reported strong feelings of camaraderie developing among the crew. In general, once the women had "proven themselves" to be capable fishers, positive attitudes prevailed.

Although gender discrimination unquestionably exists in the fishing industry, as it does in other male-dominated work, and the discrimination may well increase if a larger number of women attempt to enter fishing, currently fishermen often do not need to discriminate to constrain women from fishing. I found instead that most women do not try to break the barriers which block them from fishing. They do not want to own their own boats and become fishermen. They reproduce the boundaries between themselves and fishing and, in doing so, maintain gender boundaries. Not being a fisherman is at the core of what it is to be a woman in a fishing community. Women, by separating themselves from fishing, are defining themselves as women. In sum, heteronormative gendered rules of conduct serve as the key constraints.

A Woman Doesn't Fish: The Construction of Gender

Women, Work, and Change

Women in fishing families have always done the unpaid household and child care work that is conducted by women throughout the world. However, being a member of a fishing family often results in additional tasks. As "shore captains," fishermen's wives have been responsible for waking up and making lunch for fishermen before dawn; listening to the radio to hear about the weather, the need for errands, or an emergency; painting buoys and caring for gear; buying equipment and bait and selling catch; calling for repairs; washing clothes that smell of fish; keeping the books; paying bills and taxes; and teaching sons to fish (Sinclair and Felt, 1991; James, 1994).

Financial pressures, particularly in the previous generation of fishermen, compelled many of these working-class women to work outside the house for pay. One 70-year-old fisherman explained how there were always two people working in fishing families: "They tell about this day in the world they have two people working. We always had two people working around here. The sardine factory, the women would work in."

Until approximately 20 years ago, a bus came each morning to pick up the women from Rocky Haven and take them to the sardine processing plant. The work was hard. Standing around a table cutting and packing fish as quickly as possible to make a good piecework rate left them with sore feet, cuts, and scars. The hours were long. During the height of the season, women were often expected to work 18 hours with only a short break to go home to feed their families. Yet this work was an important way for women to be good mothers and wives by supporting both the family and the fishing industry. A fisherman's wife in Newfoundland explains her work at the fish processing plant like this: "We're fisherfolk, and I like doing my share; I feel like I'm right in there helping my husband. . . . I just love the fish. . . . I even love to touch the fish" (Davis, 1986, p. 134).

During these times, the women worked together in the community and at the plant. During their free time, they socialized. They attended meetings and dances at the Grange, weddings and parties, sewing groups and church all in the same community, all with the same people.

Particularly over the past two decades, fishing, fishing communities, and the lives of women have changed. The fish plant has been mechanized, greatly limiting the number of jobs available for women. In addition, advancements in fishing technology have led to substantial increases in income associated with fishing and thus changes in lifestyles associated with fishing. Faster, stronger boats, more efficient and durable gear, and radar and fish finders have helped to greatly increase the income of fishermen. This has led to the ability of fishing families to afford other new technologies, including better cars and trucks, air travel, cable TV, satellite dishes, and home computers. Access to these innovations has greatly decreased the isolation of fishing communities from larger American society. Not surprisingly, increased contact with life outside the community and more income have had a substantial impact on the members of fishing families. The pace of life, social networks, values, beliefs, worldviews, life expectations, and fashion among community residents have all been influenced and changed by this contact.

These social and lifestyle changes have led to corresponding changes in the type of work that women do (Connelly & MacDonald, 1983). Given the more middle-class lifestyles of fishing families today, only one woman from Rocky Haven, an employee for over 40 years, still does the dirty, hard physical work at the fish plant. Today, women in Rocky Haven do not all work together. Instead, women do many different types of work as they construct themselves in correspondence with their accepted definition of what is a good woman.

Women as Wives and Mothers

Throughout society, being a woman is closely tied with being a mother and wife (Garey, 1995). Thus, the image of a suitable woman is based on a heterosexual, feminine definition. Work, both paid and unpaid, is a primary means through which women construct their identity as women. What it means to be a "good" mother and wife, and thus an appropriate or suitable woman in fishing communities, is based on one's performance as mother and wife in relation to the family's fishermen (Davis, 1986). Being a good mother means putting your children before yourself, including preparing them for a life of fishing if they so choose. Being a good wife means understanding and supporting your husband's work as a fisherman. One fisherman's wife explains why her husband got divorced from his first wife:

> His first wife didn't want him to lobster fish. He wanted to go into lobster fishing and she didn't want him to. She wanted him to work a 9-to-5 job so there was a steady paycheck coming in all the time. . . . Then when we got together . . . my stepfather was a lobster fisherman, so I was familiar with the industry anyway. So it really didn't bother me that much, and I said if you want to do it, go ahead and do it. I have stood behind him.

This woman sees the differences between herself—an appropriate wife to her husband—and her husband's first wife—who was an inappropriate wife—as differences in the amount of support and understanding they give him as a fisherman. A fisherman who is not married makes a similar distinction between suitable and unsuitable partners:

> Most of [the wives] are very understanding about what it takes to be a fisherman. One of my girlfriends said to me once, "Why don't you go get a real job?" Obviously, she was a person that didn't understand me and what I did because when you're working these hours 7 days a week, 52 times a year, a woman has to be very understanding, I think.

In fishing communities, nearly all of the women use these definitions of wife and mother in their construction of woman. As mentioned earlier, the one woman in Rocky Haven who operates her own boat and does define her work as fishing is not married or in a relationship with a fisherman and does not have children. In other words, she is not acting in heteronormative ways appropriate for a woman. After violating this widely accepted definition of what is a "good," or even "real," woman in the fishing community, she may be more free to behave in other ways that are not appropriate for women, and to fish.

Beyond being supportive of the fisherman and fishing in their roles as wife and mother, there is much diversity in the paid and unpaid jobs that women do. As in the rest of American society, the modern women's movement and changing beliefs about the proper role of women have impacted fishing communities. At the same time, traditional views regarding women have remained. The results are different and often conflicting definitions of what a woman should be, as constructed by the work they do. Nevertheless, the commonality among their work is that women define it as nonfishing work, use it to maintain boundaries to fishing, and thereby maintain their identities as nonfishermen (i.e., women).

Women Establishing Nonfishing Businesses

Some women do work that separates them almost completely from fishing. Given the remoteness and fishing dependency of the communities, there are few paid work opportunities for women. As a result, women often start their own small businesses, including hair salons, craft shops, landscaping services, day care centers, and freelance bookkeeping. Through their own businesses, women can have an identity and success independent of their husbands' fishing and the traditional role of fisherman's wife. One woman gave the following answer to the question, "Do you do any work related to the fishing industry?"

> I keep his books. I am a hairdresser and an electrolysist. You probably saw my signs (for her business) out there.

While she does help her husband with his fishing, that is not the basis of her identity. As she is quick to point out, she has her own work and identity as owner of a beauty salon. One fisherman commented on this change:

> Of course, the women now have jobs, real jobs. It used to be that when you were out at haul and you needed something, you needed to get hold of someone you could call on the CB. . . . Now you call in and there is nobody, no women home. They are all working.

A woman who owns her own landscaping business laughed when I asked what work she does related to fishing. She answered that the most she does is to put extra soap in with her husband's fishy-smelling laundry.

These women tend to be those who have been most strongly influenced by the modern women's movement and by the middle-class lifestyle of larger American society. They choose this work because they believe that a woman should act to ensure that she and her family are no longer confined to an old-fashioned working-class fishing lifestyle. They work to make their families part of a modern, progressive, middle-class lifestyle that extends far beyond the boundaries of the fishing community. They want their children to see and experience the world, go to college, and have more options in life than fishing. Yet, while these women choose their own nonfishing businesses as a means of being progressive and modern, and do gain their own identity, status, and success through this process, it is a strategy which leaves them blocked from fishing.

Women Maintaining the Fishing Business

Other women do work associated with a more traditional role in fishing families. These women see their work as supportive of their husbands' work, the family fishing business, and the fishing industry in general. They do the work of a "shore captain" (James, 1994). But even though these women do a great deal of work for the fishing business, they are clear about defining their husbands, and not themselves, as the fishermen. One woman says:

> I am married to a fisherman. . . . My husband keeps me quite busy. . . . I never know from one day to the next if something breaks down or he seems to think of something that he needs. . . . I would say I am a gofer. . . . He has a cellular phone so that he can call me, get in contact with me—"Can you go here?" "Can you go there?" "Can you call so and so?" "Can you do this, can you do that?" . . . It ain't too bad. . . . It's his livelihood and it's our source of income. I don't mind it. It keeps me busy.

According to this woman, her husband is the fisherman and fishing is "his" livelihood. She views the work that she does, although vital to his success on the water, as purely supplementary, something to keep her "busy."

In the past generation, there have been changes in the work that women do to maintain the fishing business. One of the most significant is the acquisition of the role of political representative and lobbyist through work in fishermen's wives' organizations. These organizations were once merely women's auxiliaries to the fishing industry. The members held fund-raisers and organized dances and picnics. The role of these organizations has shifted, however. With recent state actions toward increasing fishing regulations and closing fishing waters, fishermen's wives' organizations have adopted a political agenda. The members now read, listen, and learn about the new regulations. They write and call politicians. They go to fisheries-related hearings and meetings in the state capitals and in Washington. They give testimony on the strength of the fishing stocks and the potential consequences of proposed regulations. A number of the organizations have become quite powerful in the policy-making process. Some women have been appointed to positions in the state government through their work in these organizations. The Maine Fishermen's Wives Association and the Gloucester Fishermen's Wives Association are two particularly influential groups (Clark, 1988; James, 1994), but fishermen's wives organizations have formed all along the Atlantic coast, including Rocky Haven.

The women who do political work in these organizations continue to define their efforts as an important aspect of being a good woman in a fishing family. They are fighting for the family business and fishing industry, speaking out in fishermen's interests, and keeping fishermen informed. One woman in Rocky Haven gave the following description of the political work of the Fishermen's Wives Organization:

> The wives, they can have an ear out, they can listen and can be more informative to their husbands that are out all day, whereas they probably wouldn't know what was going on because they are out working. So hopefully we can keep them informed and keep them up to date on what's going on. But also I hope that we can help other people or future fishermen that want to, like the next generation coming up.

This woman describes the political work as similar to the work of running errands. She is assisting her husband by doing work that he cannot do because he is out on the water. In other words, women's political work in fishermen's wives organizations is possible only because they are not fishermen, not out on the water. Like the women who have their own businesses, these women have new avenues for acquiring their own power, status, and identity. Yet to do so, they must do work which is in opposition to fishing. This definition of an appropriate woman also requires that women do not fish.

Women Working on Fishing Boats

Probably the most dramatic examples of how women form boundaries between themselves and fishing in the process of constructing gender are found among those women who are most closely associated with fishing and work on fishing boats with their husbands and sons. These women do work on the water. But rather than violating gender-appropriate rules for conduct, they reinforce them. Women who work in the fishing industry "justify" their behavior as part of their role as a good mother or wife and thus as an appropriate woman. In her analysis of 19th-century diaries of women who went on whaling boats, Porter (1989, p. 34) writes, "The wives who went to sea embodied the Victorian ideal of the 'wife'" by cooking and caring for their husbands on the water rather than living a life independent of their husbands on land. In her study of 20th-century women who fish, Allison (1988, pp. 254, 238) found that marriage, an arrangement of "a male captain and his wife (or 'significant other')," was the most common means for women to become involved in fishing. She explains one woman's reasons for fishing: "Glenna says that their motivation to establish a family boat was not economic, but rather to keep the family together. . . . 'My husband didn't want to make ten day trips on his own, leaving us at home.'" Women view their time on the water with their husbands or children as an extension of the caring and supportive work in the family. They do not define what they do on the boat as their job or identify themselves as fishermen. Their husbands are the fishermen and their sons are future fishermen. They are merely assisting as part of their work as mothers and wives. This woman describes going out on the boat with her sons when they were young:

> I went with the kids in the skiff fishing because they weren't able to pull the traps and things aboard. . . . I used to get seasick in the skiff when I went with the kids. I always took a sandwich so I could eat. . . . But as long as I could eat and keep something in my stomach, I was all right. But I've got used to the motion now and I'm all right.

This woman is able to overcome seasickness in order to fulfil her role as mother and help her sons fish. However, she and other women usually are not able or willing to overcome this problem in order to find work in the fishing industry for themselves. Other women explain that they go out on the boat to care and watch out for their husbands. One woman describes how she started fishing:

> I started going with him on weekends. Then my son got to the age where he graduated and moved on and I didn't want him out there alone; he's ten years older than I am.

Like Glenna from Allison's study, this woman does not view her start in fishing as her own career choice. Rather, she went out to assist her aging husband once her son no longer could.

Relatedly, women do not define the money made through fishing as theirs or attributable to their work on the boat. They go out on the boat as their husbands' assistants so that he can keep all of "his" income for the family. One woman explains how she decided to go fishing with her partner:

> He asked me if I would be interested in doing it. . . . He pays about a third of what you catch to be a sternman [helper] for tuna fishing. He was a sternman last year, and he got a third. He caught a fish a few weeks ago, and his sternman's pay was $700 just for driving the boat. I thought, why not go and bring all the money into the house? For the fish we got today, he'll be able to keep all the money. He won't have to send anybody a big check for driving the boat.

According to this woman and others, she is not the person who is earning the money. It is *his* money. She is just helping him keep it. If someone else, a man, worked as the helper, her husband would have to pay him, because he would be a fisherman who would earn an income. Women, as they see it, are merely helping by providing free labor to preclude this expense. Moreover, since women do not define themselves as earners, the notion that fishing is not their job is reinforced.

Not only do women disavow income from fishing. They also disavow any knowledge of fishing. One woman explains the relationship between her and her husband on the water as follows:

> We really don't have any trouble. We get along really well, because I know I'm not the captain of the boat. I don't know what I'm doing. I don't pretend to know what I'm doing. He goes out of his way to make me feel good.

As she defines the situation, she is not a fisherman, so she does not know what she is doing. In other words, since she does not know what she is doing, she is not a fisherman—even though she fishes.

Following this reasoning, if a woman's role as assistant results in relationship conflict, it is the woman, not the man, who stops fishing. One woman explains:

> When we first got into it, we had our own boat and I drove the boat and helped him. . . . We didn't do that very long. We found that we didn't work well together. . . . [I haven't gone] directly fishing, not for very long.

Women do not strive for success in fishing themselves. They do not aim to learn more, earn their own money, or have their own boat, independent of male family members. They are prepared to give up their fishing work if necessary. They find other avenues for success. For example, one woman who goes out on the boat with her partner every day and enjoys this work has no interest in advancing her own fishing career. Her future career plans involve going back to college and becoming a nurse.

Why do women attribute all knowledge, effort, success, income, and identity that come from fishing to their husbands? Maintaining gender boundaries is important for constructing gender. In Rocky Haven, fishing serves as the basis for gender boundaries. In a place where man is equivalent to fisherman, a woman who takes on the role and identity of a fisherman is in danger of losing her identity as a woman. One woman, who fishes with her husband every day, articulates this most clearly:

> I don't mind working like a man. I don't mind looking like a man, but I want to be treated like a lady. I have to remind [my husband]. He thinks I am one of the guys. . . . [He will ask her to pick up heavy gear on the wharf.] He will ask, "Do you think you can pick those up?" I will say, "My name is Mary, not Mark." [And he will say,] "Oh yeah, you probably ought not do that." . . . If I gave up my femininity, I know that he is the type that wouldn't miss it. I am not the type to just let him take it. I don't mind working in gravel and dirt. But if he says, "Let's go to dinner," I want him to notice that when I go out, I am not his buddy.

She even describes herself as starting to look like a man: "When you become accustomed to men's ways . . . I looked at myself in the mirror one day, looked at my hands, and I thought to myself, 'God, Mary, you are looking just like them.'"

In the evenings Mary maintains a small cake baking and decorating business. Her husband cannot understand why she would do that after working all day. She explains, "Maybe it is just what I keep as a woman." This woman clarifies her fear of losing her femininity—the very things that make her a woman—by fishing. In order to hold onto her identity as a woman, she works extra hours at night doing what is unquestionably "women's" work.

The construction of gender—the production of woman as one who does not fish—is a constant process. Women, for the most part, are not aware of this process. It is an aspect of social interaction that has endured for so long, continually, and strongly that women's nonparticipation in fishing appears natural and unalterable. Indeed, as explained earlier, when asked why they do not fish, most women give biological reasons. Men's dominance of and women's absence from fishing, while a social creation, is most easily and readily explained by those in Rocky Haven as a result of inherent biological differences.

A woman in a fishing community is one who is not a fisherman, no matter how close she is to fishing. She works in her own nonfishing business, works to maintain the family business and fishing industry, or works on a fishing boat, but a woman in a fishing community is not a fisherman. To fish is to be a man. A woman's place in fishing is only as a helper, an extension of woman-defining behavior as a good mother and wife. Greater involvement in the fishing industry threatens her very womanliness. This situation ensures that there does not have to be strong discrimination or barriers to keep women out of fishing. Women, by their very definition, do not fish. Women maintain boundaries between themselves and fishing, and as a result, the world of fishing remains a man's world.

Discussion

Theories and studies of occupational sex segregation abound. As Paula England (1984, p. 726) notes,

> Virtually every perspective in the social sciences has spawned a theory about the causes of sex segregation of jobs. . . . With such a glut of explanations, it is more of an advance to weed out incorrect theories than to propose new ones. Segregation has more causes than any single theory can depict. But we should sharpen our focus to the most important factors generating and perpetuating segregation.

Given this, what can this study add to our understanding of occupational sex segregation? The findings presented here are based on data that are not widely generalizable. Fishing is certainly not representative of all work, and Rocky Haven and lobster fishing are not even representative of all fishing industries. There are likely to be quite significant differences within other types of fisheries and within other male-dominated industries. Furthermore, the women in this study, all white and sharing a similar social class, are not representative of all women. Nevertheless, this study of women and fishing is important in showing how the construction of gender both influences choices and reinforces constraints. It is a powerful, although often hidden, force in "generating and perpetuating" occupational sex segregation and corresponding gender inequality.

As this study shows, differences in preferences and experiences in the workplace do operate to block women's entry into fishing. Parents do socialize boys and girls differently in relation to fishing. Fishermen do use forms of discrimination that likely discourage women from participating in fishing. Being a woman does limit opportunities to fish.

However, if only these factors are considered, the constraints do not appear insurmountable. Some women do fish, and those who do fish do not have particularly negative experiences. Other women, it appears, could fish if they wanted to, so it can then be reasoned that women simply choose not to fish. At the same time, it can and has been argued that while women do not fish, they gain power and status through the roles that they do fill in fishing families and communities (Thompson, 1985; Davis, 1986; Porter, 1991). Thompson (p. 3) opens his article on gender and power in fishing communities by stating:

> Fishing is commonly thought of as a man's business. Yet . . . the masculine image of the industry conceals the reality of an occupation which, by removing men to sea, makes them peculiarly dependent on the work of women ashore. And this dependence gives women not only more responsibility, but also the possibility of more power, both in the home and in the community.

A gender construction perspective does not negate traditional, choice or constraint, explanations of sex segregation. Rather, it adds to them by highlighting the subtle aspects of interaction that contribute to the maintenance of unequal treatment of girls and boys and women and men both prior to and during their working lives (Pierce, 1995). When one examines the process of gender construction in which women distance themselves from fishing and do what they define as nonfishing work, the strength and negative consequences of the segregation become clear.

The power of gender construction in maintaining sex segregation is most apparent among the women who work on fishing boats. Women are in fact working in the fishing industry, going out every day on fishing boats. Yet even when actually doing the work, the sex segregation continues. Women maintain the gender boundaries and do not define themselves as fishermen. Therefore, they do not strive to increase their involvement in the industry by owning their own boat or catching fish independent of a male family member.

This distancing work persists as values, worldviews, and lifestyle changes. Even as women question their traditional role in the family and seek to gain their own identity, status, and power outside of the family, they do not question their exclusion from fishing. Instead, they look to other avenues for success. As a result, the segregation remains firm over time and across generations. The current generation of women in Rocky Haven do not fish, just like the previous generation of women. Most signs point to a continuance of this trend for the next generation of women in fishing communities. The result is that women do not pursue success in the most lucrative and available work in a remote area. The alternatives they seek do provide some income and status, but they remain structurally inferior to men.

The durability of the definition of woman as one who does not fish, and thus women's exclusion from fishing and structural inequality in fishing communities, is likely tied to the construction of status beliefs. Gender status beliefs are cultural beliefs widely held by both women and men that evaluate one sex—men—as generally superior and more competent than the other—women (Ridgeway, 1997, p. 221; Ridgeway, Kuipers, Boyle, & Robinson, 1998). Emerging from interactions between structurally unequal individuals, these beliefs in turn reinforce unequal structural positions even as social institutions and systems change over time.

Women, as they distance themselves from fishing in the process of gender construction, are forced to play down what they know, what they can do, and what they contribute to the fishing industry. As one woman explains, "I know I am not the captain of the boat. . . . I don't pretend to know what I'm doing." However, I argue, women pretend to *not* know what they are doing and/or do not try to learn and achieve more within fishing. They must act in this way because they are held accountable for acting as women and not as (fisher)men. The result is women not just being excluded from fishing but being constructed as inferior to men in the fishing community. In the end, women simply explain that they are biologically inferior to men—too weak, too ill to fish. Women, as well as men, grow to believe and act according to the belief that women cannot and so do not fish. This belief has far-reaching consequences in a place where fishing has traditionally been considered the heart of the family, the community, and life. The consequences of these gender status beliefs endure, even as women fight against them by developing alternative means for success and power in the political arena or in their own businesses. No matter what alternatives they develop, women continue to be defined as unable to fish.

This may explain why some women, particularly those seeking a definition as modern and progressive, work to distance themselves from the concept of "fishing family" or "fishing community." They find their own work that keeps them away from their husbands' fishing and does not leave time to be a part of the fishing community. As one woman explains:

> I go to school. That's where I work. I see another fisherman's wife who also works for the school. . . . So I see her in and out. But everybody is so busy. It's not that you get together and talk about what it's like to be a fisherman's wife, any more than you talk about being anyone else's wife.

Women's ties to the community and to each other, once described as strong and important, no longer are for many women. Separation from anything related to fishing, including other fishermen's wives, may be the only way for women to avoid being inferior.

From a choice or constraint perspective, the reduction in occupational sex segregation appears to lie in the implementation and enforcement of gender equity policies and practices. Affirmative Action, Title IX of the Educational Amendments of 1972, and Title VII of the Civil Rights Act of 1964 are all ways to break down barriers and to prepare and facilitate women's movement into any job. But what can be done if the very definition of what it means to be a woman is tied to developing and maintaining distance from certain jobs? What should be done if the consequences of occupational segregation are not limited to economic inequality but are at the root of the inequality-perpetuating beliefs both women and men hold about each other? By listening to the stories of the daily lives of women in Rocky Haven and using an interactionist approach to examine the process through which the gendered construction of being a woman contributes to occupational sex segregation, this study suggests that gender-based work segregation may have more pervasive negative consequences and be more difficult to eliminate than common explanations suggest.

Acknowledgments

I would like to thank Sean Lauer, Anita Garey, Robert Zussman, and the anonymous reviewers for their insightful comments on this article. The research presented here was supported in part by a National Research Initiative grant from the Cooperative State Research, Education, and Extension Services (CSREES) of the U.S. Department of Agriculture (USDA), #95-37401-2019.

References

Acheson, J. (1988). *The lobster gangs of Maine*. Hanover, NH: University Press of New England.

Allison, C. (1988). Women fishermen in the Pacific Northwest. In J. Nadel-Klein & D. L. Davis (Eds.), *To work and to weep* (pp. 230–260). St. John's, Newfoundland: Memorial University.

Benokraitis, N., & Feagin, J. (1995). *Modern sexism: Blatant, subtle, and covert discrimination*. Englewood Cliffs, NJ: Prentice Hall.

Berk, R. A., & Berk, S. (1987). *Labor and leisure at home: Content and organization of the household day*. Beverly Hills, CA: Sage.

Bielby, W. T., & Baron, J. N. (1986). Men and women at work: Sex segregation and statistical discrimination. *American Journal of Sociology, 91,* 759–799.

Clark, M. E. (1988). Managing uncertainty: Family, religion, and collective action among fishermen's wives in Gloucester, Massachusetts. In J. Nadel-Klein & D. L. Davis (Eds.), *To work and to weep* (pp. 261–278). St. John's, Newfoundland: Memorial University.

Collinson, D. L. (1992). *Managing the shop floor: Subjectivity, masculinity, and workplace culture*. New York: Walter de Gruyter.

Collinson, D. L., & Hearn, J. (Eds.) (1996). *Men as managers, managers as men: Critical perspectives on men, masculinities, and managements*. Thousand Oaks, CA: Sage.

Connelly, P., & MacDonald, M. (1983). Women's work: Domestic and wage labour in a Nova Scotia community. *Studies in Political Economy, 10,* 45–72.

Davis, D. (1986). Occupational community and fishermen's wives in a Newfoundland fishing village. *Anthropological Quarterly, 59,* 129–142.

Ellis, C. (1986). *Fisher folk: Two communities on Chesapeake Bay*. Lexington:University Press of Kentucky.

England, P. (1984). Wage appreciation and depreciation: A test of neoclassical economic explanations of occupational sex segregation. *Social Forces, 62,* 726–749.

England, P., & Brown, I. (1992). Trends in women's economic status. *Sociological Perspectives, 35,* 17–51.

Felt, L. F., Murphy, K., & Sinclair, P. R. (1995). Everyone does it: Unpaid work and household reproduction. In L. F. Felt & P. R. Sinclair (Eds.), *Living on the edge: The Great Northern Peninsula of Newfoundland* (pp. 77–102). St. John's, Newfoundland: Memorial University.

Fraser, J. (1998). Who we are: An industry snapshot. *National Fisherman, 79,* 26–34.

Garey, A. I. (1995). Constructing motherhood on the night shift: "Working mothers" as "stay-at-home moms." *Qualitative Sociology, 18,* 415–437.

Giasson, M. (1992). Capital and workforce adaptation in Clare. In R. Apostle and G. Barrett (Eds.), *Emptying their nets: Small capital and rural industrialization in the Nova Scotia fishing industry* (pp. 232–260). Toronto: University of Toronto.

Glaser, B. G., & Strauss, A. L. (1967). *The discovery of grounded theory: Strategies for qualitative research.* London: Weidenfeld and Nicholson.

Hall, E. J. (1993a). Smiling, deferring, and flirting. *Work and Occupations, 20,* 452–471.

Hall, E. J. (1993b). Waitering/waitressing: Engendering the work of table servers. *Gender and Society, 7,* 329–346.

Halle, D. (1984). *America's working man.* Chicago: University of Chicago Press.

Hochschild, A. R. (1983). *The managed heart: Commercialization of human feeling.* Berkeley: University of California Press.

Jacobs, J. (Ed.). (1995). *Gender inequality at work.* Thousand Oaks, CA: Sage.

James, C. H. (1994). *"Shore captains" in an unsure time: Seven women's perspectives on the future of Maine's fishing industry.* Master's thesis, Tufts University.

Junger, S. (1997). *The perfect storm: A true story of men against the sea.* New York: W. W. Norton.

Kaplan, I. M. (1988). Women who go to sea: Working in the commercial fishing industry. *Journal of Contemporary Ethnography, 16,* 491–514.

Krabacher, T. (1988). Sexual division of labor, risk, and economic success along the Sherbo Coast of Sierra Leone. In J. Nadel-Klein & D. L. Davis (Eds.), *To work and to weep* (pp. 130–148). St. John's, Newfoundland: Memorial University.

Lauer, S. (1999). *Small firms, global economies: The economic sociology of the Northwest Atlantic sea urchin industry.* PhD diss., University of New Hampshire.

Leidner, R. (1991). Servicing hamburgers and selling insurance: Gender, work, and identity in interactive service jobs. *Gender and Society, 5,* 154–177.

MacKinnon, C. (1987). *Sexual harassment of working women: A case of sex discrimination.* New Haven: Yale University Press.

Martin, P. Y. (1992). Gender, interaction, and inequality in organizations. In C. L. Ridgeway (Ed.), *Gender, interaction, and inequality* (pp. 208–231). New York: Springer.

Menzies, C. R. (1991). Obscenities and fishermen: The (re)production of gender in the process of production. *Anthropology of Work Review, 12,* 13–16.

Nadel-Klein, J. (1988). A fisher laddie needs a fisher lassie: Endogamy and work in a Scottish fishing village. In J. Nadel-Klein & D. L. Davis (Eds.), *To work and to weep* (pp. 190–210). St. John's, Newfoundland: Memorial University.

Nadel-Klein, J., & Davis, D. L. (1988). Introduction: Gender in the maritime arena. In J. Nadel-Klein & D. L. Davis (Eds.), *To work and to weep* (pp. 1–17). St. John's, Newfoundland: Memorial University.

Nowack, B. S. (1988). The cooperative nature of women's and men's roles in Btsisi marine extracting activities. In J. Nadel-Klein & D. L. Davis (Eds.), *To work and to weep* (pp. 51–72). St. John's, Newfoundland: Memorial University.

Pierce, J. L. (1995). *Gender trials: Emotional lives in contemporary law firms.* Berkeley: University of California Press.

Polachek, S. W., & Siebert, W. S. (1993). *The economics of earnings.* Cambridge: Cambridge University Press.

Porter, M. (1989). "Not drowning but waving": Reading 19th-century whaling women's diaries. *Studies in Sexual Politics, 28,* 1–77.

Porter, M. (1991). Time, the life course, and work in women's lives. *Women's Studies International Forum, 14,* 1–13.

Reskin, B. (1993). Sex segregation in the workplace. *Annual Review of Sociology, 19,* 241–270.

Reskin, B. F., & Ross, P. (1992). Jobs, authority, and earnings among managers: The continuing significance of sex. *Work and Occupations, 19,* 342–365.

Ridgeway, C. L. (1997). Interaction and the conservation of gender inequality: Considering employment. *American Sociological Review, 62,* 218–235.

Ridgeway, C. L., Kuipers, K. J., Boyle, E. H., & Robinson, D. T. (1998). How do status beliefs develop? The role of resources and interactional experience. *American Sociological Review, 63,* 331–350.

Shreenan, P. (1992). On the devaluation of women's labor: Hegemonic and local ideological practices. *Alternative Routes, 9,* 44–63.

Sinclair, P. R., & Felt, L. F. (1991). Separate worlds: Gender and domestic labour in an isolated fishing region. *Canadian Review of Sociology and Anthropology, 29,* 51–71.

Thiessen, V., Davis, A., & Jentoft, S. (1992). The veiled crew: An exploration of wives' reported and desired contributions to coastal fisheries enterprises in northern Norway and Nova Scotia. *Human Organization, 51,* 342–352.

Thompson, P. (1985). Women in fishing: The roots of power between the sexes. *Journal of Comparative Society and History, 85,* 3–32.

U.S. Census Bureau. (1999). Census '90: Detailed occupation by race, Hispanic origin, and sex. CenStats Database (http://*www.census.gov*).

West, C., & Fenstermaker, S. (1993). Power, inequality, and the accomplishment of gender: An ethnomethodological view. In P. England (Ed.), *Theory on gender/feminism on theory* (pp. 151–174). New York: A. de Gruyter.

West, C., & Zimmerman, D. H. (1987). Doing gender. *Gender and Society, 1,* 125–151.

Williams, C. L. (1989). *Gender differences at work: Women and men in nontraditional occupations.* Berkeley: University of California Press.

Williams, C. L. (1995). *Still a man's world: Men who do "women's work."* Berkeley: University of California Press.

4
Domesticity and the Political Economy of Lesbigay Families

Christopher Carrington

Editorial note: For his book *No Place Like Home,* sociologist Christopher Carrington observed 52 lesbian and gay families (108 members) in their homes, followed them around town, and then interviewed them about their jobs, their domestic work, and their relationships. For eight of the couples, he spent a week living in their homes.

Although the families Carrington studied are not a random sample, he self-consciously sought a sample that would include a range in terms of both social class and race-ethnicity. Of the 108 participants in the research, 63 were predominantly Euro-American, 15 Latino/a American, 15 Asian American, 13 African American, and 2 Native American. The median household income in the San Francisco Bay area, where the study took place, is substantially higher than for the country as a whole. It was about $50,000 at the time of Carrington's study; the median household income for his study participants was $58,500, somewhat higher but not dramatically so. Household incomes ranged from $24,000 to $230,000 a year, with families from three class groupings (working/service, middle, and upper middle class). Carrington argues that "social class distinctions appear more significant to domesticity than are other distinctions like gender and ethnicity or race. However, because gender, race, and ethnicity are often conflated with class in American society, people often make the mistake of thinking of class-related differences as the product of gender or ethnic/racial differences."

Our excerpt is from chapter 5 of the book; it focuses on the egalitarian myths these couples often believe and present about their domestic lives and the ways these couples actually divide work, both in and outside of the home.

The Division of Domestic Labor in Lesbigay Families

> Sterling never cleaned toilets, he still doesn't clean toilets; he intends to clean the toilets, but right about the time when he gets to it, I have already cleaned the toilets.
>
> —Wayne Osmundsen, 35-year-old social worker

The common metaphorical use of laundry, as in the phrase "to air their dirty laundry in public," connotes several things about actual laundry, most notably a common expectation that dirty laundry should remain hidden. This chapter violates that common expectation, in both a metaphorical and in a literal sense.

Stigmatized and oppressed communities often struggle with the menacing question of how to deal with "dirty laundry." Many lesbian and gay authors feel the need to present ourselves, and our communities, to the dominant culture in ideal terms, a feeling that I have often shared. These portrayals, as opposed to the empirical realities, often reflect the efforts of lesbigay people to provide a respectable image of ourselves in a society often bent on devaluing and marginalizing us. Undoubtedly, the observations made here regarding the division of domestic work in lesbigay families violate the expectation that dirty laundry remain closeted.

The public portrayals and presentations of egalitarianism among lesbigay families do not cohere with the household realities that prevail among them. Two components of the research strategy used here expose the gap between public portrayals and empirical realities. First, the use of back-to-back interviews instead of joint interviews produces discrepancies in answers to the most routine of questions about domesticity. As Aquilino (1993) reveals, interviews often produce much higher estimates of spousal contributions to domestic work when the spouse is present than when he or she is not. Second, the fieldwork component of this research offers behavioral observations that reveal significant gaps between what participants say in interviews and what participants do in everyday life. The commitment to the ideology of familial egalitarianism within the lesbian and gay community, and among the subset of lesbigay families, is palpable. Yet the empirical reality for many of these families is something quite different, something much more akin to patterns among heterosexual families (Gerson, 1985, 1993). Moreover, when a particular family achieves something close to parity in the distribution of domestic activities, this almost always occurs under unique social conditions: great affluence, relative impoverishment, or among a distinct minority of couples with significantly diminished senses of themselves as family. In this chapter I examine each of these exceptions and what motivates lesbigay people to portray their relationships in ideal terms both to themselves and to the outside world. I will also consider what factors seem to most significantly influence the actual division of domestic labor among lesbigay families.

The Egalitarian Myth

There exists among the lesbigay families studied here a prevalent and persistent commitment to viewing both one's own relationship and those of other lesbians and gays as egalitarian. Most participants in this study, when asked to describe in general terms how they divide up household responsibilities in their relationship, relied upon the language of egalitarianism. Typical responses included: "Oh, I would say it's 50-50 around here," or "We pretty much share all of the responsibilities," or "Everyone does their fair share," or "It's pretty even." These perceptions persist even in the face of obvious empirical observations to the contrary. Many lesbigay family members fail to make much of a distinction between what they consider equal and what they consider fair. The blurring of these two quite distinct matters is necessary to maintaining the myth of egalitarianism.

I will never forget the moments during an interview with one member of a lesbian relationship, a relationship where both family members were deaf. For this interview

I hired someone adept at American Sign Language to translate. Midway through the interview the translator paused, somewhat confused by a subtle shift in meaning. In American Sign Language, the gestures for *equal* and *fair* are the same. The participant began to make a shift in describing how the family organized domestic work from equal to fair. The shift in usage came in response to a series of probes exploring the work of feeding this family. The inequality in the division of feeding work was apparent to the three of us and, I suspect, created some awkward feelings for the participant. The fact that the translator had to stop and seek clarification exacerbated the dynamic. The translator later told me he sensed great discomfort on the respondent's part, and he felt like he had done her a disservice through stumbling over the subtle transition she was making. Despite his feelings of betrayal, the stumble revealed something that exists in many families, a perception that what a family considers fair, they also consider equal. Her clarification of *fair* led to a defense of the "fairness" of the distribution of feeding work in their family, a defense premised on the difficulty and demands of her paid employment when compared with that of her partner.

Consequently, one must remain aware of the distinct possibility that intense pressures exist upon a participant's answers to questions about the division of domesticity. I think these pressures go a long way in explaining why lesbigay families, when asked about domestic activities, particularly in public settings, often joke about the matter. The humor masks the awkward feelings such questions produce. And after a few humorous exchanges, and possibly a little dig or two, the families make a concerted effort to reestablish the perception of equality. The research of Hochschild (1989) indicates that heterosexual families do exactly the same; they construct myths of egalitarianism. But there is more to the story among lesbigay families than meets the eye.

The Model-Minority Effect

Similar to other minority groups in American culture, lesbian and gay people are highly aware of the public images of ourselves. Strikingly similar to many black Americans in the 1950s, contemporary lesbian and gay Americans go to great lengths to see, and reflect upon, the media images of us within the broader culture. The African American documentary film producer Marlin Riggs notes in his film *Color Adjustments*, a film tracing images of blacks in television, that during the 1950s many black people remember calling families and friends any time a black person was to appear on television. These viewers understood that those images would shape the broader cultural understanding, if not the self-understanding, of black Americans. Black Americans hoped for positive images, images that would advance the civil rights struggle. Lesbian and gay people maintain a similar vigil. Witness the near obsession surrounding the coming out of Ellen DeGeneres on the ABC situation comedy *Ellen* in 1997. As a part of this concern, lesbigay families portray themselves using the ideals put forward by American culture, ideals propagating the myth of the egalitarian middle-class family. Appealing to those ideals obfuscates the truth about real lesbigay families that they, like all other families, struggle with real world concerns about how to balance work and family obligations, and that the dynamics that produce inequality in heterosexual families also produce inequality with lesbigay families.

The Management of Gender Identity and Domesticity

Gender looms as a significant matter in the portrayal as well as the organization of domesticity in lesbigay families. Like many other scholars of gender, I find that domestic work results not only in the creation of goods and services but also in the creation of gender (Berk, 1985; West & Zimmerman, 1987; Coltrane, 1989; Hochschild, 1989; Ferree, 1990; DeVault, 1991; Petuchek, 1992; Brines, 1994). The potential for domesticity resulting in the construction of gender identity means different things to lesbian women and gay men. For lesbians, the capacity of domesticity to construct gender carries important consequences for partners whose paid-work obligations prevent them from engaging in much domesticity. Examples abound. Many of the lesbian women employed in time- and energy-consuming occupations expressed guilt about, and made much humor of, their inattentiveness to and lack of participation in domesticity. Their partners often provide cover for them, assigning credit for domestic tasks that they really did not do, or emphasizing some femininity-producing activity that compensates.

In a number of lesbian families, that compensation comes in the form of personal appearance and fashion. One of the families I studied up close provides a vivid example. Arleen Wentworth, a successful attorney, and her partner, Dolores Bettenson, also an attorney, illustrate the dynamic. Both women work full-time, though Arlene works many more hours than Dolores. While this family relies upon cleaning services, garden services, and restaurants for much of their domestic life, many of the remaining domestic activities fall to Dolores. One of the striking differences between the two women is their personal styles and sense of fashion. Dolores leans toward more gender-neutral fashion. She greeted me at the door for the first time wearing jeans and a T-shirt. She wears professional attire for work, but emphasizes staid colors, "sensible shoes," and little makeup. In marked contrast, Arlene greeted me the first time in a bright teal-blue dress, high heels, makeup, and jewelry. The distinction was persistent with Arlene attiring herself in such a way almost every day. I remember one evening when Dolores and Arlene were to go out to a cocktail party, Dolores, sitting next to me on the couch while waiting impatiently for Arlene to finish dressing, commented: "These lipstick lesbians are certainly high maintenance, huh?"

I replied: "Yeah, what's that all about?"

"Oh, I think it's her way of getting in touch with her womanhood. She doesn't really get any other chance to do that. Being a prosecuting attorney doesn't leave much room for that."

Dolores's observation underscores the impact of one's paid work upon one's identity. Arlene expressed guilt and discomfort with the fact that Dolores did much of the domestic work in their family. Dolores placed special emphasis on the contributions Arlene did make, such as pointing out the particularly feminine bed linens that Arlene had chosen for them, as well as emphasizing Arlene's participation in occasional baking. The management of gender identity is a collective concern in many lesbian and gay families—not surprisingly, for how many of us really would want the world to think of our loved ones as deviants of one sort or another?

The Invisibility of Domesticity and the Egalitarian Myth

Much of domesticity is invisible. Many of the forms of domestic labor rest upon a foundation of unobserved efforts that consume an individual's time and energy. Monitoring the house for cleanliness, monitoring the calendar for birthdays, monitoring the catalog for appropriate gifts, monitoring the cupboard for low supplies, monitoring the moods of one's spouse, and monitoring the family finances—all are expressions of domesticity, and all are mostly invisible. The vast stores of accumulated knowledge about domestic things go unobserved by most. The knowledge of a family member's food tastes, dietary requirements, clothing size, the last gift one bought for them, work schedule, and the last time the cat received a rabies shot are all forms of domesticity and are hidden in the heads of those who hold responsibility for doing these things.

This invisibility, even to those who do it, sometimes produces seemingly inexplicable feelings of anger and resentment. Domestic work often becomes the site of enduring conflict between partners in relationships. Joe McFarland and Richard Neibuhr have been together for just under 4 years. Their relationship is "on the rocks," as Richard puts it. They reluctantly agreed to an interview. The family recently bought a house together, using money from Joe's inheritance from his previous lover, who died in the late 1980s. Both Richard and Joe conceive of their domestic relationship in strongly egalitarian terms despite what to me resembles a clear pattern of specialization with Richard doing much of the domestic labor in the family—not just much of the invisible work but the visible work as well. Richard is not happy about the situation, although he has difficulty finding the words:

> I think things are pretty equal in the relationship, although I wish Joe would appreciate my contributions more, and maybe be a little more helpful. It's hard to describe, but I feel like I do a lot of stuff to make our life better, but he doesn't really care about that. I think he thinks I'm just nagging him. If I ask him to do certain things, like, for instance, I asked him to call someone about going out to a movie on Friday night, he gets annoyed. He says that if I want to go out to a movie with someone, then I should call. He thinks that's my interest. It's funny, though, because if I don't do it, he will ask how come we're not doing anything, and complain that we don't really have many friends. I get sort of frustrated about it, but I don't push it too much. He feels like I am dominating his space, imposing on his free time too much, not respecting his boundaries. He's very big on boundaries. He gets that from his therapist, who thinks that he needs to keep his own space.

A similar conversation took place with Joe. Notice how the advice of the therapist actually influences the division of domesticity:

> CC: Tell me about continuing discussions/points of conflict or unresolved feelings with your spouse over these kinds of cleaning tasks.
>
> Joe: My therapist is of the opinion that Richard lacks empathy for me, and/or

maybe empathy for people in general, and doesn't understand that for me, time down and time alone is a chance for me to think my own thoughts, feel my feelings, expand my emotional life through reading or television. Richard doesn't have any appreciation for that. Consequently, the therapist thinks he lacks empathy. He asks me to do things that are his interest, and that's not fair to me.

CC: What kind of things?

Joe: Well, like stuff for the house. I mean, I paid for the house, or at least mostly, and I don't really care that much how the house looks. I mean, I want it clean, but a little messy is not a big deal. If he wants it a certain way, he can do it. I need my space.

Richard feels frustration because Joe won't help with domesticity. If Richard expresses those sentiments, they actually become illegitimate because they are understood as an imposition of Richard's "interests" upon Joe. Both Richard and Joe conceive of their relationship as egalitarian with the differences over domesticity actually reflecting different individual "interests." The advice of the therapist, or at least the way it gets understood and deployed in the relationship, legitimates Joe's claim to private time and relaxation and delegitimates Richard's desire for help.

Several months after these interviews I ran into Richard at the gym. He had just joined, and we talked for a while. He told me he was coming back to the gym to "get in shape, and get a man." He then reported that he and Joe had broken up and that I was part of the reason. He said he wanted to thank me for helping him to get out of his relationship. I felt perplexed, guilty, mortified. Here is my rough approximation, scribbled on the back on my workout card, of what transpired that day at the gym:

CC: I am very sorry; I certainly didn't intend any harm.

Richard: Oh, it's okay. It's not really about you but what you helped me learn about myself.

CC: What do you mean?

Richard: Well, that interview helped me to realize just how much I actually do and did for that jerk.

CC: Like what are you thinking of?

Richard: Well, like all those questions about going out and buying things for the house. You know, I did all of that. And I did it because I wanted us to have a nice home, to be a family. But being a family, he thinks, is all about me and my needs. He says I am codependent. He just couldn't appreciate what I was doing for us. The interview made it so clear just how much I had taken for granted. I actually sat down and wrote a list up, thinking of the things that you asked about. Then I realized. I confronted him with it, and he basically thinks those things are my interests, and if I want to do them, that's all about me. Well, I knew I had to get out and find someone else who appreciates me more.

The sociologist as homewrecker was not quite what I envisioned for myself. But this situation led me to wonder about why so much of domesticity is hidden from those who do it through discourses about individual "interests" and in narrow conceptions of what domesticity actually is. Families hide much of domesticity, closet it, and drape the door with the ideological veneer of egalitarianism for quite practical reasons. First, as previously suggested, they do it to avoid the stigma associated with violating gender expectations. Second, and perhaps more significantly, they do it to avoid conflicts and to preserve relationships existing in a broader socioeconomic context that does not enable families to actually produce much equality. When thinking about Joe and Richard and the demise of that relationship I can see the dilemma that many relationships face. Joe really does need "down time"; he needs his TV for relaxation. Here he describes his paid work:

> Joe: Well, it's high stress. I am working about 55 to 60 hours a week. I have to travel down to LA every other week for at least a couple of days. I constantly get called at home if things aren't going right. The project director is a total asshole—oops, sorry, I guess I should say he's difficult to deal with. Ask Richard. I vent at Richard about the guy all the time. He's your typical straight white-male loser. He is constantly second-guessing everyone, micromanaging us, and is highly insecure. You just have to learn to deal with him.
>
> CC: Travel?
>
> Joe: Yeah, as I said, I go to LA every other week for a couple of days. I actually like it. It gets me out of the office and gives me a little breathing room. It gives me that space I need.
>
> CC: What hours do you work?
>
> Joe: I usually get home about 7 or 7:30. I go in at 8:30, leaving here at about 8.
>
> CC: Do you work evenings?
>
> Joe: It depends on the cases. If a project is due, it's due. Sometimes that means I work all night. I can be at the office till midnight. It just depends.
>
> CC: Weekends?
>
> Joe: It's the same. I usually work on Saturday mornings. I try to get some time at the gym on both Saturday and Sunday, but that doesn't always happen.
>
> CC: How long a commute to work?
>
> Joe: About 30 minutes.
>
> CC: Do you think of yourself or as Richard as more committed to work/career? How come?
>
> Joe: I think I am. I don't know why exactly. He's not into it as much. He likes his work, but he's not driven by it like me. He also works in a more pleasant environment. He doesn't have to deal with as much obnoxiousness.
>
> CC: What does your partner think of your job?
>
> Joe: Well, I suspect it's a love/hate thing. I think he resents that I travel, because he thinks I am having fun, and he gets stuck keeping things going around here. I do feel a bit of guilt about that, but it really is my job that takes me down there. I also think he respects what I do, and I make good money at it. That makes our life better, especially trying to live in San Francisco. It takes a lot of money to maintain a life here, and so I really try to make sure we are earning enough. Not that I don't think Richard doesn't work hard—I know he does—but if we both worked in jobs like his, we couldn't live here, or at least we couldn't have a house of our own.

A fairly clear picture emerges here, one that many families experience. The character of Joe's and Richard's paid employment greatly determines the organization of domesticity. Richard works in human resources, as a benefits counselor, for a suburban community. He works 39 hours per week in a public-sector job with extensive family friendly benefits, most negotiated by his union. He works mostly with heterosexual women, many of whom also hold responsibility for family life. He earns much less than Joe. Joe's work exhausts him, allowing little time, much less energy, for doing family. His work frequently seeps into family time. Concealing domesticity in the language of "interests" prevented Richard and Joe from reflecting upon paid work and family conflict. In fact, concealing the matter allowed them to avoid hard choices, including the possibility of Joe seeking alternate employment, with the potential for a reduced standard of living. They also could have acknowledged Richard's specialization in domestic matters, something they both seemed unprepared to accept. Richard understood their conflict in terms of personality, without much awareness of the impact of paid work upon what happened to them.

The Egalitarian Pattern

A minority of lesbigay families do achieve a rough equivalence in the distribution of domestic work, even using a broad and inclusive conception of domesticity. Roughly 25% (13) of the families I studied approach this rough parity. The participants in these families appear to take responsibility for, as well as spend similar amounts of time on domestic matters. Interview data and field observations reveal patterns of specialization among many of these families, although they still approach equity. For instance, in several families, one person pursues much of feeding work while another manages housework and kin work. Some families go to great lengths to achieve this parity. For example, three families use quite extensive "chore wheels." Chore wheels list many of the major housework items—and in one family much of the feeding work was listed as well—but none of them listed consumption, kin work, or status work-related chores. These families share a number of distinct sociological characteristics explaining much of the parity in the division of domesticity, and to those characteristics I will now turn.

Egalitarianism: Reliance on the Service Economy

Wealthier lesbigay families often purchase much domesticity in the marketplace, therein enhancing the egalitarianism within the relationship. In contrast to working/ service-class and middle-class lesbigay families, these affluent families rely extensively on the service economy, or upon an army of low-paid workers without fringe benefits who provide much of the domestic labor. This pattern closely resembles one detected by Hertz (1986) in a study of upper-middle-class, dual-career heterosexual families who achieved greater equity in their relationships through reliance on service workers. Eight of the ten wealthiest families in this study hire someone to do housework for them. Four of those eight hire Latina women who work for an hourly rate without benefits. No family earning less than the study's median income hires someone to clean. Seven of the wealthiest ten families frequently rely either on laundry services or include laundry as a responsibility of the domestic workers who come to clean. Two families earning below the median income take laundry on a consistent basis to a laundry service. Six of the wealthiest 20 families hire someone to care for their lawns or gardens. Four families, all earning above the median income, hire someone to walk their dogs during the day. One in five lesbigay families eat at least four meals per week in a restaurant. Sixteen of those 21 families earn above the median income.

A very clear picture emerges here. Some lesbigay families achieve partial equity in their relationships through reliance on the labors of mostly working-poor people. One can see some of these workers behind the counters of taquerias, laundries, pasta shops, coffee shops, and delis in lesbigay neighborhoods, although many others one cannot see because their labors are more hidden (domestics, gardeners, laundry workers, daycare providers). These workers are for the most part Latino, Asian, African American women, and young gay men and lesbians. Their labors contribute much to the achievement of egalitarianism within the families of the affluent.

Egalitarianism and Female-Identified Professional Occupations

The egalitarian pattern emerges with notable strength among those families where both individuals, regardless of gender, work in traditionally female-identified professional occupations: primary/secondary teaching, social work, healthcare assessment (nurses, dietitians, occupational therapy), librarians, school counseling, social work, and public-sector human resources jobs. A disproportionate number of lesbians and gay men in this study work in these professions. It remains an open question whether this pattern reflects the broader population of lesbigay people (Badgett & King, 1997). Popular mythology holds that lesbigay people are everywhere, and perhaps they are, but lesbigay people in long-term relationships don't seem to be. It may well be the case that these forms of employment actually nourish longer-term relationships, providing at least one, and in the case of some egalitarian families, all family members the opportunity to pursue family matters more readily. When the primary partners in relationships work in these fields, they establish a greater degree of equality between them in the distribution of domesticity. Why?

These forms of employment often feature *real* 40-hour work weeks, and they often offer paid vacation, paid holidays, more holidays, family leave, paid sick days, flex-time, flex-place, as well as employee assistance programs offering services to families facing alcohol, drug, and domestic violence concerns. All of these family-friendly policies create a somewhat more conducive environment for doing family work. In contract, lesbigay people working in other professional occupational categories infrequently receive such benefits, or they seem reluctant to take advantage of them, even if offered. Moreover, very few people in these professions report working more than 40 hours per week for wages. This is not to say that these forms of employment are all dandy. In fact, they often feature short career ladders, glass ceilings, lower wages, and less control over the content of one's work than do male-dominated professional jobs (Glazer, 1991; Preston, 1995). In a sense, discrimination relegates lesbigay professionals into the female-dominated professions and enables them to do more domesticity. When looking at lesbigay professionals in the male-dominated occupations, including the engineers, physicians, attorneys, and middle-level managers, a starkly different pattern emerges, one encouraging a clear division of labor within the relationship. Moreover, most of the female-dominated professionals do not require one to use one's residence in order to serve clients or to entertain them very much. This reduces the amount of housework, feeding work, consumption work, and kin work within such households.

Egalitarianism and Downsizing the Family

There is one other form of the truly egalitarian family: the downsized family. These families, mostly composed of male couples, engage in relatively little domesticity. Similar to the affluent egalitarians, these families also rely on the service economy to provide domesticity, although they rely on it much less extensively. These families often live in urban environments, usually sharing a living space with multiple adults. These guys, mostly in their twenties or early thirties, are often in their first relationships. They spend very little time in the places where they live, instead hanging out in cafés, bars, restaurants, gyms, and dance clubs. They don't put much effort into feeding work, eating out at cheap taquerias and hamburger joints or eating instant ramen noodles or microwaved frozen dinners. If they engage in body building, as many seem to, they eat simple meals of vegetables, bread, and pasta when they eat at home. They don't do much consumption work, although they do make joint purchases of CDs, linens and towels, and some used furniture. These joint purchases often become emblematic of their relationships. These couples do very little kin work, calling biolegal relatives mostly, but usually on major holidays or at Mother's Day, with each person responsible for his or her own biolegal relations. Even in these austere circumstances, domesticity often comes to play a crucial role in the creation of the relationship. For instance, several of these young male couples understood the time they spent together doing laundry at laundromats as expressions of their relational identity, particularly when they mixed clothing items together for washing and drying.

The Specialization Pattern

One person specializes in domesticity in roughly three of four (38) of the lesbigay families studied. This pattern actually parallels Blumstein and Schwartz's finding that longer-term families frequently consist of one person who places more emphasis on domesticity and one who places the emphasis on paid work (1983, p. 172). In this study, the longer the family has been together, the more pronounced the specialization becomes. For instance, only among families together longer than 9 years (21 families), and mostly earning higher incomes, do I find someone working part-time by choice in order to handle domestic activities (seven families), or someone engaging in homemaking full-time (three families). Interestingly, these highly specialized, longer-term lesbigay families conceive of their circumstances as *equal*, although I suspect they really mean *fair*. They consider things fair in light of a whole series of spoken and unspoken matters ranging from the number of hours someone works for wages to the pleasures one garners from domesticity. Let me now turn to some of the central factors encouraging specialization in domesticity or in paid work within lesbigay families.

Paid employment exerts the greatest influence upon the division of domesticity in most lesbigay families. The number of hours paid work requires, where the work takes place, the length of the commute to work, the pay, the prestige, and difficulty of the work all conflate to encourage a pattern of specialization. The relative resources that each person brings to the relationship from paid work influences the division of labor. In most cases the person with less earning potential, or with less occupational prestige, picks up a disproportionate share of domestic labor. This finding parallels the "relative resource" model put forward to explain the division of domestic labor among heterosexual families (Blood & Wolfe, 1960; Brines, 1994). The pursuit of such resources (money, benefits, stock options, prestige, and networks) also takes time, usually leaving the pursuant with little time left to handle domesticity. In this sense, my findings parallel the "time availability" explanation (Acock & Demo, 1994) of the division of domestic labor. However, unlike some resource theory, my analysis does not conceive of domesticity as a great unpleasantness that the person with more resources (e.g., income, prestige, and education) forces onto the person with fewer. Such a view reduces domesticity to its unpleasant aspects and conceals its attractive ones, therein leaving us with no convincing explanation of why some people prefer, and orient themselves toward, domesticity (Ferree, 1980). Rather, I detect a pattern of family members attempting to maximize the quality of their household lives both through providing income and through providing domesticity. Among the affluent participants, each family member pursues income, and the family purchases meals, laundry, housecleaning, and so on in the service economy. Most lesbigay families can't afford this, even with both working full-time, and so they must pursue a different strategy. Longer-term families recognize the importance of domesticity to relational and family stability, and many of them pursue a strategy to attain both domesticity and financial well-being. The most obvious strategy consists of encouraging the family member with the greatest economic opportunity to pursue paid work vigorously. This has its limits, but the pattern occurs in the majority of households and becomes stronger over time.

Gravitating Toward Domesticity

Practical economic concerns and occupational characteristics play the largest role in determining who gravitates toward domestic involvement. In a few instances, those who gravitate toward domesticity "choose" employment that complements their family commitments. In most instances the character of one's paid employment facilitated participation in domesticity, with very little "choice" or much reflection on the matter. Some people appear to make conscious choices about domesticity, but the choices are constrained by economic and occupational realities. For instance, only among affluent families does the choice exist to work part-time for wages, devoting the remaining time to personal and/or family life. Similarly, those in professional careers frequently find it easier to merge work and family concerns. Some professionals make phone calls to friends and family from work, as well as arrange their work schedule to pursue domestic matters. Working- and service-class lesbigay families don't have these options. I want to emphasize the importance of context to the question of "choice" here. Some participants choose to ensconce themselves in domesticity, but few really possess that option. Some participants choose to take on a disproportionate share of domestic labor, but most simply find themselves doing the work without much sense of choice. That doesn't necessarily mean they feel unhappy or conceive of things as unfair—some do, and some don't. Rather, they often simply adjust in light of the expectations and opportunities associated with their own paid work and the paid work of other family members.

Family-Friendly Careers and Jobs

Many of the women and men in these specialized families are employed within traditional female-identified occupations (teaching, nursing, etc.). They take on a disproportionate share of domesticity, especially when they are in relationships with individuals in professional, managerial, or executive positions. The pattern is quite apparent among teachers. The summer recess, holiday breaks, the capacity to do schoolwork at home, and lower salaries all conflate to encourage teachers to pick up a disproportionate share of domestic life. Few of the teachers anticipated this state of affairs at the beginning of their relationships. The experience of one teacher, Andrew Kessler, illustrates the dynamic. In the summer of 1997, at a northern California gay resort area popularly known as the Russian River, I ran into Andrew, a third-grade teacher, whom I originally interviewed back in 1994. He has taught school for 8 years now, and is in a relationship with a computer software consultant. During casual conversation he commented on returning home from vacation to begin his "summer housewife stint." I asked, "How is it that you came to play that role?" Andrew responded:

> Well, it's kind of strange. I think it happened because I have the summer off. I wasn't really that into domestic things when we first got together. I was just out of school, and I was very gung-ho about my teaching. Part of it has to do with Darren's job. He works a lot, and he works pretty hard, and so I think I feel a little bit of obligation to try to ease the burden on him. He earns a lot, and that makes our life pretty great. It's funny, though. I don't really feel like I was forced to do the house and stuff. More like I came to like it over time. I felt a certain accomplishment about it, about keeping it nice. Darren couldn't really do that much, given the hours he works, and he travels some. So I think it fell to me to create more of a sense of home for us. Some of it is quite boring, of course, but I like some of it, too.

Andrew's experience is actually quite common among lesbigay families. Andrew did not really choose to become domestically oriented; rather, over time, he gravitated in that direction. Andrew's explanations of why he prepares evening meals, meets service and delivery people at the house, and does much of the consumption work all point to paid work, either the relative flexibility of his own career or the inflexibility of his partner's career. In Andrew's case the pull toward domestic involvement began early in his work experience, and in some ways this left him less cognizant of the ways that work influences family life. For others, the pull came later, and they have a much stronger sense of how work influences family life.

Fanny Gomez, now 44 and in her second long-term relationship as well as her second career, recently finished school and began working as a social worker. In her first relationship she did very little in terms of domesticity. She worked 60 hours per week as an accountant for a large commercial real estate firm. After her first relationship broke up, she decided she wanted to make a lot of changes in her life. Mostly she wanted to pursue a career that made her happier and that would "make some contribution to improving other people's lives." When she and her new partner, Melinda Rodriquez, moved in together, she realized that neither of them was particularly adept at domestic tasks. They wanted to eat meals together at home, but "the meals didn't seem that satisfying." Fanny decided to spend some time learning how to cook. She bought some cookbooks and attended a cooking course on Saturdays, something she would not have had the energy to do while she was working in real estate. Her new job, doing social work with elderly Latinos as part of a city-funded program, is stressful, but it has more limits. Fanny says she works 38 hours a week and "not an hour more," unlike her old job, where they knew no limits, where "my whole life was about that firm." She also receives more holiday time and more vacation time. She doesn't earn as much as she used to, but she's happier. Fanny noticed that her new job, and her new relationship with Melinda, a midlevel sales manager for a computer technology firm, brought new responsibilities on the home front:

> Fanny: We've had some fights about housecleaning over the past couple of years. She says she doesn't have time to do the stuff, and I understand that, but I don't think it's fair that I have to do it. But I think I realized that if I didn't, then nobody would. And I am here more often than she is. I get home earlier, and I leave for work later. Because I get home earlier, it's easier for me to cook and to stop by the store and stuff.
>
> CC: How is this different from your first relationship?
>
> Fanny: I never would have done that sort of thing in my first relationship. In fact, I've gone through a transition. I had no interest in cooking when I was with Janet. But in this relationship, it seems more important to me. I guess I missed the meal time that I had with Janet, and I wanted to have that again with Melinda, but Melinda wasn't into doing it, so I picked it up. I think Melinda appreciates it, though.

On the one hand, Fanny contributed to her new involvement in domestic life through choices she made about work. On the other hand, Fanny's work and the work of her new lover, Melinda, changed Fanny. Fanny's search for more fulfillment in her career brought her into an occupational context that facilitated more domestic involvement.

Fanny, a social worker, and Andrew, the teacher, are not alone. Of the 28 professionals who work as nurses, primary/secondary school teachers, counselors, social workers, librarians, and community college instructors, 18 are more domestically involved than their partners while 6 appear equally involved and 4 of those 6 are in relationships with partners in similar occupations.

In addition to the female-identified professional career tracks that seem to encourage domestic involvement, those individuals who work at home as artisans, writers/editors, or independent service contractors, as well as those who are students, retired, or underemployed, also bear a disproportionate share of domesticity. Twenty-four participants do much of their paid work at home—work ranging from accounting services to daycare to running a bed and breakfast to editing books to building furniture. Of these 24 participants, 18 carry a greater share of the domesticity. These participants often weave their paid work with their family work. Mary Ann Callihan, an artisan, builds custom Arts and Crafts style furniture out of her garage. She recounts her activities for the day I interviewed her:

> Well, I started off eating breakfast, and then loaded the dishwasher and started it. I came out to the garage to check on the custom headboard for a bed I am working on. I applied a stain to the maple last night, so I wanted to see how it turned out. Then I went back into the house and sorted some laundry and put a load in. Let me think. Then I went back out and cut some pieces of maple for the footboard that goes with this bed I am working on. That took a couple of hours. I think I went into the house a few times. I know I changed the laundry over several times. Right about lunch time, I ran down to the Castro to get some glue. I stopped by the store and picked up some groceries for dinner on the way. I got back up here, and I ate some lunch, watered the garden, and then continued working on the footboard for a couple of hours. About 4:00 P.M. I went down to deposit a check at the bank in Castro. I talked to some friends I saw in front of the bank. I got back up and folded most of the laundry. Margie got home about 5:00 P.M. I guess I started dinner while I took the car and ran over to Restoration Hardware, where they special-ordered some hinges for one of my projects. I got home and put the finishing touches on dinner. We ate, and now you're here.

Surprisingly, Mary Ann portrayed the division of domestic labor as "about 50-50" at the beginning of the interview. In contrast, her partner, Margaret Jackson, felt that Mary Ann probably did more mostly because "she's around the house more, and I think she's just more aware of what needs to be done, and she often does it." The interviews made fairly clear that Mary Ann tends to do much more domesticity. Margaret works as a personnel manager for a retail clothing store, often working into the evening and every other weekend. Margaret reports working about 55 hours per week. Determining how many hours Mary Ann works is not easy, given the blending of domestic life with her furniture work. She made $22,000 in 1994 from her furniture sales and other carpentry jobs. Margaret earned slightly more, about $25,000 the same year. Mary Ann's specialization in domesticity appears to result from the fact that she works at home, a circumstance that for her, and for many of the others who work at home, encourages greater involvement in domesticity.

In sum, many participants gravitate toward domesticity not out of choice, or because of a strong interest in domestic pursuits, or even because they possess certain skills. Rather, they gravitate toward domesticity because the character of their paid work and that of other family members encourages their involvement. Many of these domestically involved individuals have not made a big decision to focus on family life. Rather, because of many small decisions, they gravitated toward the domestic. The decision to start the evening meal because one arrives home earlier than others facilitated increased feeding work. For those who work at home, the decision to clean the bathroom or do the laundry during the day led them into increased housework.

For those with more flexible work schedules, the time to shop for consumer goods led them into increased responsibility for consumption work. Some participants do make a conscious commitment to greater involvement in domestic and family matters, and I will address them in the next section, but most do not. Their domestic careers appear to develop residually, accumulating slowly and unreflectively over the course of their relationships. They then become the experts and begin to feel the responsibility for domesticity.

Domestic by Choice

Few individuals actually choose, in a particularly conscious manner, to become more involved in family and domestic affairs. However, some do, and for a variety of reasons—reasons often reflecting growing disenchantment with paid work, or concern about maintaining an endangered relationship, or simply a love of domestic life. However, the nature of these choices varies dramatically across social class. The two men who conceive of themselves as homemakers are notable examples of choosing domestic involvement, as well as one woman, Virginia Kirbo, who works 10 hours per week. All three made conscious choices to forgo paid employment in favor of concentrating on family and community life. All three are in relationships with highly successful, well-paid individuals. These families dwell in exquisite yet labor-intensive homes. I found the daily schedules of all three quite stunning, for not only do they maintain homes thick in domesticity but these three people also expend great energy volunteering in the nonprofit sector.

John Chapman, 47, once worked as a successful graphic artist. Over the past decade he gave up his successful graphic art practice in favor of "keeping the house" and "doing good things for the community." He consciously decided that "some of the fun went out of his work, especially serving so many corporate clients." He felt that serving corporate clients created a "factorylike feel" to what he thought of as an "artistic and creative enterprise." The factorylike character of the work distracted from his satisfaction with his work, and he decided he wanted to do more work for nonprofit organizations. The rising income and career success of his partner, Theodore Fairchild, made it possible for John to do more of this kind of work, and eventually he stopped taking on new contracts.

John now does graphic work only as a volunteer. He serves on the board of directors of two of San Francisco's largest AIDS service providers. For one, he edits the monthly newsletter and maintains the website. He spends two mornings a week volunteering at a hospice for people dying of AIDS-related diseases. He has served his local Episcopal church in almost every leadership and volunteer capacity over the last decade, most recently chairing a ministerial search committee for the parish. He volunteers as a guide every other Saturday at the Conservatory of Flowers in Golden Gate Park, where he blends his personal interest in gardening with his sense of public service. He spends two nights of every month working for the Stop AIDS Project, where he takes to the streets of the Castro and "gets to tell the young ones how to practice safer sex." John and Theodore live in a spectacular Victorian residence in the Presidio Heights section of San Francisco. John maintains the house and an elaborate garden. They entertain often and always have meals at home, something that John feels is very important to their relationship. John's experience is unique, for few lesbigay families earn enough money to make such choices.

Hindered Work Opportunities

While some of the more affluent participants became disillusioned with their careers and "chose" to emphasize domestic life instead, many other participants found themselves unable to get onto career or promotional tracks or ran into glass ceilings and consequently shifted to a domestic focus. The lack of job/career opportunities resulted in a greater emphasis on domesticity for at least 11 of the families I studied. Five of these families came to San Francisco due to an employment opportunity for one member of the family. These families migrated with hopes of finding suitable employment for both partners, but this didn't always happen. Carey Becker, 43 and working part-time as a radiology technician, shares her life with Angela DiVincenzo, a special education teacher. Five years ago they moved to San Francisco from New Jersey. A suburban Bay Area school district offered Angela a position creating a new curriculum and program for special education. Carey, who worked as a full-time radiologist in back East, discovered that she lacked the proper credentials for employment in California and that few employment opportunities existed. Carey took a part-time position with hopes of finding something full-time. She never did. Initially, Carey picked up a larger share of the domesticity:

> CC: Describe the impact of significant job changes on your relationship.
> Carey: The move to San Francisco had a major impact, and I think it still does. I am still trying to get into the kind of work I would like to do, although I don't know if it's possible now. The market for radiology techs is not very hot. I have thought about what else I could do. Angela just wants me to be happy, and she hasn't put any pressure on me to find something else. The part-time position actually is 30 hours, and now that Angel's school district offers domestic partnership, I don't need to worry about going without insurance.
> CC: Did the move change what you do in the relationship?
> Carey: In some ways, it did. I do a lot more of the housework and stuff now. I don't really mind it too much. Angela works pretty hard, and I try to contribute what I can to our relationship.

Following a similar pattern, Julie Avilla moved to San Francisco with her partner, Teresa Rivera, in 1986. They came after Teresa received an offer for a midlevel management job with a San Francisco hotel. Julie found work as an attendant at a group home for severely disabled adults. Julie hated the work and switched to a sales position with a health food store for a couple of years. For the past 3 years, she has worked as a sales associate for a large bookstore. She really dislikes the work and thinks about going back to school, but "feels a bit old to be trying a whole new career or something" and doesn't really know what she would study, much less whether they can afford for her to go. Asked whether she thought their incomes influence the division of household chores in any way, Julie responded:

Sort of, but not directly. I mean, Teresa doesn't say or ever even imply that because I earn less I should do more household chores. I mean, I think I do more because it means more to me. I really get something out of it, a sense of accomplishment, of contributing something. I sure don't feel that way at work. I feel exploited there. We tried to unionize recently, and it was just ugly. The whole thing left a bad taste in my mouth, about how much the corporation that owns the store just doesn't appreciate its employees. At home, I feel appreciated. Teresa values what I do at home. She notices when I reorganize the furniture or take care of some small thing.

The poor quality of Julie's paid work life, in combination with the relative success of her partner, nourishes Julie's identification with domestic life, an arena where she feels more appreciated.

In a similar fashion, some lesbians and gay men ran into the proverbial glass ceiling at work and consequently reconceived of their careers as jobs, set limits on how much work could encroach on family, and developed a new interest in domesticity. This pattern emerged with marked strength among lesbigay professionals and managers working in predominantly heterosexual contexts. Brad O'Neil, in his early 50s, spent much of his life in computer engineering. Over the past decade he has attempted to break into an upper-level management position with his current employer. He responded thus to questions about his sexual orientation and the impact of being gay on his job:

CC: Does your employer know of your sexual orientation?
Brad: Yes.
CC: Describe the impact of this circumstance on you.
Brad: I don't know what to say. I feel like for a long time I tried very hard. I did all the right things. I worked and worked, staying late, going in on weekends. Somehow they kept passing me by for promotion. I suspect that the old straight boys think that I will not fit in, not make the decisions that they would make. I mean, maybe I am not really cut out for a high-level position. It's hard to tell. Are they discriminating against me? I think they are, but they would deny it. I look at some of the people that have moved into executive management positions, and I really wonder. In the last few years they have moved a couple of women into those positions, but I think they did that reluctantly. And I am not saying that those women shouldn't be there. They should. But, you know, I think I should also be there. Maybe there aren't enough spaces for everyone who's qualified. But the reality is, when I look around at top management, it's all straight white males and a few token straight women.
CC: How has this situation impacted your relationship?
Brad: Over the past few years, my viewpoint changed. Like I said, I realized I was not going to move up, not unless I went to another company. So I began to set some limits. I no longer go in on weekends, and I try to leave by 5:30 now. I do a lot more at home. I am trying to lift some of the burden off of Jerome, who is younger and trying to get his career going. I do much of the cooking at home, when we eat at home, and I do a lot of

the social planning for us. Jerome used to do more of that kind of stuff, but I do a lot of it now.

In like manner, Randy Ambert, a flight attendant for 15 years, realized that upward mobility was not really a possibility for him, and over time he became more vested in domestic pursuits. Listen to Randy's comments about his commitment to career:

CC: Do you think of yourself or your partner as more committed to work/career?

Randy: I think he is.

CC: How come?

Randy: He gets more out of his work now than I do. When I first started flying, it was different. I had a real sense of it as a career and that maybe I would move into management or something. But there really aren't that many opportunities for flight attendants to move up. And you certainly don't move to higher echelons of the company. I have never met a gay executive at Transglobe Airlines in 15 years, not one. So I think I lost interest after a while. A lot of people fly for a few years and then get out of it. For me, it's a job. I do what I need to do to get through it, and I find meaning in my life by doing other things.

CC: What kind of things?

Randy: Oh, the house and our friends. I collect furniture from the 1950s, and I maintain the yard, and I cook a lot. Things like that.

Unsuccessful efforts to enter or progress in paid work, whether due to lack of credentials, discrimination, or to short career ladders created disenchantment with notions of meritocracy and undivided commitment to work. As a result, the affected individuals shifted focus and infused greater effort and meaning into family matters.

Preserving Relationships

Finally, another dynamic bolstering active participation in domesticity springs from efforts to preserve a cherished relationship. At some point in their life together, several lesbigay families faced hard choices of maintaining two careers or maintaining the relationship. In most cases, these longer-term lesbigay families struck a deal. Sometimes the deal included someone turning down a promotion; in other cases the deal included a diminution of work involvement for one while the other put more into paid work. Narvin Wong and Lawrence Shoong, together for just over 5 years, faced just such a crisis about a year before I interviewed them. Narvin, a health care consultant, made the decision to do independent consulting. He saw a lucrative economic opportunity and the chance to exert greater influence over his work, and he decided to take it. The decision also meant a great increase in the number of hours that he would work. Meanwhile, Lawrence had taken a promotion to a nursing position with a large, well-funded research project. The position entailed a pay increase and was much more prestigious, given that the project was associated with a major medical research center. The position required Lawrence to work many evenings with research subjects, and diminished the amount of time he could spend at home and with Narvin. About 6 months into their new work situations, conflict began to develop at home. The conflicts initially circled around housework, but eventually expanded to questions about emotional availability and the energy available for sexual interaction. Lawrence reflects on a question about the impact of work on his family life:

CC: Describe the impact of significant job changes on family/relationship.

Lawrence: Narvin's choice to go into independent consulting created some big changes, changes in his attitude, and changes in our life together. He has very high expectations for himself. He went to an Ivy League business school, and I think he puts lots of pressures on himself to succeed. The problem was that I felt left out, sort of abandoned. I took the position at the medical center, and suddenly I wasn't around in the evenings, and I felt like our relationship just went into a spiral. I loved working at the medical center. I got to work with really great people, and the work was interesting, and I was putting in quite a few hours, more than I used to at Marin General. But after a while I began to feel like I no longer had a life with Narvin. We talked about it, and I asked him about working less on weekends and maybe trying to have a little more energy for us being together. He was pretty stubborn, though.

CC: What was he stubborn about?

Lawrence: His career and his consulting work. He just felt so strong about trying to make it go.

CC: How did that make you feel?

Lawrence: It felt terrible. For a while, I thought maybe he was no longer interested in me. I started having these fantasies that while I was at the lab, he was here, and instead of working, he was having an affair with someone. I would call, and he would get annoyed because he was trying to get work done. We talked about it, and I realized that he wasn't really having an affair, but he was just committed to his work. I think he was pretty worried about finances as well. I mean, we just bought this house, and he was giving up a good salary, and it's not like nurses make a whole lot. I mean, even with my promotion, I wasn't earning but a fraction of what he was earning.

CC: So, what did you guys do?

Lawrence: Well, I gave up the job at the lab. I mean, we talked about it, and I realized that I still wanted a relationship with him. He was in a tough place. It wasn't like he could easily go back to the hospital where he was; not at that level. You don't really go back. After a few months Narvin was making decent money, and I just decided I would rather be here at night. So I applied for a day shift position at St. Stephen's, and they took me. They were a little surprised that I was leaving the medical center, but the woman who hired me was pretty understanding. I mean, I told her that I needed more time for my relationship. Once I got back onto the day shift, things really improved. I was able to come home at a decent hour and keep things going around here and be with Narvin. Even if he spends most

	of his time in his office, I can still go in there and talk to him, and we can have dinner together.
CC:	What else did you mean by "keep things going around here"?
Lawrence:	Just taking care of stuff.
CC:	What stuff do you mean?
Lawrence:	Everything, from laundry to shopping. I am trying to get the house to feel more like a home, more lived in. Of course, he thinks I am spending too much, so I have to watch that. But, yeah, just doing a lot of stuff around here to keep things going, and to take the pressure off of him.
CC:	Did Narvin change anything after you gave up the lab job?
Lawrence:	Not really around his work. He couldn't, really. But we did agree to set times for dinner, and we always take time for brunch on Sunday and then do something together. So, yeah, I guess he gave up a bit of work time. I don't mind, though. I mean, he's happy. I thought of leaving him for a while, and I think he really dreaded that. He probably would have thrown himself into his work, but I don't think he wanted that. So I made a sacrifice. He says he'll make it up to me, and he does seem a lot more responsive to my needs now than before.

Lawrence and Narvin preserved their relationship, but not without Lawrence's willingness to place more emphasis on family life. Both of them view the choices made as practical, and both anticipate a financial gain from Narvin's commitment to his consulting business.

On the whole, those individuals who gravitate toward greater domestic involvement than their partners often share common socioeconomic characteristics. Frequently they share their lives with partners who earn more, have greater career opportunities, work more hours, and work outside the home. In addition, more domestically involved participants often work in occupations that offer real 40-hour work weeks, more flexible work schedules, the ability to work at home, more holiday and vacation time, and affiliation with colleagues who also share family obligations. Domestically involved participants seldom recognize the confluence of factors encouraging their domesticity. Instead, they rely on the vocabulary of individual choice, psychological disposition, and "interests," ignoring the social context in which such dispositions and interests develop.

Gravitating Toward Paid Work

The old adage "Nothing succeeds like success" applies to many of those participants who gravitated toward work and career. Interesting and challenging work, stable and in some cases lucrative financial opportunities, as well as ample opportunities for promotion or new positions in other settings all contributed to some participants gravitating toward paid work. Both they and their partners recognize the opportunity structures available to them, and their partners frequently encourage them to pursue those opportunities. Moreover, for a few lesbigay employees, work offers more than just a place to achieve personal and financial goals; it sometimes offers a working environment that can feel just like a family.

Career Conditions

Those gravitating toward paid employment often work in occupations and institutions that afford higher incomes, long career ladders, notable pay increases, and the potential for a great deal of agency in one's work. Returning to the case of Joan Kelsey and Kathy Atwood, one can see the influence of such factors. The week I spent living with Joan and Kathy provided a clearer picture of Kathy's career. She works as an accountant with a prominent San Francisco bank earning around $85,000. Kathy reports four promotions over her 11-year career at the bank. In the past 2 years, she received pay raises of 7% each year. She expects 8% at her next review. However, she also works 55 to 60 hours per week. She awakes at 6:30 A.M. in order to get to the train at 7:25 and to work by 8:00. During the week I stayed with Joan and Kathy, Kathy arrived home between 7:30 and 7:45 every night. Commenting on the hours, Kathy says:

> I know it's a lot. But I love it. I am highly respected at the bank. People look to me for leadership and as someone who understands the fine points. The bank has rewarded me with several promotions, and they really do appreciate my commitment. You've got to do those kinds of hours to really gain their respect, and I have done that, and it's paid off. I love my work, and we have a nice home and a great life because of it.

Kathy shares some common experiences with other participants gravitating toward paid work including a history of upward mobility at work. Among those 38 families with a discernible division of labor, when comparing the 38 people who gravitate toward paid employment with the 39 with greater domestic involvement, the former report twice as many promotions with their present employers than do those gravitating toward domesticity. Further, among the 38 work-oriented participants, 18 report taking new jobs during the course of their present relationship while only 8 domestically oriented participants took new jobs. In most cases the new jobs were upward career moves to new firms for higher pay, more authority, and/or with greater control over work content. This included four participants who started their own businesses.

While a greater opportunity for promotion characterizes the work environments of those who gravitate toward paid work, those environments also feature higher salaries and other benefits, including stock options and domestic-partnership benefits. With regard to income, 29 of the 38 work-oriented participants earn more than their respective spouses. Of the eight participants in the study with stock options, six are among those families with a specialized division of labor. The remaining two are among the highly affluent egalitarians who purchase much of their domesticity in the service economy. At the time of the interviews, 12 of the employers of the 38 work-oriented participants offered domestic-partnership coverage. Only three of the domestically involved participants worked for employers offering such benefits. Among the 12 participants receiving those benefits, 4 opted to use them for their partners. None of the domestically involved participants utilized their domestic partnership benefits for their families.

Family Support

While a positive set of work conditions encourages one to identify with paid work, the support and respect of other family members also contributed. Asking participants what their partners think of their jobs reveals something quite telling. The work-oriented respondents often speak of garnering respect from their spouses. Asking the question "What does your partner think of your job?" to the 38 work-oriented participants elicited no fewer than 12 respondents asserting their partners "respect" their work. The reverse did not occur, with only five mentioning respect as part of their answer. Consider the following answers to the question "What does your partner think of your job?"

Attorney:	I think he is very respectful. I don't really know beyond that.
Architect:	I think he enjoys the work I do and expresses an interest in what I do. We talk a great deal about my daily activities and what I do at work. He seems to express a fascination with it, and respects me for it.
Bank manager:	Well, I think she knows it's hard work and that it takes a lot out of me. She respects how hard I work. She has said that.

Note what the more domestically involved partners of the above three have to say to the same question:

Flight attendant:	Seriously, he pokes fun at it because of the stereotypes. Within the gay community even, we are perceived as cupcakes and mindless blond babes. And unfortunately he has met quite a few flight attendants who seem to fit into this stereotype. I keep looking at this and can't quite figure out why it happens. He knows that the work is hard and that the hours are long, and the frustrations can get intense. It is not work that I particularly look forward to or enjoy. Sometimes he forgets and treats it like a picnic.
Visiting nurse:	I get two messages. There are times that he is amazed by it and proud of it. Other times, I think he feels it's not work, because I do a lot of things that don't seem like work. He doesn't take it seriously and assumes that I can do things because I don't have enough to do.
Counselor:	Well, I don't know. I think because I work at home, she wonders how much I really do. I work hard, and my days are plum full. I think she envies the flexibility I have.

The above answers suggest something about the ways in which the characteristics of jobs influence dynamics within families. Higher-status jobs with higher earning potential generate feelings of respect from family members. The reverse does not occur. Perhaps some of the discrepancy is explained by the demands of the jobs. The domestically involved participants do work slightly fewer hours for paid wages. The 38 domestically involved participants worked an average of 38 hours per week, with a median of 40 hours. The full-time homemakers and the seven part-time workers bring the average down. The job-oriented participants report 46 hours on average and a median of 44 hours. I now wish I had pursued what "respect" actually meant to participants, but I did not ask. I suspect that in many cases it meant that the job, its demands, and its various rewards, both to the individual and to the family, afforded a certain amount of power to the holders of such jobs.

In many cases, both among those families where I conducted fieldwork and among those I interviewed, a kind of deference is paid to those with high-demand, high-status jobs. I recall an incident one Thursday afternoon where Sarah Lynch, a graphic artist who works at home, was busy doing the laundry, among other things. I spent much of the day hanging out at her house, and she was, to say the least, busy. She would try to answer my questions in between answering phone calls and running down the hall to change the laundry over every 45 minutes. At around 5:30, with a huge pile of unfolded laundry on the bed, she began folding at a quick pace. I asked what her hurry was:

>   CC: What's the rush?
>   Sarah: Oh, nothing really. I just want to get this done and out of the way before
>   Andrea gets home.
>   CC: How come?
>   Sarah: I just don't want her to have to deal with it. I really like us to be able to
>   have quality time when she gets here. She has enough pressure to deal
>   with at work, so I try to keep this kind of stuff out of the way.
>   CC: Do you follow this same pattern of folding the laundry before she gets
>   home, every week?
>   Sarah: Yep! I like getting it done. It feels good.

Seemingly, Sarah works as many hours as Andrea does. If one counts the domestic work, Sarah actually works many more hours than Andrea does. Sarah earns less. She works at home. Sarah was one of the respondents who earlier expressed a feeling that Andrea might harbor doubts about how much she actually does during the day. Sarah works to produce that invisibility. They both consider their relationship quite egalitarian. This led me to wonder why Sarah wanted to hurry up and get the laundry done and out of sight. Was there something that Andrea did in a similar fashion, some domestic chore hidden from Sarah's view? I could identify nothing. What I could identify was a perception on Sarah's part that Andrea deserved respite from her paid work. The fact that Sarah does laundry in such a fashion reveals the presence of a great deal of support for Andrea's commitment to her paid work.

Work as Family

Finally, a few participants gravitate toward their paid work because of a pleasant and almost familylike atmosphere at work. This doesn't happen with much frequency for lesbigay people, due largely to discrimination and the heterosexual orientation of the workplace (Woods, 1993; Friskopp & Silverstein, 1995), but six participants described their work life in quite familial terms. Four of these six participants were among the 38 gravitating more toward paid work than toward domesticity. All six share the common experience of working with many lesbian or gay colleagues in work environments affirming of lesbigay people. Carry Taglia, a human resources professional, working for a San Francisco–based clothing manufacturer, comments on her work environment:

> I work in employee benefits. It's great. I love it. The company is so supportive of its lesbian and gay employees, you know, nondiscrimination, domestic partnership, diversity programming, etc. . . . And I get to work with lots of other gay people. It feels good to go to work. The people there, I mean, I really care about them, and they care about me. And I have met so many great people, gay and straight people, there. Everyone has such a positive attitude, and even though the company is going through a restructuring, it's so clear that they want to treat everyone well, like they are people with real lives.

Carry went on to describe the extra hours she works, the commitment that she feels toward her employer, and the sense of gratitude she feels because her employer affirms her and the value of her contribution to the company's success. Carry uses the metaphor of a mother-daughter relationship to describe her working relationship with her immediate manager. Carry's gravitation toward paid work makes a lot of sense. Few lesbigay people experience such an encouraging relationship with their employer. But when they do, they respond. However envious we might feel about Carry's working conditions, we should probably maintain some critical distance, for as Arlie Hochschild's latest research, *The Time Bind: When Work Becomes Home and Home Becomes Work* (1997), suggests, the motivations for employers to create familylike atmospheres at work are mostly self-serving and rarely permanent.

In a similar fashion, Wendell Moncado works as an accountant for a nonprofit AIDS education agency. He reports working up to 60 hours per week, and feels a great passion for his work and a strong sense of solidarity with his coworkers. He understands his coworkers in familial terms. Wendell depicts his work environment:

> I really like it. I feel like I'm able to maintain a commitment to my values and get paid for it. And the people I work with are amazing. We are like a family. We look out for each other, listen to each other. Every week we have a meeting just to check in with everyone else, to see what's going on in their lives. It's very important to do that when you do this kind of work because there can be a lot of pain, and if you don't talk about that, about the losses, and a sense that you are not doing enough to inform people accurately about their risks, well, that can be quite a burden. It's something you've got to talk about. So I feel very good about my work and especially good about the people I work with.

Wendell's work environment encourages him to put in 60 hours, often working on weekends and socializing with colleagues. In some sense, work has become family for Wendell. Not that he did not experience family with his partner, Daniel, for he did. But Wendell and Daniel both experienced some sense of family through Wendell's paid work. Most of their common friends and much of their leisure time revolved around Wendell's employment. Wendell's work commitment also left Daniel with much of the responsibility for maintaining much of their domestic life. Daniel expressed resignation, but not bitterness, about this:

I have mixed feelings about it. I don't really bring it up. His work is very important to him, and it is very important work, I know that. Given how intensely he feels about it, there's not much room for changing things, and you know, I don't really push it. If he were doing something else, maybe I would feel different. But for now, I am willing to deal with it.

In both Wendell's case and in Carry's, the pull of meaningful and affable work environments encourages them to gravitate toward paid work.

Pragmatic Choices and the Sense of Fairness

I have seen a practicality in the ways that lesbigay families sort and arrange domesticity, whether the family is egalitarian or specialized. Such practicality does not create equality, however. True equality, measured with a plumb line, eludes many of these families, but that has little to do with the families per se, and much more to do with the character and quality of employment opportunities that avail themselves to these families. If the reality is that only one member of the family can make money in a fulfilling way, then lesbigay families adjust to that reality.

Many lesbigay relationships don't survive for a wide variety of reasons. I would add to that list the dilemmas of domesticity—not just the conflicts over who does what but the often overlooked fact that the opportunity to pursue domestic things is not available to everyone. If all of the family must toil at unpleasant and poorly compensating work in order to make ends meet, they do, and they try to fit domesticity in where they can. Of course, these are the families that often don't make it, and that should not be so surprising, because without the resources, time, and energy to create family, it withers.

References

Acock , A., & Demo, D. (1994). *Family diversity and well-being.* Thousand Oaks, CA: Sage.

Aquilino, W. S. (1993). Effects of spouse presence during the interview on survey responses concerning marriage. *Public Opinion Quarterly, 55*(3), 358–376.

Badgett, L., & King, M. (1997). Lesbian and gay occupational strategies. In A. Gluckman and B. Reed (Eds.), *Homo economics: Capitalism, community, and lesbian and gay life.* New York: Routledge.

Berk, S. F. (1985). *The gender factory: The apportionment of work in American households.* New York: Plenum Press.

Blood, R., & Wolfe, D. (1960). *Husbands and wives.* Glencoe, IL: Free Press.

Blumstein, P., & Schwartz, P. (1983). *American couples.* New York: Morrow.

Brines, J. (1994). Economic dependency, gender, and the division of labor at home. *American Journal of Sociology, 100,* 652–688.

Coltrane, S. (1989). Household labor and the routine production of gender. *Social Problems, 36*(5), 473–490.

DeVault, M. (1991). *Feeding the family: The social organization of caring as gendered work.* Chicago: University of Chicago Press.

Ferree, M. (1990). Beyond separate spheres: Feminism and family research. *Journal of Marriage and the Family, 52,* 866–884.

Friskopp A., & Silverstein, S. (1995). *Straight jobs, gay lives: Gay and lesbian professionals, the Harvard Business School, and the American work place.* New York: Scribner.

Gerson, K. (1985). *Hard choices.* Berkeley: University of California Press.

Glazer, N. (1991). Between a rock and a hard place: Women's professional organizations in nursing and class, racial, and ethnic inequalities. *Gender and Society, 5*(3), 351–372.

Hertz, R. (1986). *More equal than others.* Berkeley: University of California Press.

Hochschild, A. (1983). *The managed heart: Commercialization of human feeling.* Berkeley: University of California Press.

Hochschild, A. (1997). *The time bind: When work becomes home and home becomes work.* New York: Metropolitan Books.

Petuchek, J. L. (1992). Employed wives' orientation to breadwinning: A gender theory analysis. *Journal of Marriage and the Family, 54,* 548–558.

Preston, J. (1995). Gender and the formation of a women's profession. In J. Jacobs (Ed.), *Gender inequality at work.* Mountain View, CA: Sage.

West C., & Zimmerman, D. (1987). Doing gender. *Gender and Society, 1* (2), 125–151.

Woods, J. (1993). *The corporate closet.* New York: Free Press.

Part Two
Employment and the Care of Children

Nowhere has the increased employment of women been more dramatic than among the mothers of young children. A generation ago, in 1970, only 30% of mothers with children under 6 were in the labor force. By 2000, 62% were in the labor force, including 59% of mothers with infants.

What happens to children during the hours their parents work? In a few unusual circumstances, mothers work at home or take their children with them, but such circumstances are rare. In other unusual circumstances, fathers have become the primary caretakers for young children, but these circumstances are equally rare. By far the most common responses are either for children to be cared for by others (in a child care center, a provider's home, or the child's own home) while the parents are at work or for one of the parents, almost always the mother, to limit her involvement in paid employment.

The problems of providing care are particularly difficult for the parents of young children. For school age children, free public education is universally available in the United States, although problems may remain for parents trying to provide before- and after-school care. In contrast, in the United States—although not in Europe—the care of young children is regarded almost exclusively as the private responsibility of parents themselves. Child care is expensive, and young children especially require high levels of staffing. The consequence is simple: As long as care is privately funded, even if everything possible is done to hold down expenses, the cost of care will be a significant problem for many parents. Moreover, because child care is expensive and because there is little public funding available, those who provide care are poorly paid. The median wage for a child care worker is under $7 an hour, and most receive no health care benefits. The consequence is high turnover, one third of the workforce each year, which lowers the quality of care and makes it more difficult for children to form attachments to their caregivers.

In the context of women's employment and in the absence of institutional frameworks or public policy to support that employment, the presence of children creates new conflicts between work and family. To be sure, there are solutions, but each "solution" comes at a cost. Women can stay home and be full-time mothers, but this reinforces inequalities among families as well as between men and women—even if the family can support itself on one paycheck, which many today cannot. Migrants can leave their children behind, but at an obvious cost to themselves and their children. The affluent can hire full-time nannies, but these nannies may not hold the same values as the parents. If the children spend more time with the nanny than with the mother, as many do, whose culture and values get transmitted? Parents can use relatives to provide care, but doing so may create its own economic dynamic. It may be hard to change arrangements even if the parent decides center-based care would be more educational and stimulating. And although parents may think that the problem extends only through the preschool years, they may find that dealing with the work-family conflicts posed by teenage children is at least as challenging.

One way that parents can achieve affordable high-quality care is by working different shifts so that their child(ren) can be with a parent at all (or almost all) times. Today, one out of three families with children contains a parent who is working a nonstandard shift, although only a small proportion do so in order to share parenting (Presser, 2000). Francine Deutsch's article examines those working-class couples who work alternate shifts to share parenting equally. Deutsch shows how these equal sharer fathers, too, cling to some more conventional ideologies. They think of men as the primary breadwinners (even when their wives do more paid work). They claim that mothers work only for the money (in spite of the variety of rewards their wives obtain from their jobs) and that mothers really are the primary parent (regardless of how much time the fathers spend with their children). Nonetheless, in contrast to most fathers, these equal sharers change diapers, give baths, read bedtime stories, and kiss boo-boos. In the process, they become more attached to their children. What others consider biological differences between mothers and fathers, they come to view as skills developed in the course of parenting.

If studies of work and family have come to include men as well as women, they have also come to recognize differences among women. In the past, research tended toward simplistic dichotomies—comparing all women who "worked" (that is, held jobs) with all women who did not (leaving aside differences among "working women" and among "housewives"). For example, a long series of studies looked at the effects of mothers' employment on children, the effects of women's employment on divorce, and the effects of wives' employment on marital satisfaction. The simplistic dichotomy of working and nonworking women proved conceptually insufficient and, not surprisingly, often yielded findings that were neither generalizable nor reliable. In contrast, a number of the articles in this volume examine differences *among* women and do so as part of their central research design.

Nowhere are the complications—and ironies—in the relationship of work and family more striking than in regard to child care. The articles by Pierrete Hondagneu-Sotelo and Ernestine Avila and by Lynet Uttal show both the complexity of what constitutes work and the extraordinary variations among racial and ethnic groups in how this work is organized and the meanings attached to it. Implicit in both articles is the realization that the entry of women into the labor force itself generates additional demands for women workers—not as well-paid professionals but as substitute caregivers for the very children whose mothers are now holding paid positions. As a result, the entry of women into the labor force transforms not just the "exchange" between work and family but the very character of what was once one of the family's most central "functions"—the cultural production (and reproduction) of children. This task of reproduction is complicated even more by the racial and ethnic differences between the children's parents and the women who are now caring for these children.

The nannies hired by the affluent are often left with insecure employment and a feeling of alienation from the very children they are asked to care for. In Hondagneu-

Sotelo and Avila's analysis of "transnational" nannies, the ironies are powerful. The women studied have come to the United States to care for the children of other women. Yet they have left their own children behind, typically in the care of relatives. They often develop strong attachments to the children they care for, yet they insist that they would not entrust their own children to unrelated employees (like themselves).

Uttal shows the flip side of these ironies: Over the last 40 years, there has been a decrease in the use of relatives to provide care for preschoolers, and many of those who use relatives would prefer to use "quality" child care. As Uttal shows, Mexican American and African American women are much more likely than whites to regard the use of relatives as appropriate. However, this inclination does not depend solely on beliefs different from those of white Anglo women. It also depends on the *availability* of relatives who need employment. A relative who would otherwise be working in the fields or the cannery might eagerly seek to provide paid child care; a relative with a good office job would be far less willing to switch to child care. Thus, considerations of what is best for the child and of what is economically most advantageous to the parents depend, in part, on the character of the extended kin networks in which families are embedded.

Beyond variations of race and class, there are also variations over the life course. Most research has, for good reasons, focused primarily on the problems of caring for infants and preschoolers. Demie Kurz's essay moves to a somewhat later part of the life course, to the mothers of teenage children. She brings into view the many ways that the after-school care of adolescent children requires a great deal of effort, attention, and coordination. Teenagers do not "need" the kind of care, certainly not the kinds of primary care, that infants and young children require. But mothers still need to juggle a variety of concerns—whether about their teenage children's safety, their homework, or their participation in extracurricular activities. At least as important, Kurz's respondents report: "I really like getting home with the girls. That is when they talk. I really like that. If you come home later it's 'How was your day?' 'Oh, fine.'" Indeed, some even suggested that mothering an adolescent required more attention—albeit of a different sort—than mothering a younger child.

Reference

Presser, H. B. (2000, February). Nonstandard work schedules and marital instability. *Journal of Marriage and the Family, 62,* 93.

5
Halving It All: The Mother and Mr. Mom

Francine Deutsch

Editorial note: For her book, *Halving It All*, Francine Deutsch interviewed dual-earner couples, who had children ranging in age from babies to teenagers. First looking for couples who equally shared parenting, she found them in day care centers, schools, and through word of mouth. Then she called all of these couples, asking them to estimate the overall division of child care in their families. Many said they were not equal sharers, but many—at least initially—claimed to divide child care 50–50. When she investigated further, with specific questions like: "How do you divide picking up after the children? Diapering them? Feeding them? Taking them to birthday parties?" the estimates changed. Reminded of the many tasks parenting entails, many of these mothers and fathers remembered how much more of this work mothers did.

Then Deutsch added two other groups to the study: The first were those who never claimed to share parenting equally; the second was a group of alternating-shift couples—blue-collar couples in which husbands shared the care of their children by working different shifts than their wives. To be included in this latter group, the fathers had to take care of the children on his own at least 15 hours a week. While the men worked at their paid jobs, their wives were at home; while the women were at their jobs, their husbands were at home. By arranging their schedules this way, the alternating-shift couples did not have to pay for child care. They did not always share parenting equally, however. To be sure, some divided it equally (or were, in Deutsch's words, "50–50" or "equal sharers"); more divided it unequally (some in which the mothers did a bit more than half, whom Deutsch labels "60–40"), and others where the mothers did the vast majority of the child care (those Deutsch refers to as "75–25").

In the chapter we have included here, Deutsch examines the ways these alternating-shift couples divide parenting and the ways they explain and understand that division. Deutsch observed these couples. She talked to them about parenting—how they thought about it and how they behaved as parents. As Deutsch writes in the book: "I included them because their involvement debunks middle-class stereotypes that hard hats wouldn't be caught dead changing diapers. They make eminently clear that the 'revolution at home' is not simply an upper-middle-class phenomenon."

For these very same reasons, we chose for this book the chapter in which Deutsch analyses these alternating-shift couples.

If you stopped to watch at the construction site of a new office building going up in Worcester, Massachusetts, you might catch a glimpse of Stan pouring cement for the foundation. Stan is a lean, muscular, good-looking guy whose job as a laborer in the

---

construction industry means hard work for low wages. Some facts about Stan would probably not surprise you. A high school graduate, Stan is an avid Red Sox fan, thinks his mother is the world's best cook, and is known among his friends as a great storyteller. As you might expect, especially once you know that he is the father of two children, Stan worries about how to make ends meet.

However, if you believe, as I did once, that the gender revolution of today is limited to affluent, highly educated families, you might be surprised to find out what Stan does when he gets off his shift.[1] Every day at 3 P.M., Stan rushes home just in time for his wife, Maureen, to go to her job as a retail clerk at a convenience store nearby. From 3:45 until 10 P.M., when Maureen gets off, Stan is home taking care of his two daughters, 4-year-old Annie and the baby, Sarah, now 7 months old. Stan plays with them for a while, gets them their dinners, gives them baths if Maureen hasn't already done so, and puts them to bed by 8:30. Usually he washes the dinner dishes, but sometimes he leaves them for Maureen because he wants to relax after the kids are in bed. In his wildest imagination, Stan never pictured himself as the father he is today, doing all the tasks that used to be Mom's: diapering babies, giving baths, even taking his 4-year-old daughter to ballet lessons.

There's a revolution brewing in the homes of blue-collar families. Alternating work shifts has become a solution for a growing number of dual-earner couples.[2] In families like Stan and Maureen's, mothers and fathers are taking turns taking care of their children while their spouses work at paid jobs. Blue-collar fathers are taking on responsibilities that their own fathers would never have dreamed of and that they themselves had never imagined. None of these men set out to be trailblazers. "Mr. Mom," the label many of these men have bestowed on themselves, conveys their feeling that there is something topsy-turvy about it all.

Mr. Mom was the title character in a movie about a man who loses his job and stays home to take care of his children while his wife goes to work. Strikingly different from the alternating shifters on a superficial level, Mr. Mom of the movie was a high-paid executive who had lost his job. Those details were unimportant to the alternating-shift fathers, however, in the face of their identification with a man who was humorously assuming a role for which he was ill prepared. "Mr. Mom" connotes that the movie father, just like the alternating-shift dads, was acting a bit odd by doing what mothers are supposed to do. Despite the time men like Stan spend taking care of their children, they protest that they are not really the mothers. They are the "Mr. Moms." Their wives are "the mothers."

Who Are the Alternating-Shift Couples?

Approximately 23 million workers in the United States work an evening, night, or rotating shift: a fifth of all employed workers.[3] Among dual-earner couples with children under 15 years of age, the numbers are even more startling. In 51% of these families, at least one parent is working a noonday shift. These off-shifts encourage paternal caretaking.[4] Fathers are the primary caregivers of 11.4% of all preschool children whose mothers are employed and of 28% of preschoolers whose mothers work a noonday shift.[5]

Who are these fathers who are involved so intensively in the care of their children? Occupations that rely heavily on shift work are predominantly working-class occupations: mining and manufacturing, health care, fire fighting, police and correctional work, and other forms of service work.[6] The alternating-shift fathers I interviewed worked in diverse jobs; they included a bellman, a delivery man, an aircraft mechanic, an oil burner technician, a powder processor, a stock handler, a police officer, a firefighter, a custodian, a chef, two electricians, and a foreman. Their wives were nurses, pink-collar workers, retail clerks, service workers, or blue-collar workers themselves.[7]

How Do Couples Alternate Shifts?

Consider Diane and Patrick. Patrick works days as an electrician, earning about $15.00 an hour. He leaves for work around 7:30 A.M. after having breakfast with Diane and their two boys, a 5-year-old and a 3-year-old, who send him off every day with waves and kisses. Diane does "the duties during the morning and afternoon." She gets the older child off to and back from kindergarten, feeds both children breakfast and lunch, plays with them, and does some housework, although she admits housework is not her first priority: "The kids are more important than the cleaning." On most afternoons she packs them up and is off visiting friends or doing errands. Patrick gets off work at 4:30. Unlike most of the alternating-shift families, they eat dinner together before she leaves at 5:30 for her job as a sandwich maker at a delicatessen, where she works until 10 P.M. four nights a week, and from 8 A.M. until noon on most Saturdays and Sundays. When she leaves for work on weekdays, Patrick is "on." He cleans up after dinner, gives the kids their baths, takes them outside to play when the weather is nice, and puts them to bed. Before she gets home, he tries to do some housework and usually does a load of laundry.

Patrick strikes me as a sweet, earnest man. I was touched by his efforts to understand his young children's feelings and to express his own, something that was not encouraged in the male world he grew up in. Although he thinks Diane is more attuned to the emotional side of life, he keeps trying: "She's more open with her feelings and I'm more closed and more harder than she is. I've always been that way. It's really hard for me to tell about feelings. . . . I do it, but it's hard. The children know her better." Patrick's efforts and the time he spends with his sons at night have paid off: "We got to know each other a little bit. I got to be more attuned to their feelings and their emotions and stuff, so it was good."

Diane and Patrick are not equal sharers. Diane works fewer hours for pay than Patrick (about 24 hours to his 50) and spends more time with their children. In fact, when we look at the blue-collar alternating-shift families as a group, only two of them could be classified as equal sharers. As in Patrick and Diane's family, in two thirds of them mothers work many fewer hours for pay than their husbands, and the husbands work correspondingly fewer hours at home. But the variations differ in how they define their responsibilities when at home with their children. Diane brags about how much more Patrick contributes than other men who alternate shifts with their wives.

> I don't think I've ever met a man that's taken such an interest in his kids plus done house-work at the same time. It's . . . "Okay, if you wanna work at night, I'll watch the kids, but don't expect me to do the dishes. Don't expect me to put a load of wash in. . . . I'll be the father, but I won't be anything else."

She's partly right. There are a few alternating-shift fathers who do child care and nothing else. Their wives prepare the dinner, and they just warm it up in the micro-wave. After dinner, they leave the dishes in the sink. One father admitted that he called his wife at work five or six times a night, implicitly refusing to take responsi-bility: "I'll have to know where something is or what should I do. Even when she's not here, she is still kind of running the show." He acknowledges that she does 75% of the work despite their both working full-time. "I don't know how she does it. I really don't."

Although partly right, Diane is largely wrong. Many of the alternating-shift fa-thers did as much housework as Patrick, and some did a lot more. In one family of six children, a father who took care of his children three days a week while his wife worked didn't stop for a minute. After putting the youngest down for a nap in the morning, he reported,

> I usually go down to the cellar and put in a load of laundry. . . . I just kind of spend the day . . . doing whatever's got to be done. . . . I don't think I was put here to do nothing. I have to stay busy; that's why I do most of the stuff around the house. I'll vacuum the floors; I mop the floors; I do the laundry.

Other men learned how to cook instead of just heating up what their wives had pre-pared.

When we view the alternating-shift families in the light of traditional gender stan-dards, they are every bit as extraordinary as the middle-class equal sharers. Because the parents do virtually all of the child care themselves, even if fathers do a smaller *percentage* than their wives, these dads may be doing a greater total *amount* of parenting than even the equally sharing fathers. This is certainly true if we consider the time fathers spend with children by themselves. On average, the alternating-shift fathers spent 28.5 hours a week in solo care of their children, as compared with the 14.5 hours spent by middle-class equally sharing fathers.

Alternating-shift fathers resemble the equally sharing fathers on some tasks, but not others. For example, since the majority of these fathers work the early shift, they have relatively little to do with supervising children's morning routines, whereas among the equal sharers the morning jobs are some of the most equally divided.[8] Bedtime routine, however, is a different story. Fathers who alternate work shifts put their children to bed just as frequently as their wives do, just as frequently as the equally sharing fathers, and more frequently than the fathers in the 75-25 families.[9] In short, alternating-shift fathers do what needs to be done for children when their wives are not home, and that turns out to be quite a bit.[10]

The demands of children were especially intense in the homes of alternating shifters because their children were younger than the children of the equally sharing fami-lies.[11] The care required is a far cry from the stereotypical paternal jobs of rough-housing, playing sports, or teaching kids how to ride their bikes. I saw how deftly men managed the demands of preschoolers firsthand because I often interviewed the alternating-shift fathers at their homes while they fielded their young children's questions, warmed their babies' bottles, and rocked crying infants, sometimes all at once, with great aplomb.

Let's also not forget that these families can't afford paid help for housework. Men may have fought more with their wives over housework, but that was partly because they couldn't buy out of the problem the way a number of the middle-class equal sharers had.[12] Cleaning and laundry figured much more prominently in the typical day of alternating-shift fathers than in the typical day of middle-class fathers who were equally sharing.

Why Do Couples Alternate Shifts?

Money. There's no doubt about it; it is cheaper to avoid using paid child care.[13] In over 80% of the alternating-shift couples, at least one spouse mentioned money when asked why they share the care of their children the way they do. The alternating shifters have the lowest incomes among the groups I interviewed. Yet they differ in how constrained they feel. Some thought they simply couldn't afford day care; others maintained that they could have afforded it, but believed alternating work shifts was economically wise.

For some it wasn't a choice. As these parents explained:

Can't afford day care. Obviously, with three kids it would just be horrendous to pay for it.

We can't afford child care. I mean child care would be over $140, $120 a week and that's just too much because we don't make that much. With the rest of our bills, to be able to have a mortgage and vehicles and getting to and from work, and then plus trying to pay child care, we could never do it.

I mean it was just money, economics. We can't afford to pay for a babysitter five days a week unless you got a pretty good job or something. I don't know how some of these people do it.

Others reasoned that it was impractical to spend so much of their income on day care. It seems especially costly because it is often calculated as a deduction from others' incomes.[14] As this mother indicates: "I couldn't see myself working for all of this money on a weekly basis that would come in and half of it going right out to somebody else to raise my children. I didn't think it was right." A few reported that they chose alternating shifts to provide a more comfortable life for their families:

Different shifts . . . because we really wanted to build our own house and have our own house and there was no way we could do it working the same shift and not [having] more income.

We could have more and we could take them more places, take a vacation. They could even go to college.

Money matters, but money is not the only reason, or even the most important reason, that parents invoke for alternating shifts. Many of the couples believed that children should only be cared for by family.[15] Adamant about not wanting his children in day care, this father conveys what many of the parents feel:

> I've been proud of that actually. . . . Each parent is in contact with them at any given point. . . . I know people . . . just drop them off and leave them for an endless time. That to me is, you're not being a parent, you're paying somebody to do your job, and how healthy is that? "Oh, there's good day care," and all this crap. It's not as good as the real thing.

When middle-class parents object to day care, they often do so for subtle psychological reasons, because they believe it doesn't promote the child's optimal development or because they think it will damage the bond between parent and child. The blue-collar alternating-shift parents give different reasons for avoiding day care. First, they fear that terrible dangers await children who are cared for by strangers. These fears were pervasive among mothers:

> You hear too many things on the TV about what could happen and I just don't want to take the chance.

> I get nervous having to trust somebody. . . . There's too many crazy people out there, and you can never tell.

> I'm leery of having someone that I don't know real well in my house. . . . I can't see what they're doing with my daughter. . . . I'm not comfortable enough with it to put myself in that position.

And fathers said:

> I don't let people outside my family watch my kids. . . . You don't know those other people. It doesn't matter that they got a sign out that says that we're certified. . . . There's a lot of things out there that can happen to kids. . . . I don't want nothing to happen to my kids.

> . . . the fear of some of these perverts out there and stuff. We'd just as soon take care of our children ourselves.

> You hear the horror stories about child care: people hitting kids on the head with spoons to leaving them in a dark room, to tossing them in a crib and whacking them. It's so hard to know what another person's going to do with your child. . . . I'd just as soon take care of her than let some stranger take her.

> I may sound silly but you hear the horror stories all the time. Deep down inside we've always felt that we don't want anyone else to take care of our children. They're going to be exposed to enough trash soon enough anyway.

You see stuff all the time—child care people abusing children and everything.

The second reason alternating-shift parents give for avoiding day care is their resolve to inculcate their children with their own values. As one father said: "I didn't want Marie to learn things from other people. I want her to learn from us. We are not the most intelligent people in the world, but we know right from wrong." Like many of the alternating-shift mothers, Diane trusted that her husband's caregiving would reflect their shared values:

> When I go to work at night, I have a clear conscience and a clear feeling that he will do everything exactly like I would if I was home. . . . We have always said that . . . a parent has to be here at all times. . . . We both have the same understanding of how we want to raise our kids . . . with all the same goals and morals.

Repeatedly, I heard from these blue-collar parents that they didn't want strangers raising their children. Yet surely the middle-class couples who send their children to child care don't conceive of it as ceding control of child rearing to someone else. Day care may provide care for part of the day, but ultimately these middle-class parents believe that they will have more influence over their children than any substitute caregiver. Both of the criticisms leveled at day care by blue-collar families reflect their concerns about losing control over their children's care. In contrast, middle-class parents don't seem to worry about having that kind of control. They take it for granted.

Two reasons might account for this difference. First, because blue-collar families have less money, the child care that they can pay for might be worse. Their fears may have some basis in fact.[16] Second, even if the blue-collar families could avail themselves of the "best" institutional day care, they might still suffer from a relative lack of control. The so-called best institutions might reflect middle-class values and be less responsive to their concerns than to the concerns of middle-class couples.

Values are at the heart of how many of these parents talked about alternating work shifts. They conceived of parenthood as a responsibility and an opportunity to convey their own values. Although in "normal" times the mother is the direct conduit of this influence, if the mother works outside the home, responsibility shifts to the father. When driven or justified by cherished values that are shared by both parents, the alternating of work shifts is not simply a practical accommodation to financial constraints; it is a way of life that has meaning and substance.

But when husbands and wives felt they had no choice because they couldn't afford day care, the loss of time together was a bitter pill to swallow. The physical separation symbolized a spiritual separation as well. One mother, who attributed her family's arrangements entirely to financial necessity, said:

> I'd rather have him work days. I'd rather have him home at night with us as a family, not a divided family. . . . I like it when he's home at night. We're participating in the family. I like it that way. That's the way it should be.

Choosing to alternate shifts obviously creates hardships. Husbands and wives missed having time together with each other and as a family. That loss is a cost for all of the families. A few families bore the cost painfully as a symbol of the parents' inability to create the kind of family they wanted. But other parents, those who intentionally chose to alternate shifts, bore the costs philosophically, as a symbol of their willingness to sacrifice for their children and create, if not the perfect family, at least one in which they are doing right by their children. While acknowledging the price of their choice, they stress the rewards of a shared sense of purpose and moral rightness. Listen to this father of two young sons, ages 2 and 3:

> If I'm going to have kids . . . I'm going to be the one who instills their morals and ethics and I wasn't going to leave that to someone else. . . . From the start we considered parenting very, very important. . . . Whatever the sacrifice it takes as far as maybe the time me and Brenda spend together, we consider it worth it. I consider it worth it.

Theresa, a mother who had been alternating work shifts with her husband for 13 years, expressed similar sentiments:

> Before we even had the kids we had agreed we basically didn't trust anyone else. We knew how we wanted our kids raised. We knew what was important to us, what we wanted to give them. It has been a struggle because there have been times when neither one of us has been happy with the hours or the lack of sleep or the lack of contact with each other. There have been years where we've laughingly said to other people the kids have the best of Mom and Dad when they don't have much of each other. . . . Looking backwards, it's worked out, and I think that's why they're as good as they are, because we have given 100% of what they needed.

Even some parents who adopted the alternating-shift pattern only because it seemed sensible, and worried initially about the loss of time together, came to appreciate the advantages:

> I am thrilled at the way this worked out. . . . We never planned. . . . We need jobs like this because we have kids. It just worked out that way. Then after we had the kids, we saw that this is a good thing. This is not a bad thing. It's hectic and it's crazy, but I think it's good for us as a family.

In their belief that parental care is best, alternating shifters are similar to the professional families in which women sacrifice time at work to stay home with their young children. In the blue-collar families, however, it is a change in the father's life that makes parental care of children possible. When middle-class families opposed day care, the solution was usually for the mother to stay home, whereas when working-class families felt the same way, fathers' roles changed drastically. Paradoxically, staunchly adhering to some facets of traditional family life led these blue-collar fathers to assume very nontraditional roles. In doing so, they had to change.

Change and Resistance to Change

No father has changed more than David. David and Theresa have been alternating work shifts longer than any of the other couples. Theresa is an inhalation therapist who works 32 hours a week and earns $32,000 a year. David is an installer for the phone company who works 40 hours a week and earns $31,000 a year. Currently, David works days from 7 A.M. to about 4 P.M., and Theresa works the second shift four nights, from 3:30 to 11:30 P.M. The parents of three children, Veronica, 13, Betsy, 10, and Nicholas, 6, Theresa and David have been sharing the care of their children by working different shifts since their firstborn, Veronica, was $5^1/2$ weeks old.

David and Theresa's relationship is exceptionally egalitarian. She claims it is 50-50; he says it is 60-40 in her favor. But both agree that each pitches in with whatever needs to be done. On a typical day, David is the first to awaken: "My day starts at 5:30 in the morning. I get up and take a shower, put wood in the stove if it's winter-time, and then I eat breakfast. . . . I make sure that her [Veronica's] light is on. I go upstairs and get dressed and in the course of my leaving I wake Theresa up to start her day." She takes care of the morning tasks: getting the other children up, making their breakfasts, and getting them off to school. She does errands, volunteer work, or housework until Nicholas returns from kindergarten at 11:30. She gets his lunch and spends a couple of hours with him until she needs to leave for work at 2:45 P.M.

David gets home about 4 P.M. (Veronica is paid to baby-sit until he gets there.) His evenings are full. He drives the children to their activities, makes their dinners, and cleans up. Four nights of the week, he's the parent who asks about their days at school, helps them with their homework, and plays with them. He handles all the bedtimes: "I make sure the showers are taken care of, then we have some type of a snack, and then around 8:30 I get Nicholas ready. I do half-hour increments. Nicholas between 8:00 and 8:30, Betsy between 8:30 and 9:00, and Veronica . . . between 9:00 and 9:30." At bedtime he spends time with all of them, but especially with the youngest: reading, talking, calming his fears. After that, he makes the lunches for the next day, and then relaxes for a few minutes before he drops into bed. Theresa wakes him when she gets home so they can talk.

Today, David looks like the model of the new man, but he confided how much he had changed and still continues to change. He's learned the practical skills of taking care of children, has become more emotionally attuned to them, and has developed a different understanding of men's and women's roles in the family: "This is nothing that I was born with or I was brought up to see. . . . It's something I had to learn, I had to get used to."

David laughs when he reminisces about how scared he was to take care of an infant:

> I remember when we had just had Veronica. Theresa said, "Well, I'll give her a bath tonight if you give her one tomorrow night." I'm saying, "Geez, I've got to give her one tomorrow night." Now it's second nature. . . . It's something I had to learn, I had to get used to. . . . Once I started to catch steam on this thing, there was no stopping me. I told Theresa tonight I was going to make some cookies.

He learned more than just the mechanics of cooking dinner and bathing babies, however; he learned how to really listen to his children. Just the week before I interviewed him, his daughter Veronica had come home upset about a problem with a friend at school. Although at first he dismissed it, telling her not to worry, he soon realized he had made a mistake, and he invited his daughter to sit down and talk to him about what was bothering her. "It's a growing thing. . . . I'm developing, believe it or not, a soft side, but it doesn't come natural. Fathers don't have that natural ability. It's something you have to develop."

David expresses little reluctance to take on "women's work." Like many of the alternating-shift men who are unable to earn an income sufficient to support the family, he feels beholden to his wife for helping him with that responsibility. Perhaps David feels more grateful than most, because he gave up an opportunity to make more money.

A few years back David was promoted to a management position. Theresa confesses that it was a terrible period for their marriage and their family. His anger and distress about events on the job infected their home life. They decided together that it would be better for all of them if David stepped down and went back to his old job as an installer, despite the cut in pay and the need for Theresa to work more "to fill in the dollar end of it." David is very conscious of the trade-off: "I took . . . a 33% cut in pay and left. . . . If I was earning now what I was earning then, perhaps Theresa wouldn't have to work as hard as she is now."

Although David has not changed his idea that mothers are ultimately responsible for child care and fathers for breadwinning, his strong sense of fairness requires him to contribute as much as he does at home:

> I look at Theresa. . . . She is working on equal terms as myself. Theresa started out like this. . . . Her primary job is the family and running the household; the father is the outside job. When the mother steps out of that primary role and goes into another role, I feel it is the obligation of the father to step out of his primary role as the breadwinner and . . . go into the mother's part. When Theresa's at work, I am at home doing the motherly functions to the best of my ability. . . . I only consider that fair.

Virtually all the alternating-shift couples exhibited a tension between change and resistance to that change. There is no doubt that, like David, many of the alternating-shift fathers have changed their views about the appropriateness of their doing "women's work." By doing the work of the family, men learn that it is worthy of respect. Listen to this father's account:

> I've learned from this where a lot of men would never understand the respect for women. If I had never gone through this I would be in the same chauvinistic "It's a woman's job." But when you actually do what you have to do, you gain a lot more respect for what it takes.

Another father, as his wife observed, changed after he spent some time at home: "I think it was the first time he really realized it just wasn't so easy being home. . . . It wasn't the old husband come home, 'Well, what did you do all day?' Now you know what I did all day."

Women led the way amidst varying degrees of struggle with their husbands. The mounting unpaid bills helped Eileen succeed in convincing her husband to alternate shifts and pick up some of the housework, but only after her second child was born:

> When we first married, Larry felt like I was there to be his wife: to do the dishes, to clean the house, to take care of the kids. Things have changed since then. We're more equals. It's more like I'm his wife, not his slave.

Diane had an easier time with Patrick: "I always thought that he should share in the responsibilities, and he never disagreed, so I kind of just showed him the way."

Interestingly, in the alternating-shift families the wives' jobs carry leverage that they often do not in more affluent middle-class families. Because pay scales for blue-collar jobs are narrower than for white-collar jobs, when the wives of blue-collar men get paid jobs, the ratio of their income to their husbands' is often better than the wife-to-husband pay ratio among wealthier families. Moreover, upper-middle-class men do not have to acknowledge that they couldn't make it without their wives' incomes; blue-collar men do.[17]

Ironically, in these alternating-shift families the claim on men to share the work of the household derives from the belief in traditional gender roles. Because most working-class families cannot financially afford to have the mother at home, it is impossible for men to live up to a traditional standard of the breadwinner, however much they might believe in it. Failing to provide their wives with the possibility of a traditional life means that their wives can legitimately expect them to contribute to "women's work." As one mother bluntly put it:

> I don't consider myself to be a women's rights activist type person, but . . . if he wants me to stay home and cook and clean and do laundry and have meals on the table . . . that's fine, but he's going to live up to the male standard of you are the breadwinner. . . . Until that point, if I'm going my way with the financial end of this family, he's going to pull his weight with helping out with everything else that I can't be doing because I'm out 40 hours a week.

In the "economy of gratitude" that operates in these alternating-shift families, women's paid work counts. The work men do at home is often viewed as a payback for the gift they are receiving of their wives' employment.

Men who alternate work shifts receive another, even more important gift. They get to know their children, and their children get to know them. Time spent with children translates into a closeness that surprises and delights them. Fathers were thrilled to be admitted to a relationship they previously thought was reserved for mothers. One father, who thoroughly enjoyed bath time with his kids, said:

> There's other stuff that I help out and I get to see. Like when it's bath time. They love bubbles and they're always calling me in there. They take my old razor and make like they're shaving their bubble beards off.

These men are visible figures in their children's lives, in contrast to the shadowy images cast by many of their own fathers. These caregiving fathers often came from working-class families in which many of the fathers worked two or three jobs and were barely seen at home. The alternating-shift fathers work hard, too, but they are not strangers to their children. As this father said: "They've been able to bond so much more with me. . . . One of the greatest things—they really got to appreciate their Dad. . . . It has made me keep going back for more."

The remarkable changes in these families are real, but they are sometimes accompanied by resistance to change as well. A number of the alternating-shift fathers take primary responsibility for their children when their wives are at work, but abdicate if both parents are present. For example, one mother reported that she cooked and fed the children when both she and her husband were home because he was busy doing other things. When I asked what he was usually busy doing, she replied, "Watching television." Another mother said:

> On the weekends, if I'm going out to the store, I always feel guilty if I don't take them [the children] with me . . . because, oh gosh, leaving them alone with him. . . . It's not them, it's him. He doesn't like it if I leave them with him if I'm not going to work.

This resistance to changing roles when the mother and father are together is significant because it portends more traditional arrangements in the future. Many of the alternating-shift mothers who work the evening shift while their children are little plan to get day jobs when their children go to school. In these couples, I asked the mothers what they thought would happen to the division of labor if both husband and wife were working the same shift and thus were home together in the evening. Although about half of the women expected their relatively egalitarian arrangements to persist, the rest saw their husbands' backsliding as indicative of their future:

> Probably, I'd be doing most of it, because on my days off I get them to bed. I make sure they brush their teeth and they take their fluoride, and they get into their pajamas. If he could, he'd leave me their baths, too. He doesn't like to give baths.

Some still hoped. As one mother said, "I'm hoping [that the division of labor won't change]. I kind of wonder about that, though. . . . When I'm not here, he has no choice but to take care of them." But her husband's answer left little doubt about what was going to happen: "I definitely see less. I mean, I see less for myself because I just see she is so giving. She wants to be a mother." Another father had a bit more insight into his own motives: "If she was home at night, I guess there might be a point of laziness that I might acquire. When things change and you get the opportunity to take it easy, that could become a habit."

Although gender ideas in these families have changed enough to allow men to take over domestic duties when their wives are at work without any loss of manhood, often these ideas have not changed enough to really shift the ultimate responsibility. Mothers are still "in charge" of the work at home; fathers help because their wives are unavailable.

Clinging to Gender Identities

Despite the liberalization of gender ideology among all social classes over the past 15 years, there is more support for traditional gender ideology within the working class than among more highly educated groups in the United States.[18] Many of the blue-collar couples I interviewed carry with them images of an ideal of traditional family life, featuring the men going to work while their wives stay at home to tend young children. None of them live that ideal. Yet by clinging to some core aspects of that picture, they can convince themselves that they are maintaining traditional gender identities despite their nontraditional arrangements. These couples try hardest to keep intact three aspects of gender identity: the father is the breadwinner; the mother does not derive a primary sense of identity from work—she works outside the home only to ensure the economic survival of the family; and the mother is the primary parent.

The Father as Breadwinner

Ironically, even though alternating-shift men have lower salaries and earn a lower proportion of the family income than their middle-class counterparts, both they and their wives readily invoke the father's role as breadwinner. An overwhelming majority emphasized that, though both parents are employed, the men are the breadwinners in their families.[19]

There is no doubt that the alternating-shift men feel a profound responsibility to make money to provide for their families. Patrick's simple statement emphasized that there was no choice in the matter: "I have to work, and I have to be the breadwinner." Several men noted that becoming a father intensified their need to be breadwinners. Fatherhood made them feel more responsible, and for many, responsibility meant providing financially. One father, discussing how his attitude changed after he had children, said that he wanted "to do better at my job so I'd make more money." Another said: "It's made me more responsible only because now I have to provide for three more children and everything that goes with it: the home, the bills." One father was on the verge of taking a job he knew he would hate because it provided "stability and benefits." He worried that, despite the close relationship he was developing with his infant son, if he did not succeed in conventional breadwinning terms, ultimately his son would be ashamed of him:

> I mean, as far as our relationship goes, I think it's wonderful, but there's that money, success kind of thing. "Oh, what does your father do?" "He stays home and makes peanut butter and jelly sandwiches."

The most poignant statement about the father's role as a breadwinner came from a man who had been laid off. Despite taking care of his children when his wife went to work in the evening, he didn't see himself as contributing to the family: "I feel I'm not contributing anymore, I'll say, because of finances. I'm supposed to be the one to support my family." Another father, who had been laid off previously, echoed the devastating effects of the loss of the breadwinner role: "I had no self-esteem. I felt terrible about myself."

In almost all the alternating-shift families, the parents stressed men's breadwinning roles by treating the father's job as the more important job in the family.[20] Superficially, it seems to make some sense to treat the man's job as more important because in almost all the families men earned more money than their wives. But closer examination suggests that a number of couples in these families structured their work lives to enable the father to retain the role of principal breadwinner. In eight families the women's rate of pay was either higher than or equal to their husbands'. But in only two of the families did the women earn higher overall salaries. The more typical scenario was this: When women earned a higher rate of pay, their husbands worked a substantially greater number of hours. For example, in one family in which a nurse earned about $17.50 an hour to her foreman husband's $13.50, he worked 50 hours a week to her 24, resulting in his earning approximately $12,000 a year more than she. In an even more dramatic example, the mother's hourly wage rate was double that of her husband's ($14.00 an hour versus $7.00), but he worked more than twice as many hours as she, thus ending up with a higher income. It appears that couples organize family and work life to make sure that despite two incomes, and despite the woman's greater earning capacity in some families, men in the alternating-shift families are still recognized as the principal breadwinners.[21]

Like many of the alternating-shift wives, Diane doesn't dispute that Patrick is the breadwinner in their family: "We have always established that he was the head of the household. I think it was because our dads were. He just knows consciously that he's the one with the education, and he's the one that makes the most money. His job is more important than mine." In terms of overall pay, and even rate of pay, her husband *is* the principal breadwinner in their family, but as she herself points out, that was by design. After they had children, he went back to school: "We made sure that he got the education before I did, so that he would make the most money and I could just take care of the kids during the day and work at night to supplement. That was, I think, the big thing, that he is the head of the household."

The Mother as Worker

The image of the mother at home complements the ideal of the father as breadwinner. But the ideal of a mother without paid employment is problematic for these families. First, there is no way to get around the fact that these mothers are in the paid labor force. Second, in most of the families the mothers' incomes are critical to maintaining the family's economic well-being, so they do not really have a choice in the matter. Third, and perhaps most disturbing to their images of ideal family life, most of the mothers enjoy being in the paid labor force and wouldn't choose to be home full-time if that choice were available. In fact, only a handful maintained that they would prefer to be housewives. Yet the prevailing myth in these families is that the mothers work only for financial reasons.

Men in the alternating-shift families wish that their wives could be home, and believe that they would be if finances allowed. Nonetheless, almost all of their wives want to work outside the home, at least part-time. When I asked a number of the full-time working women about their preferences, initially some said that they would prefer to stay home. But when I questioned them further, most admitted that they did not want to quit their jobs entirely, but would prefer to work part-time.

> I'd rather stay working. I like to get out of the house.

> People work not just for the income but because we each are people and there are certain parts of us that need to be used. You can't just be a parent if there are other things that you're good at and need to do.

These mothers derive a variety of rewards from their paid work: a sense of independence in bringing in money, a chance to get out of the house and be with other adults, a feeling of accomplishment and recognition for a job well done, time away from children. Listen to this account receivables clerk:

> I look forward to [going to work] every night, I really do. . . . Taking off in the car by myself. . . . I really enjoy it. . . . I love it, I love my job. . . . I love doing the paperwork and working with numbers. . . . Anyone asks me a question, 9 out of 10 times I have an answer for them, and it's wonderful. I feel very successful.

The obvious satisfaction many of the alternating-shift mothers derive from their jobs contradicts the mythology that they are working only for financial reasons.[22]

Mythology often masks potential conflicts over an issue between husbands and wives. Husbands sometimes downplayed their wives' desire to work by invoking the financial need for them to be employed. One man said, "I would prefer that she didn't have to work. She only has to work because it helps supplement the family income. . . . She would have loved to be home. I would have rather had her here, but living in this state you need five incomes, so two isn't hardly enough." But his wife told a different story: "I wanted to go to work. I wanted to get out of the house."

In almost half of the alternating-shift families, wives and husbands gave very different accounts of why the women were working. The men said simply that the reason was finances, but the women gave much more elaborate answers, indicating that money wasn't the only reason. Ivy, a phlebotomist, acknowledged the need for additional income, but also revealed other motives for working: "The need to get out. . . . It is good to eat supper by yourself without somebody saying, 'I need juice.' I enjoy the two days that I do go. . . . I couldn't quite totally [stay home] even I could afford to."

Patrick and Diane were one of the few couples who had fought openly about the wife's working.[23] She explains: "He, at first, didn't want me to go to work ever. I said, 'I cannot be a person, a whole person (without working).'" He gave in, but balked again when they had two children. She held her ground: "As much as he pressured me and made me feel guilty, I was not going to give in." Nevertheless, she described the decision for her to go back to work as a mutual one, because finances had the final say. They needed her income. He still has the fantasy of her not working. When asked what he would change, he answered: "I wish she didn't have to work. . . . I'd love her not to have to work, but she works for different reasons, for money. She needs a sense of purpose, a sense of helping out. . . . It gets her out of the house."

Perhaps Patrick and Diane could have scraped by with one income. In most of the alternating-shift families, however, the economic necessity for two incomes allows the men to ignore other reasons that their wives work, reasons that would contradict their traditional ideas about family life. This mythology is reinforced because women themselves often exaggerate the financial motivations for working and their desire to be at home. One mother, a nursing assistant, complained bitterly about having to work for financial reasons: "I can't be here [at home] and I greatly resent that, just the fact that I can't be here all the time." But when asked directly if she would choose not to work at all, she responded, "No, I would have to work part-time." In fact, she was among those most enthusiastic about her job: "It would take a lot for me to leave. . . . It's wonderful when it's hectic and busy. It's very challenging. . . . It makes you realize you can have a very great impact on people." It is no wonder that men are sometimes confused.

Because of the financial pressures working-class families operate under, women are not required to make a choice between traditional family life and being employed. Freedom from actually having to make that choice means women are free to imagine themselves choosing to be home. Consequently, in some families both the women and their husbands can maintain the myth that even though the women work outside the home, paid work is not a central part of their identities.

The power dynamics underlying the suppression of this conflict are intriguing. The importance of their income to the families' survival gives these women the power to work despite their husbands' preferences. Yet the lack of conflict over this issue and the mythology surrounding it suggest the latent power of the husbands. Power can be expressed not only in whose preferences are honored but in the way conflict is managed or avoided.[24]

In truth, however, most of these alternating-shift mothers do not aspire to equal gender roles in the family. Despite being employed, women don't identify with work and breadwinning as much as their husbands do. They don't want to be in the paid labor force as much as their husbands, but they do want to be there more than their husbands want them to

Take the case of Sue, who has a clerical job in a department store, working for $7.75 an hour part-time in the evenings, and her carpenter husband, who is currently working odd jobs. In a good year when he is working 40 hours a week, he can earn $25,000 to $30,000, but times are bad, and he rarely works that many hours. The underlying conflict in this family is typical of the alternating-shift couples. He wishes she could be home: "If I can get a better job, she'll be 100% Mom then. If she wants to quit work, I'll let her. Right now, it's just for finances. That's why she works, we work two jobs." She sings a very different tune: "I just finally decided I had to go back to work. I had to get out of the house. It wasn't for financial reasons. I just had to get out. I couldn't stand being in the house anymore." Work provides quite a contrast for Sue:

> I love my job. I love my job, I really do. I'm probably one of the only people in the world who loves their job as much as I do. . . . It's the people I work with. . . . They all have

young children. We all have the same types of problems. It's more like a counseling session every night for six hours.

Although her husband began by emphasizing the financial motivations behind his wife's working, her enthusiasm for her job has not entirely escaped him. He later admitted that being home might not be her first choice: "That's what I would like. But she would just like to have a job so she doesn't have to be talking to little kids all day long, so she could talk with adults besides me. . . . That's why she likes working." When asked what would happen if he did get a higher-paying job, he predicted that his preferences would prevail: "I'd say she might quit. That's my feelings."

Chances are it will never be put to a test. Because these families can't afford to do without women's incomes, it is possible for men and even women themselves to cling to the belief that the only importance of work outside the home is to bring in income. The underlying conflicts about the real meaning of paid work, between husbands and wives and within women themselves, can remain buried. For women to earn money without embracing the work role is less threatening to traditional gender identities in the family. The financial constraints allow this myth to reign.

The Mother as the Mother

Mothers in the alternating-shift families are still regarded as the number-one parent, regardless of how much time fathers spend with their children. Dads may take over many of the functions that mothers have traditionally performed. They may feed their children, give them baths, read them bedtime stores, kiss their boo-boos, but the mother is still "the mother." Women retain this special role in two ways.

First, the mothers try to tailor their work lives so that they can be with children at times they define as key times, or they redefine the key times as those when they are available. Theresa, who has spent most of the 13 years she has been a parent on the evening shift, says of her role: "I'm very much what I consider a traditional mom in that I've had my days home. I can do the mommy stuff with the kids and volunteer in the school, or have a friend over, or be with them for whatever they want to do during the day."[25] Another mother, who works a day shift and leaves the care of younger children to her husband while she spends more time with the older ones in the evening, sees the crux of motherhood as her role with the older children: "I'm starting to feel like a true mother with the 14-year-old, with growing up and getting into high school and the peer pressure. . . . I'm beginning to really feel like a real mother, have to direct her to which the right path is."

Time is mentioned most often by mothers who work an evening shift while they have preschoolers, but expect to change their shift when their children go to school. Being there when children arrive home from a day at school is part of their image of being a good mother. One mother explained why she changed from an evening schedule to a weekend schedule: "I liked the idea of being there every day when he [her son] came home from school." She works the same number of hours and misses time with him on the weekend. But it seemed more important to her to be there at that critical time of the day. Other mothers reported similar plans:

I always said that when the kids went to school I'd rather be home during the day in case they were sick or in case they wanted to go on a field trip, and they needed a chaperone.

I'd go days, working maybe the mother hours, the school hours.

They are not called "mothers' hours" for nothing. Women want to be home at those times, and not simply because they think a parent should be there. At those key moments their husbands will not suffice, because it is their identities as mothers that are at stake. One woman put it bluntly:

Once she [her daughter] goes into school, I'll be [on] days because I don't want her coming home from school and telling just Bill what happened, or telling the baby-sitter what happened during the day. I want to be the one that she's telling these things to.

There is no doubt that by claiming this time of the day as central and insisting on her right to be there, this mother is claiming the right and the desire to be the number-one parent.

The second way that mothers retain their primary position is through the claim that they are still the center of emotional life in the family and that they should be. By and large, the alternating-shift mothers strongly believe that all mothers (including themselves) are more nurturing, closer to their children, and more attuned to their emotional needs than fathers:

As a mother, I worry more about their emotional needs.

The mother feels more strong. It's like if I had to choose, I'd do something for my kids first. . . . I don't think he sees it that way.

Moms are more tender than fathers are. My husband is compassionate, but I think I'm more compassionate than he is, and they look to me for that.

These are prescriptions as well as descriptions. Mothers should possess these qualities and hold these responsibilities in greater measure than their husbands:

As much as we try to do everything 50-50, if Freddy gets hurt and he cries, I think I'm the one that should take care of him.

Somewhere in my head I think that she [her daughter] should depend on me more.

Mothers seemed disturbed if the balance shifted too much toward their husbands. When asked about the parents' division of responsibility for their child's emotional life, one mother was reluctant to admit that it was equal: "I would hope it would be me more. . . . I don't know why I would hope that, but I would hope it would be me. . . . But I would say 50%." Another mother was disappointed that her knowledge of how to do things with her baby wasn't automatically superior to her husband's: "He taught her how to eat. I couldn't do that for some reason, which bothered me because I'm supposed to know all these things and I didn't. People told me, 'Well, you're a mother, you'll know.' I didn't."

Men seemed just as invested as their wives in retaining the notion that the mother is the primary parent. Despite spending much more time than his wife with their infant daughter because of their work schedules, one father was flabbergasted that his infant daughter would crawl to him to be comforted instead of to his wife. "It just throws me off," he said with obvious embarrassment. Other researchers have noted that even men who anchor their identities in involved fatherhood usually remain "mother's helpers" who avoid responsibility for the less desirable tasks of parenting.[26] The interesting difference in my findings is that the alternating-shift fathers often take on the responsibility for doing the tasks but still define their contribution as "helping."

Even when men were very nurturant themselves, they clung to the image of the mother as the nurturing parent. One father who does at least half of the child care and housework, including very stereotypically maternal tasks such as getting up at night to rock infants back to sleep, still wants his wife to have a more nurturant role than he: "Women can provide the softer end. . . . I mean, they don't call them the fairer sex for nothing. . . . Let her show that sympathy end of it." He is willing to do his fair share of the household work, but wants her to be "the mother," the one who nurtures. The reality is that when fathers are home, caring for young children, they become nurturers themselves, however much that contradicts their gender beliefs. As this father puts it:

> You picture the mother when the kids skin their knees, that she comes running up and hugs them and kisses the boo-boo. Well, that's something I do, and I suppose . . . the reason it's like that is because she's not here. I think if we had more overlap times she would probably do more of the traditional mother things and I would do less of them. . . . I know that when they need something, it's attended to.

In the absence of his wife, this father cared for his children just the way she would.[27] Yet many of the fathers insist that their wives provide something that they cannot:

> A mother's never going to do the same thing as a father. Even if they do the same things . . . the feeling is different.

> There's something about that sense of nurturing that the children can sense from the mother. . . . I can't probably provide for them in that way.

Even after 13 years of nurturing his children, David deferred to Theresa:

> Theresa can just zing; she's right there with them. I have to believe that's a mother's touch, something a father can work on and perhaps get, but probably never come into the capacity that a mother has. A mother's got that special—they always know what to say at the right place at the right time to kids, whereas a father is a little bit more jagged on the edges.

When the alternating-shift fathers care for their children, they believe that they are substituting for their wives. These men stress that their participation in no way detracts from the importance of their wives' gender identities in the family: "She's still the mom because, as close as we all are, if one of them falls down, if she's there, they're going to go to her first. . . . She's the mother."

Traditional Ideologies, Nontraditional Lives

Alternating-shift couples believe in an ideal family life that features breadwinning fathers and stay-at-home mothers. They are far from living that ideal. For at least part of every week mothers in these families are out in the paid workforce, while fathers are caring for their children at home. In contrast to middle-class couples, who often don't practice as much egalitarianism as they preach, these working-class couples practice more than they preach. They manage the marked difference between their behavior and their ideology by maintaining core aspects of parental gender identity.[28] Despite their nontraditional arrangements, they still regard the father as the breadwinner and the mother as the central parent.

Old notions of gender identity die hard.[29] When the mother goes to work outside the home, she does so not as a breadwinner, regardless of how much money she makes, but to help when her husband can't provide sufficiently. She goes as his proxy. Likewise, when the father cares for his children, he does it because his wife is not available. Regardless of his ability to nurture, he is merely there as her substitute.[30] It is permissible for each to expand his or her role to allow for nontraditional behavior, as long as that behavior is seen as constrained by circumstance and thus not relevant to the core of gender identity.[31] Making money doesn't make a person a breadwinner any more than doing maternal things makes a person a mother.

In one domain at least, though, gender identity is changing within this group. Although these mothers are not about to usurp their husbands' roles as primary breadwinners, they are more committed to their work roles than traditional gender ideology would allow. As we have seen, interviews with these women reveal that work provides them with a variety of satisfactions beyond the financial ones and that most would choose paid work, regardless of financial considerations.[32] The economic realities that they do face, however, mean that clashing views over this issue between husbands and wives need not be addressed.

Despite the ways in which these working-class men and their wives assert traditional gender identities, it is important to note the egalitarianism of these couples' lives. Although they may not be arguing for a genderless world in which the roles of men and women are the same, they are standing up for a world in which men and women work together to create a reasonable family life. Ironically, and perhaps without the feminist rhetoric touted by many middle-class men, the alternating-shift fathers eloquently argue for equality:

> I mean, you have a kid, it's for the both of you. You both have to pitch in and do it. I mean, it's not just, "Well, I'm the man. I'm going to work and do what the hell I want and you take care of the kid." It doesn't work that way because she's got to work, too. If we're going to make it, she's got to work, too.

In the end, it is simply a question of fairness, as this father put it:

> I think my wife works as hard as I do when she's at work, so . . . I don't think she should have to come home and do all the work when she gets home. . . . What the heck, she goes out and earns a living, too. I don't see how anybody could think it would be fair otherwise.

Notes

Portions of this chapter originally appeared in *Sex Roles, 38,* 331–332, published by Plenum Press (Deutsch & Saxon, 1998).

1. Eric Olin Wright and his colleagues conducted a rigorous study of the relation between class and division of domestic labor in the United States and Sweden. Despite extensive analyses searching for class effects, they were forced to conclude that very little of the variation in the division of labor across households can be explained by class (Wright, Shire, Hwang, Dolan, & Baxter, 1992). Their findings debunk the stereotype that working-class men do less work at home than their upper-middle-class counterparts.

2. Alternating work shifts is not an entirely new social phenomenon. In 1977, for example (the first year for which the relevant statistics are available), 14.4% of dual-earner families with preschoolers used father care while mothers worked, whereas 18.5% did in 1996 (Casper, 1998). But when you take into account the higher employment rate for mothers of preschool children in 1996, you can see that the increase in paternal care of young children is more dramatic. When you consider all preschool children living with married parents, in 1977 5.6% received primary care from their fathers some of the time, whereas by 1996, the figure had doubled to 11.3% (Casper, 1998; U.S. Bureau of Labor Statistics, 1989, 1997b).

In my study the parents of the alternating-shift couples (predominantly working class themselves) showed a much more traditional pattern in the division of labor than their offspring. In approximately two thirds of those families, fathers worked while mothers stayed at home. Two of the 46 alternating-shift parents reported that their own parents had followed the same pattern, reflecting the national trends. But many more of them reported fathers who were gone most of the time working at two or three jobs or who were absent for other reasons.

3. The numbers refer to both part-time and full-time workers (U.S. Bureau of Labor Statistics, 1997).

4. In dual-earner families with children under 15 years of age, fathers are the primary caretakers of children during mothers' work hours in 4% of the families in which both parents work a day shift, 14% of the families in which mothers work a day and fathers work a noonday shift, 21.3% of the families in which mothers work a noonday and fathers work a day shift, and 17.5% of the families in which mothers and fathers both work a noonday shift (Casper, 1997). No data are available on how many of these families intentionally choose different shifts so they can alternate child care, but many of the alternating shifters I interviewed reported that they had done so intentionally.

5. Casper, 1998.

6. Simon, 1990.

7. I did interview six other families who were alternating work shifts but had higher-status jobs. They were excluded from the analysis both because they are unrepresentative of alternating shifters and because they cannot illuminate the gender dynamics of sharing in blue-collar families. Statistical tests confirmed that the six families excluded had signifi-

cantly higher incomes, more education, and higher job statuses than the rest of the alternating shifters. This group included teachers and master's-level nurses.

8. In approximately two thirds of the alternating-shift families, the mother works the evening shift and the father works the day shift; in the other third, the father works evenings and the mother works days. In one family, the father works the graveyard shift. Equal sharers report that, on average, fathers do 50.7% of the morning routine tasks with children; alternating shifters report that fathers do 26.8%.

9. The alternating-shift fathers report doing an average of 52% of the bedtime routines, the equal sharers 48%, and the 75–25 fathers 40%.

10. A closer look reveals that because the division of labor depends on who has which shift, some alternating-shift dads put kids to bed more than their wives and supervise morning routine as much as their wives. On average, the dads who work the day shift do 69% of the putting children to bed in their families. Dads who work the evening shift contributed 47.5% of the supervision of children's morning routines, virtually the same as the equally sharing dads.

11. The average age of the youngest child was 5 in the equally sharing families and 3 in the alternating-shift families. (This difference was statistically significant when only the two groups were compared, $t(47) = 2.34$, $p<.05$. But the difference was only marginally significant ($p <.11$) in an analysis of variance comparing the four groups. Almost all (91%) of the alternating-shift fathers cared for at least one child younger than 6 years of age, and over two thirds cared for children younger than 5. Three of the fathers were caring for babies at the time I interviewed them, but many more reminisced about their baby care in years past.

Two explanations might account for the difference in the age of the youngest child in the equally sharing and alternating-shift families. First, alternating shifts is disproportionally done by families with younger children (Casper, 1997), so the sample may reflect real demographic differences between the two groups. Second, there have been a selection bias in the way I recruited participants. The affluent participants were more likely to be recruited from day care centers and schools, whereas the alternating shifters were more likely to be recruited through word of mouth. If the recruitment methods were confounded with the age of the child, then the difference between groups in my study might not reflect a real demographic difference.

12. Nine percent of the 75–25 couples, 17% of the 60–40 couples, and 3% of the equally sharing couples reported conflict over housework, whereas 30% of the alternating-shift couples reported it.

13. In 1993 there were 8.1 million families whose preschool children needed care while their mothers were at work. Over half of the families paid for that care, an average of $74 per week, or 8% of their family income. Of course, the lower their income, the higher the percentage cost. For example, if the monthly family income was between $1,200 and $2,999, paid child care constituted 12% of their expenditures (Casper, 1995).

14. See Hertz, 1986. Of course, in an egalitarian world, subtracting day care costs from women's incomes wouldn't make sense. Doing so implies that women are responsible for child care, and, as Hertz points out, it lowers the worth of women's work.

15. In a representative sample of employed mothers in Detroit, when household income was controlled, mothers who believe parental care is best were less likely to use paid child care than other mothers (Kuhlthau & Mason, 1996).

16. The relation between the cost and quality of day care is not as clear-cut as one might think. Certainly better trained day care providers and better staff-to-children ratios, which both increase the cost of care, contribute to a higher quality of care (Mocan, Burchinal, Morris, & Helburn, 1995). But the cost of producing high-quality care is not identical to the costs

that parents incur. Many child care centers are subsidized. In a study comparing the quality of care in different types of day care centers (public, nonprofit-independent, for-profit), public centers were found to provide the best care, which was also the most expensive to produce. But, on average, the cost to parents was lower in public centers than in for-profit chains, which, despite their high price tag, provided relatively low-quality care (J. Morris, personal communication, January 16, 1998).

When it comes to center-based care, the working-class parents might have the worst of all possible worlds. The NICHD Early Child Care Research Network (1997) uncovered a curvilinear relationship between family income and quality of care for children who receive center-based care. Poor and affluent children get better care at day care centers than children from moderate-income families. The working-class families' relative lack of access to subsidized day care centers means that their children fare worse than even poor children if they use center-based care.

The relation between family income and quality for family day care and home-based care (excluding father and grandfather care) was more straightforward. Families who could pay more for these types of care purchased better care (NICHD Early Child Care Research Network, 1997). When different types of care were compared overall in the NICHD study, more positive caregiving was observed in in-home care than in family day care, which, in turn, offered more positive caregiving than did centers. Fathers received higher scores in quality of caregiving than other in-home providers, such as grandparents or baby-sitters (NICHE Early Child Care Research Network, 1996). We can't assume from these data that fathers provide better care than the highest quality paid day care. But since working-class couples can't afford or don't have access to the highest quality day care, it seems reasonable to assume that fathers' care is the best way to maximize quality.

17. Blumberg and Coleman (1989) elaborate this argument. Thompson (1991) also observed that women feel more entitled to have help with domestic work if they see themselves as contributing to the breadwinning.

18. Mason & Lu, 1988; Wilkie, 1993. The working-class alternating shifters in my study endorsed more traditional attitudes than the predominantly upper-middle-class couples in the 50–50, 60–40, and 75–25 groups. The alternating-shift couples had the lowest mean egalitarianism scores of the four groups on each of the five subscales of the Beere-King Sex Role Egalitarianism Scale (education, employment, marital, parental, and social-interpersonal). Moreover, this pattern was most pronounced on the marital and parental subscales, the most relevant ones. Although both men and women were more traditional than their middle-class counterparts, the alternating-shift wives had more egalitarian views than their husbands. See Deutsch and Saxon (1998) for a more detailed statistical analysis.

19. The good provider role developed with the advent of industrialization in the early nineteenth century, and linked a masculine definition of self with the ability to provide for a family (Bernard, 1981). Today, even with so many women employed, because of the link between masculinity and providing, both men and women are reluctant to see wives as providers. Only a minority of couples think that the woman has the same kind of responsibility and obligation to provide for the family as the man (Hood, 1986; Potuchek, 1992, 1997). For example, only 12% of the 153 couples Potuchek (1997) interviewed thought of themselves as true coproviders. See Thompson and Walker (1989) for a summary of research on the gendered nature of the provider role, and see Potuchek (1992) for a detailed analysis of the meanings employed women and men attribute to their earnings.

Cohen (1993) speculated that working-class men are especially likely to see themselves as contributing to the family by providing because their jobs do not offer the intrinsic rewards available to professional men. Moreover, two studies of blue-collar women have found that even when they feel responsible for helping their husbands provide, they view themselves as secondary providers (Rosen, 1987; Zavella, 1987).

Consistent with these past findings, among the alternating-shift couples I interviewed, 18 (78%) of the men and 15 (65%) of the women emphasized that the men are the breadwinners in their families. Only one of the men and three of the women explicitly challenged that idea. Hood's category of "ambivalent coprovider" (Hood, 1986) seems to best capture the attitudes that were prevalent in my sample. Couples recognized the necessity of wives' financial contributions but were not entirely comfortable with it, especially the men.

20. Other researchers have noted that couples sometimes emphasize the relative importance of men's jobs by earmarking men's incomes for essentials and women's for "extras" (Potuchek, 1997; Thompson & Walker, 1989). (Sometimes those "extras" can be pretty essential, though.)

21. Organizing family life this way also preserves women's roles as the primary parents.

22. See Thompson and Walker (1989) for a summary of other studies of working-class couples that also show that women's needing to work for the money did not preclude their wanting to work. Lillian Rubin (1969) uncovered some similar patterns in her study of working-class families. Although women derived status from having husbands who could earn enough so that they didn't need paid work, even in the 1960s the women who were forced to work outside the home for financial reasons discovered that they liked having paid employment.

23. In two other families, either the husband or the wife reported fighting over this issue, but the spouse in each case denied there had been a conflict.

24. Komter, 1989.

25. Garey (1995) also observed that hospital nurses who work the night shift construct themselves as "at-home" mothers because they are home during the day, even though many are home sleeping.

26. Coltrane, 1996; Gerson, 1993.

27. In her (1993) analysis of the gendered nature of giving "care" in a family, Thompson says that "men are more likely to display care when there is a clear need for care, no one else is around to provide care, and the recipient is dependent" (p. 564). These are exactly the circumstances of the alternating-shift fathers. Their children need care, their wives are at work, and their children are dependent on them.

28. See Hammond and Mahoney (1983) for an example of how another nontraditional group, female coal miners, maintains a traditional feminine identity.

29. As the division of labor changes at home, "doing gender" in these blue-collar families is shifting from the enactment of different male and female behaviors to the construction of gendered meanings for what are often the same behaviors (Ferree, 1990; West & Zimmerman, 1987). As others have argued and as these families show, family is often the locus of the creation of gender (Osmond & Thorne, 1993).

30. Likewise, a study of the families of male Air Force security guards who worked off-shifts showed that although the husbands took care of their children when their wives were employed, they had not changed their ideas that mothers were ultimately responsible for child care (Hertz & Charlton, 1989).

31. Lein's (1979) intensive study of 25 dual-earner households in the 1970s found a similar result among a broader income group.

32. In several articles, Myra Marx Ferree (1980, 1983, 1984a, 1984b) has argued that the traditionalism of working-class women has been exaggerated. She has taken to task middle-class feminists who assume that working-class women would rather be home as housewives than out in the paid labor force. In fact, she showed that when middle-class and working-

class employed women and housewives were compared, the working-class housewives were the least satisfied group (1984b).

References

Bernard, J. (1981). The good provider role: Its rise and fall. *American Psychologist, 36*, 1–12.

Blumberg, R. L., and Coleman, M. T. (1989). A theoretical look at the gender balance of power in the American couple. *Journal of Family Issues, 10*, 225–250.

Casper, L. M. (1995). *What does it cost to mind our preschoolers?* (Current Population Reports: Household Economic Studies P70–52). Washington, DC: U.S. Census Bureau.

Casper, L. M. (1997). *My daddy takes care of me! Fathers as care providers* (Current Population Reports: Household Economic Studies P70–59, table 5). Washington, DC: U.S. Census Bureau.

Casper, L. M. (1998). *Who's minding our preschoolers?* (Fall 1994 update; Current Population Reports: Household Economic Studies, detailed tables for P70–62. PPL-81). Washington, DC: U.S. Census Bureau.

Cohen, T. F. (1993). What do fathers provide? Reconsidering the economic and nurturant dimensions of men as parents. In J. C. Hood (Ed.), *Men, work, and family* (pp. 1–22). Newbury Park: Sage.

Coltrane, S. (1996). *Family man: Fatherhood, housework, and gender equity.* New York: Oxford University Press.

Deutsch, F. M., & Saxon, S. E. (1998). Traditional ideologies, nontraditional lives. *Sex Roles, 38*, 331–362.

Ferree, M. M. (1980). Working-class feminism: A consideration of the consequences of employment. *Sociological Quarterly, 21*, 173–184.

Ferree, M. M. (1983). The women's movement in the working class. *Sex Roles, 9*, 493–505.

Ferree, M. M. (1984a). The view from below: Women's employment and gender equality in working class families. In B. Hess & M. Sussman (Eds.), *Women and the family: Two decades of change* (pp. 57–75). New York: Haworth Press.

Ferree, M. M. (1984b). Class, housework, and happiness: Women's work and life satisfaction. *Sex Roles, 11*, 1057–1074.

Ferree, M. M. (1990). Beyond separate spheres: Feminism and family research. *Journal of Marriage and Family, 52*, 866–884.

Garey, A. I. (1995). Constructing motherhood on the night shift: "Working mothers" as "stay-at-home moms." *Qualitative Sociology, 18*, 415–437.

Gerson, K. (1993). *No man's land: Men's changing commitments to family and work.* New York: Basic Books.

Hammond, J. A., & Mahoney, C. W. (1983). Reward-cost balancing among women coal miners. *Sex Roles, 9*, 17–29.

Hertz, R. (1986). *More equal than others: Men and women in dual-career marriages.* Berkeley: University of California Press.

Hertz, R., & Charlton, J. (1989). Making family under a shiftwork schedule: Air force security guards and their wives. *Social Problems, 36*, 491–507.

Hood, J. C. (1986). The provider role: Its meaning and measurement. *Journal of Marriage and the Family, 48*, 349–359.

Komter, A. (1989). Hidden power in marriage. *Gender and Society, 3*, 197–216.

Kuhlthau, A., & Mason, K. O. (1996). Market child care versus care by relatives: Choices made by employed and nonemployed mothers. *Journal of Family Issues, 17*, 561–578.

Lein, L. (1979). Male participation in home life: Impact of social supports and breadwinner responsibility on the allocation of tasks. *Family Coordinator, 28,* 489–495.

Mason, K. O., & Lu, K. (1988). Attitudes toward women's familial roles: Changes in the United States, 1977–1985. *Gender and Society, 2,* 39–57.

Mocan, H. N., Burchinal, M., Morris, J. R., & Helburn, S. W. (1995). Models of quality in center child care. In S. Helburn (Ed.), *Cost, quality, and child outcomes in child care centers: Technical report* (pp. 279–304). Denver: Economics Department, University of Colorado at Denver, Center for Research in Economic and Social Policy.

NICHD Early Child Care Research Network. (1997). Familial factors associated with the characteristics of nonmaternal care for infants. *Journal of Marriage and the Family, 59,* 389–408.

Osmond, M. W., & Thorne, B. (1993). Feminist theories: The social construction of gender in families and society. In P. G. Boss, W. J. Doherty, R. LaRossa, W. R. Shumm, & S. K. Steinmetz (Eds.), *Sourcebook of family theories and methods: A contextual approach* (pp. 591–623). New York: Plenum Press.

Potuchek, J. L. (1992). Employed wives' orientations to breadwinning: A gender theory analysis. *Journal of Marriage and the Family, 54,* 548–558.

Potuchek, J. L. (1997). *Who supports the family? Gender and breadwinning in dual-earner marriages.* Stanford: Stanford University Press.

Rosen, E. I. (1987). *Bitter choices: Blue-collar women in and out of work.* Chicago: University of Chicago Press.

Rubin, L. B. (1969). *Worlds of pain: Life in the working-class family.* New York: Basic Books.

Simon, B. L. (1990). Impact of shift work on individuals and families. *Families in Society: The Journal of Contemporary Human Services, 71,* 342–348.

Thompson, L. (1991). Family work: Women's sense of fairness. *Journal of Family Issues, 12,* 181–196.

Thompson, L., & Walker, A. J. (1989). Gender in families: Women and men in marriage, work, and parenthood. *Journal of Marriage and the Family, 51,* 845–871.

U.S. Bureau of Labor Statistics. (1989). *Handbook of labor statistics* (table 57). Washington, DC: Government Printing Office.

U.S. Bureau of Labor Statistics. (1997). Current Population Survey, table 6 of 1997 news release.

U.S. Bureau of Labor Statistics. (1997b). *Workers on flexible and shift schedules* (Current Population Survey, unpublished data). Washington, DC.

West, C., & Zimmerman, H. (1987). Doing gender. *Gender and Society, 1,* 125–151.

Wilkie, J. R. (1993). Changes in U.S. men's attitudes toward the family provider role, 1972–1989. *Gender and Society, 7,* 261–279.

Wright, E. O., Shire, K., Hwang, S. Dolan, M., & Baxter, J. (1992). Non-effects of class on the gender division of labor in the home: A comparative study of Sweden and the United States. *Gender and Society, 6,* 252–282.

Zavella, P. (1987). *Women's work and Chicano families: Cannery workers of the Santa Clara Valley.* Ithaca: Cornell University Press.

6

"I'm Here, but I'm There"

The Meanings of Latina Transnational Motherhood

Pierrette Hondagneu-Sotelo and Ernestine Avila

While mothering is generally understood as a practice that involves the preservation, nurturance, and training of children for adult life (Ruddick, 1989), there are many contemporary variants distinguished by race, class, and culture (Collins, 1994; Dill, 1988, 1994; Nakano Glenn, 1994). Latina immigrant women who work and reside in the United States while their children remain in their countries of origin constitute one variation in the organizational arrangements, meanings, and priorities of motherhood. We call this arrangement "transnational motherhood," and we explore how the meanings of motherhood are rearranged to accommodate these spatial and temporal separations. In the United States, there is a long legacy of Caribbean women and African American women from the South leaving their children "back home" to seek work in the North. Since the early 1980s, thousands of Central American women, and increasing numbers of Mexican women, have migrated to the United States in search of jobs, many of them leaving their children behind with grandmothers, with other female kin, with the children's fathers, and sometimes with paid caregivers. In some cases, the separations of time and distance are substantial; 10 years may elapse before women are reunited with their children. In this article we confine our analysis to Latina transnational mothers currently employed in Los Angeles in paid domestic work, one of the most gendered and racialized occupations.[1] We examine how their meanings of motherhood shift in relation to the structures of late-20th-century global capitalism.

Motherhood is not biologically predetermined in any fixed way but is historically and socially constructed. Many factors set the stage for transnational motherhood. These factors include labor demand for Latina immigrant women in the United States, particularly in paid domestic work; civil war, national economic crises, and particular development strategies, along with tenuous and scarce job opportunities for women and men in Mexico and Central America; and the subsequent increasing numbers of female-headed households (although many transnational mothers are married). More interesting to us than the macro determinants of transnational motherhood, however, is the forging of new arrangements and meanings of motherhood.

Central American and Mexican women who leave their young children "back home" and come to the United States in search of employment are in the process of actively, if not voluntarily, building alternative constructions of motherhood.

Pierrette Hondagneu-Sotelo and Ernestine Avila, *Gender & Society* (Vol. 11 No. 5), pp. 548-571, © 1997 by Sage Publications, Inc.

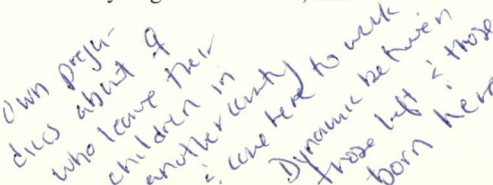

Transnational motherhood contradicts both dominant U.S., white, middle-class models of motherhood, and most Latina ideological notions of motherhood. On the cusp of the millennium, transnational mothers and their families are blazing new terrain, spanning national borders, and improvising strategies for mothering. It is a brave odyssey, but one with deep costs.

Immigration: Gendering Transnational Perspectives

We pursue this project by drawing from, and engaging in, dialogue with literature on immigration and transnational frameworks; family and motherhood; and women's work, place, and space. The 1990s witnessed the emergence of transnational perspectives of migration. Emerging primarily from postcolonial, postmodern-inspired anthropology, and explicitly challenging the linear, bipolar model of "old country" and "new world," of "sojourner" and "settler" that is typical of assimilationist models and other well-established immigration paradigms, transnationalist proponents argue that the international circulation of people, goods, and ideas creates new transnational cultures, identities, and community spheres (Basch, Schiller, & Blanc, 1994; Kearney, 1995; Rouse, 1991). Accordingly, these fluid entities become semi-autonomous spheres in their own right, transcending national borders. The new emergent cultures and hybrid ways of life resemble neither those in the place of origin nor the place of destination.

Although we welcome these insights, we raise three objections to the transnational perspective. First, we object to transnationalism's emphasis on circulation and the indeterminance of settlement. While significant segments of foreign-born Latinos regularly return to their countries for annual fiestas or to visit family members, most Latino immigrants are here to stay, regardless of their initial migration intentions. Most Latina/o immigrant workers in California are not working in industries with seasonal labor demand—agriculture employs only a small fraction of Mexicans, for example—but in urban-based jobs requiring stability of employment.[2] A glance at cities, suburbs, and rural areas around California testifies to the demographic transformation, as new Latina/o communities have emerged in neighborhoods that were previously African American or White. While some of the Latina/o residents in these diaspora communities are involved in transnational political organizations and home-town associations, many more are involved in activities and organizations firmly rooted in the United States, with local Catholic parishes or storefront Evangelical churches, Parent-Teacher Associations (PTAs) and schools, or workplace associations. Transnationalism emphasizes the ephemeral circuits and understates the permanency of Latina/o settlement.

The celebratory nature of the transnational perspective merits caution. In some of the writings, it is almost as if "resistance" is suggested merely through movement across borders and by the formation of circuits, which enhance the possibility of survival in places full of uncertainty. In these renditions, the power of the nation-state is often underestimated, and the costs—financial, social, and emotional—to the individuals involved in transnational migration may be overlooked.

A final objection to the transnational perspective is the assumption of genderless transnational migrants. In recent years, literature on women and migration has flourished (Pedraza, 1991; Tienda & Booth, 1991), but many studies that do look at women in migration—especially those informed by demography—examine gender as a variable rather than as a construct that organizes social life. With the exception of Mahler's (1996) recent work, transnationalism, like the assimilationist models that it counters, ignores gender altogether. Examining transnational motherhood, defined not as physical circuits of migration but as the circuits of affection, caring, and financial support that transcend national borders, provides an opportunity to gender views of transnationalism and immigration.

Rethinking Motherhood

Feminist scholarship has long challenged monolithic notions of family and motherhood that relegate women to the domestic arena of private/public dichotomies and that rely on the ideological conflation of family, women, reproduction, and nurturance (Collier & Yanagisako, 1987, p. 36).[3] "Rethinking the family" prompts the rethinking of motherhood (Nakano Glenn, 1994; Thorne & Yalom, 1992), allowing us to see that the glorification and exaltation of isolationist, privatized mothering is historically and culturally specific.

The "cult of domesticity" is a cultural variant of motherhood, one made possible by the industrial revolution, by breadwinner husbands who have access to employers who pay a "family wage," and by particular configurations of global and national socioeconomic and racial inequalities. Working-class women of color in the United States have rarely had access to the economic security that permits a biological mother to be the only one exclusively involved with mothering during the children's early years (Collins, 1994; Dill, 1988, 1994; Nakano Glenn, 1994). As Evelyn Nakano Glenn puts it, "Mothering is not just gendered, but also racialized" (1994, p. 7) and differentiated by class. Both historically and in the contemporary period, women lacking the resources that allow for exclusive, full-time, round-the-clock mothering rely on various arrangements to care for children. Sharing mothering responsibilities with female kin and friends as "other mothers" (Collins, 1991), by "kin-scription" (Stack & Burton, 1994), or by hiring child care (Uttal, 1996) are widely used alternatives.

Women of color have always worked. Yet many working women—including Latina women—hold the cultural prescription of solo mothering in the home as an ideal. We believe this ideal is disseminated through cultural institutions of industrialization and urbanization, as well as from preindustrial, rural peasant arrangements that allow for women to work while tending to their children. It is not only white, middle-class ideology but also strong Latina/o traditions, cultural practices, and ideals—Catholicism and the Virgin Madonna figure—that cast employment as oppositional to mothering. Cultural symbols that model maternal femininity, such as the Virgen de Guadalupe, and negative femininity, such as La Llorona and La Malinche, serve to control Mexican and Chicana women's conduct by prescribing idealized visions of motherhood.[4]

Culture, however, does not deterministically dictate what people do.[5] Many Latina women must work for pay, and many Latinas innovate income-earning strategies that allow them to simultaneously earn money and care for their children. They sew garments on industrial sewing machines at home (Fernandez-Kelly & Garcia, 1990) and incorporate their children into informal vending to friends and neighbors, at swap meets, or on the sidewalks (Chinchilla & Hamilton, 1996). They may perform agricultural work alongside their children or engage in seasonal work (Zavella, 1987); or they may clean houses when their children are at school or incorporate their daughters into paid housecleaning (Romero, 1992, 1997). Engagement in "invisible employment" allows for urgently needed income and the maintenance of the ideal of privatized mothering. The middle-class model of mothering is predicated on mother-child isolation in the home, while women of color have often worked with their children in close proximity (Collins, 1994), as in some of the examples listed above. In both cases, however, mothers are with their children. The long distances of time and space that separate transnational mothers from their children contrast sharply with both mother-child isolation in the home and mother-child integration in the workplace.

Transnational Mothers' Work, Place, and Space

Feminist geographers have focused on how gendered orientations to space influence the way we organize our daily work lives. While sociologists have tended to explain occupational segregation as rooted either in family or individual characteristics (human capital theory) or in the workplace (labor market segmentation), feminist geographers observe that women tend to take jobs close to home so that they can fulfill child rearing and domestic duties (Hanson & Pratt, 1995; Massey, 1994). Transnational mothers, on the other hand, congregate in paid domestic work, an occupation that is relentlessly segregated not only by gender but also by race, class, and nationality/citizenship. To perform child rearing and domestic duties for others, they radically break with deeply gendered spatial and temporal boundaries of family and work.

Performing domestic work for pay, especially in a live-in job, is often incompatible with providing primary care for one's own family and home (Nakano Glenn, 1986; Rollins, 1985; Romero, 1992, 1997).[6] Transnational mothering, however, is neither exclusive to live-in domestic workers nor to single mothers. Many women continue with transnational mothering after they move into live-out paid domestic work or into other jobs. Women with income-earning husbands may also become transnational mothers.[7] The women we interviewed do not necessarily divert their mothering to the children and homes of their employers but instead reformulate their other mothering to accommodate spatial and temporal gulfs.

Like other immigrant workers, most transnational mothers came to the United States with the intention to stay for a finite period of time. But as time passes and economic need remains, prolonged stays evolve. Marxist-informed theory maintains that the separation of work life and family life constitutes the separation of labor maintenance costs from the labor reproduction costs (Burawoy, 1976; Nakano Glenn, 1986). According to this framework, Latina transnational mothers work to maintain themselves in the United States and to support their children—and reproduce the next generation of workers—in Mexico or Central America. One precursor to these arrangements is the mid-20th-century Bracero Program, which in effect legislatively mandated Mexican "absentee fathers" who came to work as contracted agricultural laborers in the United States. Other precursors, going back further in history, include the 18th and 19th centuries' coercive systems of labor, whereby African American slaves and Chinese sojourner laborers were denied the right to form residentially intact families (Dill 1988, 1994).

Transnational mothering is different from some of these other arrangements in that now women with young children are recruited for U.S. jobs that pay far less than a "family wage." When men come north and leave their families in Mexico—as they did during the Bracero Program and as many continue to do today—they are fulfilling familial obligations defined as breadwinning for the family. When women do so, they are embarking not only on an immigration journey but on a more radical gender-transformative odyssey. They are initiating separations of space and time from their communities of origin, homes, children, and—sometimes—husbands. In doing so, they must cope with stigma, guilt, and criticism from others. A second difference is that these women work primarily not in production of agricultural products or manufacturing but in reproductive labor, in paid domestic work, and/or vending. Performing paid reproductive work for pay—especially caring for other people's children—is not always compatible with taking daily care of one's own family. All of this raises questions about the meanings and variations of motherhood in the late 20th century.

Description of Research

Materials for this article draw from a larger study of paid domestic work in Los Angeles County and from interviews conducted in adjacent Riverside County. The materials include in-depth interviews, a survey, and ethnographic fieldwork. We had not initially anticipated studying women who live and work apart from their children but serendipitously stumbled onto this theme in the course of our research.

For this article, we draw primarily on tape-recorded and fully transcribed interviews with 26 women who work as housecleaners and as live-out or live-in nanny-housekeepers. Of these 26 women, 8 lived apart from their children to accommodate their migration and work arrangements, but other respondents also spoke poignantly about their views and experiences with mothering, and we draw on these materials as well. We also draw, to a lesser extent, on in-depth, fully transcribed interviews with domestic agency personnel. All of the interview respondents were located through informal snowball sampling. The domestic workers interviewed are all from Mexico, El Salvador, and Guatemala, but they are diverse in terms of demographic characteristics (such as education, civil status, and children), immigration (length of time in the United States, access to legal papers), and other job-related characteristics (English language skills, driver's license, cardiopulmonary resuscitation [CPR] training).

While the interviews provide close-up information about women's experiences and views of mothering, a survey administered to 153 paid domestic workers in Los Angeles provides some indicator of how widespread these transnational arrangements are among paid domestic workers. Because no one knows the total universe of paid domestic workers—many of whom lack legal papers and work in the informal sector where census data are not reliable—we drew a nonrandom sample in three types of sites located in or near affluent areas spanning from the west side of Los Angeles to the Hollywood area. We solicited respondents at evening ESL (English as a second language) classes and in public parks where nannies and housekeepers congregate in the midmorning hours with the children they care for, and we went to bus kiosks on Mondays and Tuesdays during the early morning hours (7:00 to 9:00 A.M.) when many domestic workers, including live-in workers, are traveling to their places of employment. While we refrained from conducting the survey in places where only certain types of domestic workers might be found (the employment agencies, or organizations of domestic workers), going to the bus stops, public parks, and ESL classes means that we undersampled domestic workers with access to private cars, driver's licenses, and good English skills. In short, we undersampled women who are earning at the higher end of the occupation.

The study also draws on ethnographic field research conducted in public parks, buses, private homes, a domestic workers' association, and the waiting room of a domestic employment agency. A tape-recorded group discussion with about 15 women—including several who had their children in their countries of origin—in the employment agency waiting room also informs the study. Nearly all of the in-depth interviews, structured survey interviews, and fieldwork were conducted in Spanish. The climate of fear produced by California voters' passage of anti-immigrant legislation in November 1994 perhaps dissuaded some potential respondents from participating in the study, but more important in shaping the interviews is the deeply felt pain expressed by the respondents. The interview transcripts include tearful segments in which the women recounted the daily indignities of their jobs and the raw pain provoked by the forced separation from their young children.

Transnational Motherhood and Paid Domestic Work

Just how widespread are transnational motherhood arrangements in paid domestic work? Of the 153 domestic workers surveyed, 75% had children. Contrary to the images of Latina immigrant women as breeders with large families—a dominant image used in the campaign to pass California's Proposition 187—about half (47%) of these women have only one or two children. More significant for our purposes is this finding: 40% of the women with children have at least one of their children "back home" in their country of origin.

Transnational motherhood arrangements are not exclusive to paid domestic work, but there are particular features about the way domestic work is organized that encourage temporal and spatial separations of a mother-employee and her children. Historically and in the contemporary period, paid domestic workers have had to limit or forfeit primary care of their families and homes to earn income by providing primary care to the families and homes of employers, who are privileged by race and class (Nakano Glenn, 1986; Rollins, 1985; Romero, 1992). Paid domestic work is organized in various ways, and there is a clear relationship between the type of job arrangement women have and the likelihood of experiencing transnational family arrangements with their children. To understand the variations, it is necessary to explain how the employment is organized. Although there are variations within categories, we find it useful to employ a tripartite taxonomy of paid domestic work arrangements. This includes live-in and live-out nanny-housekeeper jobs and weekly house-cleaning jobs.

Weekly housecleaners clean different houses on different days according to what Romero (1992) calls modernized "job work" arrangements. These contractual-like employee-employer relations often resemble those between customer and vendor, and they allow employees a degree of autonomy and scheduling flexibility. Weekly employees are generally paid a flat fee, and they work shorter hours and earn considerably higher hourly rates than do live-in or live-out domestic workers. By contrast, live-in domestic workers work and live in isolation from their own families and communities, sometimes in arrangements with feudal remnants (Nakano Glenn, 1986). There are often no hourly parameters to their jobs, and as our survey results show, most live-in workers in Los Angeles earn below minimum wage. Live-out domestic workers also usually work as combination nanny-housekeepers, generally working for one household, but contrary to live-ins, they enter daily and return to their own home in the evening. Because of this, live-out workers better resemble industrial wage workers (Nakano Glenn, 1986).

Live-in jobs are the least compatible with conventional mothering responsibilities. Only half (16 out of 30) of live-ins surveyed have children, while 83% (53 out of 64) of live-outs and 77% (45 out of 59) of housecleaners do. As Table 6.1 shows, 82% of live-ins with children have at least one of their children in their country of origin. It is very difficult to work a live-in job when your children are in the United States. Employers who hire live-in workers do so because they generally want employees for jobs that may require round-the-clock service. As one owner of a domestic employment agency put it,

> They [employers] want a live-in to have somebody at their beck and call. They want the hours that are most difficult for them covered, which is like 6:30 in the morning until 8:00 when the kids go to school, and 4:00 to 7:00 when the kids are home, and it's homework, bath, and dinner.

According to our survey, live-ins work an average of 64 hours per week. The best live-in worker, from an employer's perspective, is one without daily family obliga-

Table 6.1: Domestic Workers: Wages, Hours Worked, and Children's Country of Residence

	Live-ins *(n = 30)*	*Live-outs* *(n = 64)*	*Housecleaners* *(n = 59)*
Mean hourly wage	$3.79	$5.90	$9.40
Mean hours worked per week	64	35	23
Domestic workers with children	*(n = 16)*	*(n = 53)*	*(n = 45)*
All children in the United States (%)	18	58	76
At least one child "back home"	82	42	24

tions of her own. The workweek may consist of six very long workdays. These may span from dawn to midnight and may include overnight responsibilities with sleepless or sick children, making it virtually impossible for live-in workers to sustain daily contact with their own families. Although some employers do allow for their employees' children to live in as well (Romero, 1996), this is rare. When it does occur, it is often fraught with special problems, and we discuss these in a subsequent section of this article. In fact, minimal family and mothering obligations are an informal job placement criterion for live-in workers. Many of the agencies specializing in the placement of live-in nanny-housekeepers will not even refer a woman who has children in Los Angeles to interviews for live-in jobs. As one agency owner explained, "As a policy here, we will not knowingly place a nanny in a live-in job if she has young kids here." A job seeker in an employment agency waiting room acknowledged that she understood this job criterion more broadly: "You can't have a family. You can't have anyone [if you want a live-in job]."

The subminimum pay and the long hours for live-in workers also make it very difficult for these workers to have their children in the United States. Some live-in workers who have children in the same city as their place of employment hire their own nanny-housekeeper—often a much younger female relative—to provide daily care for their children, as did Patricia, one of the interview respondents whom we discuss later in this article. Most live-ins, however, cannot afford this alternative; 93% of the live-ins surveyed earn below minimum wage (then $4.25 per hour). Many live-in workers cannot afford to bring their children to Los Angeles, but once their children are in the same city, most women try to leave live-in work to live with their children.

At the other end of the spectrum are the housecleaners whom we surveyed, who earn substantially higher wages than live-ins (averaging $9.46 per hour as opposed to $3.79) and who work fewer hours per week than live-ins (23 as opposed to 64). We suspect that many housecleaners in Los Angeles make even higher earnings and work more hours per week, because we know that the survey undersampled women who drive their own cars to work and who speak English. The survey suggests that housecleaners appear to be the least likely to experience transnational spatial and temporal separations from their children.

Financial resources and job terms enhance housecleaners' abilities to bring their children to the United States. Weekly housecleaning is not a bottom-of-the-barrel job but rather an achievement. Breaking into housecleaning work is difficult because an employee needs to locate and secure several employers. For this reason, relatively well established women with more years of experience in the United States, who speak some English, who have a car, and who have job references predominate in weekly housecleaning. Women who are better established in the United States are also more likely to have their children here. The terms of weekly housecleaning employment—particularly the relatively fewer hours worked per week, scheduling flexibility, and relatively higher wages—allow them to live with, and care for, their children. So it is not surprising that 76% of housecleaners who are mothers have their children in the United States.

Compared with live-ins and weekly cleaners, live-out nanny-housekeepers are at an intermediate level with respect to the likelihood of transnational motherhood. Forty-two percent of the live-out nanny-housekeepers who are mothers reported having at least one of their children in their country of origin. Live-out domestic workers, according to the survey, earn $5.90 per hour and work an average workweek of 35 hours. Their lower earnings, more regimented schedules, and longer workweeks than housecleaners, but higher earnings, shorter hours, and more scheduling flexibility than live-ins explain their intermediate incidence of transnational motherhood.

The Meanings of Transnational Motherhood

How do women transform the meaning of motherhood to fit immigration and employment? Being a transnational mother means more than being the mother to children raised in another country. It means forsaking deeply felt beliefs that biological mothers should raise their own children and replacing that belief with new definitions of motherhood. The ideal of biological mothers raising their own children is widely held but is also widely broken at both ends of the class spectrum. Wealthy elites have always relied on others—nannies, governesses, and boarding schools—to raise their children (Wrigley, 1995), while poor urban families often rely on kin and "other mothers" (Collins, 1991).

In Latin America, in large peasant families, the eldest daughters are often in charge of the daily care of the younger children, and in situations of extreme poverty, children as young as 5 or 6 may be loaned or hired out to well-to-do families as "child-servants," sometimes called *criadas* (Gill, 1994).[8] A middle-aged Mexican woman whom we interviewed, now a weekly housecleaner, homeowner, and mother of five children, recalled her own experience as a child-servant in Mexico: "I started working in a house when I was 8. . . . They hardly let me eat any food. . . . It was terrible, but I had to work to help my mother with the rent." This recollection of her childhood experiences reminds us how our contemporary notions of motherhood are historically and socially circumscribed and also correspond to the meanings we assign to childhood (Zelizer, 1994).

This example also underlies how the expectation on the child to help financially support her mother required daily spatial and temporal separations of mother and child. There are, in fact, many transgressions of the mother-child symbiosis in practice—large families where older daughters care for younger siblings, child-servants who at an early age leave their mothers, children raised by paid nannies and other caregivers, and mothers who leave young children to seek employment—but these are fluid enough to sustain ideological adherence to the prescription that children should be raised exclusively by biological mothers. Long-term physical and temporal separation disrupts this notion. Transnational mothering radically rearranges mother-child interactions and requires a concomitant radical reshaping of the meanings and definitions of appropriate mothering.

Transnational mothers distinguish their version of motherhood from estrangement, child abandonment, or disowning. A youthful Salvadoran woman at the domestic employment waiting room reported that she had not seen her two eldest boys, now ages 14 and 15 and under the care of her own mother in El Salvador, since they were toddlers. Yet she made it clear that this was different from putting a child up for adoption, a practice that she viewed negatively, as a form of child abandonment. Although she had been physically separated from her boys for more than a decade, she maintained her mothering ties and financial obligations to them by regularly sending home money. The exchange of letters, photos, and phone calls also helped to sustain the connection. Her physical absence did not signify emotional absence from her children. Another woman who remains intimately involved in the lives of her two daughters, now ages 17 and 21 in El Salvador, succinctly summed up this stance when she said, "I'm here, but I'm there." Over the phone and through letters, she regularly reminds her daughters to take their vitamins, to never go to bed or to school on an empty stomach, and to use protection from pregnancy and sexually transmitted diseases if they engage in sexual relations with their boyfriends.

Transnational mothers fully understand and explain the conditions that prompt their situations. In particular, many Central American women recognize that the gendered employment demand in Los Angeles has produced transnational motherhood arrangements. These new mothering arrangements, they acknowledge, take shape despite strong beliefs that biological mothers should care for their own children. Emelia, a 49-year-old woman who left her five children in Guatemala 9 years ago to join her husband in Los Angeles, explained this changing relationship between family arrangements, migration, and job demand:

> One supposes that the mother must care for the children. A mother cannot so easily throw her children aside. So, in all families, the decision is that the man comes [to the United States] first. But now, since the man cannot find work here so easily, the woman comes first. Recently, women have been coming and the men staying.

A steady demand for live-in housekeepers means that Central American women may arrive in Los Angeles on a Friday and begin working Monday at a live-in job that provides at least some minimal accommodations. Meanwhile, her male counterpart may spend weeks or months before securing even casual day laborer jobs. While Emelia, who previously earned income in Guatemala by baking cakes and pastries in her home, expressed pain and sadness at not being with her children as they grew, she was also proud of her accomplishments. "My children," she stated, "recognize what I have been able to do for them."

Most transnational mothers, like many other immigrant workers, come to the United States with the intention to stay for a finite period of time, until they can pay off bills or raise the money for an investment in a house, their children's education, or a small business. Some of these women return to their countries of origin, but many stay. As time passes, and as their stays grow longer, some of the women eventually bring some or all of their children. Other women who stay at their U.S. jobs are adamant that they do not wish for their children to traverse the multiple hazards of adolescence in U.S. cities or to repeat the job experiences they themselves have had in the United States. One Salvadoran woman in the waiting room at the domestic employment agency—whose children had been raised on earnings predicated on her separation from them—put it this way:

I've been here 19 years, I've got my legal papers and everything. But I'd have to be crazy to bring my children here. All of them have studied for a career, so why would I bring them here? To bus tables and earn minimum wage? So they won't have enough money for bus fare or food?

Who Is Taking Care of the Nanny's Children?

Transnational Central American and Mexican mothers may rely on various people to care for their children's daily, round-the-clock needs, but they prefer a close relative. The "other mothers" on whom Latinas rely include their own mothers, *comadres* (co-godmothers) and other female kin, the children's fathers, and paid caregivers. Reliance on grandmothers and comadres for shared mothering is well established in Latina culture, and it is a practice that signifies a more collectivist, shared approach to mothering in contrast to a more individualistic, Anglo-American approach (Griswold del Castillo, 1984; Segura & Pierce, 1993). Perhaps this cultural legacy facilitates the emergence of transnational motherhood.

Transnational mothers express a strong preference for their own biological mother to serve as the primary caregiver. Here, the violation of the cultural preference for the biological mother is rehabilitated by reliance on the biological grandmother or by reliance on the ceremonially bound comadres. Clemencia, for example, left her three young children behind in Mexico, each with their respective *madrina*, or godmother.

Emelia left her five children, then ranging in age from 6 to 16, under the care of her mother and sister in Guatemala. As she spoke of the hardships faced by transnational mothers, she counted herself among the fortunate ones who did not need to leave the children alone with paid caregivers:

> One's mother is the only one who can really and truly care for your children. No one else can. . . . Women who aren't able to leave their children with their mother or with someone very special, they'll wire money to Guatemala, and the people [caregivers] don't feed the children well. They don't buy the children clothes the mother would want. They take the money, and the children suffer a lot.

Both Central American and Mexican woman stated preferences for grandmothers as the ideal caregivers in situations that mandated the absence of the children's biological mother. These preferences seem to grow out of strategic availability, but these preferences assume culture mandates. Velia, a Mexicana who hailed from the border town of Mexicali, improvised an employment strategy whereby she annually sent her three elementary school–age children to her mother in Mexicali for the summer vacation months. This allowed Velia, a single mother, to intensify her housecleaning jobs and save money on day care. But she also insisted that "if my children were with the woman next door [who baby-sits], I'd worry if they were eating well, or about men [coming to harass the girls]. Having them with my mother allows me to work in peace." Another woman specified more narrowly, insisting that only maternal grandmothers could provide adequate caregiving. In a conversation in a park, a Salvadoran woman offered that a biological mother's mother was the one best suited to truly love and care for a child in the biological mother's absence. According to her, not even the paternal grandmother could be trusted to provide proper nurturance and care. Another Salvadoran woman, Maria, left her two daughters, then 14 and 17, at their paternal grandmother's home, but before departing for the United States, she trained her daughters to become self-sufficient in cooking, marketing, and budgeting money. Although she believes the paternal grandmother loves the girls, she did not trust the paternal grandmother enough to cook or administer the money that she would send her daughters.

Another variation in the preference for a biological relative as a caregiver is captured by the arrangement of Patricia, a 30-year-old Mexicana who came to the United States as a child and was working as a live-in, caring for an infant in one of southern California's affluent coastal residential areas. Her arrangement was different, as her daughters were all born, raised, and residing in the United States, but she lived apart from them during weekdays because of her live-in job. Her three daughters, ages $1^1/_2$, 6, and 11, stayed at their apartment near downtown Los Angeles under the care of their father and a paid nanny-housekeeper, Patricia's teenage cousin. Her paid caregiver was not an especially close relative, but she rationalized this arrangement by emphasizing that her husband, the girls' father and therefore a biological relative, was with them during the week.

> Whenever I've worked like this, I've always had a person in charge of them also working as a live-in. She sleeps here the five days, but when my husband arrives he takes responsibility for them. . . . When my husband arrives [from work] she [cousin/paid caregiver] goes to English class and he takes charge of the girls.

And another woman who did not have children of her own but who had worked as a nanny for her aunt stated that "as Hispanas, we don't believe in bringing someone else in to care for our children." Again, the biological ties help sanction the shared child care arrangement.

New family fissures emerge for the transnational mother as she negotiates various aspects of the arrangement with her children and with the "other mother," who provides daily care and supervision for the children. Any impulse to romanticize transnational motherhood is tempered by the sadness with which the women related their experiences and by the problems they sometimes encounter with their children and caregivers. A primary worry among transnational mothers is that their children are being neglected or abused in their absence. While there is a long legacy of child servants being mistreated and physically beaten in Latin America, transnational mothers also worry that their own paid caregivers will harm or neglect their children. They worry that their children may not receive proper nourishment, schooling and educational support, and moral guidance. They may remain unsure as to whether their children are receiving the full financial support they send home. In some cases, their concerns are intensified by the eldest child or a nearby relative who is able to monitor and report the caregiver's transgression to the transnational mother.

Transnational mothers engage in emotion work and financial compensation to maintain a smoothly functioning relationship with the children's daily caregiver. Their efforts are not always successful, and when problems arise, they may return to visit if they can afford to do so. After not seeing her four children for 7 years, Carolina abruptly quit her nanny job and returned to Guatemala in the spring of 1996 because she was concerned about one adolescent daughter's rebelliousness and about her mother-in-law's failing health. Carolina's husband remained in Los Angeles, and she was expected to return. Emelia, whose children were cared for by her mother and sister, with the assistance of paid caregivers, regularly responded to her sister's reminders to send gifts, clothing, and small amounts of money to the paid caregivers. "If they are taking care of my children," she explained, "then I have to show my gratitude."

Some of these actions are instrumental. Transnational mothers know that they may increase the likelihood of their children receiving adequate care if they appropriately remunerate the caregivers and treat them with the consideration their work requires. In fact, they often express astonishment that their own Anglo employers fail to recognize this in relation to the nanny-housekeeper work that they perform. Some of the expressions of gratitude and gifts that they send to their children's caregivers appear to be genuinely disinterested and enhanced by the transnational mothers' empathy arising out of their own similar job circumstances. A Honduran woman, a former biology teacher, who had left her four sons with a paid caregiver, maintained that the treatment of nannies and housekeepers was much better in Honduras than in the United States, in part, because of different approaches to mothering:

> We're very different back there. . . . We treat them [domestic workers] with a lot of affection and respect, and when they are taking care of our kids, even more so. The *Americana*, she is very egotistical. When the nanny loves her children, she gets jealous. Not us. We are appreciative when someone loves our children, and bathes, dresses, and feeds them as though they were their own.

These comments are clearly informed by the respondent's prior class status, as well as her simultaneous position as the employer of a paid nanny-housekeeper in Honduras and as a temporarily unemployed nanny-housekeeper in the United States. (She had been fired from her nanny-housekeeper job for not showing up on Memorial Day, which she erroneously believed was a work holiday.) Still, her comments underline the importance of showing appreciation and gratitude to the caregiver, in part, for the sake of the children's well-being.

Transnational mothers also worry about whether their children will get into trouble during adolescence or if they will transfer their allegiance and affection to the "other woman." In general, transnational mothers, like African American mothers who leave their children in the South to work up North (Stack & Burton, 1994), believe that the person who cares for the children has the right to discipline. But when adolescent youths are paired with elderly grandmothers or ineffective disciplinary figures, the mothers may need to intervene. Preadolescent and adolescent children who show signs of rebelliousness may be brought north because they are deemed unmanageable by their grandmothers or paid caregivers. Alternatively, teens who are in California may be sent back in hope that it will straighten them out, a practice that has resulted in the migration of Los Angeles–based delinquent youth gangs to Mexican and Central American towns. Another danger is that the child who has grown up without the transnational mother's presence may no longer respond to her authority. One woman at the domestic employment agency, who had recently brought her adolescent son to join her in California, reported that she had seen him at a bus stop, headed for the beach. When she demanded to know where he was going, he said something to the effect of "and who are you to tell me what to do?" After a verbal confrontation at the bus kiosk, she handed him $10. Perhaps the mother hoped that money will be a way to show caring and to advance a claim to parental authority.

Motherhood and Breadwinning

Milk, shoes, and schooling—these are the currency of transnational motherhood. Providing for children's sustenance, protecting their current well-being, and preparing them for the future are widely shared concerns of motherhood. Central American and Mexican women involved in transnational mothering attempt to ensure the present and future well-being of their children through U.S. wage earning, and as we have seen, this requires long-term physical separation from their children.

For these women, the meanings of motherhood do not appear to be in a liminal stage. That is, they do not appear to be making a linear progression from a way of motherhood that involves daily, face-to-face caregiving toward one that is defined primarily through breadwinning. Rather than replacing caregiving with breadwinning definitions of motherhood, they appear to be expanding their definitions of motherhood to encompass breadwinning that may require long-term physical separations. For these women, a core belief is that they can best fulfill traditional caregiving responsibilities through income earning in the United States while their children remain "back home."

Transnational mothers continue to state that caregiving is a defining feature of their mothering experiences. They wish to provide their children with better nutrition, clothing, and schooling, and most of them are able to purchase these items with dollars earned in the United States. They recognize, however, that their transnational relationships incur painful costs. Transnational mothers worry about some of the negative effects on their children, but they also experience the absence of domestic family life as a deeply personal loss. Transnational mothers who primarily identified as homemakers before coming to the United States identified the loss of daily contact with family as a sacrifice ventured to financially support the children. As Emelia, who had previously earned some income by baking pastries and doing catering from her home in Guatemala, reflected,

> The money [earned in the United States] is worth five times more in Guatemala. My oldest daughter was then 16, and my youngest was 6 [when I left]. Ay, it's terrible, terrible, but that's what happens to most women [transnational mothers] who are here. You sacrifice your family life [for labor migration].

Similarly, Carolina used the word *sacrifice* when discussing her family arrangement, claiming that her children "tell me that they appreciate us [parents] and the sacrifice that their papa and mama make for them. That is what they say."

The daily indignities of paid domestic work—low pay, subtle humiliations, not enough food to eat, invisibility (Nakano Glenn, 1986; Rollins, 1985; Romero, 1992)— means that transnational mothers are not only stretching their U.S.-earned dollars further by sending the money back home but also, by leaving the children behind, they are providing special protection from the discrimination the children might receive in the United States. Gladys, who had four of her five children in El Salvador, acknowledged that her U.S. dollars went further in El Salvador. Although she missed seeing those four children grow up, she felt that in some ways she had spared them the indignities to which she had exposed her youngest daughter, whom she brought to the United States at age 4 in 1988. Although her live-in employer had allowed the 4-year-old to join the family residence, Gladys tearfully recalled how that employer had initially quarantined her daughter, insisting on seeing vaccination papers before allowing the girl to play with the employer's children. "I had to battle, really struggle," she recalled, "just to get enough food for her [to eat]." For Gladys, being together with her youngest daughter in the employer's home had entailed new emotional costs.

Patricia, the mother who was apart from her children only during the weekdays when she lived in with her employer, put forth an elastic definition of motherhood, one that included both meeting financial obligations and spending time with the children. Although her job involves different scheduling than most employed mothers, she shares views similar to those held by many working mothers:

> It's something you have to do, because you can't just stay seated at home because the bills accumulate and you have to find a way. . . . I applied at many different places for work, like hospitals, as a receptionist, due to the experience I've had with computers working in shipping and receiving, things like that. But they never called me. . . . One person can't pay all the bills.

Patricia emphasized that she believes motherhood also involves making an effort to spend time with the children. According to this criterion, she explained, most employers were deficient, while she was compliant. During the middle of the week, she explained, "I invent something, some excuse for her [the employer] to let me come home, even if I have to bring the [employer's] baby here with me . . . just to spend time with my kids."

Transnational mothers echoed these sentiments. Maria Elena, for example, whose 13-year-old son resided with his father in Mexico after she lost a custody battle, insisted that motherhood did not consist of only breadwinning: "You can't give love through money." According to Maria Elena, motherhood required an emotional presence and communication with a child. Like other transnational mothers, she explained how she maintained this connection despite the long-term geographic distance: "I came here, but we're not apart. We talk [by telephone]. . . . I know [through telephone conversations] when my son is fine. I can tell when he is sad by the way he speaks." Like employed mothers everywhere, she insisted on a definition of motherhood that emphasized quality rather than quantity of time spent with the child: "I don't think that a good mother is one who is with her children at all times. . . . It's the quality of time spent with the child." She spoke these words tearfully, reflecting the trauma of losing a custody battle with her ex-husband. Gladys also stated that being a mother involves both breadwinning and providing direction and guidance. "It's not just feeding them or buying clothes for them. It's also educating them, preparing them to make good choices so they'll have a better future."

Transnational mothers seek to mesh caregiving and guidance with breadwinning. While breadwinning may require their long-term and long-distance separations from their children, they attempt to sustain family connections by showing emotional ties through letters, phone calls, and money sent home. If at all financially and logistically possible, they try to travel home to visit their children. They maintain their mothering responsibilities not only by earning money for their children's livelihood but also by communicating and advising across national borders and across the boundaries that separate their children's place of residence from their own places of employment and residence.

Bonding with the Employers' Kids and Critiques of "Americana" Mothers

Some nanny-housekeepers develop very strong ties of affection with the children they care for during long workweeks. It is not unusual for nanny-housekeepers to be alone with these children during the workweek, with no one else with whom to talk or interact. The nannies, however, develop close emotional ties selectively, with some children but not with others. For nanny-housekeepers who are transnational mothers, the loving daily caregiving that they cannot express for their own children is sometimes transferred to their employers' children. Carolina, a Guatemalan woman with four children between the ages of 10 and 14 back home, maintained that she tried to treat the employers' children with the same affection that she had for her own children "because if you do not feel affection for children, you are not able to care for them well." When interviewed, however, she was caring for 2-year-old triplets—for whom she expressed very little affection—but she recalled very longingly her fond feelings for a child at her last job, a child who vividly reminded her of her daughter, who was about the same age:

> When I saw that the young girl was lacking in affection, I began to get close to her and I saw that she appreciated that I would touch her, give her a kiss on the cheek. . . . And then I felt consoled, too, because I had someone to give love to. But I would imagine that she was my daughter, ah? And then I would give pure love to her, and that brought her closer to me.

Another nanny-housekeeping recalled a little girl for whom she had developed strong bonds of affection, laughingly imitating how the preschooler, who could not pronounce the "f" sound, would say, "You hurt my peelings, but I don't want to pight."

Other nanny-housekeepers reflected that painful experiences with abrupt job terminations had taught them not to transfer mother love to the children of their employers. Some of these women reported that they now remained very measured and guarded in their emotional closeness with the employers' children, so that they could protect themselves for the moment when that relationship might be abruptly severed.

> I love these children, but now I stop myself from becoming too close. Before, when my own children weren't here [in the United States], I gave all my love to the children I cared for [then toddler twins]. That was my recompensation [for not being with my children]. When the job ended, I hurt so much. I can't let that happen again.

> I love them, but not like they were my own children because they are not! They are not my kids! Because if I get to love them, and then I go, then I'm going to suffer like I did the last time. I don't want that.

Not all nanny-housekeepers bond tightly with the employers' children, but most of them are critical of what they perceive as the employers' neglectful parenting and mothering. Typically, they blame biological mothers (their employers) for substandard parenting. Carolina recalled advising the mother of the above-mentioned little girl, who reminded her of her own child, that the girl needed to receive more affection from her mother, whom she perceived as self-absorbed with physical fitness regimes. Carolina had also advised other employers on disciplining their children. Patricia also spoke adamantly on this topic, and she recalled with satisfaction that when she had advised her current employer to spend more than 15 minutes a day with the baby, the employer had been reduced to tears. By comparison with her employer's mothering, Patricia cited her own perseverance in going out of her way to visit her children during the week:

> If you really love your kids, you look for the time, you make time, to spend with your kids. . . . I work all week and for some reason I make excuses for her [employer] to let me come [home] . . . just to spend time with my kids.

Her rhetoric of comparative mothering is also inspired by the critique that many nanny-housekeepers have of female employers who may be out of the labor force but who employ nannies and hence do not spend time with their children.

> I love my kids; they don't. It's just like, excuse the word, *shitting* kids. . . . What they prefer is to go to the salon, get their nails done, you know, go shopping, things like that. Even if they're home all day, they don't want to spend time with the kids because they're paying somebody to do that for them.

Curiously, she spoke as though her female employer were a wealthy woman of leisure, but in fact, both her current and past female employers are wealthy business executives who worked long hours. Perhaps at this distance on the class spectrum, all class and racially privileged mothers look alike. "I work my butt off to get what I have," she observed, "and they don't have to work that much."

In some ways, transnational mothers who work as nanny-housekeepers cling to a more sentimentalized view of the employers' children than of their own. This strategy allows them to critique their employers, especially homemakers of privilege who are occupied with neither employment nor daily caregiving for their children. The Latina nannies appear to endorse motherhood as a full-time vocation in contexts of sufficient financial resources. But in contexts of financial hardship such as their own, they advocate more elastic definitions of motherhood, including forms that may include long spatial and temporal separations of mother and children.

As observers of late-20th-century U.S. families (Skolnick, 1991; Stacey, 1996) have noted, we live in an era wherein no one normative family arrangement predominates. Just as no one type of mothering unequivocally prevails in the white middle class, no singular mothering arrangement prevails among Latina immigrant women. In fact, the exigencies of contemporary immigration seem to multiply the variety of mothering arrangements. Through our research with Latina immigrant women who work as nannies, housekeepers, and housecleaners, we have encountered a broad range of mothering arrangements. Some Latinas migrate to the United States without their children to establish employment, and after some stability has been achieved, they may send for their children or they may work for a while to save money, and then return to their countries of origin. Other Latinas migrate and may postpone having children until they are financially established. Still others arrive with their children and may search for employment that allows them to live together with their children, and other Latinas may have sufficient financial support—from their husbands or kin—to stay home full-time with their children.

In the absence of a universal or at least widely shared mothering arrangement, there is tremendous uncertainty about what constitutes "good mothering," and transnational mothers must work hard to defend their choices. Some Latina nannies who have their children with them in the United States condemn transnational mothers as "bad women." One interview respondent, who was able to take her young daughter to work with her, claimed that she could never leave her daughter. For this woman, transnational mothers were not only bad mothers but also nannies who could not be trusted to adequately care for other people's children. As she said of an acquaintance, "This woman left her children [in Honduras]. . . . She was taking care [of other people's children], and I said, 'Lord, who are they [the employers] leaving their children with if she did that with her own children?'"

Given the uncertainty of what is "good mothering," and to defend their integrity as mothers when others may criticize them, transnational mothers construct new scales for gauging the quality of mothering. By favorably comparing themselves with the negative models of mothering that they see in others—especially those that they are able to closely scrutinize in their employers' homes—transnational mothers create new definitions of good-mothering standards. At the same time, selectively developing motherlike ties with other people's children allows them to enjoy affectionate, face-to-face interactions that they cannot experience on a daily basis with their own children.

Discussion: Transnational Motherhood

In California, with few exceptions, paid domestic work has become a Latina immigrant women's job. One observer has referred to these Latinas as "the new employable mothers" (Chang, 1994), but taking on these wage labor duties often requires Latina workers to expand the frontiers of motherhood by leaving their own children for several years. While today there is a greater openness to accepting a plurality of mothering arrangements—single mothers, employed mothers, stay-at-home mothers, lesbian mothers, surrogate mothers, to name a few—even feminist discussions generally assume that mothers, by definition, will reside with their children.

Transnational mothering situations disrupt the notion of family in one place and break distinctively with what some commentators have referred to as the "epoxy glue" view of motherhood (Blum & Deussen, 1996; Scheper-Hughes, 1992). Latina transnational mothers are improvising new mothering arrangements that are borne out of women's financial struggles, played out in a new global arena, to provide the best future for themselves and their children. Like many other women of color and employed mothers, transnational mothers rely on an expanded and sometimes fluid number of family members and paid caregivers. Their caring circuits, however, span stretches of geography and time that are much wider than typical joint custody or "other mother" arrangements that are more closely bound, both spatially and temporally.

The transnational perspective in immigration studies is useful in conceptualizing how relationships across borders are important. Yet an examination of transnational motherhood suggests that transnationalism is a contradictory process of the late 20th century. It is an achievement, but one accompanied by numerous costs and attained in a context of extremely scarce options. The alienation and anxiety of mothering organized by long temporal and spatial distances should give pause to the celebratory impulses of transnational perspectives of immigration. Although not addressed directly in this article, the experiences of these mothers resonate with current major political issues. For example, transnational mothering resembles precisely what immigration restrictionists have advocated through California's Proposition 187 (Hondagneu-Sotelo, 1995).[9] While proponents of Proposition 187 have never questioned California's reliance on low-waged Latino immigrant workers, this restrictionist policy calls for fully dehumanized immigrant workers, not workers with families and family needs (such as education and health services for children). In this respect, transnational mothering's externalization of the cost of labor reproduction to Mexico and Central America is a dream come true for the proponents of Proposition 187.

Contemporary transnational motherhood continues a long historical legacy of people of color being incorporated into the United States through coercive systems of labor that do not recognize family rights. As Bonnie Thornton Dill (1988), Evelyn Nakano Glenn (1986), and others have pointed out, slavery and contract labor systems were organized to maximize economic productivity and offered few supports to sustain family life. The job characteristics of paid domestic work, especially live-in work, virtually impose transnational motherhood for many Mexican and Central American women who have children of their own.

The ties of transnational motherhood suggest simultaneously the relative permeability of borders, as witnessed by the maintenance of family ties and the new meanings of motherhood, and the impermeability of nation-state borders. Ironically, just at the moment when free trade proponents and pundits celebrate globalization and transnationalism, and when "borderlands" and "border crossings" have become the metaphors of preference for describing a mind-boggling range of conditions, nation-state borders prove to be very real obstacles for many Mexican and Central American women who work in the United States and who, given the appropriate circumstances, wish to be with their children. While demanding the right for women workers to live with their children may provoke critiques of sentimentality, essentialism, and the glorification of motherhood, demanding the right for women workers to choose their own motherhood arrangements would be the beginning of truly just family and work policies, policies that address not only inequalities of gender but also inequalities of race, class, and citizenship status.

Notes

We wish to thank Maxine Baca Zinn, Linda Blum, Michael Messner, Barrie Thorne, Abel Valenzuela, and the anonymous reviewers of *Gender & Society* for helpful comments on earlier versions of this article. This research was supported by grants from the Social Science Research Council and the Southern California Studies Center at USC, and it was written while the first author was in residence at UCLA Chicano Studies Research Center.

1. No one knows the precise figures on the prevalence of transnational motherhood, just as no one knows the myriad consequences for both mothers and their children. However, one indicator that hints at both the complex outcomes and the frequencies of these arrangements is that teachers and social workers in Los Angeles are becoming increasingly concerned about some of the deleterious effects of these mother-child separations and reunions. Many Central American women who made their way to Los Angeles in the early 1980s, fleeing civil wars and economic upheaval, pioneered transnational mothering, and some of them are now financially able to bring their children whom they left behind. These children, now in their early teen years, are confronting the triple trauma of simultaneously entering adolescence (with its own psychological upheavals), a new society (often in an inner-city environment that requires learning to navigate a new language, place, and culture), and families that do not look like the ones they knew before their mothers' departure, families with new siblings born in the United States, and new stepfathers or mothers' boyfriends.

2. Even among Mexican farmworkers, researchers have found a large and growing segment who settle permanently with their families in rural California (Palerm, 1994).

3. Acknowledgment of the varieties of family and mothering has been fueled, in part, by research on the growing numbers of women-headed families, involving families of all races and socioeconomic levels, including Latina families in the United States and elsewhere (Baca Zinn, 1989; Fernandez-Kelly & Garcia, 1990), and by recognition that biological ties do not necessarily constitute family (Weston, 1991).

4. La Virgen de Guadalupe, the indigenous virgin who appeared in 1531 to a young Indian boy and for whom a major basilica is built, provides the exemplary maternal mode, *la mujer abnegada* (the self-effacing woman), who sacrifices all for her children and religious faith. La Malinche, the Aztec woman that served Cortes as a translator, a diplomat, and mistress, and La Llorona (the weeping one), a legendary solitary, ghostlike figure reputed either to have been violently murdered by a jealous husband or to have herself murdered her children by drowning them, are the negative and despised models of femininity. Both are failed women because they have failed at motherhood. La Malinche is stigmatized as a traitor and a whore who collaborated with the Spanish conquerors, and La Llorona is the archetypal evil woman condemned to eternally suffer and weep for violating her role as a wife and a mother (Soto, 1986).

5. A study comparing Mexicanas and Chicanas found that the latter are more favorably

disposed to homemaker ideals than are Mexican-born women. This difference is explained by Chicanas' greater exposure to U.S. ideology, which promotes the opposition of mothering and employment, and to Mexicanas' integration of household and economy in Mexico (Segura, 1994). While this dynamic may be partially responsible for this pattern, we suspect that Mexicanas may have higher rates of labor force participation because they are also a self-selected group of Latinas; by and large, they come to the United States to work.

6. See Romero (1997) for a study focusing on the perspective of domestic workers' children. Although most respondents in this particular study were children of day workers, and none appear to have been children of transnational mothers, they still recall significant costs stemming from their mothers' occupation.

7. This seems to be more common among Central American women than Mexican women. Central American women may be more likely than are Mexican women to have their children in their country of origin, even if their husbands are living with them in the United States, because of the multiple dangers and costs associated with undocumented travel from Central America to the United States. The civil wars of the 1980s, continuing violence and economic uncertainty, greater difficulties and costs associated with crossing multiple national borders, and stronger cultural legacies of socially sanctioned consensual unions may also contribute to this pattern for Central Americans.

8. According to interviews conducted with domestic workers in La Paz, Bolivia, in the late 1980s, 41% got their first job between the ages of 11 and 15, and one third got their first job between the ages of 6 and 10. Some parents received half of the child-servant's salary (Gill, 1994, p. 64). Similar arrangements prevailed in preindustrial rural areas of the United States and Europe.

9. In November 1994, California voters passed Proposition 187, which legislates the denial of public school education, health care, and other public benefits to undocumented immigrants and their children. The facility with which Proposition 187 passed in the California ballots rejuvenated anti-immigrant politics at a national level. It opened the doors to new legislative measures in 1997 to deny public assistance to legal immigrants.

References

Baca Zinn, M. (1989). Family, race, and poverty in the eighties. *Signs: Journal of Women in Culture & Society, 14,* 856–869.

Basch, L., Schiller, N. G., & Blanc, C. S. (1994). *Nations unbound: Transnational projects, postcolonial predicaments, and deterritorialized nation-states*. Amsterdam: Gordon & Breach.

Blum, L., & Deussen, T. (1996). Negotiating independent motherhood: Working-class African American women talk about marriage and motherhood. *Gender & Society, 10,* 199–211.

Burawoy, M. (1976). The functions and reproduction of migrant labor: Comparative material from Southern Africa and the United States. *American Journal of Sociology, 81,* 1050–1087.

Chang, G. (1994). Undocumented Latinas: Welfare burdens or beasts of burden? *Socialist Review, 23,* 151–185.

Chinchilla, N. S., & Hamilton, N. (1996). Negotiating urban space: Latina workers in domestic work and street vending in Los Angeles. *Humbolt Journal of Social Relations, 22,* 25–35.

Collier, J. F., & Yanagisako, S. J. (1987). *Gender and kinship: Essays toward a unified analysis*. Stanford, CA: Stanford University Press.

Collins, P. H. (1991). *Black feminist thought: Knowledge, consciousness, and the politics of empowerment*. New York: Routledge.

Collins, P. H. (1994). Shifting the center: Race, class, and feminist theorizing about motherhood. In E. Nakano Glenn, G. Chang, & L. R. Forcey (Eds.), *Mothering: Ideology, experience, and agency*. New York: Routledge.

Dill, B. T. (1988). Our mothers' grief: Racial-ethnic women and the maintenance of families. *Journal of Family History, 13,* 415–431.

Dill, B. T. (1994). Fictive kin, paper sons and compadrazgo: Women of color and the struggle for family survival. In M. Baca Zinn and B. T. Dill (Eds.), *Women of color in U.S. society*. Philadelphia: Temple University Press.

Fernandez-Kelly, M. P., & Garcia, A. (1990). Power surrendered, power restored: The politics of work and family among Hispanic garment workers in California and Florida. In L. A. Tilly & P. Gurin (Eds.), *Women, politics, and change*. New York: Russell Sage.

Gill, L. (1994). *Precarious dependencies: Gender, class, and domestic service in Bolivia*. New York: Columbia University Press.

Griswold del Castillo, R. (1984). *La Familia: Chicano families in the urban Southwest, 1848 to the present*. Notre Dame, IN: University of Notre Dame Press.

Hanson, S., & Pratt, G. (1995). *Gender, work, and space*. New York: Routledge.

Hondagneu-Sotelo, P. (1995). Women and children first: New directions in anti-immigrant politics. *Socialist Review, 25,* 169–190.

Kearney, M. (1995). The effects of transnational culture, economy, and migration on Mixtec identity in Oaxacalifornia. In M. P. Smith & J. R. Feagin (Eds.), *The bubbling cauldron: Race, ethnicity, and the urban crisis*. Minneapolis: University of Minnesota Press.

Mahler, S. J. (1996). *Bringing gender to a transnational focus: Theoretical and empirical ideas*. Unpublished manuscript.

Massey, D. (1994). *Space, place, and gender*. Minneapolis: University of Minnesota Press.

Nakano Glenn, E. (1986). *Issei, Nisei, warbride: Three generations of Japanese American women in domestic service*. Philadelphia: Temple University Press.

Nakano Glenn, E. (1994). Social constructions of mothering: A thematic overview. In E. Nakano Glenn, G. Chang, and L. R. Forcey (Eds.), *Mothering: Ideology, experience, and agency*. New York: Routledge.

Palerm, J.-V. (1994). *Immigrant and migrant farmworkers in the Santa Maria Valley of California*. Report for Center for Survey Methods Research, Bureau of Census.

Pedraza, S. (1991). Women and migration: The social consequences of gender. *Annual Review of Sociology, 17,* 303–325.

Rollins, J. (1985). *Between women: Domestics and their employers*. Philadelphia: Temple University Press.

Romero, M. (1992). *Maid in the U.S.A*. New York: Routledge.

Romero, M. (1996). Life as the maid's daughter: An exploration of the everyday boundaries of race, class, and gender. In A. J. Steward & D. Stanon (Eds.), *Feminisms in the academy: Rethinking the disciplines*. Ann Arbor: University of Michigan Press.

Romero, M. (1997). Who takes care of the maid's children? Exploring the costs of domestic service. In H. L. Nelson (Ed.), *Feminism and families*. New York: Routledge.

Rouse, R. (1991). Mexican migration and the social space of postmodernism. *Diaspora, 1,* 8–23.

Ruddick, S. (1989). *Maternal thinking: Toward a politics of peace*. Boston: Beacon.

Scheper-Hughes, N. (1992). *Death without weeping: The violence of everyday life in Brazil*. Berkeley: University of California Press.

Segura, D. A. (1994). Working at motherhood: Chicana and Mexican immigrant mothers and employment. In E. Nakano Glenn, G. Chang, and L. R. Forcey (Eds.), *Mothering: Ideology, experience, and agency.* New York: Routledge.

Segura, D. A., & Pierce, J. L. (1993). Chicana/o family structure and gender personality: Chodorow, familism, and psychoanalytic sociology revisited. *Signs: Journal of Women in Culture & Society, 19,* 62–79.

Skolnick, A. S. (1991). *Embattled paradise: The American family in an age of uncertainty.* New York: Basic Books.

Soto, S. (1986). Tres modelos culturales: La Virgen de Guadalupe, la Malinche, y la Llorona. *Fem* (Mexico City), no. 48, 13–16.

Stacey, J. (1996). *In the name of the family: Rethinking family values in the postmodern age.* Boston: Beacon.

Stack, C. B., & Burton, L. M. (1994). Kinscripts: Reflections on family, generation, and culture. In E. Nakano Glenn, G. Chang, and L. R. Forcey (Eds.), *Mothering: Ideology, experience, and agency.* New York: Routledge.

Thorne, B., & Yalom, M. (1992). *Rethinking the family: Some feminist questions.* Boston: Northeastern University Press.

Tienda, M., & Booth, K. (1991). Gender, migration and social change. *International Sociology, 6,* 51–72.

Uttal, L. (1996). Custodial care, surrogate care, and coordinated care: Employed mothers and the meaning of child care. *Gender & Society, 10,* 291–311.

Weston, K. (1991). *Families we choose*: *Lesbians, gays, kinship.* New York: Columbia University Press.

Wrigley, J. (1995). *Other people's children.* New York: Basic Books.

Zavella, P. (1987). *Women's work and Chicano families: Cannery workers of the Santa Clara Valley.* Ithaca, NY: Cornell University Press.

Zelizer, V. (1994). *Pricing the priceless child: The social value of children.* Princeton, NJ: Princeton University Press.

7

Using Kin for Child Care

Embedment in the Socioeconomic Networks
of Extended Families

Lynet Uttal

Child care arrangements are an essential element of parental employment. Patterns of usage of different types of child care arrangements have changed significantly in the past 30 years. Particularly noticeable is the diminishing use of relatives as the most common source of child care. Since 1958, the percentage of child care arrangements with relatives both inside and outside the child's home made by employed mothers for their infants, toddlers, and preschool-aged children has halved, from 42% to 21% of all child care arrangements in 1990. The only type of relative care that has not declined in the last 30 years is care by fathers, which remains steady at 11%. In contrast, the use of family day care homes and child care centers has more than tripled, from 17% in 1958 to 59% in 1990 (Hofferth, Brayfield, Deich, & Holcomb, 1991; Lajewski, 1959).

Despite these trends, parents continue to express a strong preference for care by relatives, especially for their infants, toddlers, and preschool-aged children. Yet the perception that relative care is an ideal substitute for parent care may exceed real preferences. Fewer parents actually use relative care than report a preference for it (Crispell, 1994). In a recent national child care survey, half of those who actually use relative care report that it is not their first choice of type of care; the preference for relative care was surpassed by the preference for "quality" child care (Hofferth et al., 1991).

Clearly, the actual use of relative care is based on a variety of reasons other than that the care is perceived as the ideal substitute for parent care. Descriptive studies of maternal and family characteristics associated with a greater likelihood of the use of relatives for child care have found that the use and preference for relative care is positively associated with the belief that parents should be caring for their own children (Hertz & Ferguson, 1996; Kuhlthau & Mason, 1996), the close proximity of relatives (Benin & Keith, 1995; Jayakody, Chatters, & Taylor, 1993; Kuhlthau & Mason, 1996; Lamphere, Zavella, Gonzales, & Evans, 1993; Parish, Hao, & Hogan, 1991; Roschelle, 1997b), lower family incomes (Crispell, 1994; Gerson, 1993; Hofferth et al., 1991; Kuhlthau & Mason, 1996; Leibowitz, Waite, & Witsberger,

1988; Stegelin & Frankel, 1993), lower maternal education (Folk, 1994; Hofferth et al., 1991), single parenthood (Folk, 1994; Oliker, 1995), families with younger children, especially under age 2 (Hofferth et al., 1991; Kuhlthau & Mason, 1996), and families with fewer children (Benin & Keith, 1995).

Another common finding is that the rate of relative care is higher for black and Hispanic families than for white families (Benin & Keith, 1995; Folk, 1994; Hofferth et al, 1991). However, it is unclear if this finding holds when the mother's employment status and the use of kin for regular, employment-related child care are controlled. Some studies find that employed mothers of color are more likely to use kin for child care than are white employed mothers (Folk, 1994; Keefe, 1996; Lamphere et al., 1993); others find that employed mothers of color are less likely to use relative care (Benin & Keith, 1995; Blau & Robins, 1991; Hayes, Palmer, & Zaslow, 1990; Roschelle, 1997a, 1997b), and yet other studies find that employed white women and women of color are more similar than dissimilar in their use of relative care (Kuhlthau & Mason, 1996).

Race differences in extended family practices are of particular interest to researchers concerned about the quality of life and economic status of low-income racial ethnic families. (The conceptual term *racial ethnic* is used throughout this article to label racial and ethnic groups that have historically experienced racism and marginalized economic status in the United States. "Racial ethnic" is a commonly used concept in the race literature that is distinct from the concept "race" or "ethnicity" and does not include whites—though all people, including whites, have a racial and ethnic identity. It has been adopted as an alternative term to using "nonwhite" because nonwhite is a term that assumes a normative model—"white"—which locates people of color on the outside of this definition.) Underlying much of this research is the common assumption that the independence of nuclear families, especially economic, is the ideal. (For a discussion of this ideal of self-sufficiency, see Thorne, 1982.) Enmeshment in social networks of the extended family is viewed as especially problematic for poor families because it obstructs achieving this ideal and perpetuates intergenerational poverty, rather than allowing any family or individual family members to rise to a higher standard of living. Because of the disproportionate focus on low-income racial ethnic families, it raises the question of whether these apparent race and ethnic differences are cultural differences or class-generated differences. Several studies have found that exchanges in the extended family networks of African Americans and Mexican Americans and the sense of "obligation to kin" persist in spite of upward class mobility (Baca Zinn, 1980; Higginbotham & Weber, 1992).

Below I analyze 31 in-depth interview accounts from a sample of African American, Anglo American, and Mexican American mothers who are employed. Like much previous research, I found that employed African American and Mexican American mothers expressed more positive views about using relative care than Anglo American mothers. In itself, this is not a surprising finding. But by using a combination of grounded theory (Glaser & Strauss, 1967) and the extended case method (Buroway et al., 1991), I identified new reasons to suggest why the families of color are more likely than Anglo American families to use kin-based child care arrangements for their regular, employment-related child care needs.

Cultural, Structural, and Integrative Explanations for Race and Ethnic Differences

Three main theories attempt to explain why racial ethnic families have higher rates of using extended kin for social support than Anglo American families. The cultural explanation states that these practices are the product of differing cultural preferences. The structural explanation conceives of them as adaptive responses to structural constraints (such as limited economic resources). The integrative explanation argues that they are due to the intersection of culturally specific values and practices (race and culture), structural constraints (race and class), and the social organization of gender (caregiving is provided mainly by female relatives). For example, cultural preferences for relative care (culture), historical racism that prevented access to public care services (race), the availability and lower cost of relative care (structure), and caregiving provided mainly by female relatives (gender) combine to increase the likelihood that racial ethnic families are more likely than white families to rely on their extended families for social support.

All three types of explanations have also appeared in child care research to explain why racial ethnic families are more likely than Anglo American families to make child care arrangements with relatives. Brayfield and Hofferth (1995) found race differences, even when they controlled for economic status and family structure in their nationally representative study of child care. Typical of research with similar findings, they concluded that the explanation for these differences was cultural: "African American mothers have different value orientations toward caregiving, child rearing, and kin support" (p. 175). Other studies have shown that racial ethnic mothers prefer child care that resembles, rather than conflicts with, the family's child rearing practices and maintains the cultural practices and values of the child's ethnic group (Auerbach, 1975; Blau, 1991; Uttal, 1996). In sum, the cultural explanation states that racial ethnic families prefer similar values and child rearing practices provided by relatives and because their cultural practices are more familistic; they are also more likely to live near their relatives.

However, cultural explanations have been criticized for failing to acknowledge that cultural practices may be adaptive responses to structural conditions, rather than real differences in cultural values (Nakano Glenn, 1983; Stack, 1974). One criticism of the cultural explanation is that it is an overgeneralization which ignores that much of the research has only studied poor racial ethnic families and confounds race and class. Alternatively, structural explanations assert that using kin is a response to factors such as low income and racism. According to this view, higher rates of kin-based child care among racial ethnic families reflect their disproportionately lower median family incomes, not cultural preferences. Kuhlthau and Mason (1996) found support for this economic explanation in their survey of 1,378 mothers of preschoolers living in the Detroit area in 1986. They found that the mother's race, as an indicator of cultural practices, was not a predictive factor of using kin-based child care arrangements. Instead, they found that regardless of the mother's race, "market-provided child care becomes more common the older the child is, the fewer the relatives who are locally available, the higher the level of family income, the higher the mother's educational level, and the weaker her preference for exclusive parental care for children" (p. 575). The greater likelihood of Hispanics and African Americans to live near relatives, to have lower family incomes and educational levels, appears to better explain why they have disproportionately higher rates of kin-based care than their culturally specific values and practices. In this explanation, residential proximity is interpreted as a structural condition rather than a cultural factor. Another structural consideration is that the use of kin for child care also allows racial ethnic families to protect their children from institutional and interpersonal racism that may be present in child care settings with predominantly white staff (Uttal, 1996).

Structural and cultural explanations differ in where they locate cultural preferences and values in their casual explanation of kin-based child care practices. The cultural explanation views the cultural preferences of individual nuclear families as determinant of child care patterns that vary by race and ethnicity, whereas the structural explanation views these patterns as practices that emerge in response to structural conditions and are not determined by the culturally specific values and practices of racial ethnic families.

Inconsistent findings about whether kin-based child care is culturally or structurally caused may also result from the failure to more carefully examine the interaction between cultural and structural factors. Beyond the study of child care arrangements, race, class, and gender scholars have proposed developing models and explanations for how racial group membership and identity, economic status and opportunities, and gender simultaneously produce certain social configurations (Baca Zinn, 1990). Roschelle (1997b) proposes using an "integrative theoretical perspective that explores the intersection of race, gender and class by examining both cultural and structural indicators of social support" (p. 107). This perspective criticizes single-factor explanations for oversimplifying complex social phenomenon, and scholars such as Maxine Baca Zinn (1990) argue that social practices can be better understood as the product of the intersections of race, class, and gender dynamics, rather than determined by a single cause—cultural or structural.

Ethnographic studies of kin-based child care arrangements reveal the multiple forces that shape child care arrangements in racial ethnic families. For example, in an in-depth interview study of employed Hispana and Anglo working-class mothers in Albuquerque, New Mexico, Lamphere et al. (1993) found that Hispana mothers used kin for child care more than Anglo mothers because they simultaneously expressed a greater preference for kin-based care (a cultural preference) and also had greater numbers of local relatives (a structural condition). Roschelle's (1997a) study of Puerto Rican extended social support networks found that in spite of continuing cultural preferences for kin-based child care, participation in social support networks was inhibited by structural constraints. Two structural factors—circular migration patterns of Puerto Rican relatives and each woman's individual struggle against poverty—restricted the ability of women to extend their support to one another in spite of their cultural preferences for kin-based child care.

Roschelle's (1997a, 1997b) finding of diminishing race and ethnic differences in kin-based child care stands alone. Most other studies have shown how a complex combination of factors, both structural and cultural, coalesce to increase the likelihood of relative care in racial ethnic families: Kin-based child care resolves tensions between gendered ideologies about the primacy of women mothering their own children and the marginal economic situations of racial ethnic families that require mothers' economic contributions to their families (Hertz & Ferguson, 1996; Kuhlthau & Mason, 1996; Segura, 1994), and the higher cost of nonrelative care combines with the low wages that racial ethnic women are paid to promote the use of relative care (Lamphere et al., 1993). Furthermore, a predominantly white child care market and distrust of this market to provide racially safe environments and/or a familiar cultural milieu encourages kin-based care as a way to stay within one's own racial ethnic group (Auerbach, 1975; Lamphere et al., 1993; Uttal, 1996). What all of these studies share is the agreement that no single factor determines the rates of kin-based care, and many factors in combination reinforce racial, cultural, class-based, and gendered practices. A major contribution of Roschelle's analysis, in spite of its unreplicated finding, is that it focuses not only on characteristics of the individual families requiring care but also on why relatives are available to provide child care (i.e., the impact of migratory patterns on participation in kin-based child care networks).

Like most of the research on the support networks of extended families, the few child care studies that have examined why employed mothers use kin-based child care have produced inconsistent findings. Clearly, no single theory has successfully established itself as the prevailing explanation. This suggests that we have yet to identify fully the appropriate model or key factors that predict the use of kin-based child care arrangements.

Methods

This inquiry emerged from a study that was designed to explore the meaning of child care arrangements to employed mothers. Upon noting race and ethnic differences in using kin-based child care, I applied the extended case method to understand this difference. In the extended case method (Buroway et al., 1991), existing theories are deductively tested and refined by comparing them with the inductive findings first generated from ethnographic research. By accounting for the case study (a type of negative case analysis), the older theory is reformulated, and a new theory and new concepts emerge. This research used in-depth interviewing to inductively discover new factors and reasons for race and ethnic differences. This method combines both traditional grounded theory method (in which theories inductively emerge from empirical data) and theory testing (in which theories are deductively assessed against empirical data).

Because the refinement of theory is based on an empirical case example, the new theory, while abstract, is still grounded theory. Yet one of the major differences is in what constitutes data. In the grounded theory method, data are typically limited to the empirical data collected through the ethnographic process (e.g., interviewing or observing people). The extended case method goes further, incorporating contextual information that comes from other sources, such as group demographic information, regional labor market statistics, contemporary political issues, and historical knowledge of specific groups. Thus, the analysis is based not only on the individual accounts but also on the researcher's knowledge of the topic, the general context of the specific case studied, and existing theoretical explanations. In this study, the final analysis combined information from interviews, knowledge about the racialized regional labor market, immigrant characteristics, and the local child care market in order to identify new factors to explain the observed race and ethnic differences in employed mothers' practices and views about relative care.

Informant Recruitment

I conducted in-depth interviews from 1990 to 1992 with employed mothers living in Santa Cruz County, California. Each participant was required to be an employed mother with at least one child not yet school-aged and residing in Santa Cruz County. Maximum variation sampling (Lincoln & Guba, 1985) was used to achieve diversification of the sample by race and ethnicity, occupation, and type of child care. Although maximum variation sampling does not allow for statistical prediction and generalization to a larger population, it does ensure that theory development is not limited to the experiences of a socially homogeneous group. This sampling technique promotes a broad exploration of experiences and issues. The sample was located through different means: Flyers were posted in public places (e.g., laundromats, health clinics), business cards with information about the study were handed out, strangers were approached and asked to participate, names were solicited through my own social networks, and referrals from each informant were collected. All but three of the informants were initially strangers to me, and each informant was paid $20 for her participation.

In-depth interviews were conducted and audiotaped in person at a location chosen by the participant (e.g., her home, my home, her office, my office, a park, or a restaurant). Interviews lasted 2 to 6 hours, and while some required a second and third meeting, most were completed in one sitting. I began each interview by asking the informant to tell me about the history of her child care arrangements, allowing for her to identify the topics that she wanted to talk about. In addition, I had a list of topics that I raised in the interview. The articulated form of interview questions varied and were modified to fit with the flow of the interview. I probed for concrete examples of and details about how she felt about her experiences.

This analysis is based on all 31 employed mothers, even though not all of the mothers actually used relatives for their regular child care needs. First, I analyzed mothers' ideal views about using kin-based child care, as well as how they felt about their actual use or nonuse of kin-based child care. Then I identified the reasons given by those who were using kin-based child care. Finally, I examined these ideals and reasons, taking into account information about the local labor market, immigrant characteristics, and the local child care market.

Characteristics of the Sample

In-depth interviews with 7 African American, 17 Anglo American, and 7 Mexican employed mothers are included in this analysis. In each race and ethnic group, the occupational representation was spread across different types of works (e.g., assembly worker, beautician, secretary, loan processor, office manager, nurse, teacher, doctor). The average number of hours worked per week was 38, ranging from 2.5 to 65 hours. Twenty-four mothers worked 30 or more hours per week, six mothers worked between 20 and 28 hours per week, and one mother who was running a business out of her home estimated that she worked 2.5 hours per week, though she had her child in 20 hours of child care per week. The children's ages ranged from newborn through 6 years. Six of the mothers were single parents, but this was not related in any systematic way to their race or ethnicity, type of child care arrangement that they used, or to their type of work. All the names I use to refer to these mothers are pseudonyms.

Child care usage was measured both by the number of hours that mothers were employed and the type of care. At the time of the interview, only six of the mothers used a single arrangement to cover their employment-related child care needs. A total of 56 arrangements were reported: 16 in family day care homes or in someone else's home (including two cared for in parent-cooperative arrangements), 16 in child care centers, 22 in the child's home cared for by a hired caregiver or the other parent, and in two cases, the child was with the mother as she worked.

The possibility of using relatives is structurally determined by whether the informants have relatives living close enough to be an available source of child care (Table 7.1). In this study, the distance of 25 miles (40 km) was used to define local relatives because of the geographical formation of Santa Cruz County. North of the county is a rural, agricultural region with a limited population. East of the county is a mountain range that separates Santa Cruz from San Jose. The 25-mile road to San Jose creates a geographical wall against easy commutes and a sense of separation. Although relatives from San Jose may be called on for occasional care, the difficult commute was viewed as an obstacle to daily arrangements. In contrast, the drive between the north and south ends of the county is straight and flat, making the 25 miles less of an obstacle. Because all of the informants in this sample were stably employed, they all had means of transportation to drive children to and from care.

Table 7.1 shows the use of relatives to cover employment-related child care needs

Table 7.1: Number of Relatives by Locality and Type of Use for Child Care[a]

Total Sample	African American (n = 7)	Anglo American (n = 17)	Mexican American (n = 7)
Number with local relatives	3	7	7
Use kin for child care			
No kin care	2	0	7
Regular	0	2	4
Back-up	2	4	1

a. This does not include two mothers with ex-husbands who lived locally and shared joint physical custody.

by frequency of use: regular care, back-up or unplanned care, or no relative care. Care by relatives was classified as a regular arrangement when mothers routinely used relatives for their employment-related child care needs, as back-up when their regular child care arrangements would not accommodate their needs (e.g., when child care centers would not take sick children or were closed but the mothers still had to work, or when they were between child care arrangements), or no care if relatives were not currently being used for either regular or back-up care. At the time of their interviews, six mothers used kin for regular child care arrangements (two Anglo American, four Mexican American). The four Mexican American mothers paid relatives for full-time care, whereas the two Anglo American mothers combined part-time paid and unpaid care by relatives and non-relatives.

African American and Mexican American mothers mentioned only women relatives as caregivers, even when they had many male relatives within 25 miles of them. Two Anglo American mothers mentioned two young adult male relatives who occasionally provided back-up care for their young children, and one Anglo American mother said that both her mother and father worked as a team to provide regular part-time child care for her son.

The (In)Appropriate Use of Kin for Child Care: Race and Ethnic Differences

A major race difference that emerged in this study was how mothers viewed using kin as a source of child care. Anglo American mothers described kin-based child care as inappropriate and even problematic, whereas African American and Mexican American mothers viewed using kin for child care as an appropriate practice even when they preferred other types of arrangements.

Only 3 of the 31 mothers in this study said that they viewed kin care as the ideal type of substitute care. Of these three mothers, only one of them was actually using her kin for child care. Lupe Gonzalez, a Mexican American mother who worked full-time as an administrative assistant, said that she hired her aunt because she believed the best substitute care for her child was her relatives. The other two mothers who desired kin care, one African American and the other Mexican American, were professionals who had relocated to Santa Cruz for their jobs, and they did not have relatives living nearby. They described their own childhood experiences in relative care as ideal and said that they would use relative care if their relatives were living nearby. Aurora Garcia, a Mexican American doctor, said,

> I come from a family that, if I lived close to my family, my mother would have taken care of [my daughter.] . . . My mother took care of children. She never took care of more than two kids. They became part of the family. . . . All my aunts have cared for children, going to the extent that one of my aunts had a little girl from birth to 15. I mean, it was a different kind of [child care] relationship that I can't find here.

In contrast to those who desired relative care but were not using it, the actual use of relatives did not indicate preference for kin-based care. Among the six employed mothers who were regularly using kin care, four had first sought or used care outside of the family. Lisa Garni, an Anglo American administrative assistant, had first looked for infant care in a child care center. Only when an extensive search for full-time infant care failed did she finally turn to her parents for part-time care to supplement a part-time infant care arrangement in a family day care home. Over the past 3 years, she continued to combine her parents' part-time care with other arrangements. She currently has all her child care needs for her 3-year-old child covered by the combined care provided part-time by her mother and father and part-time by her sister-in-law, whom she pays.

Another Anglo American mother, Elaine Ghio, had recently reduced the time her daughter went to a child care center to only mornings, and Elaine's mother now picks her up and the child stays with her grandmother in the afternoons. This change occurred when Elaine started getting behind in her child care payments because her child's father stopped paying child support, and not because Elaine preferred her mother's care. Both Elaine and her mother viewed this kin-based child care arrangement as temporary.

Similarly, of the four Mexican American mothers who were using relatives for their regular child care arrangements, only Lupe Gonzalez said that kin care was her ideal. Linda Molina, a pregnant Mexican American mother of a 1-year-old boy, did not express a preference either way for relative care of an alternative form of care because she simply did not want to be an employed mother, no matter who cared for her children. Neither of the other two Mexican American mothers viewed relative care as the best choice, even though their children had never been in any other kind of care. Maria Hernandez valued educational opportunities most when she discussed what type of care she wanted, and she went back and forth between whether the family context and flexibility of kin care outweighed the educational opportunities of a child care center. But at the time of her interview, Maria said, "I decided let's not rock the boat. Let's keep the status quo."

Relative care was used, even though it was not ideal, because relatives made themselves available to provide child care, and this was true in all racial and ethnic groups. Family care, even when it was not explicitly sought, was offered to the two Anglo American mothers, Lisa Garni and Elaine Ghio. Two of the African American mothers, Julie Lopez and Gloria Thomas, reported that their extended families provided care for their children for long periods of time, even though they lived hundreds of miles away. When Sylvia Rodriguez first mentioned to her mother that she was going to start looking for child care, her mother said, "Why are you looking?" Sylvia recalls:

> I was kind of shy. I was like, now can I just leave her here? You know, just assume that [my mother is] going to be watching them. But I think that my mom just took it upon herself, like [she said,] "Oh, let me do this," or "I'll be doing. . . ."

A subtle difference was that Anglo American mothers resisted these offers, whereas Mexican American mothers and African American mothers willingly accepted them because they felt that using relatives for child care was an appropriate and acceptable practice, whether or not it was their ideal. African American mothers accepted their families' offers to care for their children during difficult transitions, such as when one mother relocated to a new city for a new job, and another was getting resettled during a divorce. Both Julie Lopez and Gloria Thomas viewed these extended stays as child care arrangements that were necessary until each had reestablished herself. Similarly, Sylvia Rodriguez's feelings about her mother's offer to provide child care were that "this was just something that was done," suggesting that she understand the tacit availability and acceptability of kin-based child care.

In contrast, Anglo American mothers in this study vehemently rejected the idea of establishing regular child care arrangements with relatives, even when circumstances (e.g., economic problems, unavailability of care) forced them to use relative care. For example, two Anglo American mothers had set up regular child care arrangements with their kin, but one of the mothers viewed it as temporary, and the other had resisted it until she had no other options. Although five Anglo American mothers relied on kin for back-up care, they were resistant to the idea of establishing regular care arrangements with relatives. This perspective contrasted with the acceptance, expressed by both Mexican American and African American mothers, of kin care, whether they were actually using kin care or not at the time of the interview.

One of the reasons Anglo American mothers renounced using kin for regular child care arrangements was that they viewed it as an unacceptable imposition of their relatives. They did not want their own mothers to provide child care because they viewed providing child care for young children on a regular basis as incompatible with their mothers' stage of life. Even when their mothers offered their services, the employed mothers initially shied away from using them to cover their regular child care needs. Mary Turner, a professionally employed mother of two, felt strongly about this:

> I want my mother to have her own life, and I don't want her to sacrifice her life so that she can take care of my kids. I don't think that should be her role in her life. . . . I know it was in her head [to] make a big sacrifice so that her daughter could go to work, be a professional, and you know, achieve all these strong things for herself, and [my mom] was going to sacrifice herself and watch her grandchildren. And I made it really clear to her when she came up that she was welcome to spend all the time she wanted to with her grandchildren, but it wasn't going to be a job for her.

Mary articulated a view commonly presented by the Anglo American mothers in this study, and this view also cut across socioeconomic status. Working-class Anglo American women were just as likely to indicate that it was inappropriate to call upon their relatives, especially their parents, for regular child care needs. For example, Cathy Perry explained that she did not want to be obligated to her relatives, and she was not comfortable with the idea of her mother taking care of her kids.

> I don't think I'd want to be that owing to her. In debt to your mommy! I just don't like it when someone does a favor for you. There's an implied obligation that if someone does something for you, you should do something for them. I think it's better to pay for someone's services and get it over with. I'd feel this big obligation.

Similarly, self-employed Elizabeth Seymour said:

> I would hate my mom to be obliged to be a child care person. . . . She's got her own life. She comes down when she really loves to see the kids, and I certainly wouldn't want to make her be a child care person. She's left the child care years and wants to be a granny. I'd like to be nearer so we could visit them a lot and she didn't come down to work. She comes down because she really wanted to be with us and help out; obviously, she wanted to be with the kids, too. She came down for a vacation, so it wasn't a working arrangement. I don't think I'd like to work with her. Then I'd have to pay her. Then I'd have to be an employer, and I just wouldn't want that for my mom. She doesn't ever expect to get paid and . . . I wouldn't want to have to pay my Mom.

This view of using kin was very different from the view that Sylvia Rodriguez articulated about accepting her mother's original offer to provide child care for her first-born child. Rather than worrying about the obligation, Sylvia and her mother constructed the situation as if this arrangement was what is supposed to happen, rather than viewing it as undesirable.

If and when Anglo American mothers did accept their relatives' offers to provide regular child care arrangements, they limited the scope of the arrangement, as did Lisa Garni:

> My parents would probably watch him full-time, but I felt that wasn't just quite fair, encumbering their whole time, full-time. They've raised a family. . . . [They have] their commitments and the freedom to go and do the things they want to do. My father has been retired for 5 years, and not to be tied down, 5 days a week is more of a personal conviction [of mine because] I felt that it just isn't right and I think that he could get good, loving, quality care in other places and it's just more, it's just how I felt about that.

Anglo American mothers also established routines and definitions that masked and transformed the character of care by relatives. Elaine Ghio defined it as a temporary situation created by her unfortunate economic situation. Lisa Garni purposefully limited each relative to only part-time care in order to limit her sense of obligation. She also constructed reasons for the child care: Not only did she need it but her parents wanted to spend time with their grandchild. The arrangement gave them the opportunity to regularly spend some time with their only grandchild but not so much time to be a "job" or to interfere with their retirement lifestyle. This definition of the situation made the arrangement mutually beneficial. Lisa also reduced her sense of obligation to her sister-in-law by purposefully defining and structuring the child care arrangement as a business relationship. When Lisa had to find a new arrangement because her child was too old for care in the part-time infant family day care home, her sister-in-law (who was voluntarily nonemployed) offered to watch her son for free. Lisa only reluctantly accepted her sister-in-law's original offer under the condition that they formalized it as a business arrangement.

> First Susan volunteered to watch him without me paying and I said, "No, Susan, I will not do this. I have great expectations for you watching my son." I said, "You have never

really watched as a business a child before, and I have certain expectations, and I will pay you, and this is what we will do." So we sat down, and we met, and I said to her . . . my parents watch him 2 days a week and that she was to watch him Mondays, Wednesdays, and Fridays, and we sat down and I gave her my work schedule and the hours, and how much I would pay her every day, and that I would then literally end up writing her checks at the end of every week.

Lisa structured her relative care arrangements so that each relative only provides part-time care and each part-time arrangement is formally defined so that it is not viewed as "relative care." By doing this, she limited her informal familial obligation to her relatives.

Another factor that heavily influenced the rejection of relative care by Anglo American women was differences in child rearing philosophies, especially between daughters and mothers. Mary Turner also felt that her mother was an inappropriate choice for providing regular child care arrangements because she disliked her mother's child-rearing practices:

She isn't the type of person who just loves her grandkids. She's not that kind of person at all. She's not comfortable with kids. She is happy when they're asleep. When she's with Danielle . . . she doesn't interact well with Danielle. She tries to stop her from doing things, like, "Don't pull those pans out of the cupboard" or "Be careful." tries to stop her from doing things. Whereas I have a different attitude, like, "Sure, Danielle, use the knife, but let me show you how and let me hold your hand, and we can work on it together." Whereas my mother would be, "Get her out of the kitchen." She has this kind of old-fashioned attitude that I don't like at all, and she wouldn't be the type of person who would respond well to me saying I want her in there and . . . I want to change things about [how my mother is] interacting with her. She just wouldn't like that, so I prefer to let her do her things with Danielle during some time. She can take as much time with her as she wants, but I don't want her to be the primary person for Danielle.

Elizabeth Seymour also felt uncomfortable with her mother's style of child rearing. "I just feel that with my mom I may be more judgmental about the way she looks after my children."

These in-depth interviews illustrate the different views that a racially diverse sample of employed mothers hold about using kin for their regular child care arrangements. Overall, Mexican American mothers accepted the idea of using kin for child care arrangements, as did African American mothers, even though none of them were actually using relative care. In contrast, Anglo American women viewed relative care as an inappropriate practice, even when they were using relatives for their regular child care arrangements. They believed that kin care was undesirable and wished to avoid the obligations. On the face of it, this difference may appear to be simply another difference in cultural values. However, looking more closely at why Mexican American employed mothers report that they are using kin-based care reveals that this difference is not the product of cultural preferences. Even the Mexican Americans who were both positively inclined toward relative care and actually using it did not indicate that it was their ideal arrangement. Their greater willingness to engage in kin-based child care than Anglo American mothers was not predicated on preference. In the next section, I will discuss how this "willingness" reflected factors that imposed themselves from outside of the mother's individual preferences for a particular type of care.

Embedment in Extended Family Socioeconomic Networks and the Employment Needs of Relatives

When a larger context than individual preferences or needs is taken into account, new insights are discovered as to why kin-based child care is used. In particular, discussions of their embedment in extended family socioeconomic networks revealed how their relatives' economic needs contributed to their decisions to engage in kin-based child care arrangements. This insight emerges from the interviews of Mexican American mothers who were actually using kin-based child care.

Until 1988, California had a healthy, expanding economy. The availability of entry-level jobs drew ethnically diverse labor pools to northern California. Mexican migrants have historically been attracted to Santa Cruz County by the labor demands of a mixed economy of agricultural work (farm work and food processing), tourist and hotel work, manufacturing, and the new electronics and technology industries. Over the past 50 years, a stable community of second- and third-generation Mexican Americans has emerged. Although the official 1990 U.S. Census reports the county is only 10% Hispanic, locally collected statistics report an even higher presence of a Latino community: 30% in the county at large, 60% concentrated in the more agriculturally based southern region of the country (Zavella, 1997). These local numbers probably include a large population of undocumented Mexican immigrants that the Census misses. In contrast, few African Americans have moved to the region for either economic or cultural reasons. The rest of the county is (officially) 85% white, 4% Asian and Pacific Islander, and less than 1% black (U.S. Census of Population and Housing, 1990). The Anglo American population is a mix of local, long-term residents and middle-class job relocators, people affiliated with the University of California's Santa Cruz campus, and residents who use Santa Cruz as a bedroom community for the nearby San Jose "Silicon Valley" economy.

At the time these interviews were conducted in the early 1990s, unemployment was high in spite of this diversified economy, especially for the undereducated, those who didn't speak English, African Americans, and Mexican Americans. In 1990, 20% of Hispanics, 19% of African Americans, and 9% of Anglo Americans were living in poverty in Santa Cruz County (Zavella, 1997). Farm work and food processing continued to be common occupations for Mexican American and Mexican immigrant men and women.

The Santa Cruz County child care market, like child care markets nationally, is characterized by the combination of formal and informal sectors. A highly professionalized sector of licensed child care centers and family day care homes mixes with a largely invisible sector of informal care arrangements that includes undocumented immigrant child care providers and private unlicensed providers. The formal child care market and resource and referral services provided child care settings staffed by predominantly Anglo American child care providers and was used mostly by Anglo American families. While the public discussion for child care policy is well articulated at the local level, the child care market, especially for low-income families, operates at a highly privatized level (as in most parts of the country) and is not heavily influenced by these discussions.

The economic considerations that Mexican American mothers reported were based not on how they would benefit but rather how their relatives benefited from being their child care providers. The mothers viewed themselves as providing their relatives with jobs and better economic opportunities than their relatives were able to achieve in the formal labor market. This finding introduces a new type of structural explanation than previously proposed by other structural explanations, such as economic incentives, racism, local availability of relatives, and circular migratory patterns.

Three of the mothers explained how child care work was a much better way for their relatives to earn income than other forms of employment. For example, Linda Molina's 16-year-old niece from Mexico was willing to relocate to the United States for a low paid child care job because providing child care in the United States for her aunt was a much better economic opportunity than staying in Mexico. Another group who benefited from offering their child care labor to their families were older Mexican American and Mexican immigrant women with limited English. Child care work was a more attractive alternative to working in the agricultural fields, the food processing plants, factories, or hotels. For example, Sylvia Rodriguez said that her cousin (who had immigrated to the United States during high school and still did not speak English very well) was interested in working as her child care provider because the cousin found it difficult to find any employment other than low paid manufacturing and fieldwork. By working for Sylvia, she earned as much and had more control over her work. Sylvia was aware that she was providing her cousin with an economic opportunity by giving her the child care job. Similarly, Maria Hernandez' mother-in-law was able to quit physically taxing strawberry fieldwork because her daughters and daughter-in-law all brought their children to her home and paid her to care for the children:

> I've been tempted to put him in part-time [child care center] care, but then that's a problem, because [my mother-in-law] counts on babysitting money as part of her income. To her it would be a reduction in what she makes, and I'm afraid that if I did that, she probably would say, "Well, in that case, I'm not going to take care of [your child] at all," so to keep him there, we don't do that.

Maria complained that she felt her mother-in-law overcharged her, but her awareness of her mother-in-law's economic dependency made it difficult for Maria to choose to go elsewhere. She knew that her kin-based child care arrangement was not simply about her personal preference for a certain type of care, but had broader implications for the larger family network of sisters, sisters-in-law, and especially her mother-in-law. In spite of her strong desire to place her son in a preschool, she decided to wait until he entered kindergarten to give him the educational opportunities she wanted for him. Although care by her mother-in-law was not her first preference or even economically beneficial to her, Maria continued with this child care arrangement because "it's all family related, so a lot of times, you're doing favors for each other."

On the other hand, child care work cannot compete with white-collar clerical work that pays better and provides more autonomy. Because of this, younger U.S.–educated Anglo American, Mexican American, and African American women were not available to provide child care for their relatives if they were better employed in white-collar entry-level jobs. This was the case for Diane Gomez, who had four sisters living in the area. They had all been raised and educated in the United States. None of them were available to provide child care for the others because none of them were willing to quit their clerical jobs to do child care work for each other.

This study discovered that one of the major reasons that Mexican American employed mothers gave for using kin-based child care was their sense of responsibility to the economic needs of their relatives. Their child care decisions were not driven by just their needs or preferences; they also took into consideration their relatives' employment needs. Thus, these kin-based child care arrangements reflect a complex decision-making process based on a mutually beneficial arrangement between families needing child care and relatives needing better employment options. This responsibility for members of their extended families embedded employed mothers and their young children in socioeconomic networks defined not just by cultural practices but by economic needs as well.

Discussion

This study finds that there continue to be race and ethnic differences in views about using relatives for child care arrangements; and it also identifies a previously unexplored factor that can be included to better understand how culture and structure combine to create an integrative explanation for kin-based child care. This study suggests that the economic needs of those relatives who provide care and their lack of better formal labor market opportunities also help explain why racial ethnic families continue to be entrenched in child care arrangements made with relatives.

The major race and ethnic difference was not in the actual practice of using kin for child care arrangements; rather, it was the view or orientation toward the acceptability of the idea of entering into child care arrangements with relatives. Anglo American mothers viewed using kin for child care as an inappropriate and undesirable practice, whereas the Mexican American and African American mothers viewed it as an appropriate practice, although Mexican American mothers who were employed clearly did not view it as their ideal choice.

What has confused scholars using strictly cultural preferences or structural explanations (economic practices) as the primary reason for kin-based child care arrangements is that middle-class racial ethnic families do and do not rely on kin for child care. They use kin care even when they can afford nonfamily-based care, and they use nonfamily care in spite of claims about cultural preferences. Whether cultural or structural, both practices identify the reasons that originate within the immediate family needing child care. This study identifies a reason that originates outside of the immediate family—the use of their kin for child care was also shaped by the limited employment opportunities their kin had.

The identification of this external factor suggests that cultural and structural explanations are limited not only by their single factor explanations but also by the "individual needs" framework that underlies both of them. Cultural preferences are viewed as an expression of an individualistic perspective—that is, getting one's ideal met. Similarly, economic factors have been defined individualistically—that is, what the economic need is of the family requiring child care, or what the economic status and availability of the relatives providing care are. This study reveals an important and overlooked distinction between an individual (family) needs and preferences approach and an extended family embedment perspective. The finding that Mexican American women make decisions about their own needs while taking into account the needs of their relatives is similar to Higginbotham and Weber's 1992 observation that black professional women express a greater sense of reciprocal obligation to kin than white professional women. Underlying both findings is the sense of family responsibility that extends beyond the boundaries of the nuclear family unit. This study calls for shifting the focus from individual needs to the dynamic family processes that are shaped by the contexts of class, race, and gender within which they are situated. The embedment in extended family socioeconomic networks suggests a new framework and criteria used by employed mothers to make their child care choices.

These findings bring several considerations into focus: First, cultural differences in the orientation toward using kin-based child care continue to exist and influence different practices by racial ethnic and Anglo American families. Second, structural explanations not only need to include the needs of individual families but also to account for the availability of and reasons why relatives are available to provide child care. The racially stratified nature of the labor market, including the type of job opportunities, is one of these conditions. This analysis suggests that particular regions of the country with poor labor markets will also have increased supplies and practices of relative care. It is conceivable that the same processes that promote kin care for Mexican Americans in this particular study may also operate for other historically subordinated racial ethnic groups, as well as white ethnic groups that are concentrated in areas with similar economies and extended family networks. Taking the context into account may help to explain the inconsistent findings about relative care. Third, the findings of this small sample ethnographic study identify practices that reflect the combination of cultural and structural explanations, again pointing us to using integrative models for understanding why employed mothers might choose kin-based care. Finally, it suggests that in order to test this integrative model, we need to include attitudinal questions that allow us to separate idealized views from real preferences about using kin for child care, as well as demographic questions about the socioeconomic status of the family needing care and the family member providing care. Using in-depth interviews, this study discovered those factors and developed a better understanding about them for Anglo American and Mexican American mothers who are employed. However, a better understanding of African American employed mothers who have relatives living locally is still needed.

These considerations also suggest that it is again time to rethink the assumption of self-sufficient nuclear families. As new welfare policies require welfare mothers to become employed mothers in low paid labor markets, it will be increasingly important to examine how families on the economic margins make their child care arrangements with or without kin support. What is still unknown is whether the practice of using kin-based care is supportive or places families at greater risk. Another consideration is how the increasing unavailability of women relatives (Dilworth-Anderson, 1992; Roschelle, 1997a), including grandmothers (Gerstel & Gallagher, 1994; Presser, 1989), affects the quality and availability of kin-based care. Will only women in extremely tenuous economic situations be available for kin-based child care? Will this lead to increasingly unstable child care arrangements?

Understanding how individuals embedded in extended family networks take into account the needs of their extended family networks above and beyond their own individual preferences or needs is especially important in understanding racial ethnic families. In this study, preferences for different types of child care were shaped by an awareness of one's extended family's needs that went beyond considerations of convenience (what arrangements are in the best interest of the parents' need for child care) or quality factors (what type of care is in the best interests of the individual). The degree of ease with which individual families move away from or remain in relative care is complicated and requires weighing how all these factors (convenience, quality, preferences, and embedment in extended family networks) work together in order to understand which child care arrangements are established and maintained.

Acknowledgment

I would like to thank Bill Aquilino, Judi Bartfield, Deborah Johnson, and the anonymous reviewers for their insightful suggestions on this article.

References

Auerbach, S. (1975). What parents want from day care. In S. Auerbach with J. A. Rivaldo (Eds.), *Child care: A comprehensive guide: Philosophy, programs, and practices for the creation of quality services for children* (Vol. 1, pp. 137–152). New York: Human Sciences Press.

Baca Zinn, M. (1980). Employment and education of Mexican American women: The interplay of modernity and ethnicity in eight families. *Harvard Educational Review, 50*(1), 47–62.

Baca Zinn, M. (1990). Family, feminism, and race in America. *Gender & Society, 4,* 68–82.

Benin, M., & Keith, V. M. (1995). The social support of employed African American and Anglo mothers. *Journal of Family Issues, 16,* 275–297.

Blau, D. M. (1991). The quality of child care: An economic perspective. In D. M. Blau (Ed.), *The economics of child care* (pp. 145–174). New York: Russell Sage Foundation.

Blau, D. M., & Robins, P. K. (1991). Child care demand and labor supply of young women over time. *Demography, 28,* 333–351.

Brayfield, A., & Hofferth, S. L. (1995). Balancing the family budget: Differences in child care expenditures by race/ethnicity, economic status, and family structure. *Social Science Quarterly, 76,* 158–177.

Buroway, M., Burton, A., Ferguson, A. A., Fox, K. J., Gamson, J., Gartrell, N., Hurst, L., Kurzman, C., Salzinger, L., Schiffman, J., & Ui, S. (1991). *Ethnography unbound: Power and resistance in the modern metropolis*. Berkeley: University of California Press.

Crispell, D. (1994). Child-care choices don't match moms' wishes. *American Demograph-

ics, 16, 11–13.

Dilworth-Anderson, P. (1992). Extended kin networks in black families. *Generations, 16*(3), 29–32.

Folk, K. (1994). For love or money: Costs of child care by relatives. *Journal of Family and Economic Issues, 15,* 243–260.

Gerson, K. (1993). *No man's land: Men's changing commitments to family and work.* New York: Basic Books.

Gerstel, N., & Gallagher, S. (1994). Caring for kith and kin: Gender, employment, and the privatization of care. *Social Problems, 41,* 519–539.

Glaser, B., & Strauss, A. (1967). *The discovery of grounded theory: Strategies for qualitative research.* New York: Aldine.

Hayes, C. D., Palmer, J. L., & Zaslow, M. J. (Eds.). (1990). *Who cares for America's children?* Washington, DC: National Academy Press.

Hertz, R., & Ferguson, F. T. (1996). Child care choice and constraints in the United States: Social class, race, and the influence of family views. *Journal of Comparative Family Studies, 27,* 249–280.

Higginbotham, E. L., & Weber, L. (1992). Moving up with kin and community: Upward social mobility for black and white women. *Gender & Society, 6*(3), 416–440.

Hofferth, S. L., Brayfield, A., Deich, S., & Holcomb, P. (1991). *National child care survey, 1990* (Urban Institute Report 91–5). Washington, DC: Urban Institute Press.

Jayakody, R., Chatters, L., & Taylor, R. (1993). Family support to single and married African American mothers: The provision of financial, emotional, and child care assistance. *Journal of Marriage and the Family, 55,* 261–276.

Keefe, S. E. (1996). The myth of the declining family: Extended family ties among urban Mexican Americans and Anglo Americans. In G. Gmelch & W. P. Zenner (Eds.), *Urban life* (3rd ed., pp. 308–322). Prospects Heights, IL: Waveland Press.

Kuhlthau, K., & Mason, K. O. (1996). Market child care versus care by relatives: Choices made by employed and nonemployed mothers. *Journal of Family Issues, 17,* 561–578.

Lajewski, H. C. (1959). *Child care arrangements of full-time working mothers* (Children's Bureau Publication 378, U.S. Department of Health, Education, and Welfare). Washington, DC: Government Printing Office.

Lamphere, L., Zavella, P., Gonzales, F., & Evans, P. B. (1993). *Sunbelt working families: Reconciling family and factory.* Ithaca, NY: Cornell University Press.

Leibowitz, A., Waite, L. J., & Witsberger, C. (1988). Child care for preschoolers: Differences by child's age. *Demography, 25,* 205–220.

Lincoln, Y. S., & Guba, E. G. (1985). *Naturalistic inquiry.* Newbury Park, CA: Sage.

Nakano Glenn, E. (1983). Split household, small producer, and dual wage earner: An analysis of Chinese American family strategies. *Journal of Marriage and the Family, 45,* 35–46.

Oliker, S. (1995). Work commitment and constraint among mothers on workfare. *Journal of Contemporary Ethnography, 24,* 165–194.

Parish, W. L., Hao, L., & Hogan, D. P. (1991). Family support networks, welfare, and work among young mothers. *Journal of Marriage and the Family, 53,* 203–215.

Presser, H. (1989). Some economic complexities of child care provided by grandmothers. *Journal of Marriage and the Family, 51,* 581–591.

Roschelle, A. R. (1997a). Declining networks of care: Ethnicity, migration, and poverty in a Puerto Rican community. *Race, Gender and Class, 4,* 107–125.

Roschelle, A. R. (1997b). *No more kin: Exploring race, class, and gender in family networks.* Thousand Oaks, CA: Sage

Segura, D. A. (1994). Working at motherhood: Chicana and Mexican immigrant mothers and employment. In E. Nakano Glenn, G. Chang, & L. R. Forcey (Eds.), *Mothering: Ideology, experience, and agency* (pp. 211–233). New York: Routledge.

Stack, C. (1974). *All our kin: Strategies for survival in a black community.* New York: Harper & Row.

Stegelin, D., & Frankel, J. (1993). Families of lower-income employed mothers. In D. Stegelin & J. Frankel (Eds.), *The employed mother and the family context* (pp. 115–131). New York: Springer.

Thorne, B. (1982). Feminist rethinking of the family: An overview. In B. Thorne with M. Yalom (Eds.), *Rethinking the family: Some feminist questions* (pp. 1–23). New York: Longman.

U.S. Census of Population and Housing. (1990). Summary Tape File 1, Santa Cruz County, CA.

Uttal, L. (1996). Racial safety and cultural maintenance: The child care concerns of employed mothers of color. *Ethnic Studies Review, 19,* 43–59.

Zavella, P. (1997). The tables are turned: Immigration, poverty, and social conflict in California communities. In J. F. Perea (Ed.), *Immigrants out! The new nativism and anti-immigrant impulse in the United States* (pp. 136–161). New York: New York University Press.

Zinsser, C. (1991). *Raised in East Urban: Child care changes in a working-class community.* New York: Teachers College Press.

8
Work-Family Issues of Mothers of Teenage Children

Demie Kurz

The topic of care for children while mothers worked has been neglected for many years. Fortunately, a great deal of attention has been focused on the child care needs of mothers of infants and preschoolers in recent years (Hewlett, 1991). Although it has not received nearly as much attention as day care, the after-school care of children in "middle childhood" or late elementary school is now coming into focus (Belle, 1999; Hofferth, Jankuniene, & Brandon, 2000; Pettit, Laird, Bates, & Dodge, 1997). Researchers have studied different types of self-care arrangements, after-school programs, and child care by mothers at home (Posner & Vandell, 1994; Rosenthal & Vandell, 1996).

However, there has been little attention paid to the after-school hours of children 11–14 years old (early adolescence), and even less to those 14–17 years old (later adolescence) (Belle, 1999). This is undoubtedly because younger children, in contrast to older ones, can do relatively little for themselves. They need a great deal of care all day, and until recently there have been few institutionalized arrangements for their care. In addition, it has been assumed that older children are busy with after-school activities. This is often true, although Furstenberg, Cook, Eccles, Elder, and Sameroff (1998) argue that teenagers from low-income families are much less involved in extracurricular activities than are other teenagers. Also, as I will discuss, teenagers' activities are often time-limited.

What are the needs of younger and older teenagers in the hours after school? There are very few after-school programs in the country beyond fourth or fifth grade (Belle, 1999). Parents—usually mothers—who have to be at work when school is over must decide what their children will do. Go home alone? To friends' houses? To organized activities? Children also have preferences about how they spend their afternoons, and most mothers consider these (Belle, 1999). Older teenagers don't technically need care. Assuming they can be trusted, they can occupy themselves and meet their needs for food and shelter. As will be discussed, however, mothers worry about their younger and older teenagers encountering dangerous situations. According to the Carnegie Council on Adolescent Development (1995), one quarter of youths are extremely vulnerable to multiple high-risk behaviors such as pregnancy, drug use, and school failure, and another quarter are at moderate risk for these behaviors.

© 2000 by Human Sciences Press, Inc. Reprinted from *Qualitative Sociology* Vol. 23, No. 4, pp. 435-451.

This article, based on an interview study, presents data first on mothers' views of the care of their middle school and high school children and then on the strategies they use to accommodate their work schedules to their family lives. In addition, I will discuss policy questions, particularly how the issue of caring for older children relates to the failure of U.S. social policy to support care work. Unfortunately, in U.S. society, child care has too often been thought of as physical care—as filling a time slot. Since older children don't need physical care, they are not viewed as being in need of other kinds of care. In fact, for many mothers, after-school time can provide an opportunity for nurturing family relationships as well as keeping children from harmful situations. Thus, the issue of the care of older children raises the question of how much time we are willing to give to social and emotional connections with older children in families.

The Study

This article presents data from a study of parents of teenagers, their care work, and their paid work. The larger study concerns issues of how mothers raise teenagers today. I have interviewed some fathers, but primarily mothers. Thus far I have interviewed 67 mothers—36 from two random samples of parents of high school–age children in the city of Philadelphia (drawn from public and parochial schools), 15 from a random sample of mothers from a middle-class suburban community (drawn from a high school and a junior high school), and 16 from a snowball sample of mothers of children in private schools in both the city of Philadelphia and its suburbs. The sample is economically diverse. The private school mothers are from upper-income families, the suburban sample is middle-class, and the city samples draw from middle-class, working-class, and poor school districts. Twenty-four percent of the mothers are African American and almost all of the rest are white. The children of the women interviewed range in ages from 2 to 29, with a median of 15. Twenty-two percent (15) are single mothers. The great majority of these women are working at paid jobs: 60% (40) work full-time, 12% (8) work at two part-time jobs, and 21% (14) work part-time. Seven percent are not working.[1]

This article presents data on mothers only. The interviews thus far confirm that, according to mothers' reports, they are the ones who are doing the majority of the care work of raising their children. While the fathers are taking on more household tasks and helping more with child rearing, mothers carry the primary responsibility for these tasks, a pattern which is true nationwide (Coltrane, 1996).

Issues in the Study of After-School Care

The entry of large numbers of mothers into the workplace in recent decades has had a significant impact on family life. According to one estimate, between 1960 and 1986, the time that parents had to spend with children fell dramatically: 10 hours per week for whites and 12 hours for blacks (Fuchs, 1988). Currently, at least 3.5 million children in the United States ages 5 to 12 regularly spend some after-school time unsupervised by adults or older teenagers (Hofferth & Jankuniene, 2000).

Unfortunately, we don't know much about this unsupervised time for younger or older teenage children, although work by Csikszentmihalyi and Larson (1984) and Larson and Richards (1994) has given us some helpful data. In 1984 Csikszentmihalyi and Larson found that adolescents are "seldom in the company of adults" (p. 71) and spend more time with peers than their counterparts in most other cultures (p. 91). They spend half of their waking hours with their peers, in and outside of class, compared with one fifth of their waking hours with the family, only some of which is with parents (p. 71). In 1994, Larson and Richards also found that adolescents spend relatively little time with adults and that the "amount of time children spend with family declines by close to half between fifth and ninth grade" (p. 136). According to them, some of this alone time is positive; it is healthy "down time." For some of this time, however, adolescents in their study report feeling lonely, weak, and sad (p. 101). Larson and Richards and others (Nolen-Hoeksema, Morrow, & Fredrickson, 1993) believe that spending too much time alone can be a sign of trouble, a sign of an adolescent who cannot yet cope with the world and may suffer from depression or low grades (p. 103).

Researchers debate the degree to which teenagers are at risk. Some researchers assume that many teenagers are involved in risky, counterproductive behavior, which they believe has become more prevalent in recent times (Carnegie Council on Adolescent Development, 1995). Others argue that adolescence does not involve as much turmoil and risk as is commonly assumed (Offer & Schonert-Reichl, 1992). Still others argue that risk is a necessary part of adolescence, while also acknowledging that risk-taking can become dangerous (Millstein et al., 1992; Ponton, 1997). Furstenberg et al. (1998) focus on the impact of the neighborhood on the safety of adolescents. They point to the higher risks for adolescents in low-income neighborhoods and the corresponding greater effort that low-income parents must exert to keep their children safe.

Belle (1999) reviews studies of early adolescents' after-school time. On one hand, she argues against the widespread tendency to link risky and disapproved activities to unsupervised after-school time (p. 9); on the other hand, she notes contradictory findings in many studies of younger adolescents about their risks during unsupervised after-school time, with some studies finding no harmful effects on children and others finding harmful effects, particularly when young adolescents spend their unsupervised time away from home. Belle also finds that, like the Furstenberg study, other studies support the fact that "unsupervised after-school time poses particular dangers to children from low-income families" (p. 33).

One of the main issues for parents of teenagers, especially mothers, is how to assess and manage the risks their teenagers face. Mothers feel very responsible for their teenagers and, according to Larson and Richards's data, they are likely to be in better communication with their teenagers and have more emotional connection with teenagers than do their fathers. Larson and Richards's data show that "adolescents typically perceive their mothers to be more empathetic; they more often go to their mothers for social support. Even boys feel their moms are more open to listening, though boys avoid the topic of sex and dating" (1994, p. 136).

This study focuses on the caretaking work mothers do at this stage of their children's lives, particularly their concern for the safety and well-being of their teenagers during after-school hours. Almost all of these mothers worry about their children during this time, as do most parents generally (Belle, 1999). Specifically, I focus on mothers' views of teenagers' after-school time and how many arrange their work lives to accommodate this after-school time. As we will see, some find this difficult. U.S. social policies have given low priority to the family. This leaves mothers, who are held responsible for managing families while also holding down jobs in the workplace, in the difficult position of having to coordinate two systems whose requirements are often at odds with each other. In addition, mothers coordinate work and family schedules with the structure of school life, which is also not organized to accommodate the needs of families.

Mothers' Concerns about Spending Time with Teens after School

The mothers in my sample, like most mothers (Garey, 1999), want and need to do paid work, and they also want to make sure that their adolescent children, both younger and older, are engaged in productive after-school activities. Mothers are particularly concerned with their 11- to 14-year-old children, but they have concerns about their 15- to 17-year-olds as well. In this section, I examine mothers' concerns about their older children's well-being after school. I do not attempt to assess outcomes of mothers' decisions about after-school time or to determine what kind of care is best for teenagers.

After school, many teenagers are involved in activities and are productively occupied. Some of them must be transported to team practices and games and play rehearsals. Mothers must either do this or get others to do it or, if the teenagers are old enough and have access to public transportation or a car, they can transport themselves. Many teenagers are involved in activities that are time-limited, however—a sports season ends, the school play is over—and have periods of time with no activities. Some children, especially, as noted, lower-income ones, are not involved in activities.

Mothers express a number of concerns about their children's situation after the school day is over. First, they mention the opportunity that being home, or in some contact with their teenagers, provides to talk to them. Many mothers believe that their children are more likely to talk when the school day ends, and some want to be there. They want to hear about how their children's day at school went and what their concerns are, and they believe children may not talk about these things later in the day. As one mother of 14-year-old twins said:

> I really like getting home with the girls. That is when they talk. I really like that. If you come home later it's "How was your day?" "Oh, fine."

As another mother said of her 14-year-old daughter:

> You know, I'm really ready to have my own hours. I'm really ready not to come home early from work, not to come home at 4:00 (or 3:45). But that's when they talk. That's when [my daughter] talks. Up until now, she had sports in the afternoon. But she's not playing anything this winter. The other day I heard her telling someone, "Oh, I came

home from school and I felt so bummed out." And my heart sank. But I didn't get home until 6:15.

Another mother (of children 14 and 17) said:

> No one talks about staying home with older children. I think that starting when your child is 11, you should be able to come home from work at 3:00 or whenever your child gets home. That's much more important than being home with children when they are little. I like day care. It's fine that they were in day care all day. But I want to be home with my older children. That's when they talk. That's when you can process things.

The stress that mothers put on talk is more significant than might initially appear. Talking with older children can be difficult. Mothers report that teenagers are moody and that they can't count on when their children will feel like talking to them. Also, teenagers want privacy and keep things to themselves (Larson & Richards, 1994). This is as it should be, and most parents respect this, but it can make getting information difficult. Of course, given the communication patterns of teenagers, there is no guarantee that they will feel like talking with their mothers in the afternoon.

In addition, some mothers speak of the afternoon as providing an opportunity to have individual time with a child or children when they can focus on them, apart from evening and weekend schedules, which are dominated by getting family members to and from their activities, meal preparation, and laundry and other housework. Mothers may particularly want time with children who are going through some social or emotional difficulty of their own, or due to family difficulties . Some need extra support because of a disability or learning problem.

Second, mothers are concerned about their children being alone after school. This is particularly true for mothers who have only one child or for children whose brothers and sisters are not home after school or have grown up and left home. Mothers' concerns about children being alone also vary depending on the child's age, the nature of the child, and their child's preferences. Some mothers don't like leaving children home alone at all and see this in only negative terms, while others are quite comfortable with their children spending time alone. Research shows that some children like going home and having some time alone and that this is often beneficial to them (Belle, 1999). The question for mothers, however, is how much time alone is acceptable? An hour? Two hours? Four hours or longer? For the short term? For the long term?

Mothers don't want their children to be lonely. While many mothers believe that spending time alone is good for children, they worry that too much time alone may result in loneliness and be detrimental. As noted, researchers also have this concern. Mothers also want their children to do productive things, not watch television or be on the Internet all afternoon. They think that if they are home, they can make sure their children are doing homework and, if necessary, help them with their schoolwork or a school project. One mother, who had been working full-time and felt very stressed by the demands of both her family and work responsibilities, took a leave from her job to spend more time with her partner, who was ill, but also to spend more time with her high-school-age daughter, who was failing some of her courses. She found that spending time with her daughter on schoolwork dramatically raised her daughter's grades.

Third, mothers were concerned with monitoring their children's behavior and activities after school. All mothers have some fear about their children's well-being and safety. Mothers view our society as dangerous and view themselves as responsible for protecting their children from harm. Teenagers can fail to perform their best at school or fail courses, drop out of school, become harmed or injured, get in trouble with the law and be sent to prison, or bear a child. All of these things happened to the children of mothers in this sample.

Fear of harm makes mothers constantly watchful. As one mother said, "I never know when the phone is going to ring and something bad is going to happen." Several mothers simply commented, "I worry all the time." Among the things mothers worry about are drugs and sex.

> A girl can get a wrong boyfriend. It can happen overnight. These are scary times. There is so much freedom. When we were growing up, we didn't have AIDS. Now, one mistake can cost you your life. And I heard [of] one kid saying, "Oh well, if you get AIDS, it doesn't kill you for 15 years."

One woman, who wished she could be at home when her 17-year-old son returned from school, said:

> I want to know if my son is at home sleeping with his girlfriend. Even if I call, he could just answer the phone and say, "Fine, fine" (gesturing as if holding a phone in her outstretched arm), and still be sleeping with his girlfriend.

Mothers live with images of danger, including death. Some of their frightening images of what can happen to their children are based on media stories:

> I do worry. Maybe I watch the news too much, and read the paper too much. And I work in the city. You see a lot of crazy people there.

American mothers' concerns are fueled by the "culture of fear": the constant barrage of negative news, greatly exaggerated by those who stand to benefit from an overblown depiction of a social problem (Glassner, 1999). Some mothers' fears are also reinforced by the negative things that have happened to teenagers in their own communities and in their own families. One mother, who lives comfortably in a middle-class suburb, when discussing her feelings about how dangerous life can be for teens, turned and pointed to a picture of a young blonde with a one- or two-year- old daughter:

> Here is a picture of my niece. She died about a year ago of a drug overdose. She had gotten A's in school. My sister did everything, everything she possibly could. There wasn't anything more she could have done. She just had a wild streak.

Both urban and suburban women are very concerned about where their children will go after school. As one suburban woman said:

> I think you need to be around. Too many parents aren't around today for their kids. Kids have too much access to things (and too much being alone). Drugs and drinking are a problem.

Mothers are particularly concerned that their children not be in empty houses. They believe that after school, children find their way to houses where there are no adults present and engage in risky behavior. Some mothers claim that there are more empty houses because of the greater number of women who work. For them, the empty house stands as a symbol of the dangers that lie in wait after school. Almost all mothers are afraid of their teenage children being influenced by "the wrong crowd."

While all mothers are concerned about safety, however, a woman's class and race greatly affect her children's exposure to danger, with suburban neighborhoods considered to be generally safer than cities. City neighborhoods also vary considerably in terms of crime rates and danger, and middle-class white and black city mothers feel safer in their neighborhoods than poorer white and black families, who live in more dangerous neighborhoods. In their study of teenagers in working-class and poor neighborhoods of Philadelphia, Furstenberg et al. (1998) found that parents in poorer neighborhoods had to work much harder than other parents to keep their children safe. Lacking other resources, they had to rely on restrictive rules and practices to protect their children from danger. These researchers found that black parents particularly, regardless of income, were more restrictive of their children, based on their perceptions of danger and high crime rates.

One of the subjects, the 10th-grade daughter of a white working-class woman, whose neighborhood was not considered particularly dangerous, was held up near her house. Fortunately, she was not injured. An African American woman living in a poor neighborhood described how her block has changed in the last few years as older residents have died and their houses have been bought by landlords who don't keep them up. As a result, one end of her block is controlled by drug dealers. She can hear gunshots and worries that the danger will increase in the summer, as people's tempers shorten during the long hot days and nights. She and her husband have coached their children about what to do if they hear gunshots. This mother also memorizes the color of her children's clothes when they leave for school, so that if she hears from the police or on the radio or television that children have been hurt, she will be able to identify them. For the same reasons, another mother takes pains to remember the color of the clothes her daughter is wearing, and the color of the clothes of her daughter's date, before they go out.

African American women express particular fears about raising a black male in our society. When I asked one woman, "What do you worry about most with your kids?" she answered:

> I worry about school, them finishing school, and that they're okay. And with a black male in this society . . . they want to prove themselves. They want to be a man. I'm constantly

telling my son, "If somebody insults you, don't respond back, don't respond back. Walk away. You are your own person. You don't have to prove yourself.

One African American woman talked throughout the interview about "the street" and the children on the street who were likely to steal or otherwise do things that would get them in trouble with the police. She also counsels her son to "stay to yourself, stay away from the crowd," and above all, to stay out of fights. This mother, like many others, fears the bad influence some peers can have.

> The peer pressure is terrible. You can tell them all you want in the house. You can talk all the time until you're blue in the face. But when they go out on the street, the group takes over. What you said isn't there.

Anderson (1990) has described how some young black males, unable to get higher-income jobs that are a sign of manhood in our society, can resort to other, more destructive ways to demonstrate their masculinity.

It is important to reflect on the nature of these mothers' concerns. Their fears about their children's safety are real, particularly those of mothers in dangerous neighborhoods. As for their concerns about children's time alone, one can see these views as reflecting the power of "hegemonic motherhood" (Arendell, 1999) or "traditional motherhood ideology," which is based on externally imposed, outdated norms that make mothers solely responsible for their children and require them to spend almost all of their time with them. Some of these mothers may in fact subscribe wholeheartedly to the motherhood ideology.

On the other hand, one can also view these mothers as "doing the family" (DeVault, 1989), in this case constructing their family lives in response to jobs and school institutions that are inhospitable to the needs and schedules of family life. We have tended to see the times when mothers cannot be with families because of their paid work, family times, such as after school, that are out of sync with the world of work, as time that must be "filled in" or "taken care of." For most mothers, however, these are also times of nurturing their ongoing relationships with their children, and they strive to make these times benefit their families as much as possible. These mothers' concerns raise questions about family life. How much time should family members be together to be a family?

How Mothers Manage Paid Work and the Care of Older Children

In this section, I examine issues mothers face in coordinating their paid work with their older children's after-school time. Given mothers' concerns about time, how do they manage their work schedules? As noted above, almost all of these women do paid work: 60% full-time, 21% part-time, and 12% at two part-time jobs. These mothers share a strong commitment to their work. Like the mothers in Garey's study (1999), they see themselves as both parents and workers, and a high priority for almost all of them is to have some flexibility in their work schedules.

I have divided these mothers into two groups: those working at jobs that give them some flexibility in the afternoon, and those in jobs that do not. In each of these groups I examine what the mothers cite as positive and negative about their work situations. First, I describe the mothers who have tried to build more flexibility into their work schedules during after-school hours, regardless of whether they are full- or part-time. Second are mothers with jobs that require their presence from 9 A.M. to 5 P.M. or longer. It is not possible to determine exactly how many mothers were in each category. Some mothers, particularly the nurses, held jobs that required shifts— day, afternoon and evening, and night—that varied according to the week or week- end. Similarly, the women who held two part-time jobs tended to work 9 A.M. to 5 P.M. some days but not others. This description of mothers' concerns about their work schedules is not an exhaustive list of all the issues these mothers face; rather, it pre- sents some of the concerns they most frequently express.

The first group of mothers have for some time scheduled their work hours so that they can be at home when their children return from school. Some mothers work one part-time job, some two part-time jobs, which they do because it gives them the flexibility they seek. Other mothers have chosen careers or occupations that allow for hours that enable them to be at home when their children return from school, typi- cally women's traditional occupations—substitute teachers, nurses who work some hours on weekends when their husbands can be at home with the children, and those who provide day care in their own home.

These women are pleased with the flexibility that having part of the afternoon at home can give them: to be with their children, transport their children to activities, and catch up on household work. They go to their children's games, pick them up after play practice, get them to doctors' and dentists' appointments, or help them secure supplies or library books for school projects. They participate in school activi- ties and sometimes do volunteer work at their children's schools. Some value the time for helping children in trouble with schoolwork. Some, especially mothers who live in dangerous neighborhoods, feel they get to keep an eye on things.

There are trade-offs for these mothers, however. Some are afraid they will have difficulty returning to mainstream positions in their field. The suburban mothers, especially, spend a lot of after-school time as "chauffeurs," driving their children from one appointment or activity to another, until their children have their drivers' licenses. One suburban mother feels she has to be careful that she doesn't become the "neighborhood Mom." She makes it clear to neighbors who work full-time that she will not be a chauffeur to their children. Also, because they are home more, these mothers can end up doing more of the housework than they would like. This was particularly true for several women whose husbands' jobs had been downsized forc- ing them to spend longer hours at work, and leaving the mothers with little help managing the needs of the family.

Some mothers who work at nine-to-five jobs are trying to reduce their hours or work more flexible hours in order to have more time at home after school as their children leave elementary school and no longer attend after-school or other programs geared for younger children. Most of the women in this group had younger adoles- cent children, ages 11–14. Some of these mothers begin to work at their own busi- nesses from home, and some bargain with their employers for more time at home.

Sally, a physician, is cutting back her hours because, as her children have entered the teenage years, she wants more time to monitor their activities. She feels her son has been spending too much time after school on the Internet and that he has started to show disrespectful behavior toward her and her husband. She will be available for her young teenage children several afternoons a week, and she is going to reduce her weekend work hours. Another professional, a single mother, bargained with her workplace for two afternoons a week at home. Her 12-year-old's after-school program has ended. She will use the time to help him get to all his after-school activities. She also wants to keep an eye on the children he "hangs out" with.

Betty, an African American woman with sons ages 12 and 15, works part-time as a bank teller. Her husband, a chemist, works for a large firm. Betty has become dissatisfied with her job and is going to leave it, because she believes it does not give her enough flexibility for being with her children. She is going to start a daycare business in her home or possibly in another facility, and she plans to hire people to work with the children; she will be the supervisor. Betty believes this type of work will give her more flexibility to be there when her younger son gets home and to facilitate doing household tasks.

> Respondent: I enjoy being here when my younger son gets home. . . . It's when they come in the door that they want to talk. Also, I'd like to pick him up at school. I take him to school, but I can't pick him up.
> DK: What else makes you want to be home more?
> R: Well, when I am working, dinners are later and I come home more stressed out. I don't have as much control over family things. There's a build-up of housework.
> DK: So do you call home from work and see how things are going?
> R: Oh, yes, my younger son calls me as soon as he gets home. And I ask him how was his day? Are the doors locked? If I can't talk, I feel bad, like if I'm with a customer. He might start to tell me something, and I think, oh, no, how am I going to do this?

A teacher and department head at a high school had more difficulty negotiating with her supervisor, a principal whom she feels has not been supportive of her efforts to get more time with her family. Her comments also reflect her frustration at being told she has to meet the needs of other children, while potentially neglecting her own:

> R: I realized I had to start spending more time with my daughter. She needed me. She needed more time from me. She wasn't getting enough. She was acting out. So I've had to cut back at work.
> DK: We think of mothers of young children needing more time at home. But you think it's also true of mothers of older children?
> R: Yes, definitely. I've had to really argue with my supervisor about getting the time I need. And then, I told you I was the chaperon at a school event during the day. And I had to lie about that because I didn't have another personal day. So there I was, and then there were other teachers who had also lied—there we were (sighing disgustedly). Now I'm home when my daughter is home. I've taken a job to be closer to home.

> DK: And you've done that so you can be here and spend more time with her?
>
> R: Yes. You know one thing I really hate? I hate that I get told that I have to be there for other people's children—when I know that I want to be with mine. I want to be there for other people's children. But when I know that my priority is my own children, that's really hard.

These women can gain the flexibility they want for different reasons. The physician has a private practice. The woman starting a daycare business has a husband who is a professional, so she can afford to have a lower income for a while. The single mother has a fairly high-powered professional job and is able to bargain for the right to come home two afternoons a week without too much difficulty. The high school teacher, even though she was a department head, had more difficulty negotiating for additional time at home at the end of the day. Mothers who have lower-status jobs and fewer credentials found it more difficult to gain flexibility in their work hours.

A second group of mothers work nine-to-five or longer. Some have always worked nine-to-five; some only more recently. They have switched to full-time work because they have additional expenses for their older children. Many also stated that they needed extra earnings to pay for their children's college or other postsecondary education. Others, as their children grow older and they anticipate that at some point their children will leave, want to reclaim their work identity and feel they need to increase their work skills to remain competitive.

When possible, these women look for jobs that have some flexibility in scheduling their full-time work and that allow them to use the telephone. They need extra help at home. This can come from husbands, partners, children, other family members, or hired help. Some also use cell phones or beepers at home. For these women, and all of the women in this sample, the more of these factors that are present, the more satisfied they are. Help and cooperation from their husbands and children are particularly important to some of these women. Some have husbands who will help a lot, while others have husbands who will help a little or not at all.

Joan is a woman who recently switched to full-time work. She has in place most of the factors just named and finds the transition to full-time work successful so far. Joan is a white woman who is an R.N. and has a master's degree in nursing. Her children are 21, 15, and 12. The eldest attends a local college and is home on weekends. After working part-time for many years, Joan switched to full-time last year because she needed the money and also, she says, "I am a nurse." This part of her identity is secondary to her identity as a mother, but it is still very important to her, and she hopes to strengthen her credentials in nursing.

Joan, like other mothers, is very committed to her job but is also very concerned about seeing that her children are supervised and properly occupied after school. She feels that right now she is able to spend enough time on her family needs. In the interview, she cited the following factors as important in her ability to balance work and family life. First, she has a lot of flexibility at work. She can adjust her hours and her workload on a day-to-day basis. This means she can leave work early if she needs to. Second, Joan's husband helps with the housework. He is pastor of a church and does other part-time work to supplement his income. This combination enables him to be flexible with his schedule. He can sometimes be home shortly after the children return from school, and he does half of the driving of their two children to their sports events and school activities. Furthermore, Joan enlists the help of her 15-year-old daughter to look after her 12-year-old son. This serves to keep her daughter profitably occupied while having her son supervised. According to Joan, this arrangement works well, but it can create certain conflicts between herself and her daughter.

> My daughter steps into the role of mom with my younger son after school. That's fine, and she accepts the responsibility. After I come home, though, my daughter keeps playing the role of mom and telling my younger son what to do. He says, "Why are you telling me what to do?" Then they have conflicts. They have the most conflicts of the kids right now. They play on one another.

She says she also calls her daughter from work and tells her what to take out of the freezer or put in the stove for dinner. Joan says she uses the phone a lot during the day, to call her children and husband and make decisions about who will get what tasks done.

> I'm on the phone to them six or seven times a day. I talk to my husband maybe once an hour. The beeper is our lifeline—Who's going to pick this one up at the field? Who's going to drive that one there?

Furthermore, Joan's children all have beepers so she can find them at any time of day. This helps if her high-school daughter misses her curfews. At this time, Joan has carefully balanced all aspects of her life, although she is constantly "on the go," managing the household, organizing family events, and driving children to sporting and other activities. She also monitors the behavior of her 15- and 12-year-old children, to make sure they are doing all right. If they were not, she says she would reduce her time at work. While Joan is satisfied with her arrangements, she has stressful days:

> I'm tired sometimes when I come home and I don't want to go on the ballfield for two hours. Or when I walk in the house I don't always want to see four kids playing superintendent, with the house a mess, and my daughter not making dinner after I've been in a traffic jam for $1\frac{1}{2}$ hours.

Mothers who work nine-to-five or longer have tried very hard to get many of the same factors in place as those cited by Joan, in order to successfully manage work and family responsibilities. Several women with full-time professional jobs have hired people to help after school. One has hired a college student to drive her 16- and 12-year-old children to their sports teams. Another has a housekeeper who can get dinner ready and do a lot of the household work and arrangements. These women feel the kind of control Joan has, although they have obtained it by different means. In the suburbs, once teenagers have their drivers' licenses, they can do some of the driving for themselves and their siblings. One mother, who doesn't get home until 7:45 each evening, lamented the fact that the driving age had just been raised in her state. Her

16-year-old daughter, an active member of a swimming team, will have to wait another year until she can drive.

Ann, like Joan, feels she has in place most of the things she needs. She is a single mother with three children, ages 21, 17, and 11. She works as a police officer and is African American. As a single mother, she has no help from a partner, but she maintains she is satisfied with the work-family balance she has created. She credits having help from her children and the use of technology, particularly the telephone.

Ann does not have much flexibility in scheduling her work hours; however, she works only 10 minutes from home. She says she planned this so that she could always come home in case of an emergency. She has a pager and can contact her children at any time. Ann frequently uses the phone to call home, especially in the afternoon, and her children call her when they come home from school. At that time she tells them what she has prepared for them to cook for dinner. Ann says that her children know how to cook a number of things. Her children are usually not alone, and the older ones look after the younger one. This arrangement is particularly helpful when Ann has to work night shifts, which happens every third week. However, she claims that even when she is on these shifts she is still able to balance work and family responsibilities. In fact, they are easier to balance when she is on the night shift.

Some mothers work full-time because of the downsizing of their husbands' job, which can mean that a mother must take on more paid work than she had planned to. This was the case with Carol , a suburban mother who had to get a full-time job some time back because of the reduction in middle management at her husband's former company. She had a master's degree in special education and had planned for a career, but then had four children who became her priority. She was thus committed to getting part-time jobs. Then her husband, a middle manager, lost his job. While she would definitely prefer part-time work, she is glad she found a position as a school counselor that enables her to come home midway through the afternoon.

> DK: So what was your motivation for going back full-time?
> R: It was money. I would have preferred not to work full-time. I think it was
> harder on the older ones. The younger ones had never known anything
> else. And kids always know how to say provoking things and make you
> feel so guilty. I think my older one said, "Oh, Mom, we remember when
> we would come home from school and you would be on the porch waiting
> for us. It was so nice." I would like part-time. But benefits were also key.
> For five years my husband had low-paying jobs, hourly jobs. They didn't
> pay well, but they were time-consuming.

Carol feels she just barely manages to spend enough time with her children and get the housework done. Besides being stressed, she identifies another problem: She and her husband do not have enough time together, which is causing tension in their relationship. Carol feels bad about this, but says that she and her husband will just have to wait to spend more time together.

Poorer women may have to fill in as the family breadwinners more than other women. While any husband can be laid off, working-class and poorer men generally have less job security and are more likely to become injured on the job. One African American woman was taking a leave from work to care for her partner, a house painter who was injured in a fall. Another woman, who was white, had a husband who was also a house painter. He never knew when he was going to be laid off because the small business he worked for did not have enough work. At the time of the interview, her husband had been laid off for several months. This mother had started to work the night shift, which paid her more money, to make up for the loss of her husband's salary. While she actually liked the work on that shift, she felt that having to work at night made it impossible for her to participate in some family events. She was also frequently very tired.

Single parents can experience particularly difficult stresses, due both to not having help from a partner and to their greater likelihood of living in poverty. A serious problem for poorer women is the pay they receive. One single mother, Beth, is unable to work and is on disability due to a mild stroke. Her physician believes that her stroke was brought on by the fact that she had to hold three jobs at once to make ends meet.

Lack of job training can also mean that poorer women do not gain access to higher-paying jobs that may allow for greater flexibility. Several African American women regretted that they had not become RNs instead of nurse's aides. They find their nurse's aides jobs stressful, and they also must work overtime or take a second job to make ends meet. One mother of four did not graduate from high school and can obtain only low-paying jobs, some of which are located in unsafe neighborhoods and involve long commutes. She has tried to work at only part-time jobs, but her husband has been laid off several times, requiring her to get full-time jobs. Now that her children are older, she hopes to finish her high school degree, after which she plans to enroll in a local community college. It seems particularly unjust that poor women, whose children are least safe in their neighborhoods, may end up in jobs that have inflexible hours or, worse, that require them to work long hours or second jobs. In this study, several African-American mothers were under great stress as they worked overtime or at two jobs to earn enough money to support themselves and their families.

Conclusion

Researchers should give more attention to the needs of older children and their mothers. In this article I have discussed mothers' need to spend time with older children and accomplish household tasks as well as do their paid work. We must change how we conceive of care for children—not just as hours for coverage, but as time when relationships and family life are being nurtured. We must also make the multiple aspects of caring for children more visible. Those who wish to improve the quality of family life should come together to educate the public about the need for time and support for family members. As long as this work remains invisible, it will be difficult to create pressure for significant social change. Currently, the need for family time is far too often seen as the problem of individual mothers and families.

Second, mothers express the need for a variety of resources to balance paid work and their family responsibilities. One of the most important is job flexibility. Some mothers find that having flexibility in the afternoon hours increases their ability to manage the household and nurture relationships with older children. As has frequently been suggested, the government should enact legislation mandating greater flexibility at workplaces through the provision of flextime and of part-time work with adequate benefits. The school day should end later and workplaces should close earlier, to close the time gap between the two.

Third, we must continue to work to make it possible for fathers to participate more in family life. Aside from flexible work hours, assistance from husbands and partners was most often cited by mothers as helping them to balance work and family life. This must happen through nonstigmatizing policies that encourage fathers to take more time with their families. Starting from a young age, educational materials should stress gender equity. Boys must be socialized to understand their responsibilities as grown men toward their children.

Finally, social class is too often a neglected dimension of the study of work and family. Women in poverty face particular problems: lower-paying jobs with less flexibility, a greater likelihood that husbands or partners will be laid off, putting the burden of supporting the family on them, a greater likelihood of single parenthood, and extra anxiety and responsibilities resulting from living in a poor neighborhood. Poor mothers face not just a time bind (Hochschild, 1997) but a money bind, which means that families have access to fewer resources to balance work and family. It is critical that we distribute more resources to poor families so parents don't have to work extra jobs to support them. Welfare reform should be strictly monitored to ensure that it is not depriving families of needed time. Furthermore, we must improve the safety of neighborhoods. In the United States, mothers, especially poor ones, carry too much of the burden for our failure to invest in social well-being. Knowing their children are safe would lift a heavy burden off many mothers, particularly poor ones.

Acknowledgments

The author would like to acknowledge the support of the Philadelphia Education Longitudinal Study and the Philadelphia Family Study, Department of Sociology, University of Pennsylvania.

Note

1. These women are employed at higher rates than U.S. women generally. In 1995, 76% of married women with school-age children were in the workforce (U.S. Bureau of the Census 1996, p. 400). Twenty-five percent worked part-time, although because of the way part-time work is measured, many of these women can work up to 85% of a full-time schedule and still be counted as part-time workers (Garey, 1999, p. 56). The higher rates of employment in this sample are undoubtedly due to the fact that these women have older children.

References

Anderson, E. (1990). *Street wise: Race, class, and change in an urban community*. Chicago: University of Chicago Press.

Arendell, T. (1999). *Hegemonic motherhood: Deviancy discourses among employed mothers with school-aged children* (Working Paper No. 9). Berkeley: Center for Working Families, University of California.

Belle, D. (1999). *The after-school lives of children: Alone and with others while parents work.* Mahwah, NJ: Erlbaum.

Carnegie Council on Adolescent Development. (1995). Great transitions: Preparing adolescents for the new century. New York: Carnegie Corporation.

Coltrane, S. (1996). *Family man: Fatherhood, housework, and gender equity.* New York: Oxford University Press.

Csikszentmihalyi, M., & Larson, R. (1984). *Being adolescent.* New York: Basic Books.

DeVault, M. (1989). *Feeding the family: The social organization of caring as gendered work.* Chicago: University of Chicago Press.

Fuchs, V. R. (1988). *Women's quest for economic equality.* Cambridge: Harvard University Press.

Furstenberg, F. F., Cook, T., Eccles, J., Elder, G. H., & Sameroff, A. (1998). *Managing to make it: Urban families and adolescent success.* Chicago: University of Chicago Press.

Garey, A. I. (1999). *Weaving work and motherhood.* Philadelphia: Temple University Press.

Glassner, B. (1999). *The culture of fear: Why Americans are afraid of the wrong things.* New York: Basic Books.

Hewlett, S. A. (1991). *When the bough breaks: The cost of neglecting our children.* New York: Basic Books.

Hochschild, A. (1997). *The time bind: When work becomes home and home becomes work.* New York: Metropolitan Books.

Hofferth, S. L., & Jankuniene, Z. (2000). *Children's after-school activities.* Paper presented at the biennial meeting of the Society for Research on Adolescence, Chicago, March 30–April 2.

Hofferth, S. L., Jankuniene, Z., & Brandon, P. D. (2000, February 28). *Self-care among school-age children* (Working Paper). Ann Arbor: Institute for Social Research, University of Michigan.

Larson, R., & Richards, M. H. (1994). *Divergent realities: The emotional lives of mothers, fathers, and adolescents.* New York: Basic Books.

Millstein, S. G., Irwin, C. E., Adler, N. E., Cohn, L. D., Kegeles, S. M., & Dolcini, M. M. (1992). Health-risk behaviors and health concerns among young adolescents. *Pediatrics, 89,* 422–428.

Nolen-Hoeksema, S., Morrow, J., & Fredrickson, B. L. (1993). Response styles and the duration of episodes of depressed mood. *Journal of Abnormal Psychology, 102,* 20–28.

Offer, D., & Schonert-Reichl, K. (1992). Debunking the myths of adolescence. *Journal of the American Academy of Child and Adolescent Psychiatry, 331,* 1003–1014.

Pettit, G. S., Laird, R. D., Bates, J. E., & Dodge, K. A. (1997). Patterns of after-school care in middle childhood: Risk factors and developmental outcomes. *Merrill-Palmer Quarterly, 43,* 515–538.

Ponton, L. E. (1997). *The romance of risk: Why teenagers do the things they do.* New York: Basic Books.

Posner, J. K., & Vandell, D. C. (1994). Low-income children's after-school care: Are there beneficial effects of after-school programs? *Child Development, 65,* 440–456.

Rosenthal, R., & Vandell, D. L. (1996). Quality of care at school-aged child-care programs: Regulatable features, observed experiences, child perspectives, and parent perspectives. *Child Development, 67,* 2434–2445.

U.S. Bureau of the Census. (1996). *Statistical abstract of the United States, 1996*. Washington, DC: Government Printing Office.

Vandell, D. C., Corasaniti, D. L., & Corasaniti, M. A. (1988). The relation between third graders' after-school care and social, academic, and emotional functioning. *Child Development, 59,* 868–875.

Part Three
Family, Community, and Social Context

It is now widely recognized that the United States contains a remarkable diversity of family forms: single parent families, dual-career couples, three-generation households, lesbian and gay couples, reconstituted families, and childless couples as well as a rapidly dwindling number of "traditional" families made up of an employed husband, a housewife, and biological children. All these family forms, however, are contained within a single household (at least most of the time). The articles in this section broaden the analysis of families and work, even beyond a recognition of diversity within the household, by looking at the networks and communities of family life.

The articles in this section show the ways in which households depend on the help of neighbors, friends, and relatives and, in turn, provide help. They show how family is enacted in community settings. Like the activities that go on inside the household, the activities of the household in relation to neighbors, friends and kin take work. Like the work inside the home, this work tends to be invisible. It is not counted in the Gross Domestic Product and is often denigrated even by those who do it, even when touted as "community building."

The first two articles look at families in precarious positions, families who rely on neighbors, relatives, and friends. In the first of these articles, Mary Pattillo-McCoy observes middle-class African American families. Their middle-class position is fragile in large part because of the penalties of race. Living in communities on the border of poverty, they must confront underfunded schools, poor city services, drugs, and violence in their midst. They manage to maintain a hold on their class positions through support from others they know (and about whom they often harbor mixed feelings) in the community.

Continuing the discussion of teenagers begun in the last section by Kurz, Pattillo-McCoy also examines these families from the point of view of teenagers. She examines the community ties that shape teenagers' experience of family. Reflecting the precariousness of middle-class standing even among these stable African American families, Pattillo-McCoy portrays the intense competition that her young adults feel between the pull of their family and the pull of their peer group. As much as any of the articles we have included here, Pattillo-McCoy forces us to think hard about what we consider the work of the family: If we are prepared to think of parents' efforts to raise children as work, are we also prepared to think of children's efforts to do well in school and reproduce their parents' class position as work?

Pattillo-McCoy shows that the children of Groveland are raised not just by the biological parents living with them but also by kin and neighbors. She insists on the importance of fathers, even those who do not share a household with their children. Indeed, she shows the limits of census counts of households—and female-headed households—which cannot capture the elasticity of families like those in Groveland. These counts capture neither the involvement of fathers nor the extended families ties that do the work to make their middle-class status possible.

The reliance of households on wider networks is central to a number of articles in this section, especially Margaret Nelson's and Naomi Gerstel's. Focusing on white rural single mothers, Nelson examines care work and networks of support. The single mothers Nelson studied, most of them quite poor, depend heavily on the care provided by family and friends. In their relations with other single mothers, they hold tenaciously to a norm—although not always a practice—of reciprocity. In their relations with family and friends who have more privilege, Nelson's single mothers feel less need to reciprocate (at least with equivalent goods and services). They accept a great deal of help but develop a logic that sustains a belief in their own self-sufficiency. Nelson expands our understanding of care work—showing how maintaining relationships of support, developing the capacity to ask for help, and managing life as a single mother are important, but invisible, kinds of work.

In the following article, Gerstel turns to the other side of that reciprocity: the provision rather than the receipt of care. If there is a first shift of paid work and a second shift of domestic work, Gerstel shows that helping relatives and neighbors constitutes a third shift which also consumes a great deal of time and energy.[1] The gender of this third shift is, moreover, as unequal as the second shift of domestic work: "Women provide an average of 50 hours a month giving informal care outside the home, men an average of 20." This is the equivalent of women putting in almost an extra week every month.

However, as women's paid employment increases, especially in jobs resembling men's, their ability (or willingness) to do care work decreases, especially for relatives. Gerstel's findings suggest that the weakening of (traditionally understood) families may weaken the kin networks those families have helped to support in the past. Married women's increased movement into jobs that resemble those of men "begins to sever the 'kin work' that has organized and sustained what remains of the modern extended family."

Not only is gender central to kin networks. So, too, is race. Comparing blacks and whites, Gerstel suggests that the former are more likely to believe that "what goes 'round comes 'round." African Americans, employed or not, spend far more time helping people they know, especially their relatives. This finding is reinforced by other survey research showing that African Americans, like Latinas/Latinos, are more tied to family and expend much more effort helping them.[2] Such racial differences can be explained in part by class differences: Because African Americans are more likely to be poor, they need and give more. However, even as we move up the class structure, people of color still tend to do more—perhaps as Pattillo-McCoy suggests because their attachment to the middle class is more precarious. Caregiving is, as Gerstel writes, "a survival strategy as well as a demanding labor of love."

By moving to the community and the social context in which families are situated, the articles in this volume complicate the notion and location of work and family. Some, like Pattillo-McCoy, Nelson, and Gerstel, move families out of households by concentrating on close relationships within networks. Families, however, are also routinely constituted in more open community settings. Quite regularly, families are on display in public and work to ensure that their display matches the dictates of the good life celebrated by professionals, schools, and entertainment industries. Such efforts are apparent in the aisles of grocery stores, in the windows of homes with their Christmas displays, at school bake sales and PTO meetings. These public displays of family—and the efforts they require—are rarely analyzed. In the final article in this section, Marjorie DeVault makes visible work and family issues in just such a public setting: the community zoo.

Using and developing a broad definition of families, DeVault analyzes activities at the community zoo to show that the work that produces family—"as a distinctive social configuration continually brought into being through people's activities, interactions, and interpretations"—extends beyond the household. It extends into public "workplaces," like zoos and streets, parks and museums. DeVault explores an irony: Families, with the cooperation of strangers around them, coordinate in public places to emphasize their privacy. Attendance at the community zoo becomes a forum to display exclusive family membership.

DeVault echoes a theme common to this section. The kinds of families that men, women, and children produce—and perhaps the very ability to produce a family—depend on resources bound by race and class. While sociologists may analyze families as increasingly heterogeneous and as ostensibly private groupings, DeVault reminds us that public places homogenize conceptions of family experience and obscure alternatives.

Notes

1. Gerstel uses the term *third shift* to refer to the carework that families do; this is a different usage than that employed by Hochschild (1989), where she refers to a third shift as the extra work that must be done to cope with the consequences of increased time on the job and less time for the second shift of family work (like comforting children who are upset because their parents are away at work too much).

2. On African Americans see, e.g., Sarkisian et al. (2000). On Latinas/Latinos, see Gerena et al. (2000).

References

Gerena, M., Sarkisian, N., & Munoz, R. (2000, August). *Detecting distinctions: Latinas, Latinos, and care work*. Paper presented at ASA meeting, CA.

Hochschild, A, with Machung, A. (1989). *The second shift: Working parents and the revolution at home*. New York: Viking.

Sarkisian, N., Gerena, M., and Gerstel, N. (2000, August). *More or less kin: Addressing debates on care work in the African American community*. Paper presented at Conference on Carework: Research, Theory, and Advocacy, Washington, DC.

9
Black Picket Fences

Growing Up in Groveland

Mary Pattillo-McCoy

Editorial Note: Mary Pattillo-McCoy decided to study a middle-class black community because of her experiences growing up in a community much like "Groveland"—"Of my group of neighborhood and school friends, some had children young, were sporadically employed, or were lured into the drug trade, while others had gone to college, or worked steady jobs and earned enough to start a family. We started pretty much at the same place, but we ended up running the full gamut of outcomes. Some now make six figures—and others are 6 feet under. I wanted to understand these divergences."

Studies indicate that although middle-class white children are themselves highly likely to become successful members of the middle class, the same assumption cannot be made about black children. Pattillo-McCoy helps us understand why this is the case, that the reasons do not necessarily have to do with black families themselves, but rather with the neighborhoods and circumstances in which they are forced to live. Her work is unusual in helping us look at work and family issues from the perspective of teenagers as much as from that of parents.

A note about the language used in this selection: Many white Americans rarely hear Black English. Black English is not identical to Standard English; whites, however, make a big mistake if they interpret "different" to mean "inferior." Pattillo-McCoy emphasizes her conscious decision, as an ethnographer, to accurately reproduce the speech of the people she studied. In doing so she emphasizes that many middle-class black Americans are in effect bilingual: "Even though the African American bank receptionist may answer the phone in perfect Standard English, he or she may have a much different linguistic style when in the company of other African Americans." This "code switching" is only one of the many challenges that middle-class African Americans confront.

Growing Up in Groveland

The kin-based branches of the Gibbs family tree spread far and wide in Groveland. The family's trunk—Mr. and Mrs. Gibbs—moved into Groveland in 1961. They raised their six daughters there. Anna Gibbs Morris is one of the three daughters who have chosen to raise their own families in the neighborhood. Last year, Anna Morris's 19-year-old daughter, Neisha, had the family's first great-grandson, Tim Jr. The Morris family represents over 35 years in the neighborhood, with four generations, in one square block.

Much has changed since the Gibbs family moved into Groveland. One such change has been an increase in gang activity. Little Tim's father, Tim Ward Sr., is in a gang, as were many of Neisha Morris's boyfriends before Tim. Drug dealing often goes along with being in gangs. Neisha's mother, Anna, feels both anger and sadness as she watches Neisha's boyfriends fall prey to the fast life.

> I'm so sick of all this shit. 'Cause, you know, Neisha done lost too many friends to all that shit. You know, Neisha just can't take it no more. She lost two boyfriends. And she really took this last one hard. I just hate to see her go through alla that. The first one was like her first boyfriend. You know, he was a nice boy. I liked him. But they just be out there doin' they thang. And they shot him. This last one, Sugar, we just buried. You know she had waited about a year after her first boyfriend and she started seeing this boy Sugar. They shot him in the head. He was in a coma for six months. For the past six months we been goin' to visit that boy in the hospital. We all thought he was gon' pull through. And I really took this second one hard. They done lost ten friends already. Close friends, too. But still, they still choosin' these little boys who [are] out there like that. I mean, they ain't bad people, but they get caught up in all that stuff sellin' drugs.

The Gibbs family vignette illustrates the permanence of many Groveland families through changing surroundings. . . . I elaborate on the local context by focusing on the cohort of adolescents and older youth to which Neisha Morris belongs and examining the range of resources and exposures of this group.

Contextual particularities of black neighborhoods, even black middle-class neighborhoods, fuel consistent racial disparities in social indicators such as educational attainment and performance, marriage and childbearing, and levels of crime and violence. The impact of the unique middle-class black neighborhood works partly through processes of adolescent socialization. Higher poverty rates in black neighborhoods and in black communities beget greater lifestyle diversity within them. Middle-class black youth grow up with friends from a variety of social backgrounds. As a result, middle-class parents have less control over the experiences to which their children will be exposed—less than they would in a more homogeneously middle-class setting. While parents do try to control their children's interactions, other avenues continue to be alluring and enticing for their children. This is Anna Morris's dilemma: that her daughter Neisha, after losing ten friends to violence, is still "choosin' these little boys who [are] out there like that . . . sellin' drugs." While black middle-class youth have a number of resources that smooth the bumps of growing up, they also face unique roadblocks. The possibilities for downward mobility (not to mention violent death) among middle-class black youth as a result of the heterogeneous lifestyles to which they are exposed are reminders of the limited protection that middle-class status provides for African Americans.

Both Street and Descent

Theorizing from his ethnographic research in a number of poor black neighborhoods, Elijah Anderson (1991, 1994) discusses the continuum of lifestyles that exists in such contexts. At the two extremes are "decent" and "street" behaviors. "Decent" families are "loving," "committed to middle-class values," and "willing to sacrifice for their children," whereas the code of the streets revolves around the maintenance of respect, often through violent means (Anderson, 1994). "Street" families are especially prevalent (although not the majority) in poor neighborhoods, and there the code of the streets is the dominant mode of public interaction. Although Anderson's categories are related to one's material class status, "street" and "decent" are not fixed attributes of either poor people or middle-class people. Many poor families practice "decent" behaviors despite formidable material obstacles, and the middle class can act in "street" fashion. As Anderson (1991, p. 375) states, the culture of street families "is characterized by support for and encouragement of an alternative lifestyle that appears highly attractive to many adolescents, regardless of family background."

But Anderson only briefly develops the idea of the malleability of street and decent orientations and the diversity of behaviors at the individual, familial, and community levels. Families and individuals seem to be either street or decent. While decent parents want their children to be able to navigate the streets, they generally shield their children from street influences. In most cases, according to Anderson, street families produce street children and decent families raise decent children. What I aim to do in my discussion of Groveland youth is develop a much more nuanced picture of families, the choices young people make, and their outcomes. A dynamic intermediate position of balancing street and decent lifestyles is a much more common orientation in Groveland than either fully street or fully decent. While the street/decent dichotomy is useful in some ways, I argue that it is inadequate because, in daily practice, most of the "action" is going on in the middle.

The use of Black English and slang by neighborhood residents of all ages is a good example. Most studies of Black English have focused on its use in poor black communities. But as illustrated in various field notes, Black English is also widely used among the children of African American professionals and even among some of the professionals themselves, especially in casual settings. Language in Groveland constitutes a cultural arena where the significance of race is clear; Black English unites African Americans of different classes. Knowing the latest slang word or peppering stories with curse words symbolically maintains middle-class connections to the streets, especially for youth. For example, Tyson Reed explained that he not only had a different *manner* of speaking with his friends from college and his friends from the neighborhood gang; he also had a *separate set of topics* to talk about. "You just gotta know when to speak upon stuff," he advised about the craft of code-switching. But he went on to share how such linguistic maneuvers can also be confusing. "Sometimes now, I be slippin' and be forgettin' who I'm with. Like sometimes I be slippin' when I be with my ghetto-ass friends." Tyson's deliberate code-switching is part of the practice of balancing street and decent orientations that characterizes Groveland youth (and adults).

In black middle-class neighborhoods there are substantial resources to present nonstreet alternatives for young people. At the same time, the streets have a definite appeal to youth traversing the rebellious period of adolescence. And as Anderson (1994, p. 82) points out, being street-savvy "is literally necessary for operating in public." Black middle-class youth interact with friends who embrace components of both street and decent lifestyles, and neighborhood adults set both street and decent examples. Three Groveland youth—Neisha Morris, Tyson Reed, and Charisse Baker—typify the active negotiation of these two lifestyles within their family, peer, school, and neighborhood contexts. Each of these arenas is nestled within the next, going from the most immediate context of the family to a larger look at the neighborhood. All three young people share similar neighborhood exposures, but their schooling, peer, and home lives are very different.

Neisha Morris (whose family opened this chapter), Tyson Reed, and Charisse Baker are connected through family and friendship ties. Neisha has a first cousin named Ray Gibbs who also grew up in Groveland; both are grandchildren in the four-generation Gibbs clan. Ray Gibbs and Tyson are best friends, played football together at Groveland Park, and went to college together. Charisse is more peripheral to this group and probably would not recognize the other two young people on the Groveland street, but she does have a weak tie. Neisha's current boyfriend, Tim Ward, grew up in his grandmother's house two blocks from Charisse's father at the local Catholic school gym. Charisse has a crush on Tim's younger brother—a crush that her father forbids because Tim's younger brother is in and out of jail. Charisse stays informed on the gossip of Tim's relationship with Neisha, although Charisse and Neisha have never met.

Neisha Morris

Neisha's family life can be characterized by the neighborhood-based kin ties described in the first vignette. In addition to her mother's family, Neisha's father also grew up in Groveland, and his family remains in the neighborhood. Neisha's mother, Anna Morris, is a dental assistant, and her father is the supervisor of a South Side park. She has a 9-year-old brother, Nate. Her parents were married for over 15 years. They recently separated because Neisha's father had a drinking problem. Her father's unpredictable and, according to Neisha, "crazy" behavior played an indirect role in Neisha's getting pregnant at age 18. To avoid her father, she moved in with her 19-year-old boyfriend, Tim Ward, at his grandmother's home.

> [My father] was too strict on me. That's when I met Tim and I started spending the night with him every night. I got to the point where I felt like Tim took me away from my father and havin' to come home and havin' to be bothered with that.

When Neisha became pregnant, she returned to her mother's house, bringing her boyfriend along with her. By that time, Neisha's parents had separated. With Mr. Morris out of the household, Tim's income from selling drugs was a welcome help to pay the bills.

The fact that many black middle-class households are just a few steps away from financial hardship is more apparent when there is a sudden shock like Mr. and Mrs. Morris's separation. Together the Morrises made over $40,000, but the bulk of that income was from Mr. Morris's job as a park supervisor. And, as in most black families, income from their jobs was the only means of support in the Morris household.[1]

With Mr. Morris gone, Neisha's mother looked for creative ways to keep the family comfortable.

Neisha's extended family provides both positive supports and examples of negative outcomes. Many of her first cousins who grew up in Groveland run the range of possible current situations. One cousin is in jail in Iowa for assaulting someone who owed him money. Her cousin Ray decided to make some changes in his life after being shot in the stomach. He joined his friend Tyson Reed at Grambling State University, a historically black college in Louisiana. Another cousin graduated from college and is a graphic artist for a downtown design firm. Her closest cousin, Kima, has an informal beauty shop in her grandmother's home to support herself and her 3-year-old daughter.

Among Neisha's closest girlfriends there is somewhat less diversity. All three are young single mothers like Neisha, searching for career direction.

> My close friends—Libra, she's in college. She goes to Chicago State for nursing. Well, all my friends just had kids. So, Trenique's baby is 1. Deshawn is 1. And my friend Roxanne, his birthday is Thursday, so he makin' 1. So it's like Trenique didn't finish at Benton High School 'cause she got pregnant. So she went to school and got her GED. So now she in school to do hair, cosmetology school. And Roxanne, she not working either. She just trying to find out really what she wanna do with herself, you know.

As in most friendships, Neisha and her three girlfriends have much in common in addition to being young mothers.[2] The children's fathers are all in the drug business, as is Neisha's boyfriend, Tim. Drug money fills the gaps between what their parents provide, what public aid and food stamps provide, and what they need to support themselves and their children in the style to which they are accustomed.[3] "I can't take care of me and my son off no aid check, not the way he can take care of us," Neisha commented about the discrepancy between public assistance and her standard of living with her boyfriend's support. "It's like I won't have a lot of the stuff I want because my mother has to take care of her and my brother and this house." Yet Neisha knows she cannot fully rely on the unstable income of a drug dealer. "I got to do stuff for myself 'cause that [drug-dealing] lifestyle, you could have it one day and the next day it could be gone."

For the Morris family, drug money is one of the safety nets that support their once middle-income family. Because of Tim's illegal income, Neisha can avoid welfare, although she does receive food stamps. Mrs. Morris does not approve of Tim's business, but she also does not find it reprehensible. Her opinion of drug dealers was not uniformly negative.

> It all depends on that person, what they do. It all depends on the way they carry theyself. Certain of the things they do I don't see them do. See what I'm sayin'? So what I see of them might be what I like. Maybe what somebody else sees is something different.

Mrs. Morris is content that Neisha's boyfriend does not store drugs in her house and does his business away from her family. What she sees of Tim—his boyish shyness, the encouragement he gives Neisha to go back to school, and his affection toward his son—is what she likes.

The integration and balancing of street and decent orientations is apparent in the Morris family. Mrs. Morris keeps her garden colorful and her lawn meticulously trimmed. The glass table in her living room never had a smudge on it, an impressive feat with children in the house. The commitment to legal work on the part of Anna Morris, and Tim Sr.'s participation in criminal enterprise (which is also hard work) exist simultaneously. Neisha is an unmarried teen mother, but chooses not to receive welfare. The extra money she might get from public assistance would only add unwanted bureaucratic hassles and stigma to her pot of resources. And, as Mrs. Morris stated in the opening vignette, she abhors the violence that accompanies the drug business. Yet she cannot abandon her daughter, and therefore she improvises with various means of keeping the family afloat.

A description of Neisha's schooling similarly depicts the simultaneity of street and decent orientations. Neisha did not attend the local public elementary school. Instead, she was bused to a racially mixed magnet school. "I had some real high scores on my Iowa tests," Neisha remembered. "And they told me to pick another school that I wanted to go to. And that's the school my mother picked, that offered an enrichment program there." Mrs. Morris was proactive in putting her daughter in a challenging academic environment, a clearly decent strategy to facilitate Neisha's future success. However, young people do not always see the benefits their parents are trying to bestow upon them. Neisha could have continued on to the magnet high school that most of her classmates attended, but she was weary of the long commute and wanted to be with her neighborhood friends. She started at one high school and then transferred to Benton.

Benton High School is in Treelawn, a neighborhood with nearly three times the poverty rate and half the median family income as Groveland. Benton is not the closest high school to Neisha's house, but the two closer schools have worse gang problems, and one of them in particular dominated by a rival gang. The Black Mobsters are the dominant gang in Groveland, but they have little clout at the closest two high schools, which is why many Groveland teenagers choose Benton over the closer schools. Even though Benton is designated as a "preparatory academy," so that non-neighborhood students like Neisha, must achieve certain standardized test scores to get in, the overall graduation rate there is only 59%. Neisha described the mix of students at Benton.

> It's a lotta kids that's strictly into that school, strictly into going to school, all types of activities, honors, this and that. But a lotta people just be there to cut classes all day. Just to go to gym and lunch. And sometimes just come to school and don't even go in the building. And they bring down the school, the whole school. So basically it's half and half.

Neisha did graduate from Benton High, but she was not part of the honors group—not because she was not smart but because her attentions turned to her friends and to boys.

The examples set by Neisha's family, schoolmates, and neighborhood friends present various roads for Neisha to travel. Both of her parents worked in stable jobs with good incomes. They remained married for 15 years, until Mrs. Morris could no longer cope with Mr. Morris's drinking. Their home and yard were manicured. Neisha's mother chose a competitive magnet school, but also allowed Neisha to make her own decisions about high school. Of Neisha's neighborhood friends, including her cousins, some went to college and have careers, while others just made it out of high school and have started a family. Many of the young men in Neisha's life are captivated by the fast-money drug business. All of these situations have been affected by the mix of people who live in Groveland.

Tyson Reed

Tyson Reed was a member of the Black Mobsters of Groveland. The leader of the gang took a special interest in him and Neisha's cousin, Ray Gibbs, because of their leadership skills. Tyson spent a few years selling drugs and trading guns as a member of the Black Mobsters. According to Ray, many of his gang friends have "faded or disappeared." Ray elaborated:

> It's probably three things. Well, I should say four things: either in jail, still out here doin' nothin' with theyself, some died and then the other few like us probably trying to do something with theyselves, like go to school or get a job. Just get away.

Tyson and Ray have tried to get away from the gangs and drugs in Groveland by going to Grambling State University together.

Because of the schools Tyson attended, his networks are much more far-reaching than the boundaries of the neighborhood. "You gotta think about it," he instructed.

> I grew up in Groveland, but [I was] always on the West Side. I went to Presley, and kids got bused in to go there, so I knew a lotta people. Then I went to Dayton, kids got bused in to go there. Then I went Down South and went to college, so I had a lotta friends there. Not to mention in between I played football—got a lotta friends—[and] wrestled.

Tyson went to elementary school at Presley Academy, a public magnet school outside of Groveland for which there is a long waiting list. A majority of Presley students perform above national norms on standardized tests. After Presley, Tyson attended Dayton Prep, a public high school in a racially mixed middle-class neighborhood. While Dayton High School has changed over the years, and it is neither as racially mixed nor as middle class as the neighborhood that surrounds it, it continues to send over 85% of its students to 4-year colleges, and it is one of the few Chicago public schools to which college admissions officers from elite universities make regular recruiting visits. The list of magnet schools that Tyson attended was the result of his mother's insistence on a good education. Tyson's mother is a high-ranking official in the Chicago public school system. She had just received her Ph.D. a few weeks before I interviewed Tyson, and he proudly showed off her diploma. His mother's own continued schooling illustrates the stress placed on education in the Reed family.

Tyson's immediate family includes his mother and his twin sister. His father has been out of his life since he was a boy. All of what Tyson had to say about his father was filled with intense anger because of his father's absence. "I know where he at, but I don't wanna fuck with him," Tyson snapped. Even though he does not want a relationship with his father, he explicitly recognizes the problems that arise because of absent parents:

> That's a real problem right there with the black community today, with our kids and stuff. People just don't care. I mean, when the kids [are] young really it's the parents' responsibility, well, duty, to be around 'em. You know, be around they friends, be around your family or whatever. Matter of fact, outta all my friends, I'll say 90% of them either live with their mother or live with their father. Only like 10% of my friends live with both of their parents.

From his own experiences, Tyson is convinced that he would not have gotten involved in gangs or drug dealing if his father had been around.[4]

Tyson also harbors anger at his mother for having a boyfriend who seemed to try to take his father's place. At 22, Tyson has far from a close relationship with his mother, but he is beginning to realize the advantages he has gained from the kind of education his mother provided for him. He talked about this burgeoning appreciation.

> 'Cause you gotta learn how to appreciate stuff you got. I ain't never really appreciated what my mother used to do for me. Like sending me to Presley and Dayton. I ain't never appreciate that until I started to get fucked up a lot, and, you know, I really got on my own. I was like, "Damn, if it wasn't for that I'll be just as dumb as this mufucka over here." You know what I'm saying? Really, when you really think about it, you'on appreciate it 'til it's too late.

Once Tyson began to appreciate it, he started to use it to his advantage. He has just one course to complete to receive his B.A. in criminal justice at Grambling. He has plans to go to law school once he finishes college. In the meantime, he plans to work for the Chicago Board of Education, a job secured through his mother's connections.

Charisse Baker

Because Charisse is the youngest of the three youth, much of her adolescent life is still unfolding. She is 16 and lives with her mother and younger sister, Deanne, across the street from St. Mary's Catholic Church and School. Charisse's mother is a personnel assistant at a Chicago university and is taking classes there to get her bachelor's degree. Mr. Baker is a Chicago firefighter. Although her parents are separated, Charisse sees her father several times a week at the after-school basketball hour that he supervises at St. Mary's gym. He and Charisse's mother are on very good terms, and Charisse has a loving relationship with both parents. Mr. Baker is as active as any parent could be, attending the father/daughter dances at Charisse's high school, never missing a big performance, and visiting his daughters often.

Charisse and her sister are being raised by the neighborhood family in addition to their biological parents. "We [are] real close. Like all our neighbors know us because my dad grew up over here. Since the '60s." Charisse is a third-generation Grovelandite just like Neisha Morris. Her grandparents moved into Groveland with Charisse's then-teenage father when the neighborhood first opened to African Americans. Charisse's parents lived in other neighborhoods when they were first married, only to eventually settle back in Groveland a few houses down from Mr. Baker's parents. Now Charisse is benefiting from the friends her family has made over their years of residence in Groveland, especially the members of St. Mary's Church, who play the role of surrogate parents. When Charisse was in elementary school at St. Mary's, her late paternal grandmother was the school secretary, and so the Baker girls were always under the watchful eye of their grandmother as well as the staff, who were their grandmother's friends. And in the evenings Charisse's mother would bring her and her sister to choir practice, where they accumulated an ensemble of mothers and fathers.

After St. Mary's elementary school, Charisse went on to St. Agnes Catholic High School for girls, her father's choice. St. Agnes is located in a suburb of Chicago and is a solid, integrated Catholic school where 100% of the girls graduate and over 95% go on to college. Many of the students come from lower-middle-class families like the Bakers. Charisse told a story about a recent St. Agnes graduate that illustrated the importance of education at St. Agnes, as well as the economic status of its students.

> I was hearin' about this one girl who went from St. Agnes. She got a full scholarship to Stanford. And she was, you know, she was a minority. She was talkin' about how e'rybody in Stanford drivin' to school with they little Rolls-Royce and Corvettes and she was on her little ten-speed. She was like, "That's okay!" She gettin' her education.

The possibility of a Stanford scholarship, as well as the graduation statistics at St. Agnes, make it easy to understand why Charisse's parents chose it over the closer, and free, Benton High School.[5]

Most of Charisse's close friends went to St. Mary's and now go to St. Agnes with her, but her choice of boyfriends shows modest signs of rebellion. From her father's perspective, the mere fact of having boyfriends is rebellious, but Charisse still manages to have a very full social life when it comes to boys. Many of Charisse's male interests are older than she, and irregularly employed, although some are in and out of school. She meets many of them hanging out at the mall. One evening, members of the church's youth choir sat around talking about their relationships. Charisse cooed while talking about her present boyfriend, who had just graduated from high school but did not have a job and was uncertain about his future. But in the middle of that thought, Charisse spontaneously changed her attentions to a new young man that she had just met. "Charisse changes boyfriends like she changes her clothes," her sister joked, indicating the impetuous nature of adolescent relationships.

While these young men are not in gangs or selling drugs, many of them do not seem to share Charisse's strong career goals and diligence in attaining them. Some of them would not gain the approval of her parents. However, this full list of boyfriends has not clouded Charisse's focus. In her always bubbly, fast-talking manner, she declared:

> Okay, I would like to go the University of Illinois in Champaign-Urbana. I would like to major in marketing, and I'm considering minoring in communications because I talk a lot. And once I get a job, I get stable, then I can pursue a relationship. I'd like to get married, and I want five kids. 'Cause I love children. I really do. I love children.

Charisse has a clear vision for her life—school, marriage, children. The content and order of these plans subscribe to a very traditional life sequence, perhaps more traditional than anyone ever really follows (Rindfuss, Swicegood, & Rosenfeld, 1987). Her parents have made decisions about Charisse's schooling that will prepare her for college, that have instilled in her the Christian values in which they believe, and that have steered her toward a group of like-minded friends.

Yet Charisse's family, friends, and acquaintances are not all angels. "Any of my uncles might be in jail," Charisse responded when asked if she knew anyone in jail. She continued, "I know one uncle I haven't talked to. He could be on parole. And I have a cousin who I know is on parole in Detroit, so he can't see nobody." About her neighbors, Charisse recalled, "I know Harris is in jail. He live around here. You know his brother Big Tim [Neisha's boyfriend]." These relationships show that Charisse is not completely sheltered from a different, perhaps more street-oriented, crowd in either her neighborhood or her family. While Charisse's closest family and friends stress positive behaviors, her larger network provides a more diverse set of experiences and exposures.

Resources and Parental Strategies

Many Groveland parents possess financial, social, and human capital that greatly facilitate parenting, a crucial distinction between them and poor families. All three of these youth—Neisha, Tyson, and Charisse—have familial financial resources that have provided access to private schools, paid for sports equipment and dance lessons, and generated some spending money for movies, the prom, and an occasional trip or vacation. Some of the financial capital of Groveland families goes toward endowing neighborhood institutions. There are thriving local businesses; Groveland Park hosts a full summer day camp and other recreational activities; and many of the churches are well supported. These are the things that money can buy.

The families of these three youth also have important social connections to the work world. Even though Neisha dislikes her father, his job with the Chicago Park District helped her get a summer job. She admitted, "My daddy got a promotion to another park. He's a park supervisor, so I'll probably work at his park, you know, through the summer." Tyson also took advantage of his mother's connections and planned to work for the Chicago Board of Education. And Charisse's younger sister, who was not yet even 16 years old, spent her summers filing and answering phones in her mother's office, while Charisse worked at a beauty salon owned by a family friend and member of St. Mary's Church.

Finally, Groveland parents have valuable skills and knowledge—human capital acquired through both academic and on-the-job training. Parents impart these resources of information and know-how to their children. Tyson's mother's knowledge about and experience with Chicago public education surely influenced her decision to place her son in magnet schools. The fact that she attended college and graduate school no doubt facilitated Tyson's and his sister's college application process and Tyson's aspirations for law school. And because of their white-collar employment, both Neisha's and Charisse's mothers work with computers, fax machines, and other high-tech office equipment. Familiarity with such technology is now a prerequisite for future success. Groveland youth are in many ways privileged because of these resources. They enjoy opportunities that their counterparts in poor black neighborhoods do not.

At the same time, Groveland is not far removed from poor neighborhoods where resources are few, and parental strategies run up against the stubborn obstacles of underfunded and understaffed schools, crumbling housing, poor city services, drugs, and violence. The neighborhood is a part of a larger and poorer black community on Chicago's South Side. Groveland residents share many South Side institutions with other neighborhoods. The character of middle-class black neighborhoods and black communities generally increases the options, many of them deleterious, from which middle-class black youth have to choose during the rebellious adolescent period. Even though parents have strategies for raising their children that include steering them in positive directions, they cannot be with their children at all times. Charisse's covert relationships with boys illustrate that fact. Once parental strategies are chosen and enacted, there is inevitably youthful rebellion against those plans. But the shape of this rebellion cannot go too far outside of the options presented in the young person's social and spatial milieu. Some youth emerge from this course unscathed. On the other hand, many find themselves left with a variety of battle scars—gunshot wounds, criminal records, new babies, subpar educations, or one less friend.[6]

Parental strategies are quite recognizable in the life stories of Neisha, Tyson, and Charisse. All three have clear ideas about what their parents do not want for them. In response to the direct question "What do you think your parents definitely don't want for you?" Charisse and her sister answered in agreement: "No drugs. Drug addicts sittin' in a crack house, standin' on the corner tryin' to get high. With three babies! On welfare." Neisha's answer to the same questions also stressed self-sufficiency. "[My mother] don't want me to be on [public] aid all of my life." Just as they have similar understandings of what their parents want them to avoid, they also have parallel notions of what their parents positively hope for them. As Charisse put it: "That we be successful in whatever we do. So we ain't constantly callin' them for money." Neisha expanded on her parents' hopes for her success:

> I guess they just want me to really basically go to school, have a nice job, be able to take care of me without depending on somebody else to take care of me, you know. [My mother] want me to have a job and food and enjoy the finer things in life instead of just

stayin' around. Like she be sayin' she wish she coulda did this and wish she coulda did that, and I still got all them opportunities. They just want the best for me. Want me to experience more than Second Avenue. You know, more than this right here.

These parental desires are not at all surprising. Most parents want the best for their children, and prosperity is a key component of parents' "decent" plans.

Groveland parents use explicit strategies to encourage their children's expedient development into self-sufficient adults. Charisse's parents raised her in the Catholic church and school; Neisha took every dance class ever offered at Groveland Park, and she still wants to be a dance instructor, with the full support and urging of both parents; and Tyson's mother used magnet schools to get her son a solid education and steer him toward college. For the most part, these strategies were accepted by each youth, and they developed an interest in these activities apart from their parents' master plans. Yet there were some strategies that did not work, and such disagreements illustrate the different conceptions that young people have from their parents about what their lives should look like. During the rebellious period of adolescence, young people draw from both the street and decent activities available in the neighborhood environment.

Adolescent Rebellion in the Neighborhood Context

Tyson Reed resisted being pushed in the direction his mother had planned for him. He talked about the kind of son his mother wanted him to be.

> Without all the gangbanging. Without knowing the people I know. She really ain't want me to play football. She wanted me to be on the swim team. 'Cause I been swimming since I was like 3 months old. So I know how to swim real real good. And she would say, "Well why'on't you get on the swim team?" Yeah, awright, that's gay as hell. I mean, when you think about it, it ain't gay, but you thinkin', I'm a male, 17, 18, 19, 20, whatever. In college, high school. How the hell I look competin', "Oh, I'ma beat you swimmin'." When I can run up and physically hit somebody. You know what I'm sayin'? Or even basketball, you can show your abilities or something. How I look, "Oh, I'm gonna outswim you. I'm faster than you." I mean, even with track, I think it's more manly than swimming.　•

Tyson dismissed his mother's desire for him to be a studious young man on the swim team with sarcastic obstinacy. His mother's suggestion of swimming as the sport of choice indicated to him that she could not possibly understand the masculine pressures he faced as a young black male. His rebellion was based on common adolescent concerns of gender identity and a tough image.

The absence of Tyson's father compounded his search for a masculine identity and further fueled the anger toward his mother. In search of male role models and a fellowship of young men, Tyson got "plugged," Chicago slang for joining a gang. According to Tyson's friend, this was not difficult to do. His friend explained the process of becoming a Black Mobster.

> It start off like two or three people'll join a gang, but you hang with them. So you too close to 'em to let somebody beat up on 'em. Somebody mess with them, you in it. So

now they look at you as, you know what I'm saying, you with 'em. So now they want you, too. But pretty soon you start doing everything they doing. Everything they doing except being plugged. So you just plug. That's when it start.

Tyson's friend's description of getting plugged is a clear illustration that youthful rebellion can go as far as the local options allow. Tyson did not have to search far to get involved in the Black Mobsters and their drug business. There was no elaborate initiation or probationary period. Plugging was as simple as being friends with the boy next door, who was supposedly in a gang, but who himself may have been guilty of the charge only by his association with some other gang-identified friend.[7] The absence of Tyson's father, and then the departure of an uncle to whom he had been close, allowed for Tyson's exploration of delinquent neighborhood networks. His recollection of how he got involved in selling drugs interweaves the search for a male role model and the options offered by the neighborhood.

> When I really needed somebody to teach me something, my uncle was there trying to help me. But after he went to college, and I was still in grammar school by myself, it wasn't nothing else to do but go across the street and do what I had to do. Awright, my mama might have a good job, but if my homey [friend] and me go up across the street and he get on and start sellin' drugs, now you honestly think I'ma sit there? That's a form of peer pressure, I know. But you gon' see him make all that money and y'all together. You there anyway, fuck it. You might as well make you some money. That's how I felt about it, you know.

In Tyson's words, the crossroads that he faced are apparent: a young man, feeling directionless because of his father's and uncle's departures, recognizing that his mother has a good job and that that should count for something in his decision. Yet his friends are a strong force at this point in his life (the peer pressure he referred to), and fast money in the era of hundred-dollar-and-up sneakers has an almost irresistible allure. And most important for this focus on neighborhood context and options, just across the street was the short distance Tyson had to travel to make the decision to sell drugs.

In a neighborhood like Groveland, gangs and drug dealing are attractive to these middle-class youth because of the fast money they are supposed to provide. Although Grovelandites frequently describe the neighborhood as "middle class," being *black* and middle class does not allow for a lot of excess. This was definitely the situation for both Charisse and Neisha, whose families packaged financial resources—sometimes illegal ones in the case of Neisha's family—to pay the bills. To get the extra money to buy the newest sneakers or the latest hairstyle, some Groveland youth turn to the Black Mobsters and their drug business. Still, Tyson's professional mother had a high income and an average-sized family on which to spend it. What could possibly be Tyson's rationale? "Your parents give you what you need and sometime they get you what you want," Tyson explained. "But when you sell drugs, *you* get you what you wanted." Tyson's decision to sell drugs despite his family's financial resources was due in part to consumer greed and in part to the ease of opportunity, which resulted from the diverse neighborhood composition.

The higher poverty rates in black middle-class neighborhoods means that a non-trivial minority of the families in them will have fewer resources to connect their children to positive activities like dance or swimming, and buy for them the status symbols of contemporary youth consumer culture. For this more disadvantaged portion of the population, the economic attraction to selling drugs is the strongest, and the commitment to decent behaviors is most attenuated (Sampson & Wilson, 1995). Middle-class youth—eager to rebel and thrilled by the risks—are often drawn into these orientations. Their parents could provide some luxuries, as Tyson's mother could, but never enough to satisfy the wants of a consumer-minded American adolescent. Many black middle-class youth like Tyson are simultaneously in search of a male peer group and role models, excited by the sheer deviance, and desirous of the flashy material goods that an illegal income can buy. Other youth who are middle class only by the skin of their parents' teeth have clearer economic motives. For all, the opportunity for delinquent rebellion is readily available in Groveland. Tyson did not have to search far to get involved with the "wrong crowd."

Like Tyson's, Neisha's family situation affects the nature of her rebellion, which is in turn circumscribed by the neighborhood milieu. Neisha's parents stayed together for most of her childhood years, provided for her financially, and enrolled her in positive activities, and her extended family continues to give her much love and encouragement. Yet her father's problem with alcohol means that his presence often has negative consequences. When he was still in the household, he was very strict and did not want Neisha on the phone with boys, let alone dating them. Still, Neisha, like Charisse, found a way to have a thriving social life, including boyfriends. Many of the boys Neisha chose, however, have gone a similar route as Tyson. Although Neisha's mother spoke somewhat negatively about her daughter's choice of boyfriends in the opening vignette, she cannot simply forbid Neisha to date them. The reality is more complex than that. Many of Neisha's boyfriends have grown up in Groveland, and Neisha's mother has known many of them for years. She knows where they live. She knows their families. Aside from their seedy involvements, she also knows their friendly, funny, and respectful sides. These longtime neighborhood connections make it difficult to completely sever relationships with the neighborhood delinquents.

For example, Kareem, who holds a leadership position in the Black Mobsters, was one of Neisha's boyfriends before Tim. Kareem, of course, was not *born* a gang member. Before the Black Mobsters, Neisha's mother, aunts, and grandmother all knew Kareem as just another neighborhood kid. Mrs. Morris could not see Kareem and the other young men in the gang as anything but little boys. She said about them, "You know all these little boys, like Kareem and them? I ain't scared of them." How could Mrs. Morris be afraid of Kareem when he had such a humbling crush on her daughter? Neisha described her early neighborhood memories of Kareem and how they eventually started dating.

> Kareem been likin' me for the longest [time], even before he had money. I remember seein' him, he used to be sittin' on some crates over by the store with some ol' raggedy T-shirt on, and his fat just hanging. Well, this was before he had money. He would just keep on talking to me and kept on and kept on. Then, you know, he started makin' money. And

I ain't think he even liked me any more. So, you know, I wasn't even thinkin' about it. But then, he just kept tryin' to get my number and shit. Finally, I just gave it to him. And that nigga called me about a hundred times that day. He just kept tryin' to talk to me. The first time we went out he gave me $300. I was like, "What's this for?" But, you know, I really started likin' him. He really real sweet and all.

Kareem is much more than a high-ranking gang member and drug dealer. He is the fat little boy who sat in front of the store, he is "real sweet," and he has been persistent with his attentions toward Neisha. Neisha could undoubtedly find a boy in the neighborhood not affiliated with the Black Mobsters and not selling drugs, but money and power—no matter their source—have always been aphrodisiacs. The neighborhood cycle that fostered Tyson's entrance into the drug business also operates in Neisha's case by shaping her choices of young men to date.

For both Neisha and Tyson, family strategies and circumstances interact with neighborhood options. Parents use strategies to positively direct their children, but onerous family situations can undermine some of these plans and turn young people's thoughts to what else the neighborhood has to offer. The absence of Tyson's father and the frequent cruelty of Neisha's sent them both looking for alternative avenues on which to mature. Because of the diversity of local lifestyles within Groveland, and because street and decent networks are connected at several family and neighborly junctures, it was not difficult for Tyson to get plugged and for Neisha to be attracted to drug dealers.

Charisse Baker's neighborhood experiences differ in some important ways, although it is more difficult to thoroughly appraise Charisse's choices because she is younger than the other two. A number of factors in Charisse's upbringing converge to provide her parents with considerable control over the choices she can make. Her parents are separated, but her father continues to be a positive daily presence in her life. And Charisse's intense involvement in the church leaves her little time for much else. Describing how she spends her free time, Charisse joked, "I got a lot of stuff that I have to do at the church. But I don't know if that's considered work or free time." She listed her involvements in St. Mary's, including the parish pastoral council, youth group, youth council, gospel choir, and the hospitality committee. The extra parenting that she is subject to by church members makes her all the more accountable for her actions.

Charisse's rebellion, like Neisha's, is through boys. And also like Neisha's, her extended family (church and kin) know many of the residents in Groveland—the good and the bad. But unlike Neisha, whose father pushed her away from the family, Charisse and Deanne have a very good relationship with their father. This bond fortifies their conscience when choosing boyfriends and deciding what to do with them. Charisse's sister, Deanne, recalled her father's talk with her about boys.

I think one good factor is the way my father approached me about boys. He told me when I was like only 6 or 7. I mean, I was thinkin' 'bout boys but I wasn't goin' to a big long extent or nothing. He sat down, and he was like, "Deanne, boys'll tell you anything to get you in the bed." [She laughs as she remembers her father's words.] I'm thinking that's not true. You know, I'm in second grade. I ain't thinkin' along those lines. He specifically said all boys. He said they'd tell you anything. He was like, "They'll tell you they love you. They'll tell you anything to get you in the bed." He was like, "Don't do it!" He had that look on his face like if you do it, you in trouble. So I didn't do it. Later on I found out that all boys aren't bad, but a lot of them are. So I kinda got the hint.

What would happen if either Charisse or her sister were to get pregnant? Charisse answered with hesitation.

I would run away from home 'cause I think my parents would actually try to kill me. I think my daddy would kill me. I'm not being sarcastic at all. I would run away from home. I would call [my friend] Khadija and say, "Khadija, I gotta go." And I'd be up. And that's all seriousness. That's why I ain't doin' nothin', so I'on get nothin'.

Charisse's good relationship with her parents means that their words stick in her mind. While she tests the boundaries when it comes to boyfriends, she is not inclined to disregard altogether her parents' advice and lessons.

The fact that Charisse's parents have been able to more closely supervise and influence her behavior does not mean that the neighborhood context is unimportant. To the contrary, the church is also a part of the neighborhood context, as are the Catholic school and many of the people who participate in these two institutions. Charisse's family's involvement in the church and school integrates positive family and neighborhood contexts for Charisse. Just as Tyson and Neisha were easily introduced to drug dealers and gang members, Charisse's friends come from families who are paying a premium to send their children to Catholic school. The members of St. Mary's parish include Groveland's state representative, an executive at the Coca Cola Company, an executive assistant at the Urban League, entrepreneurs, teachers, and board members of community organizations. They are examples of success for Charisse to follow. At the same time, Tyson and Neisha also have positive role models in family members and friends who also exemplify hard work and success, and Charisse is by no means sheltered from the neighborhood troublemakers. Charisse knows the neighborhood gang members. She grew up with them just as Neisha did. Some of the young men who play basketball at the church gym under her father's supervision are gang members. Since Mr. Baker grew up in Groveland when the gangs were first forming, he knows many of the founding members as well as the younger cohorts. Mr. Baker's familiarity with the gangs gives Charisse and Deanne a certain feeling of security. Deanne commented, "I want people to know that that's my daddy 'cause I'on wanna be messed with or anything." These associations, and her father's lessons, make Charisse streetwise. Yet within her independence exist the rules and limitations that her parents have set for her, guiding her neighborhood relationships.

(Young) Women, (Young) Men, and Families

Neisha and Charisse are teenagers, and Tyson has just passed into his 20s. Their conceptions of sexuality, their personal understanding of gender roles, and their ideas about starting a family are in a crucial stage where what they have observed and learned will soon be translated into their own adult decisions and eventually shape their future. There is a gendered experience of growing up in Groveland. Boys and girls, young men and young women are equal beneficiaries of the resources of their middle-class parents, and so both genders have in front of them similar educational and career options and opportunities. But males and females face very different "street" temptations in the neighborhood context. The different kinds of street behaviors are themselves gendered. Boys and young men join gangs and sell drugs (as Tyson did for the somewhat gendered reason of wanting a father figure), and girls and young women get pregnant before they are married. Of course, the existence of an unwed mother means that there is necessarily an absent father out there somewhere, but this is given less attention than the woman's culpability and even her moral worth. Still, as the stories of these three youth show, street behaviors exist within a range of other activities, aspirations, and values. Neisha has "decent" plans of getting certified to work for the Chicago Park District, moving out of her mother's house (possibly to the suburbs), and raising her son with Tim Sr. She has seriously reflected on the decision she made to have a child at a relatively young age. She remembered her mother's caution: "Havin' this kid is all right, Neisha, but it ain't what you think it's gon' be." Contemplating this point, Neisha concluded, "If I woulda known what I knew now, I woulda waited." What could easily be labeled as a street behavior—i.e., Neisha's out-of-wedlock motherhood—is not nearly as unidimensional as the popular rendition might suggest.

The same point can be made when dissecting the street and decent labels as applied to certain family forms. Stressful family situations have had an impact on the routes that Neisha, Tyson, and Charisse have taken, and will probably continue to influence the choices they make as adults. Neisha's mother and father were married until Neisha was 17 years old, although her father's drinking problem meant that the Morrises were a two-parent family in name only. On the other hand, Charisse's parents separated when she was in elementary school, but her father is perhaps more involved than most fathers-in-residence. Neisha and Charisse take in their parents' experiences and examples, and their views on marriage reflect those examples. Even though the Bakers' marriage did not work out, we heard Charisse's optimism about marriage fitting neatly in her long-range plan of school, marriage, and then lots of children. Neisha, on the other hand, is more hesitant. "We was just talkin' about that a coupla minutes ago," Neisha reported, referring to a conversation she and Tim Sr. had about getting married. She continued with a skeptical "but."

> But we just both still young. I'm only 19, he only 20. So I feel like, you know, ain't no rush to get married. You know, you never know what might happen. You know, we cool for how we are now. And if we still together in a few mo' years, then we gon' get married.

Neisha's comments and those of many others in Groveland point to a tolerance and sometimes a preference for flexible family forms. Social scientists are clear on the facts—that two-parent families almost always have more resources to put toward their children's development, and that children from single-parent homes are at higher risk of dropping out of high school, having a teenage birth, and getting in trouble in school or with the law (Garfinkel & McLanahan, 1986; McLanahan & Sandefur, 1994). But his is a separate question from the family decisions at the local level. Charisse may profess her plans to adhere to the "normative" sequence of family formation, but she also baby-sits for a best friend who doesn't have a husband, and she is not ashamed of her own fatherless household. The majority of family households in Groveland (57%) are headed by a married couple. But this dry demographic does not capture the lived family fluctuations. Both the Bakers and the Morrises are still officially married. Neither couple has undergone a divorce or a legal separation. Mr. Morris moved around the corner to his mother's house, while Mr. Baker moved about a mile away. Neither husband/father is absolutely absent from the household. Who could say for sure what the response was to the "marital status" questions when the census taker came to these homes?

Groveland youth watch these elastic families, growing when a cousin or grandfather moves in and contracting with a husband's or sister's departure. There is no one way to characterize what the youth and adults believe about marriage and families. Words often follow "decent" formulations, but deeds are less dogmatic in their unfolding.[8] Tyson, whose own parents separated when he was very young and who further commented that he had very few models of two-parent families, had mainstream plans for his future family life. "That's why I always said whenever I have some kids or whatever, I'ma stay with one person. I'ma get married one time. And I ain't gon' be trippin'." The test of these beliefs will be his practice. And if his beliefs and his practice contradict one another, is Tyson to be classified as street or decent? Moreover, if "street" connotes some type of dysfunction, then even that label is problematic when applied to nonnuclear families. Mrs. Morris was acting in her children's best interest when she made her husband leave. For her children as well as for her own financial and emotional reasons, she stood by him through years of counseling and periods of sobriety, which were overshadowed by episodes of violence. Her new "female-headed household" status seems quite unlike the dysfunctional connotations of "street." Neisha's out-of-wedlock childbearing may fit more squarely in that category, but even Neisha's situation is affected by family and neighborhood pressures outside her own control. The most important conclusion to draw from these stories is in fact the least satisfying one, because it complicates the neat bipolarity of street and decent, and introduces the multiple realities that families and youth experience that influence their own choices and decisions.

Each of these three youth had some roadblocks along the way, but nevertheless, Tyson will soon graduate from college, Charisse is determined to be successful in business, and Neisha still has aspirations to be a dance instructor and will have much help in raising little Tim. Despite their rebellious forays, their street and decent balancing acts, and the fragility of the collective resources on which they depend, Neisha, Tyson, and Charisse may still be poised to duplicate their parents' middle-class status. While this is true for a good portion of young people growing up in Groveland, there are three important qualifications to such a conclusion.

First, the need to reconcile street and decent lifestyles does not end with adolescence. Adults must also maneuver the neighborhood context, as well as their peer and family relationships. While people may choose their friends, they cannot choose their relatives. Imagine the reunion of Neisha's, Tyson's, or Charisse's extended family. The possible stories and gossip—from which cousin is on parole, to which nephew graduated from college, to whose teenage daughter is pregnant, to where a sister landed a new job—run the gamut of street and decent activities. And since for many Grovelandites the extended family is the unit that makes middle-class status possible, it would be unwise for anyone to distance him- or herself from the family, even if remaining close means interacting with some unsavory characters. In all likelihood, Neisha will be able to do well only with the support of her family and the generosity of their resources. So as youth age, there are certain family imperatives, and similar friendship demands, for staying versed in both street and decent ways of life.[9]

Tyson is most explicitly determined not to lose his street edge as he grows older. Even though he is planning for law school, he stays in touch with his neighborhood friends who are still dabbling in drug dealing and maintaining their membership in the Black Mobsters. He is committed to making his future children street-smart as well. "Even if I do become a big-time lawyer, judge, or whatever, e'rybody ain't gon' be able to do that," Tyson reasoned. "So I can always know somebody in the ghetto. I'ma send my kids right over [to their] uncle such-and-such and cousin such-and-such house to let [them] know how it feel if [they] didn't have this." Negotiating street and decent lifestyles is a continuous process for black middle-class individuals embedded in especially heterogeneous neighborhoods, families, and friendship groups.

A second qualification is that a too optimistic reading of these stories disregards the fact that these three young people are the ones who are persevering. This is especially relevant for Tyson, for whom, as a young black male, mere survival has been an accomplishment. The stories of his friends who have "faded or disappeared" would be less sanguine. Neisha, Tyson, and Charisse in many ways represent those who have been or are still being successful in maneuvering their family, peer, school, and neighborhood environments. These young people are still working toward their parents' desires for them of self-sufficiency and happiness. Those who did not succeed now exist only as stories of lost friends and relatives: "Ms. Strong's daughter is on drugs," or "My cousin Ronnie got killed last year." Such reports are indicators of the uniquely perilous road that black middle-class families traverse in raising children.

And finally, the role of other factors in these young people's lives, such as personal agency and family situations, should not be underestimated. Neisha scored high enough on standardized tests to attend a magnet high school, but instead wanted to be closer to her friends, and so attended a less rigorous school. Tyson could have been his mother's angel by staying out of gangs and joining the swim team, but he chose otherwise. Charisse could still choose not to go on to college as her parents have planned for her, in favor of having a baby because she loves children. Without minimizing the importance of individual agency, the neighborhood context exists above and beyond individual and family circumstances. Choices are made within the limits of what options are presented to these young people, and many delinquent options can be realized in Groveland with great east.

In sum, then, categorizing families as either street families or decent families misses many crucial nuances. The Morris, Reed, and Baker families are all "decent."

Each employs specific strategies to guard against street influences. But is Charisse's family more decent than Neisha's because Neisha's father drinks too much, or because Charisse's family regularly attends church? Is Tyson's family more decent than either Neisha's or Charisse's because his mother holds an advanced degree and a professional job? Is Neisha's family the most decent because they have the best-kept yard, prettiest flowers, and cleanest house? Instead of demonstrating mutually exclusive categories, their lives illustrate how street and decent orientations are tangled together—in the neighborhood context, in the same family, and even within the same person. Tyson is, after all, a gangbanger with a college degree (almost). The simultaneous privileges and continuing constrains faced by the black middle class make the intermediate position of balancing street and decent a most common strategy for negotiating a variety of family situations and local and community-wide settings. All of these neighborhood-level processes operate within a mass-media and consumer-culture environment that intensifies the excitement of rebellious delinquency for youth.

Notes

1. More white families have wealth—both durable and monetary assets—in addition to income, enabling them to get by for longer periods of time when crises hit. Oliver and Shapiro (1995) report that 78.9% of black households, compared with only 38.1% of white households, are in "precarious-resource" circumstances, meaning that they do not have sufficient net worth or financial assets to survive for 3 months at the poverty line if there were a crisis that cut off income. Maintaining a middle-class standard of living (as opposed to survival at the poverty level) is even less feasible for many black households.

2. See Meriwether-de Vries, Burton, and Eggeletion (1996, p. 239) for a discussion of the "peer context" of young mothers. They state, "Embarking on the role of parent limits an adolescent's access to the social world of nonparents because economic and instrumental responsibilities for their offspring frequently preclude the expenditure of precious resources on leisure activities."

3. Edin and Lein (1997, p. 164) briefly discuss the role of men's illegal income in the survival strategies of poor women. They state, "Chronically unemployed fathers who wanted to maintain their claim on their children were powerfully motivated to engage in any kind of work, including work in the underground economy." The Morris family illustrates that such strategies are also used by middle-class families to maintain their standard of living.

4. Tyson's understanding of how delinquency is related to a concentration of single-parent families is supported by empirical evidence. Single-parent families have fewer economic resources and lack the extra pair of eyes important for monitoring youths (McLanahan and Sandefur, 1994; Sampson & Groves, 1989; Steinberg, 1987).

5. Sending children to Catholic school is a common and successful strategy among African Americans to promote upward mobility (Neal, 1997).

6. Sullivan's (1989) comparative research on young males illustrates the importance of the neighborhood context for the shape, content, and duration of youth delinquency. He shows how local employment climates affect the maturing-out process from criminal activity. In the white neighborhood Sullivan studied, young men were able to secure union jobs and desist from crime. In the poor black neighborhood, however, no such alternative to crime existed, and young men participated in crime into their young adult years. While this chapter does not examine local employment conditions, it does concentrate on the models for and access to deviant pathways provided by the local milieu.

Of course, not all adolescent socialization takes place within neighborhood boundaries. In addition to geographic neighborhoods, there are "neighborhoods of sociability" that also influence youth (Burton, Price-Spratlen, & Spencer, 1997). Parents do attempt to structure children's neighborhoods of sociability so that they further their own positive parenting goals. However, to the extent that young people have control over their circle of friends, Groveland youth are likely to befriend youth from a variety of family backgrounds because of the composition of Groveland and the surrounding neighborhoods. For example, the fact that Neisha went to high school in the Treelawn neighborhood, where the poverty rate is nearly triple that in Groveland, indicates the large sociability catchment area for black middle-class youth.

7. In *There Are No Children Here*, Alex Hotlowitz (1991) depicts the uncertainties of gang affiliation. For example, Lafayette and his friends took to writing "4CH" (for the Four Corner Hustlers gang) on their papers and on the walls, but they did not seem to be participating in any other behaviors explicitly associated with the gang. Primarily, they were posturing. Were they in a gang or not? Likewise, vague gang-labeling practices doomed one of Lafayette's older friends, Craig, who was shot and killed by agents from the Bureau of Alcohol, Tobacco, and Firearms. In the newspaper accounts, Craig was identified as a gang member even though no one in the neighborhood knew anything of such an affiliation. Law enforcement agents may have a separate set of criteria for gang membership than local residents. This is not to say that there are not initiation rites, or organizational meetings, or rules, bylaws, and mottoes that bind together fellow gang members. Indeed, Grovelandites can easily "read" the color or tilt of someone's hat to identify gang allegiances or recognize a seemingly innocent greeting as reserved for gang insiders. The point is that membership can also be very porous and sometimes impossible to escape if a young person (especially a male) chooses to have friends in a neighborhood where gangs exist.

8. Cultural theorists such as Hannerz (1969) and Swidler (1986) argue that culture is not composed solely of ultimate values, norms, and beliefs, as Kornhauser (1978) would argue. Instead, culture consists of behaviors that are shared within groups, learned by "precept," and modeled in interaction. Hannerz (1969, p. 183) writes, "As we have seen there is much verbalization of mainstream ideals in the ghetto, even from those who often act ghetto-specifically in direct contradiction of these ideals." He goes on to argue that the definition of culture must be broadened to include these behaviors, because culture is largely situational and arises in response and resistance to social, ecological, economic, and political constraints.

9. Stack (1974) elaborates on the importance of the kin network for women especially. Setting up a self-contained nuclear family severs the extended kin bond and imperils the stability of the extended network. Because the concept of the nuclear family indicates that familial resources are restricted to mother-father-children, the extended family is effectively disconnected from the possible gains made by the member now in a nuclear-family relationship. Furthermore, the person who cuts herself off jeopardizes her own ability to draw on those resources in uncertain times, although the networks often welcome back strays. Stack (1974, p. 122) summarizes this dilemma. "The life histories of adults show that the attempts by women to set up separate households with their children and husbands, or boyfriends, are short-lived. Lovers fight, jobs are scarce, houses get condemned, and needs for services among kin arise."

Even more relevant, McAdoo (1978) finds that upward mobility for African Americans does not attenuate kin ties and relationships of reciprocal exchange. Essentially, black middle-class individuals often remain connected to their less fortunate family members and friends. These connections across classes, and often across lifestyles, prompt them to have flexible "street" and "decent" orientations.

References

Anderson, E. (1990). *Streetwise: Race, class, and change in an urban community.* Chicago: University of Chicago Press.

Anderson, E. (1991). Neighborhood effects on teenage pregnancy. In C. Jencks & P. Peterson (Eds.), *The urban underclass* (pp. 375–398). Washington, DC: Brookings Institution.

Anderson, E. (1994). The code of the streets. *Atlanta Monthly, 273,* 80–94.

Burton, L., Price-Spratlen, T., & Spencer, M. B. (1997). On ways of thinking about measuring neighborhoods: Implications for studying context and development outcomes for children. In *Neighborhood poverty: Context and consequences for children.* New York: Russell Sage.

Edin, K., & Lein, L. (1997). *Making ends meet: How single mothers survive welfare and low-wage work.* New York: Russell Sage.

Garfinkel, I., & McLanahan, S.S. (1986). *Single mothers and their children: A new American dilemma.* Washington, DC: Urban Institute Press.

Hannerz, U. (1969). *Soulside: Inquiries into ghetto culture and community.* New York: Columbia University Press.

Kornhauser, R. (1978). *Social sources of delinquency: An appraisal of analytic models.* Chicago: University of Chicago Press.

Kotlowitz, A. (1991). *There are no children here.* New York: Doubleday.

McAdoo, H. P. (1978). Factors related to stability in upwardly mobile black families. *Journal of Marriage and the Family, 40,* 761–776.

McLanahan S. & Sandefur, G. (1994). *Growing up with a single parent: What hurts, what helps.* Cambridge: Harvard University Press.

Merriwether–de Vries, C. Burton, L., & Eggeletion, L. (1996). Early parenting and intergenerational family relationships within African American families. In J. Graber, J. Brooks-Gunn, & A. Peterson (Eds.), *Transitions Through Adolescence.* Mahwah, NJ: Erlbaum.

Neal, D. (1997). The effects of Catholic secondary schooling on educational achievement. *Journal of Labor Economics, 15,* 98–123.

Oliver, M. L., & Shapiro, T. M. (1995). *Black wealth/white wealth: A new perspective on racial inequality.* New York: Routledge.

Rindfuss, R. R., Swicegood, C. G., & Rosenfeld, R. (1987). Disorder in the life course: How common and does it matter? *American Sociological Review, 52,* 785–801.

Sampson, R. J., & Groves, W. B. (1989). Community structure and crime: Testing social-disorganization theory. *American Journal of Sociology, 94,* 774–802.

Sampson, R. J., & Wilson, W. J. (1995). Toward a theory of race, crime, and urban inequality. In J. Hang & R. D. Peterson (Eds.), *Crime and Inequality* (pp. 37–54). Stanford: Stanford University Press.

Stack, C. (1974). *All our kin: Strategies for survival in a black community.* New York: Harper & Row.

Steinberg, L. (1987). Single parents, stepparents, and susceptibility of adolescents to antisocial peer pressure. *Child Development, 58,* 269–275.

Sullivan, M. L. (1989). *"Getting Paid": Youth Crime and Work in the Inner City.* Ithaca, NY: Cornell University Press.

Swidler, A. (1986). Culture in action: Symbols and strategies. *American Sociological Review, 51,* 273–286.

10
Single Mothers and Social Support

The Commitment to, and Retreat from, Reciprocity

Margaret K. Nelson

For more than 25 years, Carol Stack's *All Our Kin* (1974) has shaped ideas about how survival strategies of poor, single mothers are based on relationships of exchange. A central theme in that analysis is that the give-and-take in these relationships can be understood within the anthropological perspective of the gift: Giving carries with it the obligation to reciprocate, an obligation enforced by "kin and community sanctions" (p. 14). The idea that social networks operate on the basis of reciprocity is now a well-worn, if often underexamined, assumption.[1]

The distinctiveness of the population, community, and even the time of stable welfare[2] in which Stack undertook her research raises questions about the extent to which similar relationships of mutual support would be found in areas where single mothers are white, live in the small villages and towns of a rural state, and have access to relationships with those who have greater resources than their own. Although single mothers living exclusively in rural areas are less frequently the target of scholarly investigation than are those in urban communities (for exceptions, see Schein, 1995; and Wijnberg & Reding, 1999), relationships of mutual support in the countryside are frequently romanticized. The "fictive kin" of Stack's research stands next to the barn raising as, if not a scholarly icon, a cultural one.

A substantial body of quantitative research offers more skepticism about the degree to which those in need can rely on others for support in getting by. Using a somewhat narrow definition of support networks—living in an extended family situation, receiving at least half of her income from someone other than her husband, or getting unpaid child care—Hogan, Hao, and Parish (1990, p. 810) found that although the majority of single mothers participate in a support network, "substantial proportions of single mothers fall outside such informal support systems." In a later study, limited to intergenerational support, Hogan, Eggebeen, and Clogg (1993, pp. 1444–1445) found that while unmarried mothers more often receive support from their parents than do their married peers, less than half of the single mothers receive significant amounts of this support and that "parents in poverty are significantly less likely than persons with higher incomes to be involved in either the giving or receiving of support." Roschelle (1997) similarly offers a contemporary challenge to research which claims that social support is prevalent and can mitigate against the deleterious effects of poverty (see, e.g., Stack, 1974; Allen, 1979; McAdoo, 1980) when she asserts that the "informal social support networks typically found in minority communities are not as pervasive as they were in the past" (p. xi).

Most of the quantitative studies cannot explore the issue of reciprocity. Roschelle, for example, acknowledges that her data do not allow a determination of whether "the individuals giving help to respondents are the same individuals who are also receiving that help." By focusing exclusively on intergenerational exchange, however, Hogan, Eggebeen, and Clogg (1993, p. 1455) do examine reciprocity, and they report mixed results: "Nearly half of all persons receiving intergenerational support also give support. The others do not." However, even those quantitative studies that do examine exchanges between partners in a relationship (and thus explore reciprocity to a limited extent) neither assess the quantity of goods given or received (but simply record presence or absence of giving or receiving) nor consider whether their definitions of reciprocity are shared by the actors.

Indeed, there is good substantive and theoretical reason to believe that individuals might view themselves as being in reciprocal relationships even when the available quantitative data suggest that they are net recipients. First, quantitative data cannot get at the subtlety of exchange relationships. As theorists have noted (Malinowski, 1926; Mauss, 1954; Gouldner, 1960; Levi-Strauss, 1969; Sahlins, 1972; Homans, 1974), gratitude, dependence, loyalty, and deference might serve as items of reciprocation, and these are notoriously difficult to measure. Second, the time span in most studies is quite limited. They may draw on reports of items given and received within the recent past; thus they are more likely to measure what Sahlins (1972, pp. 195–196) defines as balanced reciprocity, where "relations between people are disrupted by a failure to reciprocate within limited time and equivalence leeways" rather than what he calls "generalized reciprocity" where "the material flow is sustained by prevailing social relations" and the "expectation of reciprocity is indefinite." Some of the single mothers identified as net recipients by Hogan, Eggebeen, and Clogg (1993) might understand their current receipt of goods and services as repayment for gifts offered in the past or even as obligations they expect to fulfill. sometime in the future. They might also view themselves as net givers because the items they consider relevant to an exchange had not been measured in that study. Finally, a body of research has shown that individuals often report giving more than they receive (Komter, 1996) and that this may result from what Pahl (1984, p. 25) terms "the general concern of people not to appear too dependent on others." Even among families, where Sahlins would argue that generalized reciprocity applies, Finch and Mason (1993, p. 172) note that "people try to keep a balance between dependence and independence" in their relationships and that "[s]ome very fine calculations (which of course may not be successful) take place to try to ensure that no one becomes a net giver or net receiver, or is beholden to someone else."

In short, while Stack's (1974) research suggests that reciprocity is the norm among bounded communities of shared poverty, where what each individual has is available for all to see, her study leaves open the question of whether reciprocity is also required by those who live in quite different circumstances. The quantitative data suggest not only that support may be less available than has been assumed in the past but that, at least insofar as flows can be measured, balanced reciprocity is not invariably the norm. However, those studies leave open the question of whether "net recipients" understand themselves as such. Finally, both some quantitative research and much theoretical literature would suggest that, in fact, most individuals want to avoid an understanding of themselves as dependent and thus might strive to understand their relationships with others as having achieved some kind of balance.

This article seeks to shed light on at least some of these questions and thus to fill some of the gaps in the existing literature. Most important, I seek to understand the degree to which single mothers in a rural state require reciprocity of themselves and, more specifically, the logic of reciprocity that underlies their giving support to, and accepting support from, others. I also seek to shed light on the work involved in establishing and maintaining social support. In what follows, I first describe the setting for this research and the sample of single mothers from whom data were collected. The main body of the article is divided into two sections. In the first (and larger) I suggest that single mothers believe that balanced reciprocity should be the norm in their exchange relationships, but that they use a different understanding of the requirements of balance among different groups of people as distinguished by need and degree of familiarity.[3] In the second section I analyze the work involved in maintaining relationships of dependence and mutuality. In the conclusion I reflect on some features of the findings and consider the degree to which they can be generalized.

Methods

This study is based on interviews with 39 single mothers with at least one child under the age of 18. Initially, I located respondents through a variety of techniques such as placing notices about the research in the State Department of Health office (which handles the WIC program), at a local Parent-Child Center (a resource for young mothers and their children), and at various day care centers. Those who agreed to be interviewed were then asked to provide the names of other single mothers. The snowball sample technique was particularly appropriate for this study because it allowed my research assistants and me to interview women involved in the same networks of social support. All interviews were conducted in Vermont.

Setting

The growth in the number of single-parent families in the United States as a whole— as well as in other countries (Burns and Scott, 1994)—is a well established fact. Vermont is no exception. While an image of stable white families predominating in rural areas proves to be correct about the past, by 1990 rural areas were catching up with the rest of the country in the breakdown of the "traditional" family structure (McGranahan, 1994). As is the case elsewhere, Vermont's families headed by women are highly likely to be poor even though the majority of them are white.[4] In 1990, when 12.3% of all persons in Vermont lived in a family consisting of a female head of household and her children, almost half (42%) of the state's poor consisted of those very female heads of families and their children (Livingston & McCrate, 1993, p. 6).[5] In 1995, when the median income for all Vermont families was $44,000 (slightly above the median for all U.S. families), the median income for single mothers with children was only slightly more than a third of that—a paltry $16,000 (Institute for Women's Policy Research, 1998).

Sample

Like single mothers in the United States in general, the women interviewed in this study were quite poor, although their median family income ($20,000) stood somewhat above that found by the Institute for Women's Policy Research study 4 years earlier. (Family incomes ranged from $6,600 to $45,000.) Of the 39 women, 18 had one child, 11 had two children, and the remainder had three or more. At the time of the interview, the women ranged in age from 20 to 49 with a median age of 36; at the time at which they first gave birth or adopted a child, the women ranged in age from 17 to 40 with a median age of 24. Five of the women held no job and relied on a package of state supports (including ANFC,[6] food stamps, and Medicaid), nine of the women had some combination of part-time work and state support, and the remaining 25 relied on their own earnings and/or support from others (including child support) but received no assistance from the state. Three quarters of the women had previously been married (although not in all cases to the father of their child or children); the remaining nine women had never been married. All but five of the women lived alone with their children: three lived with a domestic partner (two with men; one with another woman);[7] one lived with another single woman and her children; and one had some other adult relative living in the household on a temporary basis. Although all of the women were white, three were raising children who were not white: One was living with her adopted Chinese daughter; two had given birth to biracial children.

Data Collection

The interviews generally lasted at least two hours; they were all taped, and the tapes were subsequently transcribed. All interviews used an interview guide and followed essentially the same format adapted to special circumstances and the flow of information. The women were asked a series of questions about their background (education, marital history, age at which they had their first child), their current living situation (who lived in the household, whether they owned or rented), and sources of income (jobs, reliance on means-tested programs, child support).

The women were also asked about access to different kinds of material and emotional support that might be necessary in the course of daily life: transportation, home repairs, financial assistance (both small and large sums), child care, and comfort or emotional support. More specifically, the women were asked whether they ever needed any of these kinds of assistance and whether they had in fact asked for assistance when it was needed. If they had requested assistance, they were then encouraged to discuss further the situation in which they had done so, to specify whom they had asked (and why), and to indicate whether the requested assistance had been received. Follow-up questions probed their feelings about receiving help and their sense of obligation to make a return gesture to those who gave them assistance. (If they did not receive help when they had asked, they were asked about their feelings about that refusal.) They were also questioned about times they needed help and did not request it.

In addition, respondents were asked to describe in more detail their relationships with individuals they named as being members of their support networks by specifying what was given to and what was received from each named person. Toward the end of the interview, the respondents were asked a set of general questions about giving and receiving which were not attached to relationships with specific individuals but probed their broader expectations about what it was appropriate to ask from, and what it was appropriate to give to, extended family members, neighborhoods, and the broader communities in which they lived.

As many of the following quotes illustrate, respondents found the interview questions thought-provoking. Although their responses make it clear that they did have "policies" to manage their exchange relationships—the logics of reciprocity discussed here—they might never have articulated these policies, to themselves or others, prior to the interview.

The Commitment to, and Retreat from, Reciprocity

Given the substantial body of theoretical scholarship which argues that reciprocity both initiates and sustains relationships, it is not surprising that the single mothers interviewed for this study expressed a strong verbal commitment to this notion.

Anne Davenport,[8] when asked whether she believed it was important to make returns for assistance received, responded, "I try really hard to . . . reciprocate [to my friends]; same with my family. I always feel obligated to give back." Similarly, Kate Harrington, when asked about her feelings about receiving assistance, said, "It's okay if we can do a barter thing—like, I would like to be able to do something for the people who help me with child care." Janet Linden said she preferred that her requests operated as "a two-way street" and that "if it turned out not to be after a couple of requests" she "would probably hesitate to request again." And Maria Nash said that when people did something for her, she would "try to do something for them. Even if they don't ask me for anything, or they don't need anything, I'll try to do something else for them."

While theory might suggest that compliance with an abstract but nonetheless real cultural norm of reciprocity alone motivates these statements, the interviews suggest that a desire to be—and to be perceived as being—independent and self-sufficient provides an equally strong motivation. Janet Linden, for example, when questioned about what she believed it was appropriate to ask of her friends and family, responded, "You're talking to a real independent person here. I don't ask for much." To the same question Cathy Earl responded, "I like to do things on my own; I like to be self-sufficient, so [asking for help is] not something that I do a lot."

In short, to the extent that single mothers could describe their exchange relationships with others as being governed by the self-imposed expectation that they would give back as much as they had received, they could sustain an image of themselves as independent agents in their own lives rather than dependent on the kindness of others. Indeed, this should come as no surprise. Sustained one-way flows (a feature of what Sahlins [1972] calls "generalized reciprocity") are often preserved for children and for those who are disabled. Self-sufficiency is a valued norm within this community of Vermonters (Nelson and Smith, 1999) as well as among other single mothers (Hertz and Ferguson, 1997).

However, the single mothers in this study faced challenges to both the commitment to balance and to that of independence/self-sufficiency. Because they lived in situations of very real need—whether with respect to the emotional demands of raising a child on their own or with respect to the material demands of getting by on limited incomes—they often found themselves drawing deeply on the resources of others. But unlike the "Flats" described by Stack (1974) or the community of homeless persons described by Dordick (1997), both of which operated on the basis of assumed need and reserved harsh judgment for those who did not reciprocate, these rural single mothers could not assume that others would be understanding of their needs. Indeed, Cathy Earl, who had suggested that she liked to be self-sufficient, indicated that she had arrived at this preference through repeated negative experiences of asking for help in the past.

Interviewer: Has there ever been a time you've needed [financial assistance] and haven't asked?

CE: Oh, all the time.

Interviewer: And why don't you ask?

CE: Because . . . you don't want them to think, "Here's Cathy again, she needs help again," you know, "she just can't make it." [My brothers] don't have any idea what it's like to be poor, to not have savings to fall back on. They've never been in that position. So there's a tendency to judge, even though they do help. They [ask,] "What's wrong with her? Why can't she make it?" They don't have any idea what it's like to be single, to be a woman, to have three kids to support.

An Overview of Three Logics of Reciprocity

Not surprisingly, then, as the women in this study discussed the manner in which they negotiated the details of their daily lives, they relied on a shifting interpretation of the demands of reciprocity (and, indeed, of the demands of self-sufficiency).

These single mothers appear to divide their world of social support into three central groupings and to apply a different logic of reciprocity to each. Those who seem to them to have similar needs—by virtue of shared life circumstances (other single mothers) or comparable situations—are singled out for a narrow kind of balanced reciprocity in which they hold themselves responsible for making exchanges of equivalent material goods and services.

In relationships with those thought to be in a more comfortable position (whether this belief is true or not), the women retain the norm and language of balanced reciprocity while freeing themselves from the obligation to make returns of equivalent material goods and services and sometimes even any return at all. Employing "strategic explanations," to the interviewer and perhaps to themselves, they provide accounts of how a very different kind of give-and-take can still be reckoned as balanced reciprocity. In particular, they either shift their understanding of what they owe to nonmaterial goods—an "economy of gratitude" and "emotion work" (Hochschild, 1983), ties of affiliation, fulfilling another's expectations—or they erase obligation altogether by asserting that the gift (and perhaps their acceptance of it) should be, or is, its own reward.

Finally, with respect to those who stand outside of intimate relationships of friendship or kinship, the single mothers shed the requirement of balanced reciprocity altogether by envisioning a world peopled by those (and here they include themselves) who should (and sometimes do) make spontaneous gestures of pure generosity.

Reciprocity in a Community of Need

Many of the single mothers in this study spoke about their involvement in rich relationships of exchange with other single mothers. As was true of the women interviewed by Stack (1974), the women shared a variety of resources including transportation, child care, small sums of money, and emotional support. And as was true of those women as well, the women in this study used kinship terminology to represent the nature of the bonds they shared with other single mothers. Speaking retrospectively and thus reversing causality—where family follows from obligation rather than creating it—Betsy Black said,

> It's always been clear to me that my friends [who are single mothers] are my family here, because I can count on them more than I can count on my own family often. I mean, I can call up and say, "Look, I need this or I need that," and they're available.

Anne Davenport similarly made a distinction between her relationship with her parents and those in her "created" family to argue that mutual obligation trumps biology:

> I have a group of friends that are absolutely amazing as far as the sacrifices that we make for one another are huge. Easter was a really good example. I had lunch with my parents, which was the traditional lunch with my parents and our minister . . . and then I had dinner with my friends. Somebody asked me what I was doing for Easter, and I said, "I'm having lunch with my parents and I'm having dinner with my real family."

As an illustration for why her friends were now her "real" family, she described how they had provided support at a time of enormous crisis:

> My friend [Joan Meyer] was in a car accident in December and [my son was hurt in the accident]. It was really difficult; it was very stressful; and everybody just took over immediately. I was not going to leave [my son's] side, but I had another child. What was I going to do with him? I had friends that immediately took over. From the day we were in the hospital, until 11 days later when we left, I didn't have to worry about where [my other child] was or who was going to take care of him because they had already made the arrangements. It was done for me.

If kinship terminology helps to bind individuals in trusting relationships, trust does not rely on an assertion of kinship alone. Perhaps even more important to the creation of trust is the assurance that those who live in similar circumstances will understand and be sympathetic about daily needs. After describing people and agencies on whom she depended for support, Kara Lattrell spoke with special warmth about her relationship with her friends Mary and Claudia. In accounting for why they offered each other support and respect, she referred to their common situation—the fact that they were all older single parents:

> You know, we're really in the same boat. I mean, all three of us are single parents and we all have one child. We were all older parents when we had our children; I mean, we weren't 18-year-olds. So I think there's a lot of that common bond . . . you know, sort of a shared life situation. It makes it easy to think about helping each other out.

Other respondents also referred to a "shared life situation" as the reason why other single mothers would understand the strains in their lives and be sympathetic about the *need* for support. Using precisely the same image as did Kara Lattrell—the "same boat"—Anne Davenport said of her friendship with Joan Meyer, the woman who had been in the accident with her son,

> Joan [Meyer]—she's the one we switch kids—we talk four times a day. I think that we really support each other. She's a single mom, and I think we're both in the same boat and we utilize each other in very positive ways. . . . I can trust her. She's not going to judge me or look at me in any different way and respects me for me.

It is perhaps because those perceived as having comparable needs (even if they aren't found in precisely the same boat) can also be relied on to understand why support is necessary, that single mothers expand their networks of a balanced reciprocity of material goods and services to include them. Thus Cathy Earl, who mentioned that she had often done without rather than abase herself before her brothers, explained that she has established a relationship of mutual support with an older woman friend who, she believes, because of her own history, will provide nonjudgmental assistance:

> You are either going to be seen as somebody who just can't make it or [is] always needy, and I think that is the real drawback in asking for help—except for my friends who are in similar situations, like other single mothers. I don't hesitate at all to ask them for help because they know what it's like. And same with Dorothy, the older woman, who lives on a fixed income, who raised her kids on welfare, and knew what it was like to be a single parent. Those are the people who I know that I can go to. They aren't going to judge me, look down on me. They're going to be there because they understand.

Carol Poirier believes herself to be fortunate in her relationship with Jack, an elderly man in her neighborhood who is lonely. "He doesn't have a lot of family. He didn't have any children. His wife's gone." He provides Carol with those vital services which, in a married couple, are often handled by the man in the house:

> He makes sure to get my trash to the dump, you know. He just, he kind of checks in. We don't spend time together, we don't do things together, but if my car didn't start one morning, I'd probably call Jack. . . . He came down when we were in [our new house] and rototilled my garden.

And when she can, and when he asks, Carol offers similar services in return:

> One day he got really sick and he couldn't go out, and he needed something from the store, and he called and said, "Could you go up to the store?" You know, [I do] that kind of stuff [for him]. [I'm] that kind of neighbor.

In *Making Ends Meet,* Edin and Lein (1997) refer to the work of maintaining relationships of interdependence between single mothers relying on welfare and low-wage work and the members of their support networks. (This work will be explored more intensively later.) However, it is important to note here that the relationships I have described are *not* automatic and that becoming a single mother does not ensure entry into a network of like-minded or similarly situated friends. Some single mothers, in fact, know no others in their same situation; others may even avoid this kind of relationship. In addition, each individual who does participate in an intimate relationship of support has to earn her place in that relationship and abide by its implicit rules. These rules include making equivalent returns, being sensitive to individual situations, and not taking advantage of momentary vulnerability.

If the members of these networks might respond to each other's extraordinary needs—as in the case of Anne Davenport's son's car accident—by and large these networks operate on the basis of a fairly balanced exchange of equivalencies within a limited time span even though the language of more generalized reciprocity—what goes 'round comes 'round—prevails. When asked whether she had drawn on support for child care during the past six months, Joan Meyer described how during more routine times the friendship network appeared to operate on a loose formula of "switch-offs":

> I ask my friends. My friends and I do switch-offs [for child care]. That's the only way any of us can afford day care. . . . Anne Davenport and Martha Hickock, we do switch-offs. . . . The other switch-off that I do is switch off with rides. If I'm going to Centerville and I have an appointment, I make it known: "I'm going there—does anybody need a ride? I have to go anyway. It's mandatory." So we try to schedule appointments around the same time frame. . . . So those types of switch-offs we do, and we do car-pooling kids. "Okay, I'm going here. Does anybody need anybody picked up during this time period?"

Similarly, Kara Lattrell described how her friendship with another single mother involved easy-going trades of goods and services:

> We're like the old, across-the-fence kind of neighbors. We trade back and forth, you know? The old roll of toilet paper goes back and forth from house to house. And . . . the cup of sugar, that kind of thing. We've traded child care a little bit, and [Mary] gives me rides sometimes now because she has a car.

She explained that it was "easy to think about helping" out Mary and Claudia, the other single mother in the same boat, as well, because she could assume that what went 'round would, indeed, come 'round:

> Because if it's me, it means that sooner or later I'll help her, and sooner or later Claudia will help me, and then I'll help Mary, and then Claudia will help Mary, and, you know . . .

As the women are questioned more fully about the details of these relationships, however, it becomes clear that emergencies and a loose language of sharing aside, a balanced exchange of equivalencies is expected. On the one hand, Cathy Earl, like Kara Lattrell, said she did not operate on a strict basis of immediate tit for tat:

> Interviewer: Do you try and keep track, for example, with your friends? If you've asked one at one point, do you try and ask someone else another time?
> CE: No, not with my friends, I don't.
> Interviewer: So you pretty much just call who comes to mind first.
> CE: Yeah.

Yet Cathy also suggested that she kept a mental balance sheet:

> Interviewer: If you needed money, for example, and your brothers weren't available to you, what do you think you would do?
> CE: Actually, Sarah has loaned me money before, so I could probably ask her, and Dorothy, for small amounts.
> Interviewer: How do you feel about receiving that kind of support from Sarah or Dorothy?
> CE: Again, actually, I feel okay about that. I always pay them back, and I've done the same for them. Like I say, they know what it's like, so it feels okay.

Anne Davenport also suggested that she tried to maintain balance because she viewed herself as having special obligations to the single mothers in her network:

> Because my group of support also involves single women, single parents, moms . . . I want to make sure that it's reciprocal. Yeah, [all that] comes into the decision: When have I last called them, are they able to handle this right now, what can I do for them in exchange, is there something I could do this week to help them out? I mean, you're always thinking about that.

The rules for survival in these relationships extend beyond maintaining balance. Anne Davenport continued her discussion of implicit norms to explain that her network expected its members would be sensitive to individual situations and would not take advantage of momentary vulnerability:

> I think everybody—community, friends, family—has different things to offer, and I think you need to be mindful that this one friend may be on overload and you cannot ask them

for any more. Joan, for example—I knew she was tired. I knew she was in pain from the accident. It wasn't like I was going to call her up and say, "Hey, want two more kids?" Even though I had a need, I wasn't going to make her life miserable because of it. Being mindful of that and paying attention to what is available and making sure that you're not asking too much, keeping an eye on that [is important].

Failure to abide by these rules can result in being thrust out of a sustaining network. Kate Harrington (about whom more will be related) described how a violation of these norms had broken up her circle of support. In her description she vacillated between taking responsibility for the dissolution of her community and a sense of grievance at being abandoned:

> KH: I've needed a lot of emotional support.
>
> Interviewer: And where does that come from?
>
> KH: Well, it's not [coming] right now. Because my community is kind of dissolving. . . . I'm in transition trying to create a new one.
>
> Interviewer: What are your feelings about asking people for that kind of support?
>
> KH: Well, prior to last week, I was comfortable with it, and now I'm not real comfortable with it because there are some things that have happened, some relationships are going through some tension, so I'm having a lot of . . . well, I'm not asking for it right now. I'm just kind of waiting it out. . . .
>
> Interviewer: How do you decide who you are going to ask for particular kinds of support?
>
> KH: . . . With the emotional support it was my little community of women friends, and I had a couple of real close friends that I could turn to. But that's dissolving, and that's in transition right now. . . . I just had two people really kind of back off of me, and my feeling was I was asking for too much, although realistically I don't believe that I was, but I think that that's what they were feeling, so they backed off. So I just lost two of my support people.

Without privileging either voice, it is worth noting that one of the lost two members of her network—another single mother—believed that Kate had violated all three norms: According to Barbara Quesnel, Kate took more than she gave, was not sensitive to availability, and took advantage of a momentary crisis:

> Interviewer: And Kate is a friend?
>
> BQ: Yes. [in an exasperated tone of voice] [laughs]
>
> Interviewer: Oh! [laughs] And what's given and received in that [relationship]?
>
> BQ: I actually do more giving than she does. She's a taker. . . . [I give her] baby-sitting, emotional support, listening to her victimized life.
>
> Interviewer: So how do you negotiate that relationship?
>
> BQ: I've had a very, very hard time pulling away from people because I don't want to hurt them. But this relationship . . . she's a taker. . . . I make up excuses why I can't do certain things for her, as opposed to being direct. . . . I met her in the crisis of my life. And she was very, very emotion-

ally supportive. I was very vulnerable. And . . . she is a very strong personality, and . . . when I'm with her, I find that I lose my voice. And she's constantly asking things of me, and I have a tendency to say yes when inside . . . it's not really what I want to do.

Negotiating Reciprocity in Relationships with Those More Fortunate

While single mothers appear to find comfort in, and rely heavily on, their equitable and balanced exchanges of material goods and services in their relationships with other single mothers (and with others who have similar needs), they also find themselves in relationships with those they determine to be more fortunate than themselves. Like the single mother friends, these other people (who include family members and friends) offered a full range of goods and services to the respondents, including emotional support, limited financial support, and help with the tasks of daily survival (e.g., transportation and baby-sitting). However, these "others" were more likely than were single mother friends to offer substantial financial support—a form of assistance which is unavailable from those who have little extra themselves. If the elements of these exchanges (that is, those with other people and those with single mother friends) are otherwise the same, the understanding of these relationships is quite different.

Having said as much, it is true that not all relationships with those more privileged (whether economically or by life circumstances) lack *elements* of a reciprocal exchange of goods and services. When possible, single mothers try to sustain the exchange of equivalencies. For example, Joan Meyer listed her mother (in addition to her friends Anne and Martha) as someone with whom she had a "switch-off":

> And my mom helps out quite a bit, which is a godsend, and with her the switch-off is that . . . when they go away, I have to go watch their house and feed their dogs and take care of their birds and do that kind of thing.

However, Joan also admitted, as did other respondents, that she could not always return equivalencies, even to her mother, because, although her mother does child care while Joan does house-sitting, her mother also provides Joan with substantial financial support.

The failure to be able to reciprocate in kind is not surprising. Recall that the single mothers *do* have acute needs and (for the most part) limited material resources with which to make exchanges. This is not to imply that the women saw themselves as dependent. Recall as well that pride in their own self-sufficiency was a significant theme in their self-accounts. In order to accept substantial assistance without assuming dependence, Joan, like the other single mothers interviewed, offered a variety of strategic explanations for their actions.

Reciprocity Through Gratitude, Emotion Work, and Affiliation

As much theoretical writing about reciprocity would suggest, exchange relationships can be balanced by repaying material goods with gratitude, emotional support, and loyalty. What is striking, however, is that it is only with respect to those identified as being more fortunate than themselves that single mothers define these not merely as vital elements of repayment for goods and services received but sometimes as the sole repayment. In asserting that these are sufficient items of exchange in some, but not all of their relationships, the single mothers both make a tacit nod to imbalance and deny it.

A simple economy of gratitude operates in some cases. Phoebe Stark first asserted that her relationships with others were "all pretty reciprocal," and she noted that she preferred it that way because she didn't want to "be obligated to people." Yet she also acknowledged that she was the recipient of gifts for which she incurred debts fulfilled in part by thanking people.

> At Christmas, . . . people are always giving stuff to my kids and I've had to [cut back]. I don't give gifts anymore, except for my immediate family. . . . We make sure that [people who give presents are] thanked, and we are grateful.

She added that in these relationships she viewed emotion work as a valuable item of exchange:

> I might give in other ways. I have a tendency to give in other ways to people, not in material ways—by being there or calling and, you know, checking on people and friends and talking.

Similarly, Kara Lattrell suggested that she recognized a debt to her brother and sister-in-law because "they're supportive of me in my situation. . . . They take my daughter and provide me time to rest and sort of recharge my body." She suggested that she paid off a portion of this perceived debt by sharing her insights:

> I give them support in different ways. I mean, sometimes we we'll talk about a problem and then we'll just discuss it. And I'll listen to them. I guess sometimes they appreciate my insight into things.

In addition to gratitude and emotion work, single mothers view affiliation with their children and, in some cases, with themselves, as available resources to meet the demands of reciprocity. Indeed, children frequently become "pawns" in equations of giving and receiving. Betsy Black simultaneously asserts her rights as a single mother to have care provided by her own mother *and* suggests that she is not left in debt because her mother derives pleasure simply from being with the grandchildren: "Because I'm a single mom, I ask [my mother] to spend time with the kids. . . . And it's a really good experience for the kids, and she loves it, of course." When Kara Lattrell was asked about her brother and sister-in-law "what's given and received in that relationship," she initially responded, "Well, let's see. I probably get more from them than I give, but I give them my kid! That's a lot!" (She then added the comment about listening.) In a somewhat different variation on this theme, Carol Poirier described a relationship between her son, Mark, and an older man, Rob, who had provided a male role model for her son:

He has cared about Mark. He was the rock that Mark—the male strength—that Mark needed, that I guess teenage boys need. He's the one that says, "Get A's, or I'll beat your head in," you know, although you wouldn't believe that he would do that. Of course Mark doesn't get A's and Rob doesn't beat his head in, but he's the one that says, "Don't screw up." Just that form of authority.

When Carol was explicitly asked, "Do you ever feel a sense that you owe him something for giving your son so much?" she first responded with reference to what Rob had received from affiliation with Mark: "No, because I know he's gotten a lot back. And he's got this 16-year-old kid that thinks he walks on water and that feels really, really good." She also suggested that she did feel "obligated to him as my own friend but not as Mark's support" and that affiliation with her could be a resource as satisfactory as affiliation with her child:

> I think sometimes it gives Rob some legitimacy because I tend to lead a normal life. And everybody goes, "Oh, Rob's so off the wall, but, you know, he's friends with Carol, so he's all right." . . . Like yeah, and I think it's helped him that way.

In this comment, Carol asserted that her single parent family was "normal" *and* set up an account sheet in which she had fulfilled her own obligation.

Before moving on to other forms of strategic explanations, it is worth noting that in making these equations, the women are putting value on precisely the kinds of skills and abilities feminist writers on caregiving and emotional work have long valorized (DiLeonardo, 1987; Abel and Nelson, 1990). It might be argued that these equivalencies cheapen the nonmaterial services—the talking, the gratitude, the affiliation—by putting a "price" on them and by making them items in exchange relationships. But it can also be argued that these equations take such activities out of the realm of naturalized abilities and into the realm of skilled work. When women "use" these skills as items of exchange, they are explicitly recognizing their intrinsic worth.

Satisfying the Giver's Expectations

A different but closely related strategic explanation involves drawing on evidence that they have satisfied the giver's expectations. Most simply, the women point to their own survival and the survival of their children as meeting a perceived desire of friends and relatives to ensure the livelihood of those they value.

Although Anne Davenport refers to her friends as her "real family," she has, indeed, been very dependent on her real parents: she has not paid them rent in years or reimbursed them for paying her fuel bill during the previous winter; she uses their car; and they baby-sit on a regular basis. While it is not easy for her to dispel her sense of dependence, she balances the account sheet by pointing to the satisfaction they derive from ensuring that their grandchildren are well-cared for:

> Because I'm an only child and because I have their only grandchildren, it's their way of feeling like they're helping. . . . I also know my parents and know them well enough to know that they would not be happy if they didn't feel like they were doing something and making sure that their grandchildren were taken care of.

In some exchanges, single mothers understand that satisfaction on the part of the giver is linked not just to "survival" but to the expectation of *specific* actions on their part. As will be shown, Betsy Black suggested that her father had learned it was enjoyable to give. She also understands that her father's pleasure is tied to the fact that she is pursuing a goal *he* values:

> My dad's helping me out. . . . I think he thinks it's really important. I know he thinks it's really important. He's very excited that I'm going back [to school]. . . . I'm sort of the only one of the four [children in the family] that has, you know, real interest in going and continuing education.

Amanda Silver makes a similar claim. During the interview she itemized some of the help she had recently received—and for which she was grateful—from members of her family:

> My father recently [helped when] I . . . just had a whole bunch of car trouble, car insurance, all that stuff. . . . My family has been very good, and when they know I'm in trouble, they help. They're very generous. My mother on her own decided that she would write me a check every month for $100 to help with the rent, for example. Or when we go visit my brother, he'll pay for both the kids' tickets and he'll pay for mine. . . . I'm really fortunate. But at the same time that's the one time I did ask for money from my dad.

When asked whether she believed she had an "obligation" to reciprocate to those family members who had helped her out, she responded affirmatively and further noted that she felt that obligation as a persistent pressure tied closely to her family's expectations of her:

> Oh, yes, that's the kicker. I pressure myself a lot about [that]. . . . Bottom line—they really would love to see me get a BA, an MA, a PhD and really really just shine the way they see shine. But I also know that they're cool and they'll be happy if I'm happy. If I get to the place where I'm happy and I'm really loving what I do and taking care of myself the way I want to take care of myself, they are there and they are willing to help me get there. So the money thing, they don't really hold it over my head too much. It's really inside my head. It's constant, though. It's constant.

When probed to explain further how she managed this constant, she responded:

> I just try to get better and better at my life. Just get better and better at my life and get happy. Yeah, I'm existing well. I'm feeding myself. I'm feeding my kids. I'm really proud of that. . . . I guess to fulfill an obligation is just to show them that I am living well and doing well by my kids.

While it is not surprising to find that the discussions of exchanges that rest on the recipient's assumption that the giver will be satisfied by ensuring her survival (and that of her children) are found with reference to relationships with parents and siblings, some single mothers used the same logic in their relationships with friends.

Martha Baldwin was asked, "When things are done for you or given to you, do you feel obligated to do something in return? Is there a sense of keeping balance?" She responded yes and then added that balance was "complicated." To illustrate what she meant, she described her relationship with a friend, Jon, who had not charged for the chiropractic work he had done on her back:

> Jon's decided not to charge me any money! . . . And there's a part of me that is like, oh, God, what can I give back to him! You know? And I've struggled with it and I've said, "Jon, please charge me!" And I've begged him to charge me, you know? And he just has this little twinkle in his eye and laughs at me. . . . One day I said, "Just explain to me why you won't charge me." And he said, "Martha, I don't know exactly why, but I just know I'm not supposed to charge you any money." . . . And I wrote him a card and I said to him that when I was young, my mother often told me that I didn't deserve things. And one of the things that she told me I didn't deserve was my son. . . . And the other thing was that I was undeserving of any financial help. . . . And at one point I realized that I didn't need to do anything [for Jon] other than just love myself. . . .What I was getting at in that card was that his giving to me like that, without my giving him anything back, just really brought all that stuff up about me being undeserving. And I knew that he knew. That's why he was doing it.

In this rendition, as in Amanda Silver's relationship with her family, Martha can repay the obligation by learning to love herself. By viewing herself as deserving, she satisfied the demands of the gift relationship.

The Giver Is Satisfied by Giving

Scholars have pointed to the ways in which employers of domestic help and child care providers often redefine employees in ways designed to minimize the costs of the work to the latter (Rollins, 1985; Romero, 1992). For example, mothers who rely on family day care providers describe those providers in ways that make giving love and daily care part of the individual's personality rather than a service requiring financial reimbursement. As one mother said in describing her day care provider (Nelson, 1990, p. 86), "[She] is just a special person with little kids—it's a mothering, nurturing thing that doesn't stop with her own."

In relationships where the shoe is on the other foot—when the *less* powerful person is in the position of receiving more in the way of assistance than she is able to repay—these same techniques are used to evade responsibility for making an equivalent return. In this new equation, the recipient describes how the giver derives pleasure from an act of generosity and argues that the pleasure thus derived is sufficient to annihilate any further obligation. One single mother says that she is not sure what she offers in her relationship with a downstairs neighbor ("I guess to some extent some emotional support") but that, in a sense, returning something of equivalent value doesn't matter because that convenient neighbor is "an incredibly giving person." Similarly, Amanda Silver can accept presents from her brother because he is "sweet, very sweet" to think of buying her sheets for her new household, and she can accept clothing from her mother because her "mom tends to like to buy [Amanda's daughter] a dress or something." Betsy Black can accept help from her father not only because she is meeting his expectations but because "he's learned that it's delightful to be able to give support." And Janet Linden, who struggles with the fact that she often feels dependent on her mother, can resolve that struggle by emphasizing her mother's (understandable) desire to help:

> My mother is not the kind of person that makes you feel as though you owe her; I think in a way it sort of nourishes her and it's very clear to me that it does, to be able to feel as though she's been helpful. And I can fully understand it because I like to feel as though I've been helpful, too.

Stretching and Resisting Reciprocity

As the women interviewed discuss their relationships with the broader community in which they live, the logic of reciprocity shifts once more. At one level, the women sound as if they believe the world should operate on the basis of an easy flow of balanced reciprocity over time. When questioned about what is appropriate to ask of the community in which she lived, Emily Beyer responded, "I feel it's appropriate to ask as little as you can get away with, give as much as you can, and somewhere along the line everybody gets what they need." Similarly, Anne Davenport, when asked about how important reciprocity was for her, spoke about a world in which there could be long delays between receiving and giving:

> I was in the lobby of the hotel one day and all I had was $60 in my hand and I needed to stay the night at this hotel. This man from Louisiana walks up to me and hands me the $4 that I need. I'm never going to see this person again, but at another point in life I may be able to do the same thing back for somebody else.

At another level, if both of these women do accept the requirement to make returns for gifts received, they acknowledge that the constraints are much looser than those that apply in their more intimate friendships: Emily has only to give what she can; Anne might some day run across a person in the same need she faced in Louisiana.

Some women assert that given their immediate needs, they should be the recipients of generosity without either having to ask or, it appears, returning the favor. Kara Lattrell, for example, tires of always having to be in a position of asking and believes that sometimes she should simply be the recipient of "pure" generosity. In explaining how she arrives at this position, she tells a story about having yelled at her child in public and then being the object of a neighbor's gossip. She examines her anger at that neighbor:

> But then, after a while I got to thinking . . . why am I angry at her? . . . And then it kind of sunk in that the reason why I was angry at her was not because she was talking about it, or not because she noticed it, or not because she was concerned about it, but because what the hell had she ever done to prevent it? And it kind of gets back to the whole thing, I mean, doesn't anybody ever think about giving me a lift every once in a while, or is it all

on me? . . . And so I still have to talk to her about that. . . . And [I want to tell her] that the thing to really look at is not how awful I was that I yelled at my kid, but how, if she doesn't want to be part of the problem, she needs to be part of the solution. And part of the solution means that . . . she has a responsibility to the kids, and having a responsibility to the kids doesn't mean just sort of saying, "Oh, hi, kid. How are you doing?" . . . but really going to a parent and saying, "Hey, you know, I noticed you're a single parent. I'll bet that's pretty stressful." And it's like, "Gee, I guess I could have your little Billy or little Susie come over to my house and play with my kid, like, you know, once a week for a couple of hours. And how would that be? That would really help you out." God! If somebody did that to me, I'd feel like I was in seventh heaven.

Amy Phelps expressed the same sentiment in a less ferocious way:

I just did [my own snow shoveling and plowing] and then eventually [a neighbor offered] to plow and that was nice. I think there's still some people out there that will see that it's just her and her two kids and maybe I can help out. There still are a few nice people like that. And that's happened to me a couple of times, so that's been great. . . . Sometimes I feel kind of weird—like you think I can't do this—and then sometimes, I guess it depends on the day, it's like, "Oh, thank you." Most of the time I don't refuse them. I say, "Thanks so much."

In short, while the single mothers want to see themselves as equal participants in a world where generous giving prevails, they also believe that being a single mother entitles them, at least temporarily, to be on the receiving end of that generosity.

The Work of Maintaining Relationships of Support

The strategic explanations discussed above are sometimes designed to sustain a (self) illusion of independence and reciprocity while the single mothers are in a position of receiving substantial material goods and services they cannot repay in kind. This should not, however, conceal the work involved in developing the capacity to ask for assistance, the efforts that go into trying to maintain reciprocity, and the learning that goes into trying to manage life as a single parent.

As noted previously, many women said that it had been difficult for them to ask for help. Not surprisingly, then, women view both acceptance of their own needs and the acquisition of the skill of seeking out assistance as concrete achievements.

Well, I really think that [asking for help is] something I never did before and I just, as a single parent, I've realized that I have to ask for the support I need. So I've learned to do that. And it may have been hard at first, but I really, at this point, feel like okay, they can say no, you know. And the financial part—that's just a small, small piece of the whole picture. Mostly what I need are [*sic*] support with the kids. And I do ask for help. . . . I just have gotten a lot better at it than I was before, particularly with my dad.

Although Betsy Black was earlier quoted as being convinced that her mother did not mind helping her out, Betsy does recognize that she has expanded her demands and that doing so took special effort on her part:

> It's easier to ask my mom [than other people]. I've gotten better at it. Like I've said, it's easier because I've been practicing. You know, the first time it was what, a couple of days with the kids and then, you know, and then a little more. This summer I'll be at school for three weeks and my mom is going to take the major portion of that.

Even those who have mastered the fine art of asking have to acquire the additional skills of judging who is available, competent, and appropriate for a given need and of maintaining some form of balance in these complex relationships. Janet Linden said,

> It's really hard to trace my thought processes because there's just an image that comes up and when I feel like I need someone to talk to, a face appears, and that's who I call, and I would be real hesitant myself to try to trace what has happened.

Amanda Silver spoke similarly about an intricate process of determining whom she could ask for assistance with different tasks of daily survival:

> I try to decide by checking in and seeing what I need. And if it's a financial thing I call my dad—or my mom. And if it's an issue of like an immediate thing or an immediate crisis or decision I would call a friend. . . . But also, if it's something I feel like my mom just wouldn't get it, I just wouldn't call her. . . . I guess it's pretty intricate . . . because then you're thinking about what is this person's relationship to you. And I guess different parts of me are out there with different people.

As these quotes suggest, Janet and Amanda, like many of their peers, have become adept at judgment and balancing.

Kate Harrington, the woman whose network was dissolving, spoke eloquently about not yet having acquired the necessary skills. While her focus in the quote below is on learning how to be a single mother—what she calls this "24-7, just me"— her comments also make it clear that she has not yet learned about how being a single mother has changed her needs—and thus her relationships within a circle of friends— and that she also has not yet learned what she can give in return for what she asks. As she considered this issue, she both assessed her own gifts and acknowledged the limits of her energies and understanding:

> Well, you know, this is kind of new. You know, before [my daughter, Mira, was born], friendships were friendships and I didn't have as many needs. Since Mira, you know, it's just kind of like trial and error. There's a lot I can do. I'm really good at giving emotional support. You know, I'm good at that. But there's a lot of other things I can do, too, that people—like my one friend didn't accept my offers to help her move. I'm also a professional massage therapist, so I try to do that when I can. . . . I have to be careful because I don't have a lot to give right now. So I have to be careful about how much I ask for because I don't have a lot. I mean, everything is pretty much going into learning how to be a single mother and handling this like 24-7, just me. So I don't have a whole lot to give out.

If Kate believes that she has much to learn, those who have already mastered these skills view an understanding of the demands of reciprocity as part of a growing maturity. Amanda Silver, after describing the intricate process of choosing whom to ask for help, describes this shift in herself:

> More and more so I feel that I reciprocate. I just try to give back. That's tricky sometimes. And as I get older I'm more aware of the balancing. I think when I was younger I just tended to take it for granted, like someone would always be there, always, always, always. And it's just not like that.

Although Amanda is more aware of balancing and sees that as being a part of her own maturation, she and other women make it clear that maintaining support networks requires enormous efforts. Recall how Cathy Earl included an older woman, Dorothy, in her close network because she thought she could empathize with her needs. But this relationship requires a lot of daily maintenance and is not simply there for the asking:

> She can consume a lot of my time, she's quite needy, and sometimes I get frustrated with her because she gets kind of possessive of my time, but she's always been there for me. . . . We have fights. You know, she'll get annoyed at me because I didn't call her, you know, I have to kind of keep constant contact with her, so it's kind of a high-maintenance relationship. If I don't call her every few days, her nose gets a little bent out of joint and, you know, she can be difficult in that respect. In the past I would let it get to me, and I would get annoyed. Now I just kind of [say], "Oh, Dorothy, get over it," or whatever and she does. It's kind of, I've learned how to handle her basically.

Finally, maintaining the strategic explanations may be its own kind of work. A failure to find a way to believe that one has—or can—repaid a gift may result in the temporary termination, or avoidance, of a relationship with an individual with whom one perceives one's self as being in debt:

> I haven't called [my friend Peter] for a long time because . . . I really want to pay [back the money I owe him] and I hate not being able. And he says, I mean, he says over and over and over again, "I know you'll pay it when you can." It's very hard for me. And so I have withdrawn. . . . I haven't talked to him in almost 6 months.

Discussion and Conclusion

The research reported here has shown that, as in other areas, single mothers in a rural state do indeed rely on others for assistance to get by, and that in accepting this help, they operate within the constraints of broadly defined reciprocity. The logic of reciprocity they apply, however, shifts with the (perceived) situation of the giver. Among relationships with others in similar life circumstances and in similar situations of need—that is, primarily, but not exclusively, other single mothers—the women interviewed held to relatively strict norms of return in what could be defined as a balanced reciprocity of goods and services within a relatively short time frame.

Most of the women interviewed for this study, however, had access to relationships with those they deemed more fortunate than themselves. In no position to give back precisely what they had received, single mothers use a logic of reciprocity that allows them to believe in their own self-sufficiency while relying on a great deal of support from others. In addition, they offer a variety of strategic explanations of how they can accept support without creating dependence: They stress their own nonmaterial gifts as items of exchange and, in so doing, recognize implicitly the value of skills frequently naturalized; they assert that their survival and that of their children should be counted as ample repayment; and they make gift-giving its own reward. Finally, in a more abstract vein, they envision a world peopled by those who should be, and indeed sometimes are, spontaneously and completely generous.

Moreover, the research shows that maintaining relationships of support—whether balanced or not—is challenging work. From their careful descriptions, the women reveal that they have had to learn to overcome shame and humiliation and that learning how, when, and whom to ask involves complex skills. The concept of strategic explanations thus should conceal neither the work that goes into maintaining these interpretations nor the possibility of their failure. When substantial gifts cannot be repaid, single mothers withdraw from relationships less because they are thrust out than because they cannot live with that kind of sustained dependence.

Having described the different logics of reciprocity, four issues bear further consideration. First, Hertz and Ferguson (1998) have suggested that single mothers can be roughly classified with respect to their access to social and material resources to create four different groupings. They suggest that the type of tight network of mutual support (described here for the relationships with other single mothers) is found predominantly among those who have high social resources but low material resources. Given this finding, the question arises of whether in describing the different logics of reciprocity I am really describing different people. The data suggest otherwise. Both Anne Davenport and Amanda Silver, to pick two examples, are deeply bound in intense relationships with other single mothers, even though Anne relies on a combination of ANFC and self-employment and Amanda holds down a secure, relatively well-paying position. Moreover, both of these two women rely as well on other people with whom they use quite different logics of reciprocity.

Second, both theory and research suggest that family has a special place in relationships of reciprocity, that the normative obligations of kinship help sustain generalized reciprocity over long periods. The question might well be raised of whether the women in this study distinguish between family and friends in their strategic explanations and believe themselves less obligated to make returns to the former. Here the answer is more complex. On one hand, assumed family obligation clearly is a factor insofar as respondents, again like Anne Davenport and Amanda Silver, find it easier to come up with a strategic explanation for making returns to family members. ("They would not be happy if they didn't feel like they were doing something and making sure that their grandchildren were taken care of." "And also I guess to fulfill an obligation is just to show them that I am living well and doing well by my kids.") Indeed, the use of kinship terms helps to bind individuals in frail relationships. The prominent cases of failed reciprocity involved relationships with nonfamily members with whom debts incurred could not be explained away. On the other hand, both

Anne and Amanda, like others, did require that explanation of themselves—suggesting that the normative obligation of family is not in and of itself a sufficient basis for receiving unreciprocated assistance. Moreover, some women—witness Martha Baldwin—could satisfy themselves with the same kind of explanations in their relationships with those bound neither by fictive nor factual kinship.

Third, the logics of reciprocity are not neatly wrapped as separate policies applied to separate people. The single mothers do require balance with those they perceive as having similar needs, and they do make stretches to a commonsense (if not anthropological) understanding of reciprocity in their relationships with those they believe to be more fortunate than themselves. However, the latter category of relationships might have exchange elements that follow the rules of balanced reciprocity as well as elements that require strategic explanations. For example, Joan Meyer makes "switch-offs" with her mother *and* rationalizes her acceptance of financial assistance as something her mother offers because "she knows I need a car to drive the children to the doctor."

Finally, as noted in the beginning, much research on single mothers has focused on those living in urban areas and often on those living in dense communities of others in similar situations. Although a couple of the single mothers in this study do live in small cities, the majority live in small towns and even, in some cases, in quite remote rural areas. The question naturally arises, then, of the extent to which these findings are distinct to such areas. Clearly, geographical dispersion marks a substantial difference from "the Flats" described by Stack (1974) or the urban neighborhoods that characterized the living conditions of the respondents interviewed by Edin and Lein (1997). Unlike women living in close proximity to one another, the women in this study *could* keep resources to themselves and conceal from others when the welfare check arrived or when they had won a small prize in the lottery. But there is little reason to believe that secrecy about earnings or income plays a major role in their lives or that they are likely to hoard goods so that they do not have to share. If there is secrecy and concealment, it seems more often to involve hiding from others just how many times one has done without. Indeed, the isolation of rural life carries its own unique burdens. While those who live in small towns or even in small cities can, like Kara Lattrell, borrow a roll of toilet paper from a neighbor or easily visit with friends, those who, like Joan Meyer, live half a mile from the nearest neighbor need a working car to manage the simplest act of sociability.

Every study of single mothers finds that their lives are marked by complex difficulties, and every author (indeed much public policy as well) struggles to find feasible solutions. Hertz and Ferguson (1997), for example, note, "It is the generosity of other individuals that aids [single mothers] during the temporary period of mothering infants," and "the problem is that there are not enough individuals among the 'rich' willing to help facilitate the aspirations of the poor by sponsoring them one by one." The findings in this article lend strength to both observations. Clearly, as single mothers discuss their relationships with family and friends, they suggest that the "rich" can help on an individual basis. Clearly, single mothers appreciate the help they receive: "I think there's still some people out there that will see that it's just her and her two kids and maybe I can help out. There still are a few nice people like that. And that's happened to me a couple of times, so that's been great." They also resent times when that help is *not* forthcoming: "I mean, well, Jesus, doesn't anybody ever think about giving me a lift every once in a while?" But these individual solutions—described by Hertz and Ferguson as a "moral obligation to be active participants in securing solutions to the dilemmas all parents face"—are, as Hertz and Ferguson also acknowledge, not a social solution. That solution—as most writers have suggested—lies in living wages *and* more generous state support. In the meantime, it is important to recognize the costs to those who struggle to maintain dignity through meeting the normative requirements of both reciprocity *and* self-sufficiency as they learn to manage "24-7, just me."

Acknowledgments

The author thanks the Middlebury College Faculty Development Fund for supporting this research; Jessica Lindert, Bethany Johnson, and Carol McMurrich for help with interviewing and transcribing; and Rosanna Hertz and two anonymous reviewers for their helpful comments. An earlier version of this article was presented at "Work and Family: Expanding the Horizons," a conference sponsored by the Business and Professional Women's Foundation, the Center for Working Families at the University of California, Berkeley, and the Alfred P. Sloan Foundation, San Francisco, March 3–4, 2000.

Notes

1. Some scholars relying on this assumption acknowledge negative outcomes that follow from the requirement of reciprocity such as limited mobility (Dordick, 1997; Stack, 1974) and the work of maintaining relationships (Edin and Lein, 1997). Many, however, focus on the positive features of reciprocal support, especially when characterizing relationships among and between African American women. To a certain extent this tendency arises in reaction to a body of literature (Frazier, 1939/1966; Moynihan, 1965; Wilson, 1987) that highlights social disorganization and welfare dependency in minority communities. Rather than seeing pathology, scholars like Dickerson (1995, pp. 6–7) emphasize "the strengths of the matrifocal, consanguineous pattern in maintaining generational continuity, providing services to kin, and resisting the negative impact of pressures outside the family" (see also Sudarkasa, 1981; Ladner, 1972; Roschelle, 1997, p. 181).

2. In 1996 Vermont received a waiver that released it from the requirement to comply with "welfare reform" until 2001 (Kitchel, 1998). The women in this study who did rely on "welfare" had thus not yet had to come to terms with the new restrictions.

3. Although this article explores relationships between single mothers and the members of their support networks, it excludes relationships between single mothers and their boyfriends/domestic partners. Because this latter set of relationships introduces a distinctive element—that of sexuality—it cannot easily be characterized within the framework of this analysis. In addition, it should be made clear that this study excludes as well professional relationships (e.g., with social workers) and relationships with those mediated by organized groups (e.g., ministers or agencies like Alcoholics Anonymous).

4. For a discussion of the poverty of rural single-parent families, see Lichter and Eggebeen (1992) and Lichter and McLaughlin (1995); for the significance of race, see Dill and Williams (1992).

5. A significant body of research demonstrates clearly that official poverty rates are understated. Not only is the poverty level itself out of date; it is not adjusted to a basic needs budget (Renwick and Bergmann, 1993). The *Vermont Job Gap Study* (Kahler, 1997) calculates the cost of basic needs for a single parent with one child and a single parent with two children in both rural and urban Vermont; it finds that a realistic account of monthly expenses ranges from $1,800 (single parent with one child in a rural area) to $2,299 (single parent with two children in an urban area). Thus it estimates that single parents require annual incomes of between $25,712 and $43,478 when the federal poverty level is pegged at $10,360 for the former group and $12,980 for the latter.

6. Vermont's welfare program is called ANFC (Aid to Needy Families with Children) rather than the more common AFDC (Aid to Families with Dependent Children).

7. Although some of the women were living with boyfriends, they spoke of themselves as "single mothers."

8. All names are pseudonyms.

References

Abel, E. K., & Nelson, M. K. (1990). *Circles of care: Work and identity in women's lives.* Albany: State University of New York Press.

Allen, W. (1979). Class culture and family organization: The effects of class and race on family structure in urban America. *Journal of Comparative Family Studies, 10,* 301–313.

Burns, A., & Scott, C. (1994). *Mother-headed families and why they have increased.* Hillsdale, NJ: Erlbaum.

Dickerson, B. J. (1995). Centering studies of African American single mothers and their families. In B. J. Dickerson (Ed.), *African American single mothers* (pp. 1–20). Thousand Oaks, CA: Sage.

DiLeonardo, M. (1987). The female world of cards and holidays: Women, families, and the work of kinship. *Signs, 12,* 440–453.

Dill, B. T., & Williams, B. B. (1992). Race, gender, and poverty in the rural South: African American single mothers. In C. M. Duncan (Ed.), *Rural poverty in America* (pp. 97–109). New York: Auburn House.

Dordick, G. A. (1997). *Something left to lose: Personal relations and survival among New York's homeless.* Philadelphia: Temple University Press.

Edin, K., & Lein, L. (1997). *Making ends meet.* New York: Russell Sage Foundation.

Finch, J., & Mason, J. (1993). *Negotiating family responsibilities.* London/New York: Tavistock/Routledge.

Frazier, E. F. (1939/1966). *The Negro family in the United States.* Chicago: University of Chicago Press.

Gouldner, A.W. (1960). The norm of reciprocity: A preliminary statement. *American Sociological Review, 25,* 161–178.

Hertz, R., & Ferguson, F. I. T. (1997). Kinship strategies and self-sufficiency among single mothers by choice: Postmodern family ties. *Qualitative Sociology, 20,* 187–209.

Hertz, R., & Ferguson, F. I. T. (1998). Only one pair of hands: Ways that single mothers stretch work and family resources. *Community, Work, and Family, 1,* 13–37.

Hochschild, A. R. (1983). *The managed heart: The commercialization of human feeling.* Berkeley: University of California Press.

Hogan, D., Eggebeen, D. J., & Clogg, C. C. (1993). The structure of intergenerational exchange in American families. *American Journal of Sociology, 98,* 1428–1458.

Hogan, D. P., Hao, L., & Parish, W. L. (1990). Race, kin support, and mother-headed families. *Social Forces, 68,* 797–812.

Homans, G. C. (1974). *Social behavior: Its elementary forms.* New York: Harcourt Brace Jovanovich.

Institute for Women's Policy Research. (1998). *State of the states: Vermont.* Washington, DC.

Kahler, E. (1997). *The Vermont job gap study, phase I: Basic needs and a livable wage.* Burlington, VT: Peace and Justice Center.

Kitchel, M. J. (1998). *Fourth annual report to the general assembly on Vermont's welfare restructuring project.* Waterbury, VT: Agency of Human Services.

Komter, A. E. (1996). Reciprocity as a principle of exclusion: Gift giving in the Netherlands. *Sociology: The Journal of the British Sociological Association, 30,* 299–317.

Ladner, J. A. (1972). *Tomorrow's tomorrow: The black woman.* Garden City, NJ: Doubleday.

Levi-Strauss, C. (1969). *The elementary structures of kinship.* London: Eyre and Spottiswoode.

Lichter, D. T., & Eggebeen, D. J. (1992). Child poverty and the changing rural family. *Rural Sociology, 57,* 151–172.

Lichter, D. T., & McLaughlin, D. K. (1995). Changing economic opportunities, family structure, and poverty in rural areas. *Rural Sociology, 60,* 688–707.

Livingston, J., & McCrate, E. (1993). *Women and economic development in Vermont: A study for the Governor's Commission on Women.* Montpelier, VT: Governor's Commission on the Status of Women.

Malinowski, B. (1926). *Crime and custom in savage society.* London: Routledge and Kegan Paul.

Mauss, M. (1954). *The gift.* Glencoe, IL: Free Press.

McAdoo, H. P. (1980). Black mothers and the extended family support network. In L. Rodgers-Rose (Ed.), *The black woman* (pp. 67–87). Beverly Hills, CA: Sage.

McGranahan, D. A. (1994). Rural America in the global economy: Socioeconomic trends. *Journal of Research in Rural Education, 10,* 139–148.

Moynihan, D. P. (1965). *The Negro family: The case for national action.* Washington, DC: Government Printing Office.

Nelson, M. K. (1990). *Negotiating care: The experience of family day care providers.* Philadelphia: Temple University Press.

Nelson, M. K., & Smith, J. (1999). *Working hard and making do: Surviving in small-town America.* Berkeley: University of California Press.

Pahl, R. E. (1984). *Divisions of labour.* Oxford: Basil Blackwell.

Renwick, T. J., & Bergmann, B. R. (1993). A budget-based definition of poverty. *Journal of Human Resources, 28,* 1–24.

Rollins, J. (1985). *Between women: Domestics and their employers.* Philadelphia: Temple University Press.

Romero, M. (1992). *Maid in the U.S.A.* New York: Routledge.

Roschelle, A. R. (1997). *No more kin: Exploring race, class, and gender in family networks.* Thousand Oaks, CA: Sage.

Sahlins, M. (1972). *Stone age economics.* Chicago: Aldine Atherton.

Schein, V. E. (1995). *Working from the margins: Voices of mothers in poverty.* Ithaca, NY: ILR Press.

Stack, C. (1974). *All our kin: Strategies for survival in a black community.* New York: Harper & Row.

Sudarkasa, N. (1981). Reassessing the black family: Dispelling the myths, reaffirming the values. *Sisters, 38–39,* 22–23.

Wijnberg, M. H., & Reding, K. M. (1999). Reclaiming a stress focus: The hassles of rural, poor single mothers. *Families in Society, 80,* 506–516.

Wilson, J. W. (1987). *The truly disadvantaged: The inner city, the underclass, and public policy.* Chicago: University of Chicago Press.

11
The Third Shift

Gender and Care Work Outside the Home

Naomi Gerstel

One of the important achievements of feminist scholarship over the past several decades has been to document the ways that women, with little recognition, contribute to the welfare of both their own families and a larger community. As a large body of research has shown, women, even employed women, do a disproportionate share of work in the home, including housework and child care (Brines, 1994; Deutsch, 1999; Garey, 1999; Greenstein, 2000; Gupta, 1999; Lennon & Rosenfield, 1994; Press & Townsley, 1998; Walzer, 1998). In this article, I want to examine yet another way in which women have, at least in the past, tended to do more than men. I examine and seek to explain the distribution and meaning of a broad range of caregiving outside the home, whether informally to relatives and friends or more formally to neighbors and strangers served by volunteer groups.

Understanding this work is central to the analysis of a number of broad issues. First, explaining differences in caregiving is fundamental to contemporary feminist theories of gender. Second, analyzing caregiving provides a means for understanding transformations in the character of extended families as well as broader communities which have been, for the most part, created and maintained by women. Finally, I will argue that analysis of gender and caregiving helps explain some central dilemmas in contemporary social policy, particularly the efforts of recent administrations to scale down the welfare state.

Since the 1970s, a central concern of women's studies and feminist theory has been gender and difference—a concern which, to be sure, has many different meanings and positions. A major strand in this thinking has been to pose gender as a dichotomy—to contrast women and men—and then to revalorize the woman who had been devalued, if seen at all. This valued woman became central to feminist scholarship in a number of fields; in this reading, she (or we) were viewed as having not only a different body but a different voice and way of thinking, a different sense of justice and politics, and a different sense of love and attachment. Those who speak of difference usually describe and then praise it. In this article, however, I do not praise difference but seek to explain it.

Increasingly, at the center of the discussion of gender and difference is women's presumed special ability to nurture and give care. A perception that women do most of the nurturing and caregiving is, of course, neither particularly new nor even particularly controversial. Not only is the current discussion of women's caregiving a reenactment of a similar discussion at the end of the nineteenth century and the beginning of the twentieth, but also grounds for a curious convergence between feminists and antifeminists. For the notion that women are different, more caring than men, has produced some curious alliances—with some neoconservative women, who defend their distinctively dependent style of life, and some feminists, who acclaim the superiority of women's relational and moral capacities, joined in a program of moral reform based on a modern cult of true womanhood.

But this is all primarily on the level of description, albeit often of a remarkably sophisticated sort. Explanation is quite another thing. Moreover, although explanation, particularly causal explanation, is altogether the dominant mode of approach in the social sciences, I should acknowledge immediately that it is not the primary intent of those disciplines that have carried on much, if not most, of the discussion of gender and difference. As a result, in looking for causal theories I must also acknowledge that to a certain degree I am imposing claims where none exist or are, at best, only implied. Nonetheless, with these caveats in mind, let me move ahead.

What I would like to suggest is that, beyond description, the discussion of gender and difference rests on four types of implicit causal explanation. The first of these is perhaps best called essentialist in that it suggests that differences in caregiving and nurturance are bound up with the biological makeup of women and men and are, by consequence, if not exactly invariant, at least deep and tenacious (for reviews, see Fausto-Sterling, 1985; Maccoby, 1998; Udry, Morris, & Kovenock, 1995). Implicitly, essentialist arguments suggest that all women are caregivers more than any men.

A second type of explanation stresses internalization—the result of differences in the socialization of girls and boys. Although a stress on internalization allows far more room for variation among women (and for overlap between women and men) than do essentialist arguments, this type of argument has more often been used to explain uniformity among women on grounds of invariance in gender-specific child rearing practices within a given society. One reading—not the only available reading but probably the most frequent—of both Nancy Chodorow (1978; 1989) and Carol Gilligan (1982) would place both in this broad camp.

A third type of explanation stresses neither biology nor internalization but the broad context of gender as a social construction at the level of a society. It stresses differences in legal structure and social expectations as well as differences in the power of men and women—in short, differences in the strength of what we might call patriarchy. Curiously, such explanations, what R. W. Connell (1987) calls "categorical theories," give a major place to power differentials but share with essentialist and internalization arguments a strong presumption that there will not be significant variations among women or significant overlap between women and men, at least within the boundaries of a single national society.

A fourth and final type of explanation is also social but, unlike "categorical theories," stresses variations in the structure of adult lives (Epstein, 1988; Lorber, 1994; Risman, 1998)—most importantly in the structure of the family and employment. Unlike essentialist arguments of all variants, this line of argument is fundamentally alert to variations among women. Moreover, this type of explanation even raises the possibility that gender may influence caregiving only through its association with other characteristics and that gender itself may have no independent effect. This final line of argument is found not only in the qualitative work of sociologists like Kathleen Gerson (1985; 1987; 1993)—in her analysis of the causes of women's divergent pathways—and psychologists like Alice Eagley (1995)—in her work on empathy and altruism—but also is deeply embedded in the very logic of quantitative, variable research.

In a brief article, I cannot, of course, address—let alone test—all four levels of explanation. Rather, the task I have set is both more limited and more prosaic. What I will argue is that we can go a significant way to explaining differences between men and women by relying solely on the final type of explanation I have just laid out—by variations in the structure of individual women's lives, in particular by variations in employment. In the past few decades, not only has there been enormous growth in the employment of women, especially Euro-American married women, but the pace of change has quickened dramatically. Women take jobs not only because they want to but because, increasingly, they have to. The escalating rates of women's participation in the labor force, I will argue, have significantly reduced both the ability and willingness of women to provide the caregiving and nurturance that others have argued are fundamental to them in the contemporary United States.

I do not mean, however, to claim that differences in employment entirely explain differences between women and men in regard to caregiving. Although employment explains a significant part of the difference, in other respects the differences in caregiving between women and men are persistent. Toward the end of this article, I return to these persistent differences and try to assess their significance for the three other types of explanation I have laid out here.

Background and Research Questions

Over the past 20 years a tremendous volume of research has demonstrated a gender-based division of labor, not only in housework and child care inside the home but also in kinkeeping (see, e.g., Marks, 1996; Rossi & Rossi, 1990; Abel, 1991) as well as in paid work outside the home (for reviews, see Bianchi, 1995; Reskin & Padavic, 1994; Roos & Gatta, 1999). However, although we know a great deal about the effects of women's employment on housework and child care, we know very little about the consequences of their employment for the other kinds of care they give, especially the broad range of care occurring *outside* the nuclear family, including, for example, extended nursing of an ailing mother, cooking an occasional meal for a bereaved friend, or volunteering in a local church soup kitchen. Even major studies of time use that have made an effort to capture the daily round and division of work in adult lives have not included analyses of the variety of unpaid caregiving that women perform, let alone related that caregiving to employment. Some of the research that I have conducted myself, over a number of years, is at least a partial exception. Drawing on this research, I can make a number of comparisons:

Between women and men: How much difference is there in the amount of care provided by women as compared with men? How much difference in the kinds of care?

Among women: How much difference is there in the amount and kind of care provided by employed women as compared with women who are not employed? To what extent is employment a key factor influencing the supply and organization of caregiving, and to what extent is gender, as a dichotomy, the key?

Between *employed* women and men in similar jobs: Does the specific character of employment matter? Do women in time-consuming, lucrative, or prestigious jobs provide the same amount and kind of care to the same people as do men in similar jobs or women employed fewer hours in less demanding or privileged jobs? How do women and men *explain* these differences?

Methods

The Sample

With the help of a number of excellent graduate students, I conducted a total of 324 interviews, primarily with married women divided into two groups—those employed and those neither employed nor looking for employment—as well as half the husbands of each group. The sample was drawn randomly from the telephone directory and was limited to Euro-Americans (86%) and African Americans (14%). With a median age of 41 years, 51% of the respondents had a least one child younger than 18 still living at home; 64% had living parents, 63% had living parents-in-law, and 49% had at least one child over 18.

The Interview

The research consisted of two parts—one quantitative and one qualitative—both necessary for the issues considered here.

The first part, administered to all respondents, consisted of a face-to-face interview with detailed standardized questions focusing on (1) characteristics of employment and (2) formal and informal caregiving. We measured a number of dimensions of employment, including measures from the NORC General Social Survey of occupational type, income, and number of hours worked for pay. In addition, we used a job centrality scale (adapted from Jencks, Perman, & Rainwater), and developed a new measure of job flexibility (see Gerstel & Gallagher, 1994). For caregiving, we used a personal network approach, first developed by Claude Fischer (1982), to assess the help provided by network members. For the purposes of this research, we turned it on its head, asking about care given instead of received. Interviewers named different types of people outside the home (like parents, parents-in-law, adult children, other relatives, neighbors, and friends) as well as volunteer groups, and asked respondents to tell us all the types of care they provided for each of them and how much time they spent giving such care to each of them.

For part of the sample we then drew on answers from the first interview and returned with a second open-ended, discursive interview tailored specifically to the experiences of the particular person we were talking to. With the intent of entering the realm of meaning, we sought the detailed accounts that individuals attach to their own involvement in caregiving.

I should note that in the very process of developing and conducting the interviews, we learned about some important aspects of caregiving and its gendered character. After asking detailed questions about what they had done and for whom, we discovered we had to reiterate that we were interested in all kinds of care, whether they thought of it as major or minor. We had to use such probes because we wanted to get at what we came to learn is a taken-for-granted kind of work, invisible not only to social analysts, it seems, but sometimes dismissed or disparaged by the providers themselves. Respondents, especially women, would often say to us, about a meal they had made for a sick friend or extensive child care they provided for one of their own adult children, "Oh, yeah, I forgot about that."

Moreover, in the process of interviewing, we found that the men (but almost never the women) would sometimes speak of "we" when they spoke about the provision of care, saying, for example, "*We* made a meal for my mother when she was sick." Upon probing, it often became quite clear that the individual who did most of the work was the wife, not the husband. Given this response, interviewers had to be trained to probe whenever they heard the word *we*. Researchers who study these issues must recognize what Peter Berger pointed out some time ago: that couples create a subjective sense of "we" to make sense and order of their daily lives. But as many since Berger have also pointed out, every marriage contains, in fact, two marriages: a "his" and a "hers," even though the two are sometimes conflated even by spouses themselves. In my research, I had to work hard to take this distinction very seriously, probing to differentiate his caregiving labor as much as possible from hers. (See Lareau, this volume, for related analysis of men's claims about family work.)

Analysis

Structural Explanations of the Distribution of Caregiving

Let me begin with an overview of the distribution or division of caregiving work. The first and simplest comparison is between women and men. Beginning with sheer quantity, there is a startling difference in the amount of time women and men spend giving informal care or care to relatives and friends. Women provide an average of 50 hours a month giving informal care outside the home, men an average of 20.

To specify, women spend significantly more hours giving care to friends and do so for significantly more friends than do men. The differences in the amount of time women, compared to men, spend providing care for relatives is even larger. Women give far more to those distantly related as well as to those more closely related. Not only do they give far more to their parents, but if there is what some call a "postparental stage," it is far more characteristic of men than women: Mothers spend a great deal of time helping adult children and are significantly more likely to do so than fathers. Mothers spend four times more hours helping adult children than do fathers.

If women give so much of this informal care, do men perhaps compensate by spending much more time on volunteer groups and activities? Men are members of a significantly larger number of groups. But they spend approximately the same amount of time working for these groups as women (an average of about 8 hours per month), and a significantly smaller proportion of the groups which men help are local, community groups (about half of women's are local while only one third of men's are). These data suggest that while men have more memberships in nonlocal groups than do women, women expend more energy making local groups that serve the community operate.

These gender differences in the amount of time spent giving care are matched by differences in the proportions of care given. Looking just at women, we find that they give many more hours of care to their relatives (especially adult children) than to their friends. In contrast, looking just at men, we find they spend slightly more time helping their friends than they do helping their relatives. Given the ascribed character of kin ties and the achieved character of friendship, these data at least suggest that men's caregiving labor is more voluntary—less prescribed than women's.

Moreover, along these same lines, while women help their own parents more than their parents-in-law, the reverse is true for men. When men are married to women who spend a lot of time helping their kin, men are likely to spend more time helping the same types of kin. When men are married to women who provide particular types of help, men are more likely to provide these particular types of help as well. We noted above an indicator of this process in the words men themselves use: men (but almost never the women) spoke of "we" when they referred to the provision of care. Husbands, in other words, do not step up to fill the gap left by wives who are employed, but rather sometimes get up to accompany their wives (employed or not) who go out to give care.[1] This suggests that wives link husbands into families and the caring that sustains them. In short, in addition to differences in the amount of care men and women provide, there are differences in the style with which they provide care.

Nonetheless, when we compare the *kind* of caregiving women and men do, we find there is not any type of care men are significantly more likely than women to provide. Women are overwhelmingly more likely to provide help with laundry, cleaning, and child care. They are also as likely as men to do other people's home repairs and yard work, or give them goods and money. That is, just as with household labor, women do a large share of what is conventionally thought of as "men's" work, but men do little of "women's" work.

Finally, there is no caregiving task which men do for a significantly larger number of people than women. Yet there are many and varied tasks which women do for a significantly larger number than men. Women's caregiving, then, has more breadth and depth than men's.

Stated bluntly, my findings suggest there is very little *division* of labor. To be sure, women *and* men spend a good deal of time doing the work on which families and communities depend. But, compared to men, women give more care. Women spend more time giving that care. Women give more kinds of care. Women give to a larger number of people.

If there is very little division of labor in caregiving, perhaps that is because it is part of a wider division of labor in the family. Men do paid work; women do unpaid work. But what happens when women work for pay?

Put simply, here I am interested in comparing three groups: employed men, employed women, and women who are not employed. (I had too small a sample of men who are not employed, a conceptually significant but numerically smaller category, at least among married couples within the prime years of employment.) If gender—as a dichotomy—were the entire story, employed women would look like non-employed women. If employment—or experiences of adult life—were the source of gender difference, employed women would look like employed men. Or, if not all employed women did, at least women in jobs with characteristics similar to men would.

Although I will not present the specific findings here, let me summarize: My analysis shows both that there are differences among women and differences between women and men.[2] Employment is clearly associated with both the kind and quantity of care—with the number and kind of people helped and the hours spent helping them. Compared with employed women, the "traditional woman" who does not work for pay does much more unpaid caregiving work. In particular, she is especially likely to do "kin work"—providing care for her family by blood and marriage. However, employment does not significantly reduce "friend work." In fact, the trend is in the opposite direction: Employed women provide somewhat more help to friends than do those not employed. And the type of task a housewife does is different from what an employed woman does. Employed women continue to help out, but especially with the kinds of help that consume not time so much as economic resources. They give more money and gifts while housewives do more time-consuming, hands-on chores, like child care, for those outside the household. Employed women are beginning to look a little like employed men.

But the "traditional" man—who holds a paying job—continues to do significantly less than his employed female counterpart. He helps fewer relatives and fewer friends and spends fewer hours helping both relatives and friends. Compared with employed women, employed men also belong to a smaller proportion of local volunteer groups. So, too, employed women are significantly more likely to do many kinds of labor for the people they know—not only preparing meals or helping with child care but also giving material aid, whether goods or gifts, more often and to significantly more people than do employed men. In fact, there is no kind of help employed men are significantly more likely to give. To put it simply, the discussion to this point would seem to suggest two things: First, the characteristics of women's adult lives clearly do shape both the amount and character of caregiving they perform; second, even when employed, women are different from men.

Perhaps the difference in men's and women's caregiving is not so much a consequence of employment per se but of the kinds of jobs women often hold. If their jobs took more hours or were better-paying and more central to their lives, perhaps their caregiving would begin to resemble that of men in similar jobs even more. I assessed this by examining the relationship between characteristics of employment and caregiving.

This analysis produced two sets of findings—parallel to those I found in comparisons of all women with all men. First, job characteristics as a group do shape caregiving. Second, the effect of gender remains quite strong, even controlling for type of employment. More specifically, women—like men—in more prestigious, time-consuming, and lucrative jobs that are more central to their lives spend significantly fewer hours helping relatives—especially parents and adult children—than those in jobs less demanding or prestigious. But overall women still do significantly more than men in these same kinds of jobs.

Let me summarize and situate my findings to this point. I have shown that caregiving remains women's work far more than men's. As many have suggested, women are—compared with men—keepers of the modern (or "postmodern"?) extended family. They are also, as I have already suggested, the keepers of friends, neighbors, and even those strangers served by local volunteer groups. They put a great deal of time into these "labors of love." To put it quite starkly, women add more than *an extra work week to their monthly load* by caring for those outside their households. For many, then, the labor I have documented is a "third shift" because women do so much of it and because women do it in addition to the "first shift" of paid work and what Arlie Hochschild (1989) has called the "second shift" of housework and child care.

At the same time, the changing structure of women's lives is very clearly changing the structure and organization of caregiving. As I have shown, employed women, compared with housewives, do less unpaid work for extended family by blood and marriage. But they do at least as much for those outside the family, be they strangers in the community or neighbors and friends. In fact, employed women are *more* likely to help at least one friend than are housewives, and they spend more time helping friends overall.

I would like to suggest that these findings speak to the weakening of families, at least as we have traditionally understood them. The strongest and most consistent findings in this study concern the attenuation of care for kin. Both employed wives and husbands not only help a smaller number of relatives, but they spend much less time than housewives helping parents and adult children as well as other kin. Moreover, when wives enter "privileged" jobs, they are particularly likely to pull back from kin. As they pull back, so, too, do their husbands, whose caregiving is often contingent on that of their wives. In this sense, then, married women's increased movement into the labor force and their assumption of jobs that resemble those of men begins to sever the "kin work" that has organized and sustained what remains of the modern extended family.

There may be a number of explanations for these findings with regard to kin versus non-kin. Most obviously, we know that housewives are more isolated than those who are employed (Fischer, 1982). Compared with the employed, then, they simply do not know those outside of their families to whom they might provide care. While the employed do have such access to non-kin, they may have less time and energy—but more material resources at their disposal—to help them (which helps explain why we find that they give help in ways not requiring hands-on labor, especially to non-kin). Note that one might expect that employed women have less access to kin because, for example, they live at a greater distance from them. But my research suggests that is not a primary explanation. The findings I presented control for geographic proximity of kin.

More generally, while recent changes in women's work lives may turn them away from their extended families, I have also provided some evidence that women's employment does not turn them away from the larger community—quite the reverse. Much discussion of caregiving artificially restricts its view to help given to relatives, especially aged parents, but does not assess the provision of care to others, especially non-kin. As a result, it appears that employment constrains women's involvement with those outside the nuclear family. This is because so many conceive of the extended family as the only alternative to the nuclear family. As I have suggested, this is too simple and narrow a view. By encouraging voluntary rather than prescribed ties, employment transforms and to some extent diminishes (though it does not abrogate) the giving of care. In fact, women's employment may produce a wider social integration beyond the family.

Overall, then, employment explains a significant amount of the difference between women's caregiving and men's. But it does not explain the entire difference either in the amount of caregiving or the kind. Perhaps with more extensive and refined measures of variations in adult lives specified at the level of individuals, I would explain even more of the difference. But, even with such measures, I suspect I could not explain it all. Moreover, while the documentation of differences of the kind I make here involves fundamentally quantitative questions, the explanation of these differences is of a different sort and requires a different kind of data. For these explanations, I turn to the open-ended interviews and words that the respondents themselves chose to explain difference.

Essentialist Explanations of Difference

In searching to explain caregiving, my respondents themselves often espoused a variant of essentialist views. Many women, both housewives and employed women, explained their caregiving by saying things like: "I guess it's just my nature" or "It's the way I am, my nature."

Not a single man used that phrase, at least when describing his own caregiving. But they did use it to explain their wives'. As one husband described his wife:

> She is very helpful to folks. She has always been a very helpful person. People come by, and she'll feed them and take care of them. Takes care of people. Like my folks, she runs errands for them. And my brother will sleep over a night or two, and she makes him meals. Sometimes she feels she's getting put upon a little bit, but her nature is that way.

The term *nature* is a complicated one, of course, and I am not sure if my respondents—women or men—intend its specifically biological sense or a somewhat looser sense in which the term is used to refer to character more generally. Most likely, they meant both, without having thought out the distinction very clearly. In any event, the importance of this distinction is more on an interpretive level than on an explanatory one, critical to understanding how women make sense to themselves of their caregiving, but less important in understanding the causes of difference. Put a little differently, the resort to *nature* seems to me to have a clear ideological use. It is a turn of language that justifies gender differences and gender inequalities by normalizing them and making them appear invariant. The ambiguity around the two senses of nature serves only to make their claim stronger in everyday life.

There is, however, another suggestion that a number of my respondents made that seems to me a more promising line of investigation. In the quite typical words of one woman in a demanding position, a 50-year-old lawyer:

> Well, my mother may be a pain sometimes, but she is very frail now and needs me. She expects me to help her. And, you know, she took care of her mother. So I have to help her. Nobody else will.

This brief excerpt from a long interview is interpretively dense. Certainly we can see in it a morality centered on issues of connection, an injunction not to turn away from someone in need, to respond to particular people by understanding their particular situations—a morality of precisely the sort that Gilligan and others suggest is essential to women. But what I would point out is that this morality is not vested simply in the woman herself. While she said she helps her mother because she feels she should and also out of love, she also said she helps because *her mother expects her to.*

In contrast, when men spoke of their motivations for caregiving, they would often speak in far more abstract and lofty terms. For example, one 45-year-old man, also a lawyer, explained his caregiving quite simply: "I want to make the world a better place to live." Here, what is critical from my point of view is not simply the abstract character of the formulation but the abstract character of the obligation itself. Unlike the woman I just cited, the man speaks of free-floating obligations. He does not mention—or cannot think of— anyone in particular who holds him to those expectations.

In this sense, the difference between the ethic of care that women articulate and the ethic of care that men articulate may have nothing whatsoever to do with essential differences and surprisingly little to do with differences even in socialization. Rather, they may be realistic responses to variations in the expectations generated, day in and day out in adult life, for women more than men.

If women and men develop different ethics of care in response to different expectations, so too they may develop different practices of care in response to a broad context of domination and dependency—a context from which employment provides only a partial and uncertain escape. To use the words of one woman, speaking of the great deal of care she gave to a friend who had recently been very sick, "I just feel that we need other people." Then she said, "I really believe what you give is what you get back." Many women, but not men, in explaining their caregiving, spoke of it as a form of social insurance, saying, "I might need help one day." or "You know, I have to admit that I think, oh, I will need someone to take care of me someday, too." Perhaps men do not talk about caregiving in this way because they take the receipt of care for granted, do not recognize the work it entails, or feel entitled to care in both the short and long run. In contrast, women are less certain. Here, women's caregiving becomes both altruistic *and* self-interested, resting on a norm, and practice, of reciprocity in both the short and long run.

Caregiving and Power

By turning to another aspect of my data, I can further elaborate on this point. I have focused on gender and employment, but in the quantitative analysis, I also found that African Americans, employed or not, especially women but also men, spend far more time helping people they know, especially kin, and volunteering than do Euro-Americans. In fact, the difference between Euro- and African Americans was as large as the difference between women and men. This resonates to much literature which suggests that African Americans are more embedded in community life than equally situated Euro-Americans. (For summary and analysis of this literature, see Sarkisian et al., 2000.) This, in concert with the findings I have already discussed, also suggests that those less powerful in American society (African Americans and women) may engage in caregiving as a technique of empowerment and survival. One African American woman, after recounting to me the large number of hours she spent on caregiving, smiled and explained, "Well, what goes 'round comes 'round." Caregiving, then, is a survival strategy as well as a demanding labor of love.

This material on African Americans and Euro-American women, like that on employed women and housewives, speaks to another meaning of gender and difference: that of differences among women rather than differences between men and women. But it is not just another meaning. On the one hand, it speaks against the homogenization of all women or the strict dichotomy between women and men. It forces us to reject a single image of "woman, the nurturer." On the other hand, it provides added strength to the argument that differences which do exist may rest in social relations and inequalities of power—that caregiving may originate in (and constitute an adaptive response to) the experience of an uncertain or subordinate social location.

Conclusion

This analysis has a number of implications beyond the particular contours of caregiving. Some of the findings are particularly consequential for recent social policy. The current administration, committed to decreasing the "public" role in caregiving and welfare, is calling for increased reliance on "private" volunteer services. In this, as an assistant secretary at Health and Human Services has observed, families are to become "the first line of defense" in the care of the needy. Recent administrations have pressed for numerous policies toward this end, whether through changes in health care (like the shortening of hospital stays) or changes in employment policies (like the Family and Medical Leave Act). Providing only *unpaid* leaves to covered employees, the FMLA allows families to provide care, but does so without ensuring the income that caregivers often need and want to support their families. Those who can take leaves have someone else they can rely on for income. Thus, though touted as "gender-neutral," this act bolsters the gendered division of family caregiving. It is women—especially married women with husbands to support them—who take family leaves to provide care for family members (Gerstel & McGonagle, 1999). Economist Barbara Bergmann (1997, p. 27) has disputed the efficacy of recent "family friendly" policies, like those promoting leaves that support women's exits from jobs or child care subsidies limited to families at home, arguing: "Such family friendly policies, like 'family values,' can push us in a retrograde direction. Policies that appear to make life easier for women, and that may even be welcomed by a majority of women, may cement women's inequality." We can go further. Among the affluent, policies like the FMLA cement gender inequality. They also cement class inequality. While the affluent can afford to give care to their families, those less affluent can ill afford to give such care.

Such pressure on families, again especially on poor women, is further intensified by recent welfare reforms. The movement from AFDC to Temporary Assistance to Needy Families (TANF), while claiming to strengthen the nuclear family, makes it especially hard for poor mothers to give care to their loved ones—be they young or old (Gerstel, 2000; Loprest, 1999; Oliker, this volume and 2000). Because "what goes 'round comes 'round," welfare leavers lose not only time to give care themselves but also the informal care they had come to expect from others.

These growing pressures and inequalities in caregiving coincide with a growing demand for care. In addition to an expansion of the poverty population as a whole, demographic trends have increased the ratio of the dependent to the population able to help. Decreased family size is reducing the number of family members available to provide care, while increasing longevity is expanding at least the elderly population most likely to need care. Thus, younger generations will be under growing pressure to provide private volunteer care. Overall, then, a growing proportion of families in the United States—in effect, women—are called upon to do an increasing amount of caregiving.

While the current administration, like the one before it, is attempting to return the growing demand for caregiving to "the family," I have shown that a rising number of women are less available to provide such care, especially to their families. Increasingly, caregiving can no longer simply be assumed to be a private or "family affair." This creates a structural problem for those who engage in a politics of privatizing care.

But the employment of women creates another political problem as well. Not only does the employment of women make it more difficult to provide care privately. It may undermine the ideological support for doing so. Using a set of questions on attitudes, I found that women—those very family members whom the state is hoping to count on—are more favorably disposed than men to the *public* provision of care, both from government and employers. In this limited sense, then, employed women remain the very moral guardians not only of their families but also of the larger community that some nineteenth- and twentieth-century feminists describe and praise. However, employed women are significantly more likely than women who are not employed to be favorably disposed to the provision of public aid as a substitute for their own labor of care. Moreover, compared with housewives and employed men, employed women who do continue to provide care feel more burdened as a result of doing so. In other words, structurally, politically, and psychologically, the lives and views of many contradict the policies proposed by the current administration. Because employed women—a growing majority—want (and need) more public support at the same time that the recent administrations have stressed the development of more private care, the current direction of public policy will serve to create not only greater pressure on women but a growing vacuum of care. Ironically, as Oliker (this volume) suggests, these changes may further undermine an ethos stressing the importance of giving care.

Finally, my discussion has implications for the contrasting perspectives with which I began this article. My analyses offer considerable support for social structural perspectives on gender difference. The fact that employment has a significant effect on caregiving suggests that the predispositions formed in early years of life also are subject to and reinforced (or undermined) by the constraints and opportunities increasingly characteristic of women's adult lives. If differences were simply rooted in early development, or even in some set of general cultural expectations that attach caregiving to women, we would not expect to find the significant differences between employed women and housewives or among women in different types of jobs. But we do. By one reading, I have shown that women's employment reduces the differences between women and men. By another reading, however, I have shown how employment generates differences among women not only in the extent of caregiving but also in its direction and form.

However, the social sources of difference I have emphasized by no means eliminate the effect of gender. Whether because of internalization, expectation, anticipated need, or even an unmeasured structural factor other than employment, women may be more disposed than men to focus on close ties (whether with relatives or friends) and more inclined to assist those in the local community who seek help. Where "traditional" women are more likely to direct care to kin, employed women are more likely to direct their care to wider networks beyond kin. In whichever form, however, women may not only feel burdened but may also obtain some culturally affirmed sense of identity as well as power and material rewards by doing the work that sustains community. I am suggesting that we need to further decompose both conceptually and empirically that wide range of phenomena we typically package as "gender" in order to fully understand the sources of difference.

In conclusion, then, women are different from men. I would argue that we must recognize difference. It has been a powerful analytic tool and important source of sisterhood. But I would also insist that it is malleable, that it is rooted in a division of labor and subject to a set of social relations that developed in the 19th and 20th centuries but is, even in the face of resistance, coming undone in the 21st. In making theory, feminists should not abandon the exploration of difference but be self-conscious about its political uses. Insisting on difference sometimes means making women and their work visible. But it may also constrict our possibilities. Fitting nicely with a new conservatism, difference is often substituted for and is used to legitimate inequality. And finally, to come full circle, I would argue that insisting on difference is often used to trivialize the important family and community work we do by making it seem somehow God-given or natural.

Acknowledgment

Research for this article was funded by the Rockefeller Foundation. I would like to thank Sally Gallagher, Dan Clawson, and Robert Zussman.

Notes

1. For an elaboration of this argument concerning the ways the women in men's lives shape men's caregiving, see Gerstel and Gallagher, 2001.

2. Here I began to use the methods of ordinary least squares and logistic regression with dummy-coded variables that allow me to compare the effects of gender (at least among the employed) and employment (among women), while controlling for and examining the effects of other important social factors like race, the presence of young children, and the geographic proximity of kin, all factors associated with employment. (For a more detailed discussion of some of these methods and findings, see Gerstel & Gallagher, 1994; Gallagher & Gerstel, 2000.)

References

Abel, E. (1991). *Who cares for the elderly? Public policy and the experiences of adult daughters*. Philadelphia: Temple University Press.

Bergmann, B. (1997). Work-family policies and equality between women and men. In F. Blau & R. Ehrenberg (Eds.), *Gender and family in the workplace* (pp. 277–280). New York: Russell Sage Foundation.

Bianchi, S. (1995). Changing economic roles of women and men. In R. Farley (Ed.), *State of the union* (Vol. 1, pp. 107–154). New York: Russell Sage.

Brines, J. (1994). Economic dependency, gender, and the division of labor at home. *American Journal of Sociology, 100*, 652–688.

Chodorow, N. (1978). *The reproduction of mothering*. Berkeley: University of California Press.

Chodorow, N. (1989). *Feminism and psychoanalytic theory*. New Haven: Yale University Press.

Connell, R. W. (1987). *Gender and power: Society, the person, and sexual politics*. Cambridge: Polity/Blackwell.

Deutsch, F. (1999). *Halving it all: How equally shared parenting works*. Cambridge: Harvard University Press.

Eagley, A. (1995). The science and politics of comparing women and men. *American Psychologist, 50*, 145–158.

Epstein, C. (1988). *Deceptive distinctions: Sex, gender, and the social order*. New Haven: Yale University Press.

Fausto-Sterling, A. (1985). *Myths of gender: Biological theories about women and men*. New York: Basic Books.

Fischer, C. (1982). *To dwell among friends: Personal networks in town and city*. Chicago: University of Chicago Press.

Gallagher, S., & Gerstel, N. (2000). Connections and constraints: The effects of children on caregiving. *Journal of Marriage and the Family, 62* (August).

Garey, A. I. (1999). *Weaving work and motherhood*. Philadelphia: Temple University Press.

Gerson, K. (1985). *Hard choices: How women decide about work, career, and motherhood*. Berkeley: University of California Press.

Gerson, K. (1987). Emerging social divisions among women: Implications for welfare state politics. *Politics and Society, 15,* 213–221.

Gerson, K. (1993). *No man's land: Men's changing commitments to family and work.* New York: Basic Books.

Gerstel, N. (2000, May). *Family power and family policies: FMLA and TANF.* Paper presented at Conference on Power in America: The Big Issues. Leroy Neiman Center Group. UCLA.

Gerstel, N., & Gallagher, S. K. (1994). Caring for kith and kin: Gender, employment, and the privatization of care. *Social Problems, 41,* 519–538.

Gerstel, N., & Gallagher, S. K. (2001). Men's caregiving: Gender and the contingent character of care. *Gender & Society, 15,* 197–217.

Gerstel, N., & McGonagle, K. (1999). Job leaves and the limits of the Family and Medical Leave Act: The effects of gender, race, and family. *Work and Occupations, 26,* 510–534.

Gilligan, C. (1982). *In a different voice.* Cambridge: Harvard University Press.

Greenstein, T. (2000). Economic dependence, gender, and the division of labor in the home. *Journal of Marriage and the Family, 62,* 332–335.

Gupta, S. (1999). The effects of transitions in marital status on men's performance of housework. *Journal of Marriage and the Family, 61,* 700–711.

Hochschild, A, with Machung, A. (1989). *The second shift: Working parents and the revolution at home.* New York: Viking.

Lennon, M. C., & Rosenfield, S. (1994). Relative fairness and the division of household labor. *American Journal of Sociology, 100,* 506–531.

Loprest, P. (1999, August). How families that left welfare are doing: A national picture. *Urban Institute,* Series B, #B-1.

Lorber, J. (1994). *Paradoxes of gender.* New Haven: Yale University Press.

Maccoby, E. (1998). *The two sexes.* Cambridge, MA: Belknap Press.

Marks, N. (1996). Caregiving across the lifespan: National prevalence and predictors. *Family Relations, 45,* 27–36.

Oliker, S. J. (2000). Examining care at welfare's end. In M. H. Meyer (Ed.), *Care work: Gender, labor, and welfare states* (pp. 167–325). London: Routledge.

Press, J., & Townsley, E. (1998). Wives' and husbands' housework reporting: Gender, class, and social desirability. *Gender & Society, 12,* 218–228.

Reskin, B., & Padavic, I. (1994). *Women and men at work.* Thousand Oaks, CA: Pine Forge Press.

Risman, B. (1998). *Gender vertigo.* New Haven: Yale University Press.

Roos, P., & Gatta, M. (1999). The gender gap in earnings: Trends, explanations, prospects. In G. Powell (Ed.), *Handbook of gender and work* (pp. 95–123). Thousand Oaks, CA: Sage.

Rossi, A. S., & Rossi, P. H.(1990). *Of human bonding: Parent-child relations across the life course.* New York: A. de Gruyter.

Sarkisian, N., Gerena, M., & Gerstel, N. (2000). *More or less kin: Addressing debates on care work in African American communities.* Paper presented at Carework Conference, Washington, DC.

Udry, J. R., Morris, N. M., & Kovenock, J. (1995). Androgen effects on women's gendered behavior. *Journal of Biosocial Science, 27,* 359–368.

Walzer, S. (1998.) *Thinking about the baby: Gender and transitions into parenthood.* Philadelphia: Temple University Press.

12

Producing Family Time

Practices of Leisure Activity Beyond the Home

Marjorie L. DeVault

This article presents my analysis of an occasional, local, and apparently rather trivial activity—the "family outing" to the zoo—but I want to suggest that it can be read as part of a larger story, about the changing character of middle- and working-class family life. Part of this large story revolves around time—how much time parents can and do spend with families (Hochschild, 1997), for example, who is overworked and why (Schor, 1992), and how to provide for the "quality time" that most Americans believe is so crucial for children's development (Daly, 1998). Policy makers take up these questions in the context of an emergent discourse of "work/family" (or sometimes "work/life") issues. Such developments are signals of a large social transformation in the organization of work and family life—arising in large part from the establishment of middle-class wives and mothers as relatively permanent members of the labor force. As in the early industrial period, this large change is accompanied by uncertainties and anxieties about the reproduction of future generations, and it motivates attempts to develop a model (or models) for family life that will fit with a restructuring economy. Research on the "time bind" in contemporary family life (Hochschild, 1997)—and widespread discussion of it—points toward larger areas of concern: How will ordinary people sustain those experiences that make up "family life" as so many have known it in the industrial period? What do the middle classes want to preserve, and why? Not, apparently, starched and pressed collars, home-baked cookies, or even (but much more controversially) child care at home. What, then, will come to be defined as essential to family life—and for whom?

The research I report on here is concerned with some of the things that parents do with the "family time" they have with children, and—in a very preliminary way—with how their practices are shaped by larger social structures—not only by work hours, schedules, and pressures but also by the organization of the public spaces that family members might inhabit together and a discourse of family life that swirls around those spaces. Though I can only sketch in these larger contexts and their consequences at this point, my intention is to identify some openings for connecting this ethnography of a local setting to broader political-economic relations (as outlined in Smith, 1987; and DeVault, 1999, ch. 3).

The notion of "the family outing" is a concept with a class and cultural bias built into it. I do not mean that only middle-class families go to the zoo; in fact, the zoo appears to be one of the more "democratic" spaces in which families gather. What I mean is that the idea of the outing calls up a particular image of family life, an image that minimizes collective economic support and emphasizes a terrain of consciously constructed emotional expression (and discipline)—the "modern" view of marriage and family life. Many North Americans seek this mode of family experience, work extremely hard to achieve it, and derive intense pleasure from their sense of family connectedness. This model of family life is also encouraged and enforced by public discourses of family life, through advice directed to mothers, references to "quality time," public images of family, and the activities of social workers and other family educators. For example, a social worker tells me that when she taught "parenting skills" she regularly "prescribed" an outing to the zoo. She went on to say, however, that few of her low-income clients were able to comply with the advice; such an outing requires substantial resources (transportation, entrance fees, money for snacks and souvenirs) and, perhaps more important, a good deal of time and energy for planning and execution. This kind of explicit instruction is less common than a more general imperative for parents to attend to children's development, conveyed through focused advice literature and disseminated even more widely through various media. For example, nearly every city newspaper publishes a calendar of events, many identified as especially appropriate for children or families, and in most cities of any size, one finds monthly publications directed specifically toward parents and offering a smorgasbord of sites, services, and products for producing family time. Thus, an outing to the zoo is the kind of activity that has come to be seen—by experts and those parents oriented to expert discourse—as fundamental to satisfactory family life, even though in practice many family groups cannot accomplish such activities routinely or do not wish to.

My reference to this kind of family outing as an "accomplishment" signals the theoretical foundations of my approach. My intention is to analyze family ethnomethodologically, as a distinctive social configuration that is continually brought into being through people's activities, interactions, and interpretations, situated within powerful discourses of family life (Gubrium & Holstein, 1990; Griffith & Smith, 1987; DeVault, 1991). Such an approach recognizes biological, economic, and legal connections as critical resources for constituting family relationships, but it also implies that these connections are mobilized and given meaning only through interactive interpretive processes. A social sense of the primordial character of family experience is held in place, like other social realities, through collective practices of sense-making (Garfinkel, 1967) that establish the routine grounds of shared experience. Thus, family relations are sustained through the social practices of many actors in a multitude of social settings. The largely invisible work practices of mothers, fathers, and other caretakers are central to the constitution of family; but so are the practices of social workers (like the one I referred to above), teachers, employers, and others. The family outing, then, is constituted not only by its central actors—parents, children, and other participants such as relatives and friends—but also by those who produce its context: the social workers, educators, journalists, and others who write about family life, and also the planners, administrators, and entrepreneurs who create and maintain sites for family recreation. In the analysis that follows, I focus on the work practices of adults who conduct family outings with children, but I attempt to pursue the analysis of those practices in a way that keeps their contexts in view.[1]

This kind of analysis depends on a "generous" definition of work (Smith, 1987) and builds on the work of scholars who have brought into view the various kinds of work that contribute to the day-to-day construction of family life. In addition to wage work that supports the household economically, unpaid family work at home includes not just child care and basic sustenance but less visible effort such as coordination and planning, emotion and kin work, and the production of intimacy and sociability (e.g., DeVault, 1991; Hochschild, 1983; Di Leonardo, 1987; Carrington, 1999).[2] Some scholars have recognized that the work which produces family extends beyond the household into public settings such as schools, courtrooms, and health-care institutions (Smith & Griffith, 1990; Gubrium & Holstein, 1990), though Gubrium and Holstein note that these public faces of family life have been relatively neglected by family scholars. The small body of research that does consider family work outside the home has focused on family members' (usually obligatory) participation in the formal organizations, such as workplace and school, that govern contemporary life. The emergent discourse of work/family concerns, however, suggests an increasing awareness of the links across ostensible boundaries between homes and other organizations.

Many fewer scholars have considered the constitution of family through voluntary, collective leisure activity in public, the kind of activity I refer to here as a "family outing." Sociologists of leisure tend to focus on the individual (Olszewska & Roberts, 1989; Wimbush & Talbot, 1988), despite the fact that those living with children spend much of their leisure time in family groupings of various sorts. This pattern no doubt reflects the fact that for parents (and especially mothers), such outings must be considered an ambiguous mix of "leisure" and "work." Some studies show that middle-class (and perhaps other) parents (again, especially mothers) devote considerable effort and thought to such activity (Seery, 1996; Daly, 1998). And Jack Katz (1996), in a study of laughter in a hall of "funny mirrors" in France, suggests that it is the family grouping and its constitution (highlighted in a distorted reflection) that has the social power to bring participants to the moment of laughter. Parents themselves do not necessarily think of such activities as work and may not even think of them as efforts requiring any distinctive label. "Outing" is my term; those I've talked with rarely name such activity, or do so much less formally. However, they do speak of "getting out," "doing things," and wanting children to "see all kinds of things."

While there are many possible destinations for family outings, the zoo provides a particularly rich example. It is a loosely structured site, organized and managed in the contemporary moment for multiple purposes (recreational, educational, and environmental), but still bearing the traces of a colonialist history of exploration and conquest (Ritvo, 1987; Mullen & Marvin, 1999). It is a site that is strongly associated with familial experience, perhaps because it offers varying pleasures to people of all ages. It is also a site that is methodologically convenient, since it brings together many family groups, each constructing its own version of the activity given the resources and restrictions of a particular zoo.

Methods and Data

The core of my analysis describes, on the basis of naturalistic observation (Adler & Adler, 1994), how family activities at the zoo are conducted, with a focus on parents' practices of coordinating the experience. Drawing on a tradition of sociological study of public life (Goffman, 1971; Lofland, 1973; Brooks Gardner, 1995), I consider how family groups move into and through the zoo, what they can be seen doing while there, and how they manage their activity as one group among many. The observational data are supplemented by informal interviews conducted at the zoo and some data drawn from another interview study concerned more broadly with the conduct of various outings.

I collected observational data with help from several assistants.[3] Our procedure was relatively simple: in sessions of 1-2 hours, we walked around the zoo, mingling with other visitors and watching them carefully. Observations were relatively unstructured but focused on the movement of groups through the setting and how movement is coordinated, the group members talk with one another about what they see, and their interpretations of zoo exhibits. At the end of an observation session, we jotted brief notes to preserve the outlines of what we had seen. Later (but as soon as possible), we wrote much more detailed accounts, recording as much as we could remember about the composition, conduct, and conversation of the groups we had observed. This procedure meant that we appeared to be zoo visitors ourselves; in fact, our conduct was shaped by our research purposes. We generally tried to "follow" a particular group through several exhibits, standing near enough to see and hear their activity and moving from one exhibit to the next at about the same speed. Sometimes we stationed ourselves for an extended period at an exhibit that was especially popular, watching groups flow past. Most of these observations were conducted at two relatively modest zoos in two northeastern cities, one small and one large; though both zoos drew some visitors from surrounding communities, neither was the kind of "major" regional zoo that often serves as a prominent tourist attraction. We have made observations at a few smaller and larger community zoos in other cities, as opportunities arise, and I have observed occasionally at other animal venues (e.g., an aquarium, a demonstration farm).

After completing about 50 hours of unobtrusive observation, I obtained permission to do more systematic data collection at the big-city zoo. During several days of observation, I watched while family groups viewed various exhibits and took verbatim notes on their conversation. Though not as complete as tape recordings would be, these notes provide more reliable detail than notes taken from memory about the talk occurring among family members. In addition, I conducted informal interviews of about 10 minutes or so with 25 visitor groups resting at the picnic area. In these conversations, I inquired about the relationships among those who composed the visiting group, and asked several general questions about their experiences, beginning with "What brought you to the zoo today?" and following up with questions such as "What have you done during your visit?" "Do you come to the zoo often?" "Did you have any kind of plan when you arrived?"

Findings

Our observation procedure did not involve any overt attempt to determine whether a group was "actually" a family. Most of the groups we watched were "family-like" groups of adults and children together. However, we also made notes about adult couples, lone visitors, and occasional groups that seemed obviously not to be families (one such case, e.g., was a group of seven or eight girls of about the same age, supervised by an adult woman and wearing nametags of some sort; another was a group of six adults who appeared to have developmental disabilities, shepherded through the zoo by two adults without obvious disabilities). My use of scare quotes above (in "'actually' a family") signals the problematic character of this judgment: even if we had perfect knowledge of the people we saw, what criteria would make them family or not? I have not adopted the standard methodological procedure in family studies, whereby the analyst decides, however thoughtfully, on some definition for a family—based perhaps on biological or legal connections, perhaps on members' self-definitions—and includes only those groups that fit the selected model. Such procedures seem to ensure that some of the diversity of family experience will be lost. My procedure here carries the opposite risk: that I may include in the analysis some groups that others would not identify as family. But this ambiguity seems to me more consistent with people's actual experiences of social relationships than with the often false sense of precision that is produced by more standardized research techniques. I do not mean to dismiss the question of who is family too glibly—if I knew more, I would provide more detailed stories about the groups I observed—nor to imply that any zoo-visiting group becomes "family." However, I ask the reader to accept some uncertainty about the matter as one of the costs of looking at family activity naturalistically in a public setting.

I conducted informal interviews partly in order to address this question, and the interview data confirm that the zoo is populated primarily by groupings that would be considered family by almost any definition, although many of these groupings diverge from the nuclear family model consisting of parents and their children alone. Of the 25 groups I interviewed (on Saturday and Sunday afternoons), about half fit this parent-and-child family form. Most others were groups of parents and children with extended family members (aunts, uncles, grandparents), or groups made up of several families (or several parts of families) together. Only four of the groups I spoke with consisted of adults alone, and only two were made up of individuals without any family ties; two groups of adult visitors without children were based on sibling relationships.

Some groups that don't look much like the idealized family at the zoo in fact would count as "actual" or legal families. For example, two women together turn out to be a mother and daughter: the daughter, 28 years old, uses a wheelchair and, as they tell the story, depends heavily on her mother for mobility. They've come to the zoo for a treat before she endures another in a series of painful surgeries. Other groups that look unproblematically familial turn out to be something else: for example, a woman and young boy are simply "friends." The extended interviews I've conducted with parents suggest that groups in these kinds of settings sometimes include children's friends as well as the immediate family. These kinds of observations point to a unit of social organization that seems to have a robust reality, though it is rarely noticed as a distinctive form; we might call it a "familial grouping."[4] It is a unit that is brought into being when adults travel to public settings with children in their charge; adults in these groupings have the authority and responsibilities of parents and adopt many parental practices, though they are not actually or legally parents to all the children in the group.

In this analysis, I focus on the observable practices through which adults and children in such groupings jointly accomplish their time at the zoo.[5] Parents (or other adult companions) use the zoo as one of many sites that situate children within a public world, a world of objects known in common. At the same time, practices of family recreation constitute the particular family grouping as a significant one, with its own unique experiences of such public space. I begin by examining what appears to be a fundamental lesson of the zoo visit: the development of a shared orientation to a "viewable" nonhuman landscape. I first analyze parents' and children's practices, and then examine the zoo as an ensemble of exhibits and texts that constitute a shared landscape. In the third part of the analysis, I return to the practices of family members to show how the boundedness and uniqueness of a particular family group is preserved within such settings.

The Coordination of Looking

The core activity of a zoo visit is viewing the animals, as presented in their enclosures. Some live in rows of small, simple cages; many, now, are presented in larger pens, designed to simulate their natural habitats. Directions for viewing are provided by signs posted near the exhibits; these identify the species on view, usually providing as well some information about the species or, less often, about individual animals.

I was struck, when I began the fieldwork, by the simplicity (one might even say banality) of most talk among zoo visitors, which was primarily concerned with the work of seeing. While it might seem a simple matter for a family group to stand at an enclosure and see the animals it contains, a close look at their activity reveals that they work assiduously at this accomplishment. Much of the talk among groups consists of announcements and directives. For example:

> There were a few small groups standing at low fences by the ponds, commenting briefly on the birds. One child announced, "A flamingo, a flamingo!" Elsewhere, I heard a father note, "It's a toucan." Others were just locating the birds, with comments like "There's one," or "Look at that."

This excerpt illustrates both generic pointing talk ("Look!" There!") and species naming ("LIONS!"). These simple exchanges among family members coordinate and comment on their joint looking. Their talk ensures that they look together. Sometimes seeing is more challenging, and family members work together to accomplish the viewing of each exhibit. For example:

> The boy spotted the snowy owl before his father did, and pointed it out. It was behind some shrubbery, and the dad suggested they move to the other side of the cage for a better view.

This kind of coordinated looking is characteristic of virtually all zoo-visiting groups, whether they are families or not. Within these family groupings, however, it can be seen as one of the myriad ways that parents socialize children by locating them within a larger public world. It contributes to the child's stock of social knowledge and gives a sense of shared practice and of participation in a social ritual. As in most childhood activity, there is an intensity behind the pleasure of both children and their parents and focused work aimed at achieving appropriate forms of participation.

The development of appropriate looking as a skill can be seen most clearly in the activities of the youngest zoo visitors, guided by their adult companions, as they learn how to view the exhibits. We saw many couples touring the zoo with infants, positioning their children in order to direct their gaze appropriately. Sometimes infants were transported in strollers, and positioning was accomplished through the orientation of the stroller; other parents lifted infants up to the exhibits, holding them close to ensure an appropriate view. Talk can reinforce these positional strategies, even when children are quite young, as in the following example:

> A white man holds a toddler. He's soft-spoken and rarely initiates talk to the child, but always responds. The child is surprisingly verbal, but only in single syllables:
> "Buh."
> "Yes, that's a bird."
> "Moh."
> "That's right, there's another one." (I thought he'd said monkey, but his dad knew.)
> "Wah."
> "Yes, there's some water."
> "Eee."
> "Yes, the bird is eating."
> "Moh."
> "Yes, there are some more birds." And after a moment's silence: "Look, there's a monkey."

As children become more independent, they begin to look on their own. The activities of toddlers, however, sometimes reveal that they have not yet learned to attend to all the cues that direct viewing at the zoo. While more mature visitors know that exhibits are contained within the zoo's enclosures, and look there for "viewable" contents, very young children may seem equally fascinated by more mundane features of the environment. They stoop down to pick up rocks from the pathway or fondle interesting paving stones; they study and ask about guardrails and enclosures, maintenance areas and equipment, and so on. Parents' responses (and nonresponses) give clues about the significance of such features, as in the following exchange:

> A man with two boys, one about 10 and the other in a stroller, walk past an unlabeled pond.
> The older boy asks: "What's in there?"
> "Oh, it's just a pond, I think."
> "But what's in it?"
> "I don't know. Turtles, probably, something like that."

Learning to look properly in this environment (as in any situation) means coming to understand that some features deserve attention, while others are "just there"—essential but to be treated as meaningless. (The child learns, for example, to see the animal, but not the cage.) Thoroughly socialized viewers rarely exhibit such lapses, and in the occasional cases when they do, their embarrassment underlines the felt "wrongness" of undisciplined viewing. For example, in one wooded area of the zoo—a large enclosure for deer—squirrels frolic on a bird feeder. We saw a grandmother fall behind the rest of her family because she was watching the squirrels; as she turned to catch up with them, she muttered to herself, "I shouldn't be looking at squirrels. I can see them any time."

Such responses reveal not only an awareness of the boundaries of appropriate viewing but also some consciousness of the zoo visit as public activity, subject to evaluations by other visitors. Parents responding to children in these situations can often be seen providing remedial displays (Goffman, 1971). In these situations, "performance" takes over momentarily, revealing the potential tensions between family experience and the requirements of public activity. For example:

> A boy asks his father about a recess in the wall, rather than the exhibit; the man glances around self-consciously as he shrugs off the question.

> Parents are disciplining their kids for climbing on some rocks; one boy begins a tantrum, and his parents exchange looks with the observers.

Consciously or not, this behavior seems concerned with doing zoo visiting "properly." It also points to the way that this kind of activity is in a peculiar way simultaneously "private" and "public." I will return to this idea later.

The Zoo as an Ensemble of Texts

Interpretive signs provide information about zoo exhibits. These aids nearly always indicate species names and habitats, sometimes supplemented with information about notable features of a species or its behavior. Some signs control behavior, usually through gentle prohibitions: "Please do not toss coins into the wetland. They could harm the animals." Or, on the stalls of the farm animals: "We bite." A few give credit for exhibits to corporate sponsors. All this textual material exists as a possible resource for use in visitors' interaction, with the exhibits and with one another. Given the increasing commitment of modern zoos to environmental education, and their considerable sophistication in the design of exhibit space and interpretation, one might expect to see visitors studying these informational placards carefully, in order to glean full educational value from the exhibit. In fact, most signs are used, for the most part, in simple, direct ways, to reinforce and make meaningful the proper gaze discussed above.

> Father: We're not seeing the hornbill.
> Mother: [or maybe it was the daughter] Yes, there it is.
> Father: (studying the placard): No, it has a very large beak.
> Mother: Yes, look. It's up there.
> Father: Oh, yes, so it is. Well, look at that.

Often, parents seem to use signs to produce authoritative talk with their children—typically, to announce a species name or, less frequently, to provide some fact about the animals on display. For example, one sign labeled a group of ring-tailed lemurs:

> As families approach this exhibit, much of their talk deals with identification: Kids frequently refer to the animals as raccoons and parents usually correct them. "No, it's not a raccoon. It looks like a raccoon, but it's something else."

These didactic moments tend to be brief and relatively thin, however. For example, as one family group moved on to the ruffed lemur, a father announced:

> "This is another kind of lemur. They're just like the lemurs we saw before, except they're different."

Signs, and the phrases they provide, often seem to operate as a kind of pivot around which collective conversation turns, rather than as fully processed, meaningful information. These kinds of talk organize a collective experience, even if they do not produce the kind of nature education their designers might have imagined. For example, at one enclosure a group of small animals are identified most prominently by an unusual characteristic: They are labeled as "barking deer." Many viewers read this phrase aloud, and I overheard one group in which an entire conversation went something like this:

> A mother, announcing: "Barking deer. Hmmm."
> Another adult woman, with the group, sounding very surprised and interested: "Barking deer?"
> The mother again, shaking her head with wonder, and confirming her original comment: "Barking deer."
> And finally, one of the boys with them, about 6, kind of sing-songing, to no one in particular: "Barking deer, barking deer."

Some parents add information to that contained in the official signage, often drawing on texts from outside the zoo. For example:

> The sign at the falcon's cage is titled "WHOOSH," and many of the people who approached the cage while I stood there read out, "Whoosh," as they arrived. A couple of

parents read off the sign to their children: "This is the fastest animal on earth." One person, drawing on a local news story, commented (I think to another adult), "That's like at the MONY tower." A few minutes later, a parent developed a more elaborate version of this comment for a child: "There are very few of these in the world, and do you know where two of them are? They're living at the MONY tower downtown. That's right, they came there and they made their nest right on the tower."

These kinds of practices—dependent on parents' (usually) more sophisticated literacy—produce distinctive, hierarchical relations of knowledge/authority within these family groups. Parents use information gleaned from texts to instruct children; thus, in most cases they appear, "naturally," to know more than their children. In a few cases, however, children are the ones who use signs more skillfully. Occasionally, for example, we've observed interactions in which children seem to be interpreting signs for non-English-speaking parents.

Animals have a pervasive presence in many North American children's lives, and animal texts beyond the zoo are important anchors for the zoo experience; indeed, some parents report that they bring children to the zoo so that they can see the "real animals" they have read and talked about. Animals are standard, ubiquitous characters in children's stories, and they provide material for very early cultural learning (dogs go "bow-wow;" ducks go "quack"). Soft stuffed animals are popular toys, and animal characters speak to children from the TV screen. Disney texts sometimes serve as reference points from outside the zoo, as when a mother summarizes: "So you saw Timon [the meercat]—you can tell ———— you saw Timon. And you saw the Lion King, too!" Such references seem more common at the smaller-city zoo, where concessions are provided through an on-site Burger King, with Disney-themed logos and souvenir cups (on "themed environments," see Gottdiener 1997).

Some family groups seem to use the zoo in more sustained and focused ways, drawing on interpretive signs in ways closer to their designers' intentions. In my informal interviews at the big-city zoo, for example, I talked with several groups of parents and children for whom animal study was a sustained hobby of sorts. These children collected animal books at home, prided themselves on their knowledge of animal life and habits, came to the zoo more frequently than others, and seemed concerned with more complex links between sights at the zoo and a wider field of knowledge. These activities required parental support, of course, and were sometimes presented as joint interests of adults and children. But most of these parents spoke about them "on behalf" of their children, with language pointing to (and constructing) children's individual interests and concerns: "He's interested in animals." "She wants to be an animal doctor."

Featured exhibits at the zoo—whose signage focuses on the lives of individual animals with eventful life stories—provide rich sites for such sustained study. At the big-city zoo, for example, signs identify individual gorillas, explicate their family relationships, and point to incidents that have viewable consequences (as when a young gorilla cuts its arm). Zoo educators, animal keepers, or volunteers are frequently stationed near these exhibits during peak weekend hours; they model sustained attention to individual animals and provide for occasional visitors the kind of information that accumulates with sustained study. These textual and organizational resources provide for varying degrees of orientation to individual animals in these special exhibits. For the youngest and casually involved visitors, such an orientation may simply involve locating "the baby," or noticing that the young gorilla "has a boo-boo." Older children who take an interest may pick up quickly from volunteers the kind of surveillance that treats the gorillas as social groups with patterns of interaction.

I interviewed one family grouping, a mother and two daughters, who had made a regular routine of gorilla study. They come to the zoo three or four times a month and spend much of their time watching these animals. The older daughter, 11 years old, began to explain; her sister, only one, then recited the gorillas' names. When I turned to their mother, she chimed in, "Oh, I like the gorillas," and added, "My kids have no choice; this is the only pet they're going to get." But even more casual and sporadic visitors can develop a feel for sustained observation, as when I watched two adults wait patiently while a teenaged girl tracked a pair of playful adolescent gorillas from one exhibit window to another, returning periodically to report on their activities to her parents and a zoo volunteer stationed at the exhibit.

These kinds of involvement appear to develop primarily around exhibits featured by particular zoos, usually exhibits of animals with some social life that can serve as a narrative resource for interpretive material. While the gorillas are the centerpiece of the large-city zoo's featured tropical forest exhibit, the smaller-city zoo features a collection of elephants and an elephant breeding program whose successes have been prominently featured in local media. Thus, some parents and children arrive to view this kind of exhibit with considerable background knowledge gleaned from textual materials outside the zoo.

The Construction of Family Space in Public

However they use the resources of the setting, family groups must coordinate their movement around the zoo, from one exhibit to another. They move from place to place not as autonomous individuals but in amoeba-like collective formations. The practices of moving together, like those of looking together, vary with the ages of children in family groups. Infants and toddlers are often carried or ride in strollers, so that parents can rely on such equipment to keep children nearby and position them in front of viewable sights. As children get older and begin to move about independently, they tend to circulate around adults and older children in their groups. A common pattern we observed involved a parent or parents walking relatively slowly and directly from one place to another, while young children "buzzed" around them, like little satellites. Sometimes family members hold hands as they walk along, but it is much more common for the group simply to maintain proximity, using talk or eye contact to monitor the positions of others. For example, parents can usually be observed watching children and often call to those who stray too far away. Children, often running ahead of the rest of their group or lingering behind, reluctant to leave an attractive exhibit, look back or ahead from time to time, making sure they haven't lost the rest of the group. Occasionally, we see parents making explicit rules about positioning. For example:

> I look back and see another group approaching from the front gate, kids in the lead. Dad, raising his voice: "Now here's the rule. You can only run so far ahead. We have to be able to see you."

Much more frequently, members seem to rely on unspoken or at least firmly established expectations that need no reiteration. Though unspoken, the mutual monitoring involved is obvious, as when a mother focuses her gaze on a small child 20 feet away, shifting position slightly as the child moves so that she is always in view; or when a small boy, absorbed in an exhibit, looks up to see his parents walking on, and follows as if tied to them by an invisible string.

These practices mark families as groups, so that as they move about the zoo, they recognize each other's boundaries. Like individuals on a crowded public street, who notice each other just enough to avoid collision, they display a collective awareness of other groups, respect the territories of other groups, and expect to enjoy the same respect themselves. Over and over, we could see groups arriving at an exhibit area and positioning themselves in a cluster, so as to maintain their proximity. They often seek an "open" area, so as to stake their claim to a relatively "private" space. (Like understandings of properly "viewable" exhibits, these practices develop with age and experience: thus, parents monitor the behavior of children, directing them to open areas and positioning them in ways that respect boundaries the youngest children may not yet notice.) Members of these groups attempt not to breach the boundaries of other groups, and they engage in subtly signaled apologies when boundaries are disrupted, as we did in the following example:

> As we left the building, I noted how we encountered another group coming in. We were walking two by two, and they were four or five people spread out in a row. There was that awkward kind of moment, where our group was pointed right into the middle of theirs. Everyone hesitated just a moment, I think, and then they spread apart slightly, and we walked through the middle of their line. There was just a bit of eye contact, as if they were giving permission and we were acknowledging that.

Conversation at the zoo occurs almost entirely within rather than across such family boundaries. Although various groups are in close proximity and can easily hear conversation in other groups, each group constructs its own realm of talk and practices a version of "civil inattention" (Goffman, 1971) with respect to other groups. Thus, each group creates a sphere that has a "private" character even in this often densely crowded public setting. Katz (1996) noted similar behaviors in the fun house, where bystanders watched patiently while family groups looked into the funny mirrors, standing aside and never participating in the group's collective laughter.

These practices are most striking in the situations where privacy is most difficult to sustain. Every zoo seems to produce a few especially crowded sites, where many viewing families cluster around the most popular exhibits. In these areas, family group boundaries loosen and become more permeable (though they don't dissolve completely). Thus:

> Four large, adult elephants came parading out with a baby elephant wandering around at their feet. As soon as she was visible, the crowd unanimously "Ahhh!"ed. I could hear a number of women in the crowd say, "Isn't she adorable?"

Even within these crowds, however, one finds family groups (or sometimes subgroups, since larger families are more likely to become segmented in these crowded settings) constructing smaller "private" conversations within the brouhaha of the larger crowd. For example:

> One of the bears was pacing, and a mother and son (about 10 years old) were discussing its behavior. The woman said that the bear was confused and that that was why he was pacing. The son started giggling and repeated the "confusing" part, while his mother laughed. A few others in the crowd then began commenting on the same "confused bear."

Information flows easily across groups in these crowded settings, and this example illustrates how "family" conversations in these settings are sometimes enhanced by information obtained from observing other groups. But these hearings rarely produce interactions across groups.

> The lion male was roaming around the cage, putting on an interesting show for the crowd, and there was quite a crush near the glass. Some boys were debating whether the lion could see them, and I noticed a young girl listening intently to their speculations and asking her parent, "Can they see us?"

Strikingly, as in this example, when a member hears something interesting in another group, any comment on that hearing is nearly always contained within the hearer's family. The child asks not the one commenting but her own mother if the lion can really see them; a father overhears and then tells his own child that the racoonlike animal is a lemur.

Only two kinds of moments seem likely to stimulate brief talk among apparently unacquainted adults; both could be seen as moments of departure from an idealized zoo visiting routine. When children misbehave, or cry long and loudly, parents often exchange sympathetic glances and sometimes offer reassuring remarks. For example, a mother whose child has been screaming for several minutes, grimaces at another mother nearby: "Having a bad day." And the response: "I know what that's like. I've had plenty of bad days myself." In addition, boundaries appear vulnerable in the face of animal displays of sexuality and mess. When children comment on animals' sexual organs or display interest in prominent turds, adult visitors almost always glance nervously around, grimacing or giggling uncomfortably with adults in nearby groups. (Sometimes adults simply ignore their children's comments about these displays, another indication that these exhibits don't fit well with adult conceptions of "proper" viewing. And sometimes they carry on "adult conversations," as when two couples exchanged remarks about a pregnant lemur—"Whoa, is she pregnant!" "Oh my god, look at that!"—without inviting children to respond.)

From time to time, I have tested the strength of the family boundaries on talk by offering conversational overtures to parents in nearby family groupings. Typically, parents respond to an initial conversational offering, briefly (the zoo is a friendly place, after all), but decline to pursue talk beyond a one-time exchange; in response to a follow-up remark, they nod politely and turn away, attending assiduously to their children and signaling to me that our conversation should end. This conversational pattern means that the collective activity of looking/watching is contained in family groups—members do not usually speak about exhibits to those in neighboring groups—and therefore what's seen at the zoo is constructed as "the family's" experience.

Discussion: Family as Socially Organized Practice

This analysis provides a view of family-as-it-happens, a view of activity that is quite familiar but almost entirely taken for granted. Conceptually, I have tried to illustrate an ethnomethodologically-based approach to family studies that focuses on activity and interpretation. Rather than treating family as an objective entity, defined from outside, this approach treats family as discursively organized practice, a mode of action rather than a state of being.[6] The value of such an approach lies in its ability to capture the fluidity and diversity of family life as it actually occurs in the world, beginning with the sites where family is happening, rather than with notions of family "form" that are more durable in scholarship than in the world (Smith, 1993).

These data provide one example of how small groups of individuals actively constitute themselves as family. I do not mean that people go to the zoo with this explicit intention; they are simply doing something that families often do (perhaps something that they think is "good" for families to do, along the lines of spending "quality time" together). What's important, analytically, is that they are engaged in a kind of "standard practice" of family life. Zoo visiting produces a distinctive kind of family experience: It locates a group as one among many, doing something understood as "properly" familial. It orients group members, collectively, toward a larger world of nature, and thus positions children within a shared world of nature and human activity. It is conducted in public, and yet its character reinforces the enclosed and at least "quasi-private" quality of family experience.

I would suggest that this kind of activity conveys relatively unnoticed but profound social messages. Though the zoo visit may be experienced by participants in myriad ways—with pleasure, boredom, or indifference; as simple fun, nature education, or a difficult ordeal; and so on—its core activities virtually always involve family members in practices that define and reinforce a series of significant boundaries: between humans and animals, between properly viewable and insignificant sights, and between family and others. My analysis of family activity at the zoo brings into view a kind of parental work that pervades everyday life, situating very young children within a world-known-in-common—a foundation for the related work of "developing the child" (Noble, cited in Smith, 1987). This kind of work pervades life with children. In contemporary, highly stratified societies, it is discursively organized in increasingly elaborate ways.

Zoos are usually publicly supported, relatively accessible spaces for the broad mass of urban families. Still, not every family goes to the zoo. Participation in this kind of activity is organized in part by money and time. One must find time for a zoo visit and arrange transportation to the site. In addition, the zoos studied here charge admission, a fee that seems nominal to some and prohibitive to others (though the big-city zoo has a "free hour" once a month—a considerably diminished version of the "free day" that has been traditional at many urban museums). Participation is also organized culturally. While the zoo is widely seen as an especially appropriate place for spending family time, it is no doubt located differently in the repertoires of different family groups and within a wider field of cultural experiences that are understood hierarchically (some families might choose a more commercial attraction or a more "natural" wildlife sanctuary). The local parenting magazines I mentioned in the introduction contain not only calendars of family activities but also an array of advertisements that reveal an increasing variety of commercial spaces for family activities, including new suburban spaces that seem directed at more affluent parents and children. Participation is also organized through residential geographies, including the recreational facilities available in various locations and the continuing economic and racial/ethnic segregation of U.S. cities. For example, the two zoos in which most of these data were collected are both located in multiethnic cities, but they contrast in interesting ways that reveal the racialized structures of public settings in the United States. One zoo is located in a section of the city recognized as mostly white, and zoo visitors are nearly all white. The other is located on the edge of a predominantly African American neighborhood in a large, older urban park. Here visitors are a more visibly diverse group. This zoo appears to be more accessible and comfortable for racial/ethnic minority visitors, and perhaps also less comfortable for whites accustomed to homogeneous settings. Zoo staff allude to this dynamic with references to "suburban" visitors who may be anxious about an "urban experience."

Despite such social divisions, ideas about the family outing manifest a characteristic feature of public imagery and discourse about families—its tendency to represent family experience in homogenized ways that obscure social differences and inequalities (Rapp, 1982; DeVault, 1991). Realms of family life—as lived by some—typically appear as terrains of choice and autonomy, where members of the society share aspirations and equally participate in fundamental human experiences of connection, responsibility, and pleasure—any parent, this illusion suggests, can enjoy taking a child to the zoo.

It has been important to bring into view the invisible work parents (and especially mothers) do to produce and sustain family life. However, a potential pitfall in focusing on parental work practice is that such effects can appear to depend on effort alone. Indeed, family education directed at parents considered "at risk" often seems to rely on such illusions, as in the social worker's comment quoted at the beginning of this article. My intention here is to locate an extended parental work process within the complex of structures and institutions beyond the home: to bring into view the "workplaces," as it were, that shape the efforts of parents in various ways.

We can see in this analysis that public spaces are often populated by clusters of individuals connected through family ties. Their public activity is organized strongly by their orientations to the ostensibly "private" experiences of family. Similarly, as family members move in and out of their residences, their experiences are organized not only by family ties but also by the contexts in which they live. The work of "developing the child" extends outward into the social world that surrounds each household, as parents and children venture into yards and streets, offices and shops, parks and museums. The worlds surrounding particular households are quite different, however—sometimes rich and welcoming for parents and children, sometimes bleak and dangerous—and so are parents' capacities to move with their children beyond local settings. Thus, some children easily gain a sense of knowledge, comfort, and mastery in a wider world, while others live in social worlds that are considerably more constricted.

I began by noting that the family day at the zoo appears to be a fleeting moment of pleasurable frivolity, but it has, in fact, a larger significance. Like any slice of social reality, it is not only local and immediate but also part of the structural and systemic relations of the wider society. My largest aim in this study is to illustrate how these small moments of family life can be "opened up" to connect with larger political economic concerns. I mean to show that a family outing to the zoo is produced through collective activity in the broadest sense, as family members engage in constant interplay with other realms of activity that constitute the structural features of contemporary life: the shared economic and cultural circumstances of household members, public facilities and their differential accessibility, industries of education and entertainment, and the professions that produce knowledge about parenting and family life. People practice family—artfully, creatively, with intention—in local settings, in more diverse groups than family scholars may acknowledge. And their intentions and craft are formed within material and discursive contexts that shape and channel those efforts in ways that family scholars have yet to fully recognize and explore.

Acknowledgments

Earlier versions of this paper were presented at Boston College, the 1998 Sloan Foundation/BPW/Wellesley College conference "Work and Family: Today's Realities, Tomorrow's Visions," and the writing workshop in the Syracuse University Department of Sociology. I'm grateful to members of those audiences, and to Naomi Gerstel and Dan Clawson, for probing questions and helpful comments.

Notes

1. My attention to context reflects the "institutional ethnography" approach recommended by Smith (1987), which allows analysis of how local activities and settings are coordinated through linkages to "ruling" institutions. (See also DeVault, 1999, ch. 3; Campbell, 1998; Grahame, 1998.)

2. Carrington's recent addition to this literature is especially interesting; it shows how some gay and lesbian couples, barred from legal marriage, work to produce home and family through a range of elaborated domestic pursuits.

3. My thanks for fieldwork and early discussions of the project to Sarah Pitcher, John B.

Thomas, and Andrew Roth-Wells.

4. Thanks to Rosanna Hertz for a conversation in which we "discovered" this grouping.

5. I do not consider preparatory activities, transportation to the zoo, or the ways that parents and children later share their zoo experiences in talk and activity elsewhere—although all of these are certainly important in the construction of these experiences.

6. The word "family," I would argue, should be an adjective rather than noun.

References

Adler, P. A., & Adler, P. (1994). Observational techniques. In N. K. Denzin and Y. S. Lincoln (Eds.), *Handbook of qualitative research* (pp. 377–392). Thousand Oaks, CA: Sage.

Brooks Gardner, C. (1995). *Passing by: Gender and public harassment*. Berkeley: University of California Press.

Campbell, M. L. (1998). Institutional ethnography and experience as data. *Qualitative Sociology, 21,* 55–73.

Carrington, C. (1999). *No place like home: Relationships and family life among lesbians and gay men*. Chicago: University of Chicago Press.

Daly, K. J. (1998, November 6–7). *Deconstructing family time: From ideology to lived experience*. Paper presented at Alfred P. Sloan Foundation/BPW Conference Work and Family: Today's Realities and Tomorrow's Visions, Boston.

DeVault, M. L. (1991). *Feeding the family: The social organization of caring as gendered work*. Chicago: University of Chicago Press.

DeVault, M. L. (1999). *Liberating method: Feminism and social research*. Philadelphia: Temple University Press.

Di Leonardo, M. (1987). The female world of cards and holidays: Women, families, and the work of kinship. *Signs, 12,* 440–453.

Garfinkel, H. (1967). *Studies in ethnomethodology*. Englewood Cliffs, NJ: Prentice-Hall.

Goffman, E. (1971). *Relations in public: Microstudies of the public order*. New York: Basic Books.

Goffman, E. (1979). *Gender advertisements*. New York: Harper & Row.

Gottdiener, M. (1997). *The theming of America: Dreams, visions, and commercial spaces*. Boulder, CO: Westview Press.

Grahame, P. R. (1998). Ethnography, institutions, and the social organization of knowledge. *Human Studies, 21,* 347–360.

Griffith, A. I., & Smith, D. E. (1987). Constructing cultural knowledge: Mothering as discourse. In J. Gaskell and A. McLaren (Eds.), *Women and education: A Canadian perspective* (pp. 87–103). Calgary, Alberta: Detselig.

Gubrium, J. F., & Holstein, J. A. (1990). *What is family?* Mountain View, CA: Mayfield.

Hochschild, A. R. (1983). *The managed heart: Commercialization of human feeling*. Berkeley: University of California Press.

Hochschild, A. R. (1997). *The time bind: When work becomes home and home becomes work*. New York: Holt.

Katz, J. (1996). Families and funny mirrors: A study of the social construction and personal embodiment of humor. *American Journal of Sociology, 101,* 1194–1237.

Lofland, L. H. (1973). *A world of strangers: Order and action in urban public space*. New York: Basic Books.

Mullen, B., & Marvin, G. (1999). *Zoo culture*. Urbana: University of Illinois Press.

Olszewska, A., & Roberts, K. (Eds.) (1989). *Leisure and lifestyle: A comparative analysis of free time*. London: Sage.

Rapp, R. (1982). Family and class in contemporary America: Notes toward an understanding of ideology. In B. Thorne with M. Yalom (Eds.), *Rethinking the family* (pp. 168–187). New York: Longman.

Ritvo, H. (1987). *The animal estate: The English and other creatures in the Victorian Age.* Cambridge: Harvard University Press.

Schor, J. B. (1992). *The overworked American: The unexpected decline of leisure.* New York: Basic Books.

Seery, B. L. (1996). *Four types of mothering emotion work: Distress management, ego work, relationship management, and pleasure/enjoyment work.* Doctoral dissertation, Pennsylvania State University.

Smith, D. E. (1987). *The everyday world as problematic: A feminist sociology.* Boston: Northeastern University Press.

Smith, D. E. (1993). The standard North American family: SNAF as an ideological code. *Journal of Family Issues, 14,* 50–65.

Smith, D. E., & Griffith, A. I. (1990). Coordinating the uncoordinated: Mothering, schooling, and social class. In G. Miller and J. A. Holstein (Eds.), *Perspectives on social problems: A research annual* (Vol. 2, pp. 25–42). Greenwich, CT: JAI Press.

Wimbush, E., & Talbot, M. (Eds.) (1988). *Relative freedoms: Women and leisure.* Philadelphia: Open University Press.

Part Four
Policy, Politics, and Working Families

Conflicts between work and family are not the inevitable result of economic or technological "progress." Neither are they simply the consequence of the unconstrained choices of individual women and men, pulled in different directions by inherently contradictory goals. Rather, as the articles in this section show, the conflicts between work and family are driven, in large part, by political decisions, based on collective choices in which those with more power exercise more influence. There is, however, nothing inevitable about these collective decisions and it is likely that over the years ahead they will be challenged by social movements of various sorts, including, most importantly, feminist and union organizations.

To be sure, individual women and men do make choices about how to organize their own work lives and family lives, but they do not make these decisions under circumstances of their own choosing. Their choices about where to work and when to work, to have children, to raise their children one way or another are limited by the options they confront. Most obviously, their choices about where to work and when to work depend on the requirements of the jobs available to them: on requirements for mandatory overtime, on requirements for travel or for weekend work, on the flexibility (or, more often, inflexibility) of working hours. Less obviously, the choices women and men make—about work, about their children, even about their marital relationship—also depend on public policies and political decisions.

Most readers on work and family concentrate on the *adaptations* of individual women and men to conditions that are, themselves, never examined. This collection tries to expand the discussion of the relationship between work and family by looking at some of the processes that create those conditions. While the previous section located families in networks of neighbors, friends, and kin, this section looks at the ways in which broader political and public policy shape the relationship between work and families.

Feminists and the New Right are perhaps the most visible participants in debates of work and family policy. It would, however, be a mistake to imagine that they are the only participants. Business and industrial leaders have, of course, had a long standing interest in the size, availability and, not least, compliance of their labor force. In the past, they have been able to secure such a labor force with, for the most part, little explicit attention to what we now think of as work-family policy. As women have come to make up an ever larger part of the labor force, creating new issues for employed men as well as employed women, business and industrial leaders can no longer afford to neglect such policy. They have adapted and dramatically transformed, for their own purposes, many of the work-family issues first raised by feminists. Often working behind the scenes, business and industrial leaders have probably been the most important influence on policy makers, including both Republicans and so-called New Democrats.

The legislation that most explicitly addresses work-family conflicts is the Family and Medical Leave Act (FMLA) of 1993. More than a decade in the making, and previously vetoed by President Bush (the elder), the FMLA was the first law signed by President Clinton. It gives workers, men and women, the right to take up to 12 weeks of leave to care for a newborn child, or for any child, spouse, or parent with medical problems. Workers are guaranteed that they will be able to return to their old job or to an equivalent job without penalty. The law is limited, however, in that—unlike the benefits provided by almost every other industrial society—the leave it guarantees is *unpaid*.

If the FMLA leans, however weakly, in the direction of progressive politics, it has been more than counterbalanced by conservative policies, above all by so-called welfare reform. For most of the twentieth century, most of welfare in the United States was organized around an effort to support the mothers of dependent children who were not in the labor force. In the welfare reforms of the 1990s, the effort has moved dramatically in the direction of coercing former "welfare mothers" to find jobs. With strong support by a Republican Congress, and with the signature of a Democratic president who had promised "to end welfare as we know it," the 1996 Personal Responsibility and Work Opportunity Reconciliation Act included a host of punitive provisions aimed to reduce the number of mothers receiving welfare. Most important, with very limited exceptions, adults receiving benefits, even mothers of infants, are required either to find a job or enter a job-training program.

We could imagine a welfare reform that addressed work-family conflicts by providing free childcare of high quality to all children or by substantially raising the minimum wage. Imagine that, instead of welfare reform, Congress had decided to raise the minimum wage. At the $5.15 minimum wage rate mandated for 2001, someone who works full-time all year long will earn $10,712. But to stay above the poverty line in 1998, a family of four needed an income of $16,660. If the minimum wage had been raised to the 1968 level, adjusted for inflation, it would be $7.61; if it were also adjusted for the growth in productivity, it would be $11.57, more than double today's rate. If the minimum wage in the past decade had increased at the same rate as the pay of chief executive officers of major corporations, workers would now be guaranteed a minimum of $22.80 an hour. In the 1990s, however, the goal of welfare reform was not to end poverty so much as to end welfare, even if that came at the expense of the poor.

In the article that begins this section, Stacey Oliker argues that welfare reform's requirements for paid work diminish family ties and other networks of the poor. Welfare's end "marks a break from work-welfare programs under AFDC because it repeals the small amount of *discretion* [her emphasis] that poor single mothers used when deciding how to allocate resources to work and care. Work now must come first. . . . In welfare's last days, women had little discretion to favor caregiving over earning. But they used their small space of discretion to favor caring over earning." She is even more pessimistic about "welfare reform" than many others, emphasizing not only the weakness of networks among poor mothers but also the likelihood that new welfare regulations will further erode an ethos of care.

Ellen K. Scott, Andrew S. London, and Nancy A. Myers also focus on the consequences of welfare "reform," especially on domestic violence. Using rich interviews from more than 2 years of fieldwork, they examine the work and family consequences of welfare reform, especially for those women who reported past domestic violence. The 1996 welfare reform requires mothers to provide paternity data on the fathers of their children and sets strict limits on welfare eligibility—a maximum of 5 years in a woman's lifetime, and a maximum of 2 years in any one stretch. Most of the women Scott and her colleagues interviewed were willing to report paternity data, despite the fact that it increased the probability that the fathers of their children would assault them. As one mother explained, she was willing to provide information if it would benefit her daughter. The father, she reported, "has broken into my houses and kicked my ass" and if he knew she had provided paternity information, "He'd probably come over and kick my ass," but her daughter is "worth an ass kicking . . . 'cause she deserves to have money." Even though many were willing to report their children's fathers, welfare reform made the women more dependent on their abusive ex-partners, not only when they faced an end to welfare but even when they were "successful" in finding low-wage work.

Welfare "reform" was introduced by political conservatives drawn from both political parties. Naomi Gerstel and Dan Clawson discuss an alternative political force—union members and union leaders. An analysis of unions shifts our perspective. It invites us to rethink not only the character of conventional work family policies (child care, flextime) but also, and perhaps more important, what should be included under the general umbrella of work-family policies—including health benefits, provisions for overtime, even wages. An analysis of unions also shifts our understanding of whom policies serve (as well as what policies should be). In particular, an analysis of unions moves away from a narrow focus on professionals and managers to a broader analysis that includes the working-class women and men often ignored in the policy-making process. At the same time, Gerstel and Clawson argue for a more nuanced understanding of unions. They reveal striking differences *among* unions with regard to involvement in family issues.

If public policy shapes the character of work-family conflicts, so too must we think about how "how women's and men's commitment to work and/or family affects political commitment." Rebecca E. Klatch studied these issues for a sample of 1960s student activists of both the left and right. For the activists she studied, both paid work and family obligations create a turn to private needs away from collective concerns.

Taken together, the readings in this section show some of the many ways that "the personal is political." Women and men do make individual decisions—about where and when to work, about how to raise their children—but their decisions have broad implications for public policy and are made under conditions shaped by economic power and political forces.

13
Challenges for Studying Care after AFDC

Stacey Oliker

The end of Aid to Families with Dependent Children (AFDC) challenges us to learn what happens to care in single-mother families once paid work becomes mandatory. The importance of studying family processes may seem obvious, but there has been little concern about the nonpecuniary dimensions of family life in public discussion of welfare. The debate over ending AFDC centered on paid work. The issue of care for children and dependent elders in poor families rarely entered the debates on ending the AFDC safety net. Concern with care for children in single-mother families has receded from public discourse over several decades, although it was central when AFDC was created early in the century (Gordon, 1994). Ironically, welfare ceased to be a "work and family" issue just as a policy domain of work and family issues expanded in U.S. politics.

Now that Congress has abolished AFDC, mandated work, capped and set time limits on federal support, and devolved authority over eligibility and programs to the states, citizens and scholars are asking how the end of AFDC has affected poor families. Reasonably, their first questions are about the economic impact of welfare's end, since proponents of a federal safety net predicted calamitous economic results (Edelman, 1997). Less reasonably, we have heard few questions about the noneconomic impacts of abolishing the safety net. How does ending AFDC affect parenting, nurture, supervision, tutelage, and care in the families of single mothers who are mandated to become self-sufficient breadwinners? How do poor single mothers balance work and family after AFDC?

This article suggests some challenges facing researchers who will examine care after AFDC. The challenges come from several sources. One is the diversity in post-AFDC policy among the states. Welfare has not ended in most states yet, and everywhere it is ending differently. Second, sociology is just beginning to offer frameworks for studying caregiving (Finch & Groves, 1983; Abel & Nelson, 1990; Cancian & Oliker, 2000). We need more inspiring ideas about the dynamics of change in patterns of care. And third, some of our usual methods of registering change in caregiving, whether qualitative or quantitative, may be less reliable in a period of change.

Although my aim is to suggest how we can meet these challenges, I will do this by imagining harsh changes in care at welfare's end. The vision I create counterbalances the optimism that prompted the move to end welfare and responded to the phenomenal drop in welfare rolls and the increases in employment that followed. An example of this optimism was the prediction that single mothers could handle the transition to mandatory work because they had rich networks of support to rely on (Kaus, 1992; Mead, 1992). After AFDC was abolished in 1996, this argument found a defensive echo among those who insisted that poor communities would "pull together" in adversity, as they've always done.

My pessimistic predictions counter these optimistic ones by emphasizing the weakness of networks of support among the poor and the ways that mandatory work could constrict them. Against the optimism that has greeted plummeting welfare rolls and growing employment rates, I will show how a mandatory shift of priorities from care to work can hurt families, even if we have the improbable experience of an endless economic boom, like the one undergirding current welfare rolls and employment rates.

Both the challenges I identify and the dynamics I envision derive from a qualitative study of work and family patterns in the last years of AFDC (Oliker 1995a, 1995b). During the late 1980s and early 1990s, I studied work-welfare programs in two states' largest cities, where I observed welfare programs and interviewed program workers and participants. At that time, work-welfare reforms were under way, creating various kinds of pressures on single mothers to find employment. However, even programs that sanctioned mothers for insufficient work effort preserved a safety net under children's benefits. Now no safety net is required. I draw the ideas about change that could follow AFDC from my findings on how single mothers on AFDC balanced obligations to work and family, as well as from others' studies of families in poverty, work-family relations, and social networks.

The conceptual framework of social network analysis is especially fruitful for exploring caregiving in the context of family resources and supports. I will use my qualitative study, network analysis, and studies of poverty and of work-family relations to tie propositions about changes in caregiving to changes in the social networks of single mothers.

Social network analysis explores how the *structure* of social relationships influences action. For example, network scholars often pay attention to the density of ties (whether members of one's network know each other). The same perspective can take account of the *content* of network exchanges, for example, the kinds of care that are exchanged or beliefs about caregiving that network members convey (Fischer et al., 1977; Wellman & Berkowitz, 1988). Below, I will suggest how the end of welfare may affect the size and density of poor single mothers' personal networks and how it may affect the caregiving and supports for care that network members exchange.

Few states have ended welfare and mandated work as thoroughly and precipitously as Wisconsin, which has cut its welfare rolls by 93% (Stephenson, 1999). Because of this, the best national and local coverage of family life after welfare focuses on Milwaukee, Wisconsin's largest city. For this reason, and in the absence of academic studies of family life after AFDC, I use newspaper coverage of Milwaukee as my source of examples of projected changes after AFDC.

Economic Impacts of Ending Welfare

I pay minimal attention here to paid work and concentrate on family, mainly because we have research formations in place to learn about what happens to poor single mothers in the marketplace, but fewer strategies of studying care. We're already learning what is happening to low-income single mothers in the market, and I can summarize it succinctly: More are employed than before (at least, in on-the-books jobs—as opposed to the ubiquitous informal paid work that was common under welfare). While official employment rates are higher, jobs are unsteady, and, steady or not, wages remain low for most. Many paid workers are poorer than they were on welfare (Cancian et al., 2000; Pawasarat, 1997; Primus et al., 1999). Wage rates start low and remain low over time, especially for AFDC leavers who enter the lowest wage jobs (Burtless, 1998). And these are the results for the single mothers who left AFDC the fastest—who are better educated, have more job experience, and have smaller families to support (Cancian et al., 2000). When the time caps set by Congress go into effect, those with the least human capital and the biggest problems with health, substance abuse, and dependent care will be unsupported and in the job market.

Work Mandates, Discretion, and Norms of Care

In my qualitative study of single-mother families during the last years of AFDC, I used the rubric of a "moral economy" to think about how single mothers allocate their resources between earning and caring (Oliker, 1995a). The idea here is that while economic interests shape the moral economies of poor single-mother households, so do nonpecuniary considerations of the needs of loved ones for care. Family allocations of resources and efforts are shaped by family and communal commitments, as well as by economic pressures. In devising strategies of balancing work and family, single mothers are guided by communally negotiated and reinforced commitments to care as well as by motives of economic gain.

Johnetta (a pseudonym) is one of the single mothers I interviewed. She lost a job during the period when she and two sisters took turns commuting to the South from different states to care for their seriously ill mother and cope with the effects of racist medical neglect. "I had to be here two weeks, and then I would go down there for about two weeks, and we'd come back and go there." During the depression Johnetta suffered after her mother's death, her adult daughter moved in to care for her. Now her daughter was pregnant and Johnetta was contemplating how she could help her daughter, comply with work-welfare requirements, deal with her school-age children's health problems, and persuade another day care center not to expel the emotionally disturbed toddler nephew who was in her care. "What can you do? You can't just walk away and say, 'Well, I don't give a damn.'"

This interview took place before welfare ended in Johnetta's home state. At that time, if she continued to let obligations to others take priority over her work-welfare obligations, the state would cut off her grant, but her children would continue to receive theirs. Not so after AFDC.

The end of welfare marks a break from work-welfare programs under AFDC because it repeals the small amount of *discretion* that poor single mothers used when deciding how to allocate resources to work and care. Work now must come first. Work, or children do not eat. Work, or risk losing custody of children who are not supported financially. In welfare's last days, women had little discretion to favor caregiving over earning. But they used their small space of discretion to favor caring over earning when they decided it was in their children's interest or in the interest of another loved one.

Carol is another single mother I interviewed in my work-welfare study. She had successfully packaged on-the-books and off-the-books employment to stay off AFDC during much of her young children's lives. Carol had moved to the city she lived in now for its better jobs and to get her children out of dangerous Chicago housing projects. She had even managed to hold onto a few part-time jobs during the period that her son was hospitalized and recovering from a serious injury. Though her mobility in previous employment would not have seemed likely to encourage optimism, Carol liked working and was optimistic about what hard work could bring her family. She suppressed her worries that her children "need their momma, too," when she believed she could do better for them with work.

After a fire displaced Carol's family to a new neighborhood, the balance of commitments shifted for Carol. The new neighborhood was more dangerous, so the children needed more supervision, but Carol did not know neighbors who could keep an eye on the children or her place. "I don't have anybody who can watch [my kindergartner] get off the bus and stay on [to baby-sit]." The recent accident and fire and new vulnerabilities had her worried and often panicked when she was at work.

Finally, Carol pared down employment to one part-time job, remained eligible for AFDC, and adopted a commonplace inner-city strategy of care: She kept her children inside, and when they were not, "I'm watching every two, three minutes making sure they in front." She kept to herself: "I don't socialize with too many people. The less company you keep, the better off you will have stuff in your home." And she avoided taking jobs that interfered with her new level of supervision, postponing full-time work until her children were both in school all day. "I want something better, but I'm at a standstill now because of the kids." Her "standstill" did not involve standing still, but it did mean less income and optimism; she traded them deliberately in her children's interest.

I interviewed Carol before welfare ended. If she were in the same circumstances now, when everyone in her state must find work, her job history and drive would probably place her among the former AFDC recipients who find work. But whatever the level of crime in her neighborhood, however her children are handling the crises in their family, and however panicked and worried Carol feels at work, the choice she must make would be clear. She must keep working. The balance between work and family commitments would be set for her.

The balance would be set, too, for Sandy, who had held a job throughout her toddler's first 2 years but finally left it and drew AFDC when her employer moved her to the late shift and she fell asleep when she was bathing her toddler. Others who risked getting fired, and sometimes were, when they went to work late because the baby-sitter was late, or when they left early to shadow a teenager who was falling into dangerous habits, would also have the balance reset to make work the inevitable priority.

Welfare allowed the very poor to adopt an ethos of attentive caregiving that more affluent women pioneered a century before. I clearly heard the ethos in accounts of single mothers in my AFDC study, for example, when they defended putting off day care and taking a job "until she can talk," in order to be able to monitor care by asking the child questions. I heard it in the accounts of those who added hours to their work day by taking multiple buses to day care and work, rather than depend on unreliable relatives. And I heard it in the bitterness expressed by mothers who had denied children's needs for their time and attention in order to support them, but who still remained poor.

Gwen, for example, was the mother of a 13-year-old girl who had started getting into trouble at school. After years of working irregular shifts as a nurse's aide, "thinking, you know, it'll get better, I just have to make another paycheck," she began to rethink her commitment: "Where have I gotten with all that experience? . . . Not a damn place. . . . I would have been better off if I would have spent my time every day being at home with her. Who am I benefiting? I decided work is really important, and [I was] really neglecting her."

Judging the stresses her low-paying job caused to be "child abuse," Gwen had finally left the job, spent more time with the child who was in trouble, and made plans to get schooling for a job that would leave them better off. After AFDC, she would not have such choices. Without a choice, I wonder how long Gwen could have faced the damage she believed her long work hours were causing her daughter.

Though we still lack data on life after welfare, I can offer a contrast to Gwen's stance in a story from a *New York Times* series based on extensive interviews. Michele Crawford, still on her job 13 months after leaving welfare in Milwaukee (a rare achievement among the hundreds interviewed for the series), was lauded by the Wisconsin state legislature as a role model for her young children. She told the *Times* reporter, however, that her children were acting up in school and hurting from the lack of attention from their mother: "I sometimes feel like I'm not taking care of my family like I should." But Crawford's account also "took an uncharacteristic turn toward the bitter": "Right now, I've got to concentrate on myself and what I've got to do. . . . I'm sorry my kids are taking it the way they are. They're acting like little selfish brats" (DeParle 1999). Among others who have no choice about long hours away from children, the turn toward acceptance of neglect may not always be uncharacteristic.

After welfare, work must come first. If work takes inevitable priority, women must surrender caregiving practices that are deeply invested with meaning, that are normative, constitutive of identity in a community, understood to be beneficial, and unlikely to be replaced. Renouncing the priority of care may require psychological denial in order to cope with the pain of loss and failure. Whatever the psychological motives, it seems plausible that the imposition of regular decisions to subordinate caregiving to earning may encourage those who believed in doing otherwise to minimize the damages this causes. At welfare's end, mothers who had reviled their children's child care options may come to view poor day care centers or care by irresponsible relatives as adequate. The result here would not just be changes in caregiving practices but changes in individual attitudes toward care and, eventually, in communal norms.

We might better imagine the way an *ethos of care* changes in a community or society if we conceive of how communal norms are reinforced in communal networks. So, before treating the large realm of ethos, I will explore the microstructures of social networks and relations among network members.

Personal Networks: Size, Composition, and Resources of Exchange

Although optimists take for granted the capacities of personal networks to cushion adversity, we should examine the effects of the end of welfare on networks of support. Ethnographies of poor communities in past decades did show that poor families were embedded in close-knit kin-based networks of support, exchanging child care and other material and emotional supports for care, and enforcing norms of good care as well (Martin & Martin, 1978; McAdoo, 1986; Stack, 1974). Ethnographies in recent decades, however, question the extensiveness of kin supports for poor families. Ethnographic studies of teenage mothers, new immigrant families, and urban single mothers suggest that regardless of ideals of "familism" in poor communities, many families lack the support of kin or close friends (Kaplan, 1997; Mahler, 1995; Roschelle, 1997).

Quantitative studies of large, national, representative sample surveys conducted over two decades uniformly suggest that the poor are not richer than others in support from kin. To the contrary, they find that families in poverty, and minority families in particular, have smaller networks of extended kin. Affluence, not poverty, increases the size of networks of support, the frequency of contact with kin, and the amount of help and economic and emotional support that families receive from others (Hofferth, 1984; Hogan, Eggebeen, & Clogg, 1993; Hogan, Hao, & Parish, 1990; Kaplan, 1997; Mahler, 1995; Roschelle, 1997). Just as important for my argument, the large-scale studies show that the poor who receive support are also more likely to *give* support to others than the nonpoor who get support, and this too may affect care (Hogan et al., 1993; Roschelle, 1997).

The quantitative studies do confirm that single mothers (especially minority single mothers) are more likely to live with kin than are wives. Yet, while many single mothers receive some kind of support from parents, a third of them receive none (Hogan et al., 1993; Roschelle, 1997). The poor are repeatedly found among those who had *no one* who exchanges either advice, child care, or household help. And it is mothers of very young children who receive help from kin. Single mothers with older children are far less likely to be aided by kin. Taken all together, studies of family and kin in poverty suggest we need to look closely at the ways poverty both elicits and limits reliance on kin supports.

My qualitative study in welfare's last days, along with others in this period, found mostly small personal networks of exchange among single mothers, anchored by and largely centered on the relationships of single mothers and their mothers (Edin &

Lein, 1997; Kaplan, 1997; Minkler & Roe, 1993). Still, many of the mothers I interviewed received rich supports for caregiving from the members of their small networks, especially from their mothers. Above all, their mothers provided child care. Some mothers of single mothers were primary child caregivers; others provided part-time or back-up care. They prepared for holidays and did other tasks of homemaking and kin-keeping for which employed mothers could not spare the time. And they supported maternal care by being primary confidantes and consolers for their daughters. Whether their mothers lived with them or not, single mothers were likely to include only their mothers, along with their children, among those they listed as "most a part of my life." After mothers, grown daughters, aunts, fathers, and brothers (in that order) were the kin network members who provided resources in support of caregiving.

Boyfriends rarely provided regular care for children, and neither did children's fathers. Boyfriends were sometimes good sources of emergency care, though, more often than fathers were. Close friends who helped with care were also not very common. The mothers I interviewed were often reluctant to ask friends for child care because it usually meant a trade of child care they could not easily manage.

In my study, like the larger surveys, a large minority of families lacked networks of support. *No one* provided them with resources that supported their caregiving, yet having a network of close kin and friends was not necessarily an advantage. Some women gave so much help and money to people in their network that they were deprived of time and resources for care as often as they were enriched. And some networks only extracted time and resources from single mothers, rarely ever supplying them. The single mothers whose extended families were rife with substance abuse, homelessness, and mental illness gave care, help, and money continually; they and their children bore the costs. Gwen, who earlier described her paid work as abusive to her child, had not been able to depend on her hard-living family for help. One reason she had delayed leaving her job to care for her daughter was her hope of saving enough money to move out of state, away from predatory siblings.

Although much of this article will concentrate on how the end of welfare threatens the stability of networks and thus their support of care, the end of welfare can also constrain women's *exit* from networks and personal ties that inflict harm or extract too many costs. Before welfare ended, single mothers moved out of the homes of mothers whom they believed hurt their children with excessive discipline. They broke ties with siblings who lured them back into drug use, boyfriends who demanded money or beat them and their children, and children's fathers who wanted to renew abusive relationships. After welfare, when unemployment and eviction are greater threats, the meager resources of money or help that these ties offer may sustain them. The end of welfare could encourage damaging dependencies, as single mothers struggle to keep their families afloat.

Before welfare ended, neighbors sometimes served as nonintimate, but nonetheless useful, ties for purposes of caregiving. Since AFDC enabled some single mothers to be at home with their children, there were often neighbors around who could informally "keep an eye" on children as they walked home from school, waited at home for an employed mother's return, or played outside. Worldly mothers knew what an independent child's "messing" looked, smelled, or sounded like and would report to a child's or teenager's mother before the police or landlord figured it out or before a child was deeply committed to trouble.

Work mandates should clear most adults out of neighborhoods during the day, and so informal urban mechanisms of safety and surveillance may not persist. These informal networks are also more threatened if unstable jobs, without the meager stability of the welfare grant, cause more evictions, as appears to be the case in Milwaukee (Derus, 1988). Without the AFDC safety net, few mothers will risk losing jobs to stay home to resolve problems, as did some women I interviewed, or to make surprise visits to entrap unsuspecting teenagers or neglectful baby-sitters, as did others.

Mandatory work may also affect caregiving by changing what network members give as support. In the absence of a safety net for periods of unemployment, network members who want to keep families together may view money, rather than care, as the essential exchange to offer. Like single mothers who are mandated to work, those most involved with single-mother families may voluntarily shift their investment from care to work in order to contribute to family subsistence. Personal networks and family financial resources may remain stable, even as exchanges of care diminish.

Reciprocity and Network Stability

Observers of families embedded in extended networks of kin often admiringly invoke the expression "What goes 'round comes 'round," forgetting that it extols giving as well as receiving support. Studies of social networks emphasize the constitutive principle of *reciprocation,* and my study also suggested its importance (Fischer et al., 1977; Uehara, 1990; Wellman et al., 1988). Single mothers who received help from mothers or others also gave help to them. For example, one single mother whose mother took care of her grandchild took care of her mother during a long illness. Another woman took her brother's children any time he "dumped them" because he lent her his car when she had night shift work. (She eventually was dropped from a training program that provided care for her child, but not for the nephews who were in her care.)

In addition to direct reciprocation, the mothers I interviewed also participated in another kind of reciprocation, which network theorists call "generalized" exchange. In networks that feature generalized exchange, reciprocation is indirect. Over time, one gives commensurably with what one gets, but does not necessarily give back to the giver (Uehara, 1990; Wellman et al., 1988). In my study, for example, one grandmother had provided shelter, comfort, and child care but asked little in return. Still, it was the tie to her mother that encouraged the woman I interviewed to take in and care for a cousin's child. This single mother was estranged from her drug-addicted cousin, but her mother called on her to help her sister's family. Other members of the kin network showed their appreciation in various ways.

As the large-scale surveys also suggest, in my study, women whose network members were also poor had burdensome obligations to reciprocate, as well as obligations to care for others which would not be reciprocated any time soon (Roschelle, 1997).

Before welfare ended, single mothers weighed those obligations against the work obligations and sanctions imposed by work-welfare programs. They sometimes used welfare for a time, to meet their commitments to family and kin, and to accept the economic sacrifice that entailed. By fulfilling their obligations, they completed the round of exchanges that kept their networks of support intact.

At welfare's end, single mothers who are compelled to find work or face losing their children will be less able to find the time to reciprocate the help others give them. The low-wage job market they enter will leave most of them no more able financially to replace the care they once provided by purchasing services, like home health aides or taxi fares. Will increasingly asymmetric exchanges in close kin networks damage close relationships and constrict networks? In networks of generalized exchange, which is the form of exchange in many but by no means all kin networks, the answer may be no, at least in the short run. The failure to reciprocate is more likely to damage looser-knit networks, like friendship networks, in which direct and immediate exchange predominates ("You take my kids this weekend, I'll take yours next") (Uehara, 1990).

The tighter weave of kinship networks allows its members to view reciprocation in the much longer run. *In the long run,* however, studies of social networks suggest that stark asymmetries undermine even the more trusting and committed ties of generalized exchange. Those who give a lot but do not receive begin to feel exploited or just "burn out" (Minkler & Roe, 1993; Stack & Burton, 1994; Stack, 1974).

This long-run dynamic may explain anecdotal evidence in Milwaukee that publicly registered homelessness among whole families has increased in the aftermath of welfare, but not enormously. There have been much greater increases in the numbers of single mothers entering shelters as single women (whose children have been placed in others' care) and in the numbers of homeless teenagers (the children most likely to be first "liberated" from care) (Huston, 1998). These may be first, but not ultimate, patterns of adaptation to welfare's end. Doubling up in housing has long been a first, unstable step toward homelessness (Gerstel et al., 1996; Rochefort, 1998; Torrey, 1997).

Social network scholarship suggests that mandatory work in low-paying jobs may limit mothers' capacity to reciprocate without enabling them to substitute money for time—purchasing services in place of giving of themselves. The absence of discretion to limit work in favor of family obligations thus may diminish caregiving by diminishing capacities of reciprocity.

If networks of flexible, generalized exchange do constrict, and single mothers desperately try to rebuild networks of survival among kin and nonkin, immediate obligations to reciprocate are likely to intensify, and these will be harder to meet under a regime of mandatory work. Desperate network builders will inevitably draw in others desperate enough to depend on mere velocity of exchange.

As Carol's strategy suggests, before AFDC ended, single mothers' moral economies were often suffused with a wariness of those who are not proven friends. Some avoided getting involved with men as boyfriends, some avoided neighbors or associates. Census sample data that show increases in coresidence with nonrelatives, especially boyfriends, may suggest that need is already eclipsing older cautious strategies (Jencks & Swingle, 2000).

Network Characteristics and the Ethos of Care

The networks that are rebuilt amid pressing need after the constriction of older networks are likely to be more heavily composed of people who are not bound by the moral obligations of close kinship and who consistently have few resources to share. However, voluntary networks are harder to build and to sustain among people who have desperate instrumental needs of one another. Such networks are likely to be looser-knit than kinship networks are, and thus they break down easier (for example, because there is no one in the role of the aunt who sits feuding siblings together at a holiday meal). In the looser connections of such networks, network capacities of communal reinforcement are weaker, and this may weaken a communal ethos of caregiving. In this dynamic, both the structural and the communal supports for caregiving erode—reducing the supply of care and also its centrality.

The reinforcement of a communal ethos of care can thus erode as tight-knit networks constrict and looser or smaller ones replace them. But a communal ethos can also weaken in tight-knit and solidary networks. If the ability of families to give care declines because work must take first priority and family crises threaten the possibility of government intervention to protect children by removing them, network members who are intent on keeping families together share the mother's incentive to redefine adequate care. That is, if children cannot be nurtured, supervised, taught, and protected, communities and individuals who want to keep families from breaking up can help to do so by revising norms of care and perceiving that children can do all right without these privileges.

If communal networks cannot generate resources to prevent a decline in care in poor families, their interests in keeping families whole may favor silences about poor care or even revised norms of care. We could see fewer reports of child neglect and abuse even as rates increase, and we could hear fewer accounts of poor care in qualitative field work, even if we listen carefully. For researchers, the usual ways of registering change—whether by official data or respondent accounts—may fail us.

Conclusion

In conclusion, when welfare is no longer available, but wages are insufficient to purchase good substitute care, the domestic moral economies that favored caregiving over earning may be impossible to re-create. Personal networks of support may weaken, as the capacity of single mothers to reciprocate declines. The close-knit networks that remain may concentrate on the exchange of material subsistence rather than caregiving. The norms of care that personal networks transmit and reinforce in an era of meager social provision may change once provision ends. Communal support for subsistence and keeping families together may become paramount. And reliable strategies of care in poor urban neighborhoods may become less accessible. Through such dynamics, caregiving declines and the social ethos of care does, too.

This grim portrayal of the prospect of deteriorating care after AFDC presents a number of challenges for researchers who will examine life after AFDC. For those who have been waiting to begin research until the remnants of AFDC in their states have finally disappeared, this article suggests that we should begin now. Long-term study of moral economies and network patterns before and during the end of AFDC may be crucial for capturing what happens afterward, for changes in care may quickly be normalized. If respondent accounts become less reliable, long-term study will address that problem, and the ways accounts of care change becomes a worthwhile subject in itself.

If this turns out to be a period of change in family arrangements, personal communities, and strategies and ideas about caregiving, qualitative researchers are well positioned to contribute to the sociology of caregiving and of work-family decisions in poverty. We are able to explore emergent meanings, adaptations that become norms, and the unexplored nuances of exchange in networks. Quantitative studies of caregiving will depend on us to refine concepts and questions about families and care that they incorporate into large impact studies.

Large-sample studies, on the other hand, may be the first to register changes in household and network forms and patterns of exchange that qualitative researchers will want to explore. For example, the above-mentioned census sample finding that single mothers live more often with nonrelatives now than in 1996 invites the qualitative researcher to find out how live-in boyfriends or doubled-up households affect child care coverage, child abuse, children's contact with fathers, and elder care. This early finding on life after welfare inspires us to use qualitative methods to explore why the first changes preceded or substituted for increases in moves to live with relatives. (I would guess that these patterns reflect the slow movement of most states to end grants: The prospect of insecurity may encourage coresidence with boyfriends. The final cutoffs of aid—still not widespread—may radically escalate coresidence with kin. Single mothers who can live peaceably with kin may already do so.)

We will need a range of strategies to study caregiving at welfare's end. Sociologists are well able to meet the challenges that the issue presents to researchers. The most daunting challenge will be drawing public attention away from the bottom line of jobs and incomes to the other resources from which people make families. Persuasive qualitative research may be just what it takes to revive a concern in poverty policy for families as sites of care and to make work and family policy a cross-class policy domain.

References

Abel, E. K., & Nelson, M. K. (Eds.) (1990). *Circles of care: Work and identity in women's lives*. Albany: State University of New York Press.

Burtless, G. (1998). Can the labor market absorb three million welfare recipients? *Focus, 19,* 1–6.

Cancian, F. M., & Oliker, S. J. (2000). *Caring and gender*. Thousand Oaks, CA: Pine Forge Press.

Cancian, M., Haveman, R., Meyer, D. R., & Wolfe, B. (2000). *Before and after TANF: The economic well-being of women leaving welfare*. Madison: University of Wisconsin Institute for Research on Poverty.

DeParle, J. (1999, December 30). Bold effort leaves much unchanged for the poor. *New York Times.*

Derus, M. (1988, January 18). W2 families squeeze in together. *Milwaukee Journal-Sentinel,* F1.

Edelman, P. (1997, March). The worst thing Clinton has done. *Atlantic Monthly,* 43–58.

Edin, K., & Lein, L. (1997). *Making ends meet.* New York: Russell Sage Foundation.

Finch, J., & Groves, D. (Eds.) (1983). *A labor of love: Women, work, and caring.* London: Routledge & Kegan Paul.

Fischer, C. S., Jackson, R. M., Steuve, A., Gerson, K., & Jones, L. M. (1977). *Networks and places.* New York: Free Press.

Gerstel, N., Bogart, C. J., McConnell, J. J., & Schwartz, M. (1996). The therapeutic incarceration of homeless families. *Social Service Review, 70,* 543–572.

Gordon, L. (1994). *Pitied but not entitled: Single mothers and the history of welfare, 1890–1935.* New York: Free Press.

Hofferth, S. L. (1984). Kin networks, race, and family structure. *Journal of Marriage and the Family, 46,* 791–806.

Hogan, D. P., Eggebeen, D. J., & Clogg, C. (1993). The structure of intergenerational exchange in American families. *American Journal of Sociology, 98,* 1428–1458.

Hogan, D. P., Hao, L.-X., & Parish, W. (1990). Race, kin networks, and assistance to mother-headed families. *Social Forces, 68,* 797–812.

Huston, M. (1998, December 12). More women in shelters. *Milwaukee Journal-Sentinel,* B1.

Jencks, C., & Swingle, J. (2000). Without a net: Whom the new welfare law helps and hurts. *American Prospect, 11,* 37–41.

Kaplan, E. B. (1997). *Not our kind of girl.* Berkeley: University of California Press.

Kaus, M. (1992). *The end of equality.* New York: Basic Books.

Mahler, S. J. (1995). *American dreaming.* Princeton: Princeton University Press.

Martin, E. P., & Martin, J. M. (1978). *The black extended family.* Chicago: University of Chicago Press.

McAdoo, H. P. (1986). Strategies used by black single mothers against stress. In M. C. Simms & J. Malveaux (Eds.), *Slipping through the cracks* (pp. 153–166). New Brunswick, NJ: Transaction Books.

Mead, L. M. (1992). *The new politics of poverty.* New York: Basic Books.

Minkler, M., & Roe, K. M. (1993). *Grandmothers as caregivers.* Newbury Park, CA: Sage.

Oliker, S. J. (1995a). The proximate contexts of workfare and work. *Sociological Quarterly, 36,* 251–272.

Oliker, S. J. (1995b). Work commitment and constraint among mothers on workfare. *Journal of Contemporary Ethnography, 24,* 165–194.

Pawasarat, J. (1997). *The employer perspective: Jobs held by the Milwaukee County AFDC single-parent population (January 1996–March 1997).* Milwaukee: University of Wisconsin–Milwaukee Employment and Training Institute.

Primus, W., Rawlings, L., Larin, K., & Porter, K. (1999). *The initial impacts of welfare reform on the incomes of single-mother families.* Washington, DC: Center on Budget and Policy Priorities.

Rochefort, D. A. (1998). *From poorhouses to homelessness.* Westport, CT: Auburn House.

Roschelle, A. R. (1997). *No more kin.* Thousand Oaks, CA: Sage.

Stack, C. B. (1974). *All our kin.* New York: Harper & Row.

Stack, C., & Burton, L. M. (1994). Kinscripts: Reflections on family, generation, and culture.

In E. N. Glen, G. Chang, & L. R. Forcey (Eds.), *Mothering: Ideology, experience, and agency* (pp. 45–66). New York: Routledge.

Stephenson, C. (1999, December 12). Hardest cases define welfare's next challenge. *Milwaukee Journal-Sentinel*, A1.

Torrey, E. F. (1997). *Out of the shadows*. New York: John Wiley.

Uehara, E. (1990). Dual exchange theory, social networks, and informal support. *American Journal of Sociology, 96,* 1305–1344.

Wellman, B., & Berkowitz, S. D. (Eds.). (1988). *Social structures: A network approach.* Cambridge: Cambridge University Press.

Wellman, B., Carrington, P., & Hall, A. (1988). Networks as personal communities. In B. Wellman & S. D. Berkowitz (Eds.), *Social structures: A network approach* (pp. 130–184). Cambridge: Cambridge University Press.

14
Living with Violence

Women's Reliance on Abusive Men
in Their Transitions from Welfare to Work

Ellen K. Scott, Andrew S. London, and Nancy A. Myers

The 1996 Personal Responsibility and Work Opportunity Reconciliation Act (PRWORA), commonly referred to as "welfare reform," poses special problems for women who are the victims of domestic violence. The ideological foundation of the new form of aid, known as Temporary Assistance for Needy Families (TANF), is "work-first." In addition to the goal of getting welfare recipients into jobs or activities geared toward getting them jobs quickly, three additional goals aimed to change aspects of recipients' reproductive, marital, and parental behavior. These other goals established by the TANF legislation were (1) to provide temporary assistance to needy families to help support work and child care; (2) to "prevent and reduce the incidence of out-of-wedlock pregnancies," and (3) to "encourage the formation and maintenance of two-parent families." Ultimately, PRWORA aims to promote "self-sufficiency," or shift support from the state to reliance on informal networks.

The federal legislation allowed states to establish sanctions for failure to comply with various provisions of TANF, including the loss of cash benefits, Medicaid, and food stamps. However, states were also allowed the option of implementing various forms of "good cause" exemptions from work requirements and sanctioning policies.

Acknowledging that there is a high incidence of domestic violence among welfare recipients (Raphael, 1999), and that for many victims of domestic violence welfare constitutes a critical safety net allowing them to leave abusive relationships, Congress amended PRWORA with the Family Violence Option. The FVO allows states to create a good cause exemption for women who have experienced domestic violence. For those states which choose to adopt such a good cause exemption, they could opt to exempt women from work requirements, time limits, and/or the requirement that women report paternity for their children. However, to date, not all states have adopted this form of exemption, and there is little information about how those that have are implementing them. Ohio, where the research for this article was conducted, is one of the states that have not adopted the FVO. Given that many women do not disclose past or present domestic violence to welfare caseworkers (Raphael & Tolman, 1997), many advocates are concerned that even in those states which have adopted the FVO, these exemption policies will not be able to reach those they are intended to help.

For many women who leave violent relationships, welfare receipt is a critical resource. Domestic violence is a common reason for the initiation of welfare, which many women utilize for relatively short periods as they establish and transition to independent living arrangements (Davis, 1999). Using data from the ethnographic component of Manpower Demonstration Research Corporation's Project on Devolution and Urban Change (henceforth Urban Change), we sought to investigate domestic violence in the context of welfare reform. Because most of the literature we were familiar with focused on the manner in which domestic violence constituted an obstacle to women's ability to meet the mandated work requirements within designated time limits, we too initially focused our own research on that set of concerns. Interestingly, inductive analysis of our qualitative data (which we detail below) revealed an additional concern which has *not* been a particular focus of attention thus far in the literature on welfare reform and domestic violence, one that we also did not anticipate. That is, the extent to which women's attempts to meet the mandated work requirements inadvertently increased their dependence in a variety of ways on informal social networks, which, for formerly or currently battered women, include abusive partners. In analyzing the data from a small sample of welfare recipients in Cleveland, we found that a significant number of women told stories that led us to believe they were increasing their dependence on men who had been abusive to them as they diligently attempted to follow the requirements of the new welfare regulations. This dependence was practical and instrumental; these were not relationships which were likely to be formalized in marriage. Although the explicit policy goal of the federal welfare legislation is for women to marry as a route out of their "dependency" on the welfare system, due to past experiences of abuse, many of the women in our study were not willing to marry or to remarry former husbands. Given the limited options available to them and their reluctance to marry, some of these women were forced to be increasingly dependent on social networks that included abusive men in order to try to achieve "self-sufficiency." Thus, in this article, we explore some of the issues of concern in the literature on welfare reform and domestic violence, and we present some of the data that suggest to us a new and vital point for further research.

The data for our study come from more than two years of fieldwork with approximately 40 welfare-reliant women in Cleveland, part of the multicity Urban Change study. We recruited 12–15 welfare-reliant families residing in each of three neighborhoods—two predominantly black and one predominantly white—with moderate to high concentrations of poverty. Our respondents are predominantly unmarried women; however, like the national welfare population, our sample includes some married women. In the first round of ethnographic data collection, mostly in 1998, we established baseline information about the women's lives. At that time, all the women were receiving welfare. In that interview, we did not ask specific questions about experiences of domestic violence. However, in many instances, stories of domestic violence emerged in the course of the in-depth interviews, which typically lasted between four and six hours. In the second round of in-depth interviewing, mostly in 1999, we again met with women for four to six hours and repeated many of the original questions we had asked. However, in this round we added a specific module of questions that addressed their experiences with domestic violence and the ways in which those might impede the mandate of welfare reform that women report paternity to the welfare department and that they enter the workforce. We conducted a third in-depth interview in the summer of 2000, but as of this writing those data are unanalyzed. Between the main interviews, we have kept in regular phone or in-person contact with each respondent. We try to touch base with respondents every 6 to 8 weeks, but for a variety of reasons this is not possible with every respondent. We conduct lengthier check-ins when respondents find employment, have a family crisis, or experience other important life changes. To date, we have experienced relatively little sample attrition, despite the difficulty involved in maintaining contact with some of the women.

As of the second round of interviewing, the Cleveland ethnographic sample consisted of 23 black women and 17 white women living in three distinct neighborhoods of concentrated poverty. Fourteen of the 17 white women and 10 of the 23 black women in our sample reported having experienced abusive relationships with husbands or boyfriends in their adult lives. With more than half of our ethnographic sample indicating that they had at some point in their adult lives been the victims of domestic violence, this sample corresponds with other studies of welfare recipients, which have found that, depending on how abuse is defined, as many as 60% report past abuse (Raphael, 1999). For many of the women in our sample, the abuse of which they spoke occurred in past relationships, though they were often still connected in a variety of ways with those who had been abusive. Because the abuse was more typically in the past, the concerns of the women in our sample tended to differ considerably from those of women who are currently in abusive relationships.

Paternity Reports and the Fear of Violence

In an effort to increase the collection of child support, PRWORA mandated states to collect information on the names, social security numbers, addresses, and workplaces of the fathers of the children on the TANF rolls. Women who do not provide this information can be denied welfare. Child support enforcement raises particular concerns for women who have left or are trying to leave abusive relationships. Prior research suggests that women in currently or formerly abusive relationships fear retaliation from men who are angry that they have been reported to the welfare department. That literature also suggests that women who have left and have not disclosed their own location to abusive men fear that men may be able to locate them and threaten their safety or the safety of their children. Finally, the literature indicates that women fear that such reporting and the enforced collection of child support could lead to custody or visitation battles and thereby increase the risk of physical or emotional violence for themselves or their children (Allard, Colten, Albelda, & Cosenza, 1997; Davies, 1997; Roberts, 1999).

In our study, even in cases where women might have felt concerned for their safety or their children's safety if they provided information about the whereabouts of the fathers, it did not occur to them to raise this issue with caseworkers. Nor did their caseworkers raise it with them. It is not clear that in a short meeting with a stranger, women would be willing to open up about a history of domestic violence, which is still perceived to be intimate and often shameful. Indeed, their need for the benefits was greater than their fear of the potential for retaliation or violence by fathers of children. We consistently asked women what would happen if they did not provide the information requested about fathers. Repeatedly, women told us in no uncertain terms: "They will cut you off"; "They will sanction your check"; "They were going to sanction me. Well, actually, you get terminated. They cut you off"; "I would not get any benefits"; "You have to cooperate, or you lose it"; "We would be denied. We wouldn't get any type of benefits."

A primary concern in feminist literature on welfare reform has been the fear of retaliatory violence against women reporting their children's fathers. In our sample of 23 women who reported past abuse, few women expressed any great concern about having to provide information about paternity. Similar to the reports of victims of domestic violence in another study (Pearson, Thoennes, & Griswold, 1999), many women in our sample reported that they were happy to give the information to the child support enforcement units in the hope that the fathers might be forced to take more responsibility for their children. This is perhaps mostly a measure of the immediacy of the danger these particular women felt themselves to be in. For many, the abuse was sufficiently in the past that their worries about providing identifying information to the welfare department about former abusers were diminished.

Marcy,[1] a 23-year-old black woman, told us she gave the welfare department everything she knew about her kids' father. When asked how she felt about revealing that information, she responded:

> Hey, I didn't make them by myself. I don't feel I should have to take care of them by myself. . . . Get the man involved, you know what I'm saying?

Glenda, also a black woman in her early 20s, said she gave whatever information she had on the fathers of her children because "They don't do nothing for the kids. They don't come around. . . . I just call them sperm donors." Jannelle, a 37-year-old black woman, said she was "just thrilled" to reveal information about paternity. As far as she was concerned, "It's their [the fathers'] problem!" And Janice, a 32-year-old white woman, concurred:

> It felt good. I really want them [child support enforcement] to get them [the fathers]. I really do. And if I had any information now, I'd give it to them.

Gloria, who is black and 27 years old, reported everything she knew about her kids' fathers.

> You want to play pappa, or whatever, you gonna pay child support, and you gonna take care of 'em, as far as, 'cause you not gonna come and get my child, and play pappa to my child, and you not [pay]. You pay support because you are the one who let welfare take control of the situation and pay for your child.

Brenda, a 26-year-old white woman, agreed to provide the information requested about the father of her daughter, and she said she even felt pretty good about doing so. But later in the interview Brenda also acknowledged that she had also found out he was abusive toward his ex-wife and had sexually molested his stepdaughter. As a consequence, Brenda cut off all contact with him, even though she wanted the father to "have to pay child support." She did not want him to find out where she lived, and she sought the assurance of the welfare department that he would not be able to use her paternity report to track them down. It was only after being told "he won't be able to find you through us" that Brenda agreed to give them all the information.

A minority of the women in our sample faced immediate threats of physical violence. Some of them were nonetheless willing to report paternity *if* doing so would benefit their children. Gayle, a 40-year-old white woman, had been abused for 12 years by the father of her child, her former husband. She felt she had no choice but to tell them *who* the father of her child was, but she also told them that she did not know *where* he was. They tracked his address and sent him a request to come to the child support enforcement office. In order to avoid potential retaliation from him, Gayle contacted her former husband and convinced him that she had not given child support information about his location, that they had gotten it from when he served time in jail. She presumed that if he thought she had provided the information, there might be serious repercussions for her:

> He probably would get drunk and cuss me out and shit. . . . He's been known to kick my doors in. He's broken into my houses and kicked my ass, you know. I don't want to take a chance for what, you know? He'd probably come over and kick my ass. . . . If he gets drunk, he could do anything.

When asked if she thought they would actually collect child support from him, would she be more inclined to provide the information requested, Gayle responded:

> Ya, if my daughter was gonna get something out of it, then I would. So she's worth an ass kicking, I guess. If I had to take an ass kicking for it, 'cause she deserves to have money.

This is just one of the many instances in which women expressed their willingness to put themselves in danger or to suffer great hardship if it meant that their children would somehow benefit.

Work and Marriage

Discussions about the intersection of domestic violence and welfare reform have focused predominantly on the question of how domestic violence might be an obstacle to women's ability to meet the new work requirements of welfare. Under the new regulations, women are required to work or participate in work-related activities. (In Cleveland, the requirement is 30 hours per week for single parents and 35 hours per week for married couples.) The women in our sample corroborate what other researchers have found: Frequently batterers forbid their partners from working, or they make it extremely difficult for them to maintain employment through both direct and indirect intervention (Browne, Salomon, & Bassuk, 1999; Davis, 1999; Raphael, 1999). Winnie, a 42-year-old black respondent, went to school to become a nurse's aide. She often did not want to go to school because her partner had been hitting her, but she said, "I always got up and went." The abuse intensified as she came closer to completing the program. "The last couple of weeks, when I was just about in finals, he just started picking, picking, picking, and I thought I wasn't going to finish." Karen, another black respondent, was one of several respondents who told stories of being fired from jobs due to the disruption and harassment of jealous, abusive partners. One partner made it difficult for her to get a job because he would stop her from leaving the house. Cindy, a 44-year-old white woman, told us that her husband "sabotaged every job I ever had." He would cause so much disruption in the family that her daughters would not let her leave them and go to work; he would start fights with her at work, or he would start fights with the people she worked with; he would show up at her workplace and check up on her. The abuse also made it impossible for her to function well enough to get to work and do her job.

Even when injuries were not significant enough to prevent women from going to work or to school, the humiliation and shame often prevented them from appearing in public immediately after a bad beating. They preferred to risk the loss of a job rather than have to explain their injuries to their coworkers. Gayle and a number of other women talked about exhaustion as an obstacle to work. Their husbands or boyfriends would keep them up all night, either in arguments, or simply disturbing their sleep for other reasons.

A number of our respondents told us that work was a welcome escape from the abusive fathers of their children. Work was a source of relief. As Alice put it:

> It's so much more easier. I felt so much more better when I was working, about myself, about my situations at home. I used working more or less as an excuse to get away from their father. You know, so I really dug into my work. I'm a good worker.

Yet, despite women's desire to work, sometimes failure to provide promised childcare constituted another means by which men intentionally and unintentionally prevented them from doing so. Alice also said that she had to depend on the father of her children for child care. Since his care was consistently inadequate, she found herself routinely having to quit her jobs. Wendy said that when her kids were young, 2 and 3 years old, she was in a training program for medical assistance. Her husband would not watch the kids, although he said he would: "They would end up being left alone. . . . So as soon as I found out, I would be back home and had to say good-bye to that." The obstructions of abusive men are clearly significant obstacles for many welfare-reliant women who are attempting to meet the requirements that they engage in work-related activities and find a job within a specified time limit.

The 1996 welfare reform legislation explicitly encourages single women with children to rely more on personal networks than on the state, especially by forming two-parent families through legal marriage. Because of their experiences of domestic violence, many women in our sample did not consider marriage to be a realistic or desirable option. They told us quite simply that they would not consider marriage again in the future. The risks were too great. Other women said they would consider marriage only in specific and idealized circumstances. Some of the women who objected to marriage were in relationships with men and might even consider living with them. However, they thought that the legal ties of marriage were too complicated if it were to go bad; hence most said they would opt not to marry. When asked if she would consider marriage again, Melissa, a 28-year-old white woman, said, "No. That was a real simple question." She might consider marriage sometime down the road, but certainly not within five years, and if she did marry, "there would be a lot of ground rules set down, 'cause I just can't, you know, I won't deal with crap from anybody. . . . I personally don't need to go through it again, and my kids definitely don't need to go through it again." Janice said that she would never consider marriage again: "Once the paper's signed, they think they own you."

In light of the explicit intention of welfare reform to encourage marriage, these are striking findings. The experiences women had in marriages (and other relationships with men) in which there was an all-too-common use of violence and emotional abuse to control them convinced them that marriage was not a reasonable alternative for the future. Compounding their own experience was the fact that they witnessed this same kind of abuse and maltreatment in the relationships their mothers, sisters, cousins, aunts, and friends had with men. They might have relationships, but at least as long as their children were still living at home, many women thought that legally binding relationships did not make a lot of sense. It seemed unlikely that any changes in the welfare laws would change their minds given the intensity of their past experiences with abusive men.

Unintended Consequences of Welfare Reform: Increased Dependence on Abusive Men

Although women did not see marriage as viable with the men who were or might be in their lives, women had many other forms of complex social relationships with men who had been their husbands or boyfriends, who they had lived with, and who were the fathers of their children. These men often lived nearby, as did their kin, who were also still connected to the women in our sample and their children in various and complex ways. For many women in our sample who were no longer being abused by the fathers of their children, but were still in contact with them in their limited and often isolated social networks, a different concern emerged from our reading of the data. That is, many women who no longer felt that they were in immediate danger from, or were directly controlled by, the fathers of their children found themselves relying on these men who had been abusive to them in order to enable them to meet the work requirements of welfare and the demands of their impoverished lives. These findings indicate that we ought to be more concerned about the ways in which women might become more dependent on their social networks, *which often include abusive men,* in order to comply with work requirements.

The women in our sample have few resources to draw upon. That's why they were on welfare. Despite their reluctance to be in a position of relying on marriage or other private forms of support and assistance (which women reported their mothers, siblings, women friends, and other relatives were hard-pressed to provide), we found that in fact women may be increasing their reliance on the very men who have caused them to decide that marriage was not a viable option. Our data suggest that women may be forced to call on their limited support networks, especially fathers of children, as they seek to comply with welfare's work requirements. Alternatively, women may seek new relationships with men that place them in situations of dependency and risk. The stories below are some of those which suggested to us this possibility of increased dependence on formerly or potentially abusive men.

Wendy thought she was eligible for permanent disability, yet she reported: "I want to go to work so desperately." She felt that by working her kids could "see that no matter what happens to you, you can still get up and go to work." However, the obstacles to her working were significant. Wendy has two children, both born in the 1980s. Wendy's son was very, very hard to care for—he was diagnosed with bipolar disorder and schizophrenia—and she had great difficulty finding someone to help her when she was working. Wendy herself had numerous health problems: asthma, anxiety disorders, a back injury, and a foot injury. Although she started and finished a course in nursing assistance, she was unable to obtain employment as a home health aide because she was awaiting surgery for her foot injury and could not be on her feet all day. (She did work at a video store, under the table, in order to help make ends meet.)

Wendy talked often in the interviews about being convinced that her son's medical and emotional problems would make it impossible for her to find help caring for him. Thus, it was often the father of her two children who would step in when she needed a hand. When she could not manage the kids anymore during a Christmas vacation, off they went to their father's house. When she thought about who could handle her son if she got a permanent job, she thought of his father. Even though she did not trust him, she was even less trustful of strangers: "When I start working, I don't know, because it is hard. Even the county providers do not take children like [him]. They will not be responsible for his medication. And he's on such powerful drugs. . . . So, no, I can't trust just anybody with them." She was convinced that no one would be willing to care for her son with his behavior problems. Their father also did a lot of the routine transporting of the children to and from school, since he had a car and Wendy did not. Further, Wendy's own medical problems forced her to be more dependent on her ex-husband to care for the children. When her foot was in a cast, she asked him to pick up their son at school when he got kicked out for threatening another child.

Wendy felt forced to rely on the children's father even though she had good reason to fear doing so. He was an alcoholic and also abused other drugs. He had been a machinist, but he lost his job due to his drinking. She divorced him when the children were under 5 years old, but they got back together and remarried when he quit drinking. He began drinking again, and shortly thereafter he became abusive to her and the children. She kicked him out once again. Wendy reported that he physically abused her son and emotionally, physically, and sexually abused her. She described his hitting and choking her on a routine basis, as well as raping her: "I would be waking up in the middle of the night and he would be having sex with me, with me bein' asleep. Or I'd wake up and I would be up in the air and he would be choking me." She said that he also beat her son: "His dad would choke him until he was blue in the face. Hit him with his fist in the chest, knock him across the room, hit him in the shoulders." Wendy also reported that, more recently, her ex-husband had "french-kissed" their daughter, and her son had caught his father watching his daughter take a shower.

Several months after this interview, Wendy told our interviewer that her ex-husband had beaten their daughter and was sentenced to two years probation as a consequence.

Toward the end of the second year of the study, Wendy discovered that her foot had serious problems that would require more than surgery. She was on pain medication, which confused her and made her feel high all the time. As a consequence, the kids were spending more time with their father, although her daughter was reluctant after he beat her. Wendy said she anticipated having to rely on him even more to care for the kids, given the severity of her foot problems.

Gayle was in an abusive relationship for twelve years with the father of her child. She attributed her own decision to stay for as long as she did to the "way I was raised. . . . I just thought that [if] . . . you had a family, you know, you stay together and that was it." These views, similar to those of many of the conservative authors of "welfare reform" legislation, could not survive the severe abuse she experienced:

> He broke a couple of my ribs, broke my nose, pushed my teeth up into my face. I broke my hand punching him in the head. He choked me until I passed out. Thought he killed me and left me there. Black eyes all the time. . . . I just hate him.

He never abused their daughter, but one of the reasons she eventually left was she was afraid that there was nothing to stop him from eventually turning on her. The father still saw his daughter frequently, and Gayle lived close to her former father-in-law and saw him often. Gayle had been on welfare since 1984, and the father of her child did not help her financially. Gayle had a GED and an associate degree in administrative assistance. When we first interviewed her, she was hoping to become employed as a receptionist; however, she had not been able to find a job in that field despite filling out many applications. She had recently taken a job working in a thrift store, and she was still receiving food stamps and Medicaid.

During the first two years of Gayle's involvement in the Urban Change study, she went through many crises involving great instability in her life. Within a few months of taking the job in the thrift store and receiving transitional benefits, Gayle was cut off all her benefits because she neglected to turn in some paperwork. For Gayle, the loss of Medicaid constituted a crisis—she was asthmatic and relied heavily on her benefits for her many trips to the hospital, some of which involved overnight stays and even a week in the hospital. She was counting on finding a job with health benefits within the year, but in the meantime she relied on her transitional Medicaid benefits. She also lost her housing and had to move in with her former father-in-law for a period of time while waiting for subsidized housing to become available. He helped considerably with her daughter. He helped his granddaughter get to school in the morning, and he stayed at the house with her after school until Gayle could get home from work. Gayle relied on her car for transportation to and from work; however, she was having car problems and she could not afford to get the car fixed. She was trying to get the welfare department to pay for repairs for her, but that was taking some time to arrange.

Shortly thereafter, Gayle lost her job at the thrift store and went back on welfare. She applied for many jobs and hoped she could find a job doing delivery, if her car would hold up. As she described the ups and downs of her search for work and her health problems, she talked about relying first on her ex-husband's father for child care and then on her ex-husband to keep her car running and also to watch her child. Her ex-husband lived with his father, so when her daughter was with her grandfather she was often also with her father. Although Gayle distrusted the father of her daughter because of his drinking, she thought that the grandfather would ensure things would be okay. Gayle had not wanted her ex-husband to know where she lived, but she eventually had to reveal the location to him so he could come repair her car. For Gayle, there seemed to be no exit from this cycle of searching for employment, searching for reliable child care, and attempting to keep her car functioning. Her safety net as she struggled to survive and make ends meet, for herself and her daughter was the man who had abused her for 12 years and his father.

Heather, the only teenager in our sample at baseline, left her mother's house when she dropped out of school in the eighth grade. She moved in with her boyfriend, Tim, and lived with him for two years in an abusive relationship until she came home one day to find him "in bed" with her cousin. Heather met Tommy the day after she left Tim. They have been together for 4 years. Tommy has been in and out of jail, and Heather has had other boyfriends. She has two children and is uncertain of paternity with both children. However, Tommy is the social father of her children, regardless of paternity. Heather likes the fact that Tommy is a good parent. He spends time with the kids, unlike many fathers, she notes.

However, Heather is not satisfied with their relationship because he is unable to keep a job and thereby provide for her and the children. She said that was the main problem that she and Tommy had, and she frequently expressed considerable frustration about this in interviews. She often threatened to leave him because of it. Fed up, one more time, with Tommy's inability to find work, Heather kicked him out again. At that point he "went off," breaking her phone: "Pull me up by my neck, tried smothering me, tried to cut me with a knife and shit." Although this incident occurred in the first year of the study, at the end of the second year Tommy was still in Heather's life, as were other men. One of the other men may have been the biological father of the second child she was carrying in the second year of the study. Without a GED or much work history, through sanctions and facing the probable end of her time limit for welfare receipt, Heather found herself relying on this rather complicated network of boyfriends in order to take care of herself and her children. She also moved in and out of her mother's house and various apartments of her own numerous times in the first two years of the study.

Kate, a 22-year-old white woman, comes from an extremely disadvantaged background. Her mother was murdered when she was 3 years old, and at the time of the first interview her father had been in prison for 8 years for child molestation. Kate was raised mostly by her grandparents, but she also spent 3 years in foster care after her grandmother passed away.

She became pregnant with her first child when she was 15. She lived with the father of this child and his parents, then she lived with him in an apartment. When she was 7 months pregnant, "he started like getting abusive or whatever," so she left to live with her sister. She had two more children by another man, Ted, who was also abusive. She eventually went to a battered women's shelter because Ted "had a nervous breakdown and . . . just flipped and stuff."

Despite this, Kate was also quite dependent on Ted. At the time of the baseline interview, three months after leaving the battered women's shelter, Kate was living in an apartment that welfare and the women's shelter had helped her get into. She was living with her three children, a woman friend, and with Ted. Kate thought Ted would help her with the big things—enabling her to meet her dream of owning a house and a beauty salon—and he was the one she depended on for day-to-day help. "He still helps me, as in buying my kid's diapers. . . . He helps me pay my lights and gas and my phone bill."

Kate had few options other than to rely on Ted. In doing her budget during the baseline interview, Kate said that she could not get any help from her father and that her sister helped her out sometimes; however, "I always got to pay her back or something." Mostly, when she needs something, she said she relied on Ted: "My kids' dad, he's the one that helps me, gives me a little bit of money every now and then." When asked from whom she could borrow $20 to $50 for a couple of weeks, Kate said: "I wouldn't have to borrow it from Ted. He'd just, I'd just keep it."

Despite his continued attempts at controlling her, at the time of the initial interview Kate still seemed to think marrying Ted was possible. He had given her a ring, and she said that they would "probably try to get married in the year 2000." But she was reluctant to consider it further until "he straightens his act up." At the time of the interview, Ted had a good job hanging drywall with his father, which Kate was happy about despite the fact that she said that she almost always had problems with him, that he was almost always critical of her and that she was "always mad at him for something."

A year later Kate had ended her relationship with Ted, and although she previously had totally objected to abortion, she decided to have an abortion when she found out she was pregnant with another child fathered by Ted. She did not want Ted to have another reason to be tied into the family because he "was totally violent. He used to beat me up."

Kate also had a new boyfriend, Juan, but Kate told our interviewer that whenever a man moved in with her she would fall behind on her bills, so she would not let anyone move in with her now. By the end of the summer, however, Kate was pregnant with her fourth child, Juan's baby. Because she was trying to establish a compatible relationship with Juan, she expressed some regret that when she went on welfare she had to report Juan to child support. However, she felt no such remorse about reporting Ted:

> So I felt kind of bad doing it for him [Juan], but my other kids, go for it, whatever you can get, take it all. I don't even care if I see one penny of it, you know. Go ahead. I mean, her father, Ted, makes $500 to $600 a week. He don't give me $5 for diapers. Nothing. I don't get nothing from him.

Kate said that she was in the process of trying to get child support from Ted, and as a result she feared confrontations with him when he came to the house to see the kids.

Although Juan would not or could not maintain a job or provide much financial assistance to Kate and her children, which ultimately became a major strain in their relationship, he was there to protect her and do other things around the house:

> Ted is the one that was abusive, but I've got Juan here, and I know if he comes over to see the kids, I don't do it unless Juan's here. You know, if he wants to come by and pick up the kids and take them to the park, whatever, you know, he's got to wait till Juan comes home 'cause there's no confrontation. If Juan's there, he ain't gonna say nothing to me.

At the end of the second-year interview, Kate volunteered more and more information about the violence in her relationship with Juan and the problems it was causing for her. A few months later, as the violence in Kate and Juan's relationship continued to escalate, Kate reported trying to break up with Juan, thus provoking more of his violent behavior. After one confrontation, Kate called 911 and the cops came and arrested Juan. Juan had an outstanding warrant against him for selling some fake drugs to an undercover cop, so this report was consequential for him. Kate and Juan broke up but later got back together. Our last interview with Kate was when our interviewer was driving her to the police station to report an incident of domestic violence. She was unclear what she would do: "I don't have to sign anything when I come here. You know, I can just come here and talk and see what their plans are."

At 24, with four children under the age of 4, Kate had scarcely been in the labor market, and she faced reaching her limits for welfare receipt within months of this last interview. Her hope was that this relationship with the father of her fourth child would work out. Even as she was being driven to the police station to file a report against him, she pondered whether she had to resort to this and concluded that she could just go see what her options were once she got to the station. Like the policy makers in Congress when they revised the welfare laws, Kate believed that marriage might be the best path out of dependency on the state, but she also knew that this would hardly be a path to self-sufficiency. When weighing her alternatives, in light of a realistic assessment of her human capital and the likelihood that she could support her four children through her own employment, she concluded that the fathers of her children, particularly Juan, were her best bet. But these were tough choices she was weighing—to hang in there and risk further abuse, potentially escalating violence that would threaten her and her children's safety, or find some other way that was not apparent to her from her current vantage point. Given the options, one understands her extraordinary hesitancy and her rationalization for not going through with the charges, as she was driven to the police station.

Conclusion

In the current context of time-limited welfare and benefits tied to work participation, if women are unable to find decent child care or jobs that pay a living wage, they will be increasingly dependent on the men in their lives. We do not yet know the extent to which these will be abusive men who are currently, or in the past were, abusive to them. Nor do we know the extent to which current policies will increase the risk of dependence on abusive men in future relationships. While to date this has not been central to discussions in the literature on domestic violence and welfare reform, this dynamic appeared frequently in the stories told by women in our small Cleveland sample. We think it is a critical issue to raise for further exploration in research and discussion among policy makers.

For women facing the possibility of reaching their welfare time limits or being sanctioned for failure to comply with work requirements, domestic violence has additional consequences. Hence, it is critical that welfare departments take seriously the need to develop flexible policies that can accommodate women in these circumstances and also that they find ways to identify such women and link them to needed services. The latter may be the more critical and difficult task. The following example from our fieldwork illustrates the potentially grave difficulties identifying battered women.

The week we were finishing this article, a full 2 years into our study involving ongoing contact with respondents as well as in-depth interviews on an annual basis, one of our interviewers reported to us that she just had a case of domestic violence revealed to her while she was conducting the third annual in-depth interview. The story is as follows. Maria had been physically abused by her boyfriend (the father of her two youngest children) for the past 8 years, up until February 2000 when he moved out of the house. Maria said she was beaten at least once a month during that time, sometimes resulting in trips to the hospital for stitches. Our interviewer perceived herself to have good rapport with Maria, which was demonstrated in the many intimate details Maria had shared about her life. Our interviewer reported being surprised that this was disclosed now. Maria had other opportunities to talk about the abuse, but most of them were while she was still living with the batterer. Maria had been asked questions on domestic violence in our open-ended interview the previous year, as well as in a self-administered questionnaire that asked her about incidents of domestic violence in the previous 12 months. In both instances, she responded "no" to each question about past or present experiences of abuse. One factor contributing to her reticence may have been the coming and going of the abusive boyfriend during the interview, making it impossible to talk about the violence. This has been a problem at times in Cleveland and other sites of the Urban Change study.

Not coincidentally, we suspect, 5 months after the last incident of violence when her boyfriend finally moved out of the house, Maria disclosed the abuse to our interviewer. Sadly, in her account of the abuse, she blames herself. When asked what led up to the abuse, she responded that it was because she never knew when to shut up, she always had to have the last word in an argument. Our interviewer reported that Maria recounted the domestic violence in front of her 13-year-old daughter, with her daughter corroborating the reasoning she was giving for having been beaten. They seemed to be making a joke of it, talking at least lightly, if not cavalierly, about the 8 years of abuse. Further, when prompted to do so, her daughter affirmed her mother's interpretation that she had provoked the violence. Maria also said that she would like her boyfriend to move back in if he would just get a job. She did not stipulate that he stop hitting her. She has also just found out that she is again pregnant by him, so we might predict there is a high likelihood that he will be moving back in.

In discussing this case with our interviewer, we suspected a number of reasons why Maria chose not to disclose the abuse until now, despite the high level of rapport between her and our interviewer. She may have been afraid her boyfriend would retaliate if he found out she had disclosed the abuse. She may have felt ashamed of the fact that she was being beaten, and she clearly blamed herself, which would likely contribute to her tendency to feel shame and humiliation. She may have been surviving the abuse by denying either the fact of the violence or the extent of the violence. Denial becomes much more difficult if one acknowledges the violence to someone else. Finally, for Maria, as it seems for some of our other respondents, perhaps the violence was also routinized. If normative for her, there is not much to talk about. When she did disclose it, she did so in a fairly lighthearted, offhand manner. However, this does not explain why she answered no to direct questions about abuse and violence. Again, perhaps this was due to the presence of the abuser. In fact, her lighthearted manner could also be another defense mechanism as she struggles with the feelings of shame and humiliation so common to battered women.

Our experience with having a case of domestic violence disclosed 2 years into a study involving extensive contact between interviewers and respondents raises both methodological and policy issues. Given that most studies cited in the literature on welfare reform and domestic violence involve single contacts, or at least significantly less contact with subjects than we have had in the Urban Change study, and given that most welfare caseworkers asking questions to identify cases of domestic violence will likely meet with recipients for much shorter periods, we have reason to be very concerned about whether we are capturing the extent of the problem either in our research or in our attempts to provide public assistance. This is particularly true for those women who are currently being abused, and those are the women about whom we should be most worried and for whom we should seek the most flexible policies. If the shame, denial, and fear that battered women typically experience keep them from disclosing an ongoing history of domestic violence to someone they have been talking with for two years and with whom they have demonstrated a great deal of trust, why do we think this is going to be easy to identify in a welfare office in a half-hour meeting? This poses an extraordinary conundrum for policy makers.

Acknowledgments

We would like to thank Manpower Demonstration Research Corporation for the opportunity to collect these data under the auspices of the Project on Devolution and Urban Change. We would also particularly like to thank Kathryn Edin, director of the multisite ethnography for Urban Change, as well as Gordon Berlin and Barbara Goldman from MDRC and our national collaborators for their support of this work. We thank Lorna Dilley, Ralonda Ellis-Hill, Karen Fierer, Vicki Hunter, Leondra Mitchell, Samieka Mitchell, Kagendo Mutua, Laura Nichols, and Sarah Spain, who worked with us to recruit the sample and conduct the ethnographic interviews. We also thank Karen Fierer for developing an annotated bibliography on welfare reform and domestic violence. Finally, although unnamed, we would like to thank the women who shared their stories with us. Each has contributed to this article in ways more significant than the authors can begin to acknowledge.

Note

1. All names of respondents are pseudonyms. All ages given in the text are from the baseline interview unless otherwise specified.

References

Allard, M. A., Colten, M. E., Albelda, R., & Cosenza, C. 1997. *In harm's way? Domestic violence, AFDC receipt, and welfare reform in Massachusetts.* Boston: University of Massachusetts, McCormack Institute, Center for Survey Research.

Browne, A., Salomon, A., & Bassuk, S. 1999. The impact of recent partner violence on poor women's capacity to maintain work. *Violence Against Women 5*(4), 393–426.

Davies, J. 1997. *The new welfare law: Child support enforcement.* National Resource Center on Domestic Violence and the National Network to End Domestic Violence, Harrisburg, PA.

Davis, M. F. 1999. The economics of abuse: How violence perpetuates women's poverty. In R. A. Brandwein (Ed.), *Battered women, children, and welfare reform: Ties that bind.* Thousand Oaks, CA: Sage.

Pearson, J., N. Thoennes, & Griswold, E. A. 1999. Child support and domestic violence: The victims speak out. *Violence Against Women 5*(4):427–448.

Raphael, J. 1999. Keeping women poor: How domestic violence prevents women from leaving welfare and entering the world of work. In R. A. Brandwein (Ed.), *Battered women, children, and welfare reform: Ties that Bind.* Thousand Oaks, CA: Sage.

Raphael, J., & Tolman, T. (1997). *Trapped by poverty, trapped by abuse: New evidence documenting the relationship between domestic violence and welfare.* Report available from www.ssw.umich.edu/trapped/pubs

Roberts, P. 1999. Pursuing child support for victims of domestic violence. In R. A. Brandwein (Ed.), *Battered women, children, and welfare reform: Ties that bind.* Thousand Oaks, CA: Sage.

15
Unions' Responses to Family Concerns

Naomi Gerstel and Dan Clawson

Job obligations often make it difficult to take care of families, and family responsibilities often interfere with jobs. At least four related forces shape this tension: the preferences and families of individual women and men and the powers and policies of three institutions—the state, employers, and labor unions. Individual preferences have been well researched as have many state and employer policies. Most discussions, however, have neglected unions and the workers they represent. By analyzing work-family issues from the perspective of unions, this article seeks to reinvigorate the class component. Such an analysis provides an understanding of the ways—and for whom—family benefits at the workplace have been construed and constructed.

Union members represent a diverse population not often captured in studies of work-family issues. While much research on work-family issues focuses on either the poor or the affluent (Lambert, 1999), a study of unions provides access to experiences of both the middle and working classes. Twenty-five percent of union members are college graduates; 75% are not. While many studies of family benefits focus on women, unions contain both women (6.5 million) and men (9.9 million). So, too, a study of unions moves beyond the focus on white employees, who dominate the research on work-family issues. Unions cross racial lines: Of the women members, 1.1 million are black and .6 million Latina; of the men, 1.3 million are black and 1.0 million Latino.[1] Analyses of unions, then, have the potential to broaden our understanding of "working families" and the social movement infrastructure necessary to promote workplaces broadly responsive to those families.

This article makes several broad arguments. First, analyses of unions force us to shift our perspective—rethinking both what should be considered under the general umbrella of work-family policies as well as the contours of specific policies, whether child care or flextime. This focus shifts our understanding not only of *what* the policies should be but *whom* the policies do and can serve. Under the impact of movements that began in the 1960s and continue to the present, we have learned, and continue to learn, just how different the world looks if we put front-and-center the perspectives of women, African Americans, other people of color, gays and lesbians. However, the class component has been the least developed in recent years. Approaching work-family issues from the perspective of ordinary wage workers, and from the perspective of the organizations that represent their collective interests, helps reinvigorate the class component.

Second, we argue for a more nuanced understanding of unions, their circumstances and stance. In attempts to explain who obtains work-family benefits, most researchers have treated unionization as a dichotomy: They analyze whether union members have more family benefits than those who are not members. And they write either that unions—as bastions of male privilege, as embattled collectivities—do not and cannot support these issues or, conversely, that unions—as key players in progressive politics—have become important advocates of these emerging work-family issues. Our interviews revealed striking differences *among* unions: a small number make work-family policies, as we conventionally understand those, central to their contract negotiations, training, and legislative agendas; others do not (or have very little success when they try). For this area, as for so many others, we argue the union/nonunion dichotomy may conceal as much as it reveals.

Finally, and most tentatively, we ask *under what conditions* have unions either neglected work-family benefits or served as vehicles for their implementation. While no one has examined this question directly, some scholars have addressed closely related issues and relied on two broad theoretical perspectives—one emphasizing culture; the other, structure. Emphasizing the importance of cultural shifts in the development of legislation promoting work-family solutions, Burstein and Wierzbicki (2000) argue that changes in the definitions of the problem and in public opinion led to such new legislation. Addressing the union context itself, other even earlier work suggests that broad cultural systems, including men's patriarchal attitudes, have historically pushed unions away from embracing family issues (Hartmann, 1976; Feldberg, 1987). From this perspective, members' expectations—whether about the validity of family expectations or their rights to demand family benefits in the workplace—are central in explaining whether they seek and obtain such benefits.

While respecting the contributions of a cultural approach, Milkman (1990) emphasizes a structural perspective in her insightful analysis of gender and unions. She, too, argues that unions are not monolithic, explaining variation by the historical period in which the union took form and expanded. Extending Stinchcombe's (1965) analysis of organizational inertia, she argues that four waves of unionization produced four distinct cohorts of labor organizations—craft, craft/industrial, industrial, service—each of which brought a growing "openness to alternative ideologies and modes of organizing in general" and, more specifically, "openness to demands from women and feminist approaches" (p. 94)

While Milkman uses this structural model to explain the extent to which women are members and leaders of unions, we argue that these factors, in turn, help explain the degree of union support for work-family issues. Perhaps most obvious among these is the gender of members. Because women workers still tend to have more responsibility for domestic demands than do men, we expect those unions with a higher proportion of women in their ranks would put issues like child care and paid family leave higher on their agenda. Simultaneously we expect that it is not simply the gender of the workers that matters but that of the leaders as well, for those unions with a higher proportion of women leaders will have the power, personnel, and commitment to advocate for greater work-family benefits.

Finally, we add to gender another structural factor: the strength of unions themselves. While the other three factors help explain the extent to which unions make work-family benefits a priority, this focuses on a union's ability to win that priority.

These four factors—member expectations, gender of members, gender of leaders, and union strength—are highly correlated. Milkman's analysis helps explain why these factors are correlated. For our purposes, this makes it difficult to disentangle the effects of each. Our aim, however, is not a precise specification of the contribution of each factor. Instead, we want to explain variation among unions by beginning to specify which union conditions are associated with the promotion of family concerns.

This article begins with a brief review of the literature and discussion of our methods and then is divided into two main sections. The first examines the range of work-family policies that an analysis of unions brings to the fore. The second critiques the dichotomous understanding of unions and analyzes why and which unions do (or do not) win substantial work-family benefits.

Literature Review

Very little literature, to date, examines union responses to work-family issues.

The literature that does exist can be divided into two sets. The first addresses those institutional factors associated with the availability of work-family benefits. These include analyses of unions, typically almost in passing, as one among a number of factors shaping these benefits. Even here, the findings are inconsistent. Both Galinsky (2001) and Glass and Fujimoto (1995) found that unionized workplaces were more likely to provide a range of family benefits. Glass and Fujimoto (1995, p. 398) also found unions "somewhat more successful in gaining family benefits in predominantly male workplaces despite the lesser caregiving responsibilities of men." A similar gender bias was found by Gerstel and McGonagle (1999), who found no effect of union membership on taking family leaves; yet, when examining the length of family leaves, they found union membership significantly increased the length of men's leaves but had no impact on the length of women's. Although they did find that a higher rate of unionization was associated with more generous provision of conventional fringe benefits, Deitch and Huffman (2001), Osterman (1995), and Knoke (1996) found no significant effect for unionization on family benefits. In a rare study focusing on a range of unions, Budd and Brey (2000) suggest that while unionization may not have an effect on actual family leave taking, union members—compared with those not in unions—do appear to obtain better information about the FMLA, and they are more likely to use that information to positive effect. For example, union members are less likely than nonunion members to worry about losing their jobs because they take a family leave. However, Kelly (1999) found that unionization had a negative effect on employers' adoption of maternity leave policy both before and after the passage of the FMLA, although as Osterman (1995) points out, this negative association may be a result of the fact that major American employers have developed family policies as a way to avoid unionization. Overall, existing studies provide inconsistent and limited results. More important, the existence of policies can tell us neither about workers' views of those policies nor the social and political processes by which employers came to offer them or unions sought to win them.

The second set of literature focuses on unions themselves to document the practices of those particular unions that have made considerable progress on issues relating to work and family (Cobble, 1993, 1994; Clawson, forthcoming). Much of the work on unions themselves comes out of the AFL-CIO Working Women's Department, the Coalition of Labor Union Women, and the Labor Project for Working Families. Most of the union research, like the Survey of Working Women, is based on a volunteer sample and is directed toward mobilizing (see, e.g., AFL-CIO Working Women's Department, n.d.). Other existing work, like that by the Labor Project, is equally important but aimed at documenting the "best practices" that select unions have been able to achieve (Grundy & Firestein, 1997; Grundy, Bell, & Firestein, 2000). However, this literature does not address variation among unions or those characteristics of workers and their unions that lead to these "best" practices. Though no one has studied its relationship to work-family benefits, research does suggest that one important characteristic is likely the union's strength. Not only is it important whether unions assign priority to family issues; it is also important whether unions have the strength to achieve their aims. That strength is determined in significant part by unions' ability to organize and represent a substantial fraction of the workforce (Bronfenbrenner et al., 1998; Freeman & Medoff, 1984; Western, 1997).

To find material directly relevant to variation in the provision of work-family benefits, we must turn to a broader literature on organizations rather than on unions themselves. Employers are no more monolithic than unions: Certain employers are likely to support particular benefits whereas others do not (see, e.g., Baron et al., 1986). Some organizational researchers have predicted that the proportion of women—as either workers or employers—likely shapes the availability and provision of work-family benefits. While the findings are not altogether consistent (see, e.g., Knoke, 1996), Auerbach (1990), Goodstein (1994) and Seyler, Monroe, and Garan (1995) all find a higher percentage of women employees predicted various family supportive benefits. As Galinsky (2001) and Deitch and Huffman (2001) both suggest, the relationship may be curvilinear, with organizations that have a predominance of women less likely to provide the more expensive family benefits, such as paid family leaves. Other organizational studies have suggested that it is not simply the representation of women among workers but rather the presence of powerful women in positions of leadership who can push for the implementation of such benefits. Thus, in her national study, Galinsky (2001, p. 211) finds that having a larger proportion of top executive positions filled by women is associated with the provision of such benefits as flextime and on- or near-site child care.

These analyses of organizations provide useful models and clues for analyses of unions. On the other hand, they typically consider a conventional and rather narrow view of family benefits. These policies, and the very definition of work-family issues they entail, come from or are at least shaped by the needs of corporations (Gross, 2001) rather than the workers themselves.

This article uses a different organizational lens, that of unions rather than employers. We ask: what is the role of unions in helping employees deal with family responsibilities? What explains variation among those unions?

Method: Sample and Interviews

Material for this article comes primarily from a set of interviews we conducted with a purposive sample of key informants. Through a series of contacts and phone calls, we attempted first to identify the most knowledgeable and centrally positioned person at every major union. We then interviewed one or two well-informed people at the national headquarters of all but one of the unions that have 300,000 or more members. Finally, we supplemented that by interviewing key informants at a few other unions (one national, three local, one at AFL-CIO headquarters) that were identified by our respondents as having the most innovative family policies, for a total of 23 interviews. These informants are in unions that collectively represent 68% of all U.S. union members (calculated from Gifford, 1998).

We developed a detailed interview schedule that covered general work-family policies and a number of specific policies, including child care, family leaves, elder care, and alternative work schedules. The interview covered three broad elements of union activity regarding each of these policies: efforts to win better contract language; programs to educate members and increase utilization of existing options (both those secured by the contract and those based on state policy), and activities to promote passage of government programs and legal protections. While we used these questions to frame all interviews, the respondents guided us through as we probed particular areas. We conducted interviews, all of which we taped in full, over the phone or in person; they lasted from 30 minutes to almost 2 hours, depending in part on how much the person we contacted knew and how much their union was actually making progress on work-family policies.

Generating our sample and interviewing were informative, both about the character of union activity and our study. To verify that we had identified the key informants at large unions and to identify other unions with innovative programs that merited attention, we asked our informants at the end of their interviews to give us names of people whom they thought it would be useful for us to call. A small number of names came up over and over again.

We supplemented the face-to-face interviews in several ways. In addition to arranging and attending a 2-hour meeting to discuss child care with AFL-CIO officials and representatives of a number of national unions, we asked informants to complete a self administered mail questionnaire about basic characteristics of their union, including, most importantly for our purposes here, the proportion of members who are women. All unions supplied this information on gender composition of membership; for most it is hard data, but some unions do not collect the information and therefore estimated it for us. These data are recoded into three categories: high (more than 50%), medium (25–50%), and low (less than 25%). We used this breakdown because, on average, national union membership is 40% women and because each of these categories (high, medium as well as low) contains approximately one third of the unions in our study.

For information on the gender composition of union leadership, we obtained data from Yong-Dal Chung (2001). Using the 1997 Bureau of National Affairs *Directory of Labor Organizations* (Gifford, 1997), he determined what proportion of executive board members were women for each national union. Applying these rankings to the unions in our study, we combined them into two categories: those in which more than one quarter of the leaders are women were ranked high (one third of unions); those with less than one quarter women were categorized as low (two thirds). We did not use a middle category here because there was a dramatic break from those categorized as high (in which at least 25% of leaders were women) to the top of the next category (in which only 14% of leaders were women).

No such systematic measure is available for the other two variables of interest: union strength or union success in obtaining work-family benefits, especially child care and family leave. Ideally these variables would be measured at the level of the local (not the national) union, which is where most union contracts are bargained. The AFL-CIO is a federation of 67 national unions, but together these unions have more than 40,000 union locals, some of which may represent several groups of workers, each with a separate contract. Within a given national union, some locals are strong, others weak. Some may have negotiated excellent work-family benefits; others have won little or nothing. For these two variables we therefore relied on assessments by three experts. None are members or employees of any of the unions included in our study. Because all three are centrally placed and therefore easily identifiable, they provided their rankings only with a promise of complete confidentiality (since no union would be happy to be ranked low on either of these variables). For both these variables, the experts divided unions into high, medium, and low groupings. They stressed the limitations of these assessments, emphasizing that a single ranking cannot capture the range found within many unions. We concur. More research is needed, especially at the local level. But the initial research findings reported here can help to guide and inform future work, and some attempt at systematic assessment is better than none at all.

We are confident that we identified and were able to interview key union people as well as key experts for our assessments, but it is important to note that we only know what our informants think and told us. They were remarkably open, generous with their time and knowledge. Much of that knowledge, nonetheless, comes out of a culture of activists who have jointly developed a paradigm over the years. We have very little data on locals, and we do not have any data directly from members themselves—either what they themselves might say to us about these policies or what family benefits they actually obtain.

Viewpoints: The Social Construction of Work-Family Issues

The conventional issues that the growing cadre of researchers interested in work-family issues tend to address include child care, family leave, alternative work schedules, and elder care. The first thing we learned is that many unions don't share that "conventional" perspective: "When you look at a union contract, there's lots in there that's a work-family issue, for instance, your pay, your insurance, your hospitalization, your pension, your days off." Many of the things that professionals take for granted, another informant suggested, "you don't realize are work and family issues until workers no longer have them—for example, sick leave or vacation or disability pay—all of which are things that for the most part were originally union-negotiated benefits." One union survey found that "one third of low-wage women don't even have paid sick leave [for themselves], much less have it for their children." In that context, some unions are justifiably proud of the benefits they have won and conscious of the ways they improve family life:

> One of the most striking differences between unionized workers and nonunion workers is in the area of benefits. Our typical member with 13 years of seniority has 4 weeks paid vacation, and that's for men and women. Thirteen paid holidays is the average for our typical member. So you're talking about 6-7 weeks of paid time off, which is significantly higher than comparable nonunion workers. That's a big family issue, having that kind of time off.

We also take for granted that health-care benefits, for example, will be extended to all family members, but unions often have to fight for this:

> There have been times in the history of our union when employers have proposed that we negotiate benefits simply for the individual worker, and that if anyone is concerned about dependent coverage, he or she can pay for their own dependent coverage, and we have always insisted that we negotiate for the full family, and that has been a potential division for our membership, because not everyone in our membership has dependents. But we have insisted that all of us fight for all members of families.

Some ranged even more widely, including as work-family issues "contaminants coming out of the mill into the community," the learning disabilities of the children of lead workers, the 8-hour day, voter registration, and food banks.

This broadening of what is included in "work-family" is open to opposing interpretations. One hypothesis would be that it is a defensive posture most likely to be adopted by those whose unions have done relatively little to address child care or family leave and who can only claim success by including a very broad range of issues on the work-family agenda. These unresponsive unions, however, are not the only ones who argue the work-family agenda should be broadened. Indeed, to cast their response as simply defensive is itself a defensive posture on the part of those academics and policy makers who have established a circumscribed perspective (for a related point, see Gross, 2001). This limited perspective may be shaped by middle-class privilege, which takes for granted what unions and workers have to fight hard to win.

At the same time, a number of our informants did address precisely those issues that the conventional analyses of work and family consider central to their agenda. Most important for them were alternative work schedules, child care, and family leave.[2] Although we have separated these issues for purposes of analysis here, they are related issues that our respondents often would discuss simultaneously, even conflate, for purposes of their own analysis. With regard to all three issues, informants spoke of specifications necessary to make these issues relevant to the lives of a range of employees and suggested that all too often they are construed and constructed to serve the needs of those other than workers or only very privileged workers.

Alternative Work Schedules

About one in five employees now work "nonstandard" schedules (Presser, 2000). A growing number of researchers debate the use and meaning of such schedules—one variant of "flextime"[3]—asking whether workers choose them as a way to take care of family responsibilities or whether such schedules are taken involuntarily, at the behest of the employer rather than the worker. In her recent ethnographic piece, Deutsch (2000) found many who choose equal parenting also choose shift work as the only means to such equality. But these equal sharers are still a relatively rare group. Suggesting this is not primarily a result of workers' own choices, or at least their parenting, Galinsky found that "there are complex reasons that couples work different shifts, not just child care" (2000). In fact, Presser (2000) finds that "complicated work schedules" are most often determined by *employer* demand rather than personal choice, and Lambert (1999) concludes her review of low-wage workers by suggesting they have little choice about their work schedules (see also Golden & Figart, 2000; Kahn & Blum, 1998).

Perhaps the most important point our respondents make about flextime is that it must be recast if it is to be of value for workers. We found a wide range of responses about this issue, from those who argue that flextime entails an attack on workers and is a policy to support corporate interests and profits to those who see it as a policy their members very much needed and wanted. An informant at a union that represents many public sector clerical workers said:

> The need and the desire for it is huge, and I think people feel that if they get some of that flexibility it makes them feel so much less stressed, and it makes them feel that their employer understands that they're trying to work and do a good job at work and do a good job at home, and when they don't get that from their employer, they're very angry.

In contrast, an informant at a predominantly male union representing factory workers reported that one of their most important recent campaigns had focused on resisting flextime:

> In 1999 [a major employer] had put a stake in the sand saying giving flexible work hours was their chief goal in the negotiation, to get 24/7 coverage so that they could run their factories around the clock, compete by using all of the productive capacities all the time. Our members just said . . . the slogan was "Seven Day—No Way." It really became a work and family issue. How can you have a family life if you're working five shifts and seven days a week? It just doesn't compute. And we were able to resist the company's demands for that. We organized a very aggressive campaign to educate our members about what the company's proposal really was and to let people know what the effect of that would be, that there was going to be some more money on the table, but it would really disrupt their family life. At the end of the day the company didn't even propose it. When we got to negotiations, they had got the message; they knew if they put that on the table it was going to cause a huge problem.

Another noted the growing recognition even among women of the problems with flextime:

If you're a young person, or if you're a woman with a number of children, it may appeal to you because you think, this is going to allow me to make better child care arrangements. But what ends up happening is it just makes you work for straight time rather than your overtime hours, and they still end up working, because we find that there's more work than there are people usually. Employers don't hire enough people to do the work, and so they always have to make people work more. So what happens is they end up doing away with overtime altogether and working people all week long on these flexible schedules, and it depresses the amount of money people make and the amount of pensions. Our standard position, every time I go into a local I always ask what do you think about alternative work schedules, and they go, uh-uh, no, no, no, we'll do anything but that. That, I would say, is the majority. There's always a few people who say I would love to have an alternative schedule.

Another informant noted one key to the differences we found: The issue "is actually control over work hours as opposed to flextime. . . . The real issue is whether you make those decisions yourself or whether those are all management decisions."

The importance of who has control over time emerged when a union succeeded in negotiating a change in the rules on the use of personal days. Instead of giving more than a month's notice for emergencies, workers were permitted to give notice up until the time their shift started. The managers who negotiated this benefit

got more than 55 calls, from managers screaming and yelling at them, telling them they gave away the company to the union, the company was going to go down the toilet, there goes productivity. And yet on our [union] side, all I was getting was phone calls from males saying, this was the best thing you ever could have done to negotiate for me in terms of my family. I've now got flexibility.

Even when flextime means some control over their time, it may be a very limited control within oppressive constraints:

When I talk to working women and ask them, do you have flexibility, and they say, oh, yeah, I've got a flexible work schedule; I work nights and my husband works days. So the fact is people have a painfully contracted view of what flexibility means; it means I don't have to pay a baby-sitter because somehow we can always manage to have someone at home, but I haven't seen my husband in four years.

Workers often face mandatory overtime and may be working 60–70 hours a week with no right to refuse overtime. On the one hand, this is oppressive and disrupts family life; on the other hand, workers may see it as necessary to survival and be angry if the union tries to limit overtime. When that happens, sometimes "our members want to rip our heads off—'Are you crazy? I want that overtime!'—I'm sure they don't want to work 80 hours, but they want the money." Unions historically insisted on overtime pay, one informant said, as "a penalty that companies paid for taking people away from their families. That's really the concept of overtime."

Overtime and flextime, then, are viewed as competing ways to frame and regulate the organization of work time; many (though not all) unions prefer the former and believe that the latter has become, in the hands of employers, a means to squeeze still more time, at less cost, from workers. And employers now can claim to do so in an increasingly legitimized manner that is under the umbrella of the fashionable concept of "flextime."

Not all workers, however, want the money from overtime. Unscheduled mandatory overtime is especially disruptive, since workers cannot predict when they will be able to pick up their children. One of our informants told us about a creative job action. The National Labor Relations Board has ruled that workers may not engage in a "partial strike" of any kind; they must either work the full hours the employer demands, day in and day out, or they must go on a complete strike. In *Valley City Furniture*, for example, the employer, in violation of the act, had unilaterally increased the work day by one hour; the union refused to work the extra hour in protest of the company's failure to bargain about the longer workday. The NLRB ruled that "the union, by trying to bring about a condition that would be neither strike nor work, was attempting to dictate the terms and conditions of employment" and therefore the employer had been justified in firing all of the participants in a one-day stoppage (Gross, 1995, pp. 115-116). Recognizing this, a union local with an all-women workforce coordinated an action that does not qualify as a strike:

> A group of women had mandatory overtime, meaning that at the end of your shift your supervisor could come up to you and say you have to stay two more hours. So the women who had children called their baby-sitters, who said, "I'm sorry. I can't stay." So what the women were doing as a group, they made a decision as a group—I'm talking 500 or 700 employees—they started having the baby-sitters drop the children off at the plant. The security guards were, what are we supposed to do with these kids? When the women were confronted by the managers, they would say, I would be put in prison and my children would be taken away from me if I leave them at home alone. I cannot do that. You told me I had to stay, so they're going to come here. It was basically a showdown.

The variation from one union to the next—with some organizing job actions to disrupt and prevent overtime, while at others members "want to rip our heads off" if the union tries to limit overtime—indicates how impossible it is to specify "the" union position on flextime. Large-scale quantitative analyses that compare union and non-union workers are likely to find no overall union effect, when the reality may well be strong effects that vary from one union to the next.

Child Care

It is not just flextime that evokes mixed responses. For very different reasons, there is hardly unanimous support of child care. The very term *child care* conceals a range of policies—from the institutional child care provided by employers (for which there is very little support) to the availability of vouchers that members can use for kids of various ages in various settings (which receives much more support). Many suggested that on-site child care is impossible for most workers to afford.

> A lot of times, work site centers are real model programs—they are higher quality, they might be accredited, they might have a lot of the bells and whistles because the corpora-

tion or, in some cases, the state, wants it to be a showcase. People know it's not going to be affordable, so what good is it to them?

One union that has negotiated funds which helped set up over 50 centers has found that "one of the ongoing struggles has been that it's difficult for our members to afford them. So what we've wound up with is a wonderful management center for high-level professionals, but we don't represent the professional group, so this is a problem." Similarly, at another union our informant sits on a committee that allocates money from a fund in response to applications; a key criterion is that many proposals are in practice for executives: "The child care tuition is so high, the occupational people aren't going to take the benefit from it."

Even if cost were not a consideration, an on-site child care center may not be what workers want: "If you have a chemical factory, do you really want to have a child care facility on-site?" Others talked of how workers preferred kin over strangers to take care of their kids. Also, "folks are more interested in having their children go to child care near their home than near their work. If you live in a suburb, bringing your child into the middle of downtown is not most people's first choice."

Referral services were also regarded as problematic. One union introduced such a program as part of a package that included other initiatives; it reported that "the counseling referral was not used and was less than .1% utilization." The problem was that "basically it's advice on how to get child care you can't afford." In another case, two unions jointly negotiated a program that provides assistance not directly to workers but rather to child care centers or providers. Contributions might be used to train providers or to extend the hours of an existing center. A couple of unions mentioned programs where, often at employer initiative, child care is provided on-site when a school holiday is a work day. These seemed popular both to workers and employers; presumably such programs help employers reduce absenteeism.

Across many settings, subsidies seem the most popular program. At one union the employer established a fund to provide subsidies to employees, "but that fund ran out real quick." A large local provided some type of child care benefit to 8,000 children, but had benefits requested on behalf of 29,000 children. Within the subsidy program "the most popular and needed program is the informal—where you can pay anyone other than yourself or your spouse, i.e., your mother-in-law, your neighbor, your cousin, your friend's baby-sitter, up to $100 a month for that kind of care." Even though subsidies are the most popular, unions face potential opposition if they make them a priority:

> Subsidies are much more expensive; they're harder to win. I do think maybe subsidies is the only place that some people think: why should that person get another $1,000 a year just because they have kids? My kids are older now, but I'm trying to send them to college, and I don't get that money. So a subsidy is a little bit tough sometimes to justify, although we have won them in places.

As this comment suggests, variation exists not only between unions but within unions—whether between men and women, young and old, or those with children at home and those without.

Family Leaves

For a number of reasons, there seems to be less variation in union support of family leaves. There is less variation because leaves are likely to be needed by the large majority of union members at some point in their life course (to take care of a sick child, a sick parent, or a sick spouse). In addition, one of our informants noted that FMLA has "been easier than some issues." This is only "partly because the union talks about it." At least as important is that "it's gotten a lot of attention in the commercial press."

Moreover, there is probably less variation because the law is not the "Family Leave Act" but rather the "Family and Medical Leave Act." Researchers (Gerstel & McGonagle, 1999; Armenia, Gerstel, & Fisher, 2000) found that since the passage of the FMLA, women are much more likely than men to take job leaves to care for other family members; in contrast, men are significantly more likely than women to take leaves to care for themselves. Especially in heavily male unions, the individual or medical aspect of the leave is at least as important as the family aspect of the leave.

Perhaps most important, because the law now mandates that employers provide family leaves, there is less need to prioritize this benefit in bargaining, although some unions have fought for and won extensions beyond the law (e.g., paid leave). Given recent legislative progress on family leaves, union members often saw their role in this area more as one of monitoring, education, and lobbying than contract negotiations. With regard to family leaves, then, unions play a different but important part: They serve as a key mechanism through which state policy is developed, disseminated, and ensured. As our informants suggested, unions provide the means to translate policy into action.[4]

A number talked about lobbying in the early 1990s to get the FMLA passed; more talk of lobbying now for paid leaves and longer leaves for a wider range of employers (those with fewer than the current minimum of 50 employees). While many unions are working for an expanded legislative agenda, even more pointed out that just getting the current law enforced is itself an important part of their role. As executive director of 9 to 5, Ellen Bravo (1995, p. 13) notes: "Enforcement has been greatly weakened over the years so little monitoring is done to see if businesses are complying."

Others discussed their role as providers of information about the current law. As one commented:

> I have had people numerous times call on the phone, either members or staff reps, and they say we have a case where this person was in a car accident and they've been going for physical therapy and now they've used up their fourth day off this year and so they're getting a warning. And you say, oh no, no, no, they're not! It says in FMLA that it qualifies.

With the support of the FMLA, the union is "always successful" in such disputes, in part because the union simply knows the law better than many employers do and runs "a lot of workshops" to be sure union members and staff are well informed:

> Employers are very frequently not going by the law, don't know what the law is, don't understand it. Employees are confused, too, but there does seem to be a fairly decent recognition that there is a law out there that says something about this, and maybe I should ask my union rep. . . . Sometimes they'll have us fax them some of the regulations from the Department of Labor which they show the employer, and a lot of times the answer is, oh, really?

Given misinformation, and misuse of information about the law, unions did still work to ensure its broad use and interpretation:

> We want to expand the scope of the interpretation to the extent that we can, and the companies want to narrow it. It's just a totally converse relationship. . . . We keep encouraging local unions to negotiate into their contracts these gray areas.

Others made it clear that they played an active part in enforcing existing law so there would be fewer violations. One spoke about the union's role in a recent court case:

> We filed suit on this issue of family and medical leave. We went to court and there was an out-of-court settlement agreed to on this issue, but we were told we could not advertise this. But the company was violating FMLA right and left. You name it, they were violating it.

The union knew there was a problem, but was not aware of its extent until an anonymous source in management sent the tip-off and supporting materials. Workers "were saying, I have to go down to Florida—my parent just had a heart attack," and the company was refusing permission, as well as requiring unreasonable documentation prior to any approval, "just violations right and left in terms of being unreasonable."

> The company was so mad about the FMLA, they felt it put their absence control plan totally down the toilet; immediately [the company] tried to implement a very restrictive absence control plan in retaliation for the FMLA—so we had to work to get rid of that, which we finally did; it was part of the court settlement. But it was such an enormous fight. It took up a huge amount of our time.

Why Benefits Are (or Are Not) Won

While many of our informants emphasized the range of family benefits unions supported and won, some unions were more supportive in general of these issues—and won more—than others. Of the 13 national unions that our external experts assessed, four negotiated and won a high level, two a medium level, and seven a low level of work-family benefits.

Why such variation? Several possible explanations need to be evaluated. The first emphasizes cultural expectations; the remainder, structural factors. (1) Work-family issues are a top priority for some but not most members. (2) Gender of members is crucial; women care far more about the issues than do men. (3) The members (who, by this point, are more than 40% women) are eager for these benefits, but the leadership (which is often male, white, older, entrenched, and concerned above all with holding onto their jobs) has resisted making any effort. (4) Unions have tried to win these benefits, but the resistance of employers, especially combined with the weakness of unions, has limited the gains.

We use two sets of data to address these explanations for variation. First, we present our informants' comments about each of the explanations. Second, we use expert assessments of, and quantitative data about, 13 national unions to analyze the factors associated with union success in obtaining work-family benefits.

Members' Expectations

Many of our informants emphasized the power of culture, rooting their explanations in members' expectations. Most union leaders we interviewed agreed that the membership is not aggressively demanding either child care or family leave:

> When I travel, I don't hear this groundswell of excitement about family medical leave.

> Because you're only going to get as much at the table as the membership pushes for in the workplace.

> To be honest with you, the work and family issues (with the exception of the 7-day campaign)—day care facilities, getting extra FMLA paid time off, getting additional holidays and vacation time—it's close to the bottom of the list. Job security is always the number one issue. Improving health care and improving pensions is almost always ranked number two and number three.

Some reported that they had done surveys, showing these were not the priorities that members list:

> It's not as hotly felt an issue as other things. . . . In other words, if we didn't get it, we weren't going to get elected out of office. The members weren't really holding our feet to the fire about this.

> We do a survey, and we ask them what their priorities are, and we'll list some family issue stuff in there, and it will fall low on the list of priorities.

> I think that what we find over and over again is that if you do a survey of the membership in a particular local or council, you will find that child care might rank at best third, maybe fifth. Number one would be wages, number two would be benefits and health care. There might be some other things going on, but even among people who are desperate for better child care and can't afford what they have, wages and health care are going to come first, in part because with higher wages you could buy better child care, and then you add in everyone who doesn't have a child care need right now. I think child care will never be first, but that doesn't mean it's not incredibly important to people.

Several factors limit the likelihood that a substantial fraction of the membership will see family benefits, especially child care, as a union priority. The first is that child care "is a distinct period in any worker's life." Second, not only is it most pressing only when the children are young, but in order to be employed at all workers must find a way to care for their children; those that are unable to do so are (probably) no longer in the workforce.

> People find that at one particular point or three or four particular points it's a crisis for them, that they *have* to find a solution—so they find a solution. So the next month if you ask them, they might be back to wanting wages again, because whatever they found, at least they have some level of comfort there because they keep getting to work every day, and if they don't keep getting to work every day, they are no longer there to respond to the union's survey.

At least equally important are members' cultural expectations: Most do not feel that it is their right or privilege to demand help from others, especially employers, with their families. That is an individual responsibility:

> It's still the culture of the society that people believe that if you have kids, then it's your problem, that people really haven't broken through yet that society should be taking some responsibility for working parents' responsibility for their kids. If you can't handle it, you shouldn't have had them. I think that's still the norm out there.

As one informant noted:

> People still believe that things like child care are their own burden. They are not society's burden; they are not their employer's burden; it is not the union's job. It's just something they have to do. They chose to have these kids, and they just have to deal with it.

Union leaders who are committed to these issues compellingly argue that member survey responses are misleading, dramatically understating the issues' potential. Members, these leaders argue, do not feel entitled to expect employers to address their problems:

> You've got a membership that has been trained to think that the most that they can expect out of their employer is money as opposed to benefits: Give me better pay, and I'll make the arrangements.

Members think that way for a simple reason: "Because it's their reality."

> That's why, in poll after poll, you'll find out women or men are not likely to list child care as an employer benefit as something new to put high on their list; they're far more likely to identify higher pay or health care as top priority. That doesn't mean they don't have acute problems, but there's just not the history that makes you think that employers will take this up. If your employer won't even allow you to get your kid covered to go see the doctor, why would you expect that your employer is going to provide quality child care?

Thus, even though there is an acute need for child care, there is also a lack of what an economist would call "member effective demand," and this shapes and constrains union activity. If members aren't asking for it, why should unions make it a priority? And if staff or leaders wish it to be a priority, will members support them?

While these assessments of our respondents seem convincing, we do not have quantitative measures or outside experts' assessments of variation on this cultural dimension. Consequently, we cannot more systematically address the extent to which this factor influences the level of benefits fought for and won.

Gender of Members

A central operating assumption of most, if not all, of our key informants, is that women's presence in the union is key to the ability to make family issues a part of the union's agenda and contract negotiations. This assumption appeared again and again in the interviews:

> I'm absolutely sure that in most places you're going to find women behind these initiatives.

> Our union is predominantly male, and now I'm speculating. However, it could be that the lack of excitement is due to the fact that perhaps they're not the primary caregivers.

> After all, we *are* a construction union. We don't have many women. Of course, we are very concerned about these issues, but they are not our highest priority; we are concerned more to support the AFL-CIO, since these issues don't affect our members.

Albeit quite limited, our more quantitative data also suggests that the gender of union members matters. The three unions with low female membership (<25%) all have low work-family benefits, and three of the five unions with high (>50%) proportions of women members are high in work-family benefits (while two are medium). Of the four unions with medium proportions of women members (25-50%), three have low work-family benefits and one is high.

A view stressing the centrality of gender reinforces the understanding of family caregiving as women's responsibility. To be sure, this view is rooted to some extent in the reality of experience: A great deal of literature shows that women far more than men provide care for children as well as other kin and are responsible for arranging that which they do not provide (see, e.g., Gerstel & Gallagher, 1994; Gerstel, 2000; Di Leonardo, 1987; Rossi & Rossi, 1990). Union informants see that reality. However, especially among the married, men financially support their children, at least in large part, and younger men (as a number of our informants emphasized) are doing at least somewhat more of the work of parenting. They are or could be stakeholders in these policies. Consequently, with a changed perspective, these work-family policies would be viewed as financial benefits fitting comfortably within a male breadwinner role.

Moreover, from our intensive interviews, it became evident that "gender" appeared to have its impact through structure, which was subject to change and which many of our informants saw changing. Some men took a lead on these issues, but

If you scratch beneath the surface you see that these men have been the sole support of their children because their wife died or because they got custody of their children, and when they're in the same position that we're in of having primary responsibility for the family, all of a sudden they get it.

The rise of single-parent fathers had created a new constituency, and with them taking a visible stance "it was not a women's issue, it was a member issue." One enthused: "I've been amazed at the increase in calls I get from fathers who are the sole support of their kids." In one key city, two of the men who had been very active in pushing for better benefits both had wives who had recently died of cancer. At a meeting on work-family issues, one of the leading women activists said with a laugh, "I hope we don't have to all die for you guys to get it."[5]

The Importance of Leaders

Women are 40% of union members but a smaller proportion of leaders and a much smaller proportion of top leaders—for example, they are 13% of the AFL-CIO Executive Council. Based on more general organizational analyses that find women executives are more likely than their male counterparts to advocate for work-family benefits, we expect that the presence of women leaders in unions might also be significant. Some of our informants articulated such views: "My feeling is that this is 90% an issue of lack of women being in positions of power in the trade union movement to shape an agenda, and a lack of men leading on it." Although this was the most extreme formulation of the position, several informants argued that women's presence in leadership makes a significant difference, and they expect these issues to assume a higher priority as more women move into leadership positions.

Our data do not allow us to disentangle the effects of gender of membership from gender of leadership—all the unions with a high percentage of women leaders also have a high percentage of women members, and all of the unions with a low percentage of women members also have a low percentage of women leaders. Although we must be cautious about interpreting these data, gender of leadership does appear to be related to the level of work-family benefits won: Of eight unions with low proportions of women leaders (<15%), seven have low levels of work-family benefits (though one has high benefits); of five unions with high (>25%) levels of women leaders, three have high, and two have medium, levels of work-family benefits.

However, only a minority of our informants in the intensive interviews highlighted gender of the leadership as a key factor in explaining union support for work-family benefits. It is true that these issues did not tend to be a priority for most union leaders and they were not mobilizing their constituency around these issues. At the same time, though, it cannot be said that they were holding back a wave of protest. A number felt that the leadership was not out front on the issue, and they linked that position back to the membership. They suggested leaders would be prepared to support campaigns if the members wanted to do so. As one informant said,

Even if the president is not fabulous but just okay, if there are women who are pushing I think it makes a difference because most sort-of 'okay' men are not going to stick their necks out if there's not a constituency that's saying to them this is an issue that we want you to follow through on.

Union Strength and Employer Resistance

As we have argued, both cultural expectations and social characteristics of members and leaders are important for winning family benefits. At the same time, the resistance of employers, especially combined with the weakness of unions, can obviously limit any gains.

Central to overcoming employer resistance, our informants argued, was showing them the ways that family benefits are in their interest. One union faced employer complaints about worker absenteeism and tardiness.

> The union said we have an idea: We suspect that a lot of the absenteeism and tardiness and distraction have to do with people's concerns about their families outside of work, while they're at work. Let's put together a program that addresses those concerns and put some concrete support in it, i.e., money, and we think that's going to address your concerns as well.

Similarly, one union found that it had won paid family leave at only a handful of locals, and "It was in units where worker retention was important. It was either in remote areas or in industries where they were struggling with trying to hire qualified workers or workers who would stay." In fact, sometimes the employers "were the ones who proposed the language."

As more general literature on work-family benefits has shown, employers may grant benefits which they believe inexpensive but are reluctant to grant any benefit that they think will cost a significant amount of money. Resource and referral programs, and altered tax treatment of child care expenses, are relatively cheap for employers, "so they're easy to win. Subsidies are much more expensive; they're harder to win." But the cost of a program is not always a simple matter. The strength of the employer's opposition is crucial, with victories most likely when the employer can see (or be shown) some benefits for their bottom line.

As important, however, is the strength of the *union*, itself determined in large part by organizing. For example, we interviewed officials at two local unions because they had won the best child care benefits; both represent a high proportion of workers in their jurisdiction. In an interview, one of us made the remark that it takes innovative ideas to win, and the informant immediately responded, "It takes innovative ideas, but it also takes power to get the employers to do it." An informant reported that at her international, the local with the best policy has "got a good part of their market up there organized. You can't do this if you've got 20% of the stores organized, because you have no clout." When we asked an informant at a union with one of the two best policies why they had been able to win the benefits, the response was, "We are an active union. The members are extremely active and participate." Our follow-up query asked why members were active on these issues and not others, and the informant rejected that formulation:

I don't think that's the particular way to look at it; our members are active, period. . . . When you've successfully, continually, and aggressively organized non-union [establishments], you're able to maintain an increased standard of living for the members, and so that's our top priority. We're able to continue to grow so the standards have been able to include things like child/elder care. Does that make sense? If you do not continually organize, you become less and less powerful where you are. If your power diminishes, you're unlikely to be able to negotiate new programs like child/elder care. We're a fighting union. We have one of the highest quality-of-life experiences for [industry] workers in the country, and it's because we are constantly organizing our members to stand up and be involved in constantly organizing non-union properties. That's the core of our existence, and that's why we're able to do breakthrough things like this.

Although it is again very difficult to disentangle the effects of union strength from other structural factors, the data from external experts at least do not disconfirm our speculation that the strength of unions matters for the winning of work-family benefits. Three unions were classified as low in strength; all three have low levels of work-family benefits. Six unions were classified as medium in strength: two have high and four have low levels of work-family benefits. Four unions were classified as strong: Two have high and two have medium levels of work-family benefits. Although obviously limited, these data, too, lend some support to the view that structure—here the strength of the union itself—is important for explaining variation among unions in their support for work-family benefits.

Conclusion

Unions have been almost invisible in academic analyses of work and family issues. At least two factors contribute to this. First, academics have neglected unions in general, and thereby have missed an opportunity for fresh insights; second, unions have not—*yet*—played a major role in shaping the work-family agenda.

By now it is not news that issues look different depending on the standpoint of the observer. But despite frequent references to "race, class, gender" analysts frequently neglect class and rarely remember unions, workers' most important collective organizations and voice.[6] A union perspective advances our understanding of work-family issues in four ways.

First, why does the conventional framing of work-family issues include child care, family leave, and flextime, but exclude many other issues? Why has the field drawn the lines where it has, and should the lines stay where they are? Because we too were absorbed in the perspective of the field, we initially did not think to ask these questions. We would now suggest that what a group sees as a work-family issue depends on its circumstances. If a benefit can be taken for granted, or if it seems clearly beyond reach, people will not (routinely) think of it as a work-family benefit; instead, attention will focus on benefits that are contested but within reach. For professionals and managers, sick pay, vacation days, and family health care can now typically be assumed, but child care and family leave are less certain. For workers and unions, sick pay (for the worker—never mind to take care of a child), health benefits for family members, and vacation days are uncertain but winnable (and can, of course, have a huge impact on family life); hence, union leaders' insist that these should be counted as work-family issues. Across unions, we find support for these benefits—like vacation days or family health care—that have *not* been conventionally understood as family issues. In some subset of unions, we find strong support for precisely those issues—like child care or paid family leaves—that are conventionally understood as work-family concerns.

Thus, our second argument is that unions—like employers, families, and workers—are not monolithic. Hoffman (1987) argued some time ago that, when studying consequences for families, it rarely makes sense to simply ask whether a woman is employed or not (instead of asking about the character of her employment). In a similar vein, Baron et al. (1986) have insisted it makes little sense to treat a job as a job (using job titles or broad occupational categories) when assessing the benefits associated with employment arrangements (see also Kalleberg et al., 1996; Lambert, 1999). So too, we found, it rarely makes sense to refer to "the" union position. Hence, it is counterproductive to use a dichotomous variable about union membership in quantitative analyses of work-family issues. Some unions bitterly oppose flexible schedules; others push for them. Most unions put child care low on their priority list; some fight for some forms of child care. Meaningful evaluations of unions must take into account this variation.

Third, from the perspective of workers and unions, the first necessity for any benefit is that it be affordable. To the affluent, it may seem obvious that parents would want the highest possible quality child care. But if a top quality day care center charges more than workers can pay, it is less help than lower quality, but affordable, benefits. So, too, what one group of workers assumes is "top quality" may not be viewed in the same way by other workers. The most successful union child care benefits offer workers a range of options. One union, for example, reimburses members $100 a month for informal care and up to $225 a month for licensed care (which is considerably more expensive); nonetheless, the informal care subsidy is much more popular. Recently the union has added a new element: if an unlicensed provider attends a union-sponsored training program, the reimbursement to the member increases by $25, from $100 a month to $125 a month. The union is recognizing that workers prefer informal care, but it is working to increase the formal skills of those that provide such care.

Fourth, although collective bargaining contracts are one important means to obtain family benefits, workers win their greatest advances when the state becomes involved. The Family and Medical Leave Act is a good example. Although the FMLA covers only about half of all workers, that is still substantially more than are covered by collective bargaining contracts. The law is weak, but unions can and do build on it in at least two ways. First, using the law as a base, unions negotiate to extend the benefits provided by the law; they negotiate, for example, paid leaves or longer leaves. Second, because employers often ignore the law, government monitoring is ineffective, and workers rarely know their rights or how to enforce them, unions help workers enforce the rights legally won. The law itself, and the campaign to pass the law, increase public awareness and thus make it more likely that workers will approach the union seeking assistance. Workers and unions thus benefit from the public awareness generated by a campaign driven primarily by feminist organizations like the Women's Legal Defense Fund (now called the National Partnership for Families) and NOW.

The neglect of union perspectives comes not only because of an academic blindspot regarding unions, but also because unions have not yet had a major impact on these issues. In 1989 a Bureau of National Affairs study projected that "work and family concerns may become the dominant issue of the 1990s for the American labor movement" (Bureau of National Affairs, 1989, p. 4). That has not yet happened. Our interviews indicate the potential for unions to play a significant role in a transformed and invigorated social movement focused on work-family issues. That will not happen if unions wait for members to raise this issue as a priority. We do not yet have a public culture where workers feel entitled to demand work-family benefits.

One response to this situation might be to blame the members, or to sit back and wait for a general cultural shift. Those feelings de facto shape the responses of some union leaders, who would like to move on the issue but feel that their hands are tied. Others, however, make a compelling counterargument and have actually carried through the victories that demonstrate their case. These leaders argue that in fact the potential demand is there, if workers and the union could break through the sense that they have no right to expect good work-family policies. Once a policy is in place, they argue, it will develop a powerful constituency, so the problem is "only" how to win that entering wedge.

The union that won one of the most impressive child care programs did so primarily because of the efforts of one leader.

> I felt very strongly that this was an issue that we all needed to address through using our collective power, and all of us were looking at it as a personal problem and workers were looking at it as a personal problem because there weren't widespread policies. People would think, what can the union do? They [wanted] more wage increases, more holidays, and they wouldn't think about child care because there weren't a lot of models out there.

Rather than simply accepting this, she pushed hard to make this a union priority, even *without* evidence that members viewed this as one of the most important issues. Because of her position as one of the leaders of the bargaining team, she was in a position to say to the employers:

> No settlement without [child care]. Basically, that's what I had to say. [The employers] said, "This is not going to be a strike issue if we don't give it, and it's not going to be a deal breaker." And I said, "How do you know? You could put this either way: I could say this is not that great, it's not going to be a deal buster for your side either. Your employers are not going to not approve this whole package if you added [a small amount] for child care. And no, I'm not recommending to the negotiating committee that they approve this unless you say yes."

With the threat of a strike over the issue, with child care as a potential issue that would prevent an agreement from being reached, employers accepted a fund, with payments equal to a small percentage of payroll. Once the fund was won, it *created* a constituency and a sense that workers had a right to expect this, such that now there is no going back (at least not without a major fight). As one informant noted about one of the largest existing programs:

> Last year we served 8,000 children with some type of child care benefits, but we had benefits requested on behalf of 29,000 children. So we could use 1% or 1.5% of payroll. The fact that this large amount of people are requesting child care or some type of benefit—whether it's after-school care or weekend care, summer camp, whatever—[means that] if the employers try to take this away right now there would be an absolute uproar.

Our interview with another union that has won a similar benefit indicates that they had a strikingly similar experience. Although members wanted the benefit, demand for it was not especially pressing. Once it was won, however, the union was surprised at the enthusiasm of the response:

> We set up an application week in which we intended to open the first day at 7:00 A.M., first come first served, and there were people standing outside the office at 3:00 A.M. in the dark in [a dangerous downtown area] with their children, waiting to apply. We realized how insensitive that was of us. The next year we had an in-person application week run by lottery, so if you came in anytime during that week, you would be a participant in the lottery and we would award your benefits in the order in which your numbers were pulled out of a hat.

As these examples suggest, unions have the potential to serve as social movement entrepreneurs, mobilizing resources that could make work-family issues a priority in the populations that have been least able to win benefits. A charismatic and committed union leader (often a woman), along with women members and union strength, makes that all the more likely. Historically, social movements mushroom when they break out of their past confines and tap into new constituencies and networks. This is what happened to the labor movement in the 1930s, as the craft base of the past gave way to industrial unions (Bernstein, 1970); to the student antiwar movement, when it moved outside elite institutions and expanded into the mass of public colleges and universities (Gitlin, 1980); and to the gay liberation movement, when it moved beyond respectable professionals and incorporated the bar scenes of San Francisco and New York (D'Emilio, 1983). These past expansions have changed the character of movements, redefining the issues and introducing new cultural styles, with the initial core group often opposed to this transformation and uncomfortable with the new participants. Work-family issues, programs, and victories have been primarily associated with professionals and managers. A movement would gain much momentum by expanding its base to more fully include the groups currently represented by unions. Doing so would change the movement's issues and priorities, make some of the current leaders uncomfortable, and have the potential to create a far more powerful movement. At the same time, including work-family issues would lend new momentum to labor unions themselves, challenging some entrenched leaders but increasing unions' appeal to women and younger workers, two of the demographic groups unions are striving to incorporate.

An earlier version of this article was presented at the Sloan Conference on Work and Family and UC, Berkeley, March 2000, San Francisco. We would like to thank the Political Economy Research Institute for supporting this research, and Robert Zussman, Mary Ann Clawson, David Smith, and three outstanding anonymous reviewers for comments and suggestions. We also thank those we interviewed, who were generous with their time, and outside experts (who asked to remain anonymous), who provided assessments for two of our key measures.

Notes

1. These figures include not only members of labor unions but also members of employee associations similar to labor unions, such as the National Education Association. Data are for 1999 and come from the Bureau of Labor Statistics web site (stats.bls.gov/news.release/union2t01.htm). Other racial groups are not included in these calculations.

2. To be sure, respondents mentioned other conventional work-family issues, like elder care, domestic violence, and homework, but they figured far less prominently in most discussions and, especially given space constraints, we have not focused on them here.

3. As Carre et al. (2000) point out, a wide range of terms has been used to describe the various forms of nonstandard employment, including alternative, flexible, nontraditional, and market-mediated. In this section, we use both "flextime" and "alternative work schedules" to refer to the range of shifts and time on the job.

4. As Budd and Brey (2000) show in their analysis of a national sample of workers, union members have greater knowledge about their rights under the FMLA than do those not members of unions.

5. Given our argument that the relevant factor is structural—primary responsibility for raising a child—rather than biological, our theory would be better tested by data on the percentage of members who had primary custodial responsibility for children, but those data are not available.

6. For economics, Freeman and Medoff (1979, p. 69) found that the percentage "of articles in major economic journals treating trade unionism dropped from 9.2% in the 1940s to 5.1% in the 1950s to 0.4% in the early 1970s." We know of no comparable study for sociology, but would expect comparable results.

References

AFL-CIO Working Women's Department. No date [1998?]. Fact sheets. Web site www.aflcio.org.

Armenia, A., Gerstel, N., & Fisher, G. (1990). *Taking time off for family: The FMLA and gender neutrality.* Paper presented at Work and Family: Expanding the Horizons Conference, San Francisco.

Auerbach, J. (1990). Employer-supported child care as a woman responsive policy. *Journal of Family Issue, 11,* 384–400.

Baron, J., Blake, A. D., & Bielby, W. (1986). The structure of opportunity: How promotion ladders vary within and among organizations. *Administrative Science Quarterly, 31,* 248–273.

Bernstein, I. (1970). *The turbulent years: A history of the American worker.* Boston: Houghton Mifflin.

Bravo, E. (1990). *The job-family challenge.* New York: Wiley.

Bronfenbrenner, K., Friedman, S., Hurd, R. W., Oswald, R. A., & Seeber, R. L. (Eds.) (1998).

Organizing to win: New research on union strategies. Ithaca, NY: ILR/Cornell University Press.

Budd, J. W., & Brey, A. (2000). *Unions and family leave: Early experience under the Family and Medical Leave Act.* Unpublished paper. Bureau of National Affairs.

Budd, J. W., & Brey, A. (1989). *Work and family and unions: Labor's agenda for the 1990s.* Special Report #20. Washington, DC.

Burstein, Paul, & Wierzbicki, Susan. (2000). Public opinion and congressional action on work, family, and gender, 1954–1990. In T. Parcel & D. Cornfield (Eds.), *Work and family: Research informing policy.* Thousand Oaks, CA: Sage.

Carré, F., Ferber, M., & Golden, L. (2000). *Nonstandard work: The nature and challenges of changing employment arrangements.* IL: Industrial Relations Research Association.

Chung, Y.-D. (2001). *The two faces of unionism: A dual closure approach to contradictory behavior in U.S. labor unions.* Doctoral dissertation, North Carolina State University.

Clawson, D. (2001). *The next upsurge: Labor fuses with social movements.* Unpublished manuscript.

Cobble, D. S. (1993). *Women and unions: Forging a partnership.* Ithaca, NY: ILR Press.

Cobble, D. S. (1994). Recapturing working-class feminism: Union women in the postwar era. In J. Meyerowitz (Ed.), *Not June Cleaver: Women and gender in postwar America, 1945–1960* (57–83). Philadelphia: Temple University Press.

Deitch, C., & Huffman, M. (2001). Family responsive benefits and the two-tiered labor market. In R. Hertz & N. Marshall (Eds.), *Work and family: Today's realities and tomorrow's possibilities.* Berkeley: University of California Press.

D'Emilio, J. (1983). *Sexual politics, sexual communities: The making of a homosexual minority in the United States, 1940–1970.* Chicago: University of Chicago Press.

Deutsch, F. (1999). *Halving it all: How equally shared parenting works.* Cambridge: Harvard University Press.

Di Leonardo, M. (1987). The female world of cards and holidays: Women, families, and the work of kinship. *Signs, 12,* 440–453.

Fantasia, R. (1988). *Cultures of solidarity: Consciousness, action, and contemporary American workers.* Berkeley: University of California Press.

Feldberg, R. L. (1987). Women and trade unions: Are we asking the right questions? In C. Bose et al. (Eds.), *Hidden aspects of women's work* (pp. 299–322). New York: Praeger.

Freeman, R. B., & Medoff, J. (1979). The two faces of unionism. *Public Interest, 57,* 69–93.

Freeman, R. B., & Medoff, J. (1984). *What do unions do?* New York: Basic Books.

Fried, M. (1998). *Taking time.* Philadelphia: Temple University Press.

Galinsky, E. (2001). Toward a new view of work and family life. In R. Hertz & N. Marshall (Eds.), *Work and family: Today's realities and tomorrow's possibilities.* Berkeley: University of California Press.

Galinsky, E., Bond, J. T., & Friedman, D. E. (1990). The Role of Employers in Addressing the Needs of Employed Parents. *Journal of Social Issues, 52,* 111–136.

Gerstel, N. (2000). The third shift: Gender and care work outside the home. *Qualitative Sociology, 23,* 467–483.

Gerstel, N., & Gallagher, S. K. (1994). Caring for kith and kin: Gender, employment, and the privatization of care. *Social Problems, 41,* 519–538.

Gerstel, N., & McGonagle, K. (1999). Job leaves and the limits of the Family and Medical Leave Act: The effects of gender, race, and family. *Work & Occupations, 26,* 510–534.

Gifford, C. D. (1997). *Directory of U.S. labor organizations.* Washington, DC: Bureau of National Affairs.

Gifford, C. D. (1998). *Directory of U.S. labor organizations*. Washington, D.C.: Bureau of National Affairs.

Gitlin, T. (1980). *The whole world is watching: Mass media in the making and unmaking of the New Left*. Berkeley: University of California Press.

Glass, J., & Estes, S. B. (1997). The family responsive workplace. *Annual Review of Sociology, 23,* 289–313.

Glass, J., & Fujimoto, T. (1995). Employer characteristics and the provision of family responsive policies. *Work and Occupations, 22,* 380–411.

Golden, L., & Figart, D. M. (Eds.) (2000). *Working time: International trends, theory, and policy perspectives*. London: Routledge.

Goodstein, J. (1994). Institutional pressures and strategic responsiveness: Employer involvement in work-family issues. *Academy of Management Journal, 37,* 350–382.

Gross, H. (2001). Work/family and globalization: Broadening the scope of policy analysis. In R. Hertz and N. Marshall (Eds.), *Work and family: Today's realities and tomorrow's possibilities*. Berkeley: University of California Press.

Gross, J. A. (1995). *Broken promise: The subversion of U.S. labor relations policy, 1947–1994*. Philadelphia: Temple University Press.

Grundy, L., & Firestein, N. (1997). *Work, family, and the labor movement*. Changing Work in America series. Radcliffe Public Policy Institute, Cambridge, MA.

Grundy, L., Bell, L., & Firestein, N. (2000). *Labor's role in addressing the child care crisis*. Foundation for Child Development Working Paper Series.

Guthrie, D., & Roth, L. M. (1995). The state, courts, and maternity policy in U.S. organizations: Specifying institutional mechanisms. *American Sociological Review, 64,* 41–63.

Hartmann, H. (1976). Capitalism, patriarchy, and job segregation by sex. *Signs, 1,* 366–394.

Hoffman, L. (1987). The effects on children of maternal and paternal employment. In N. Gerstel & H. Gross (Eds.), *Families and Work* (pp. 362–396). Philadelphia: Temple University Press.

Hyde, J. (1990). Women and maternity leave: Empirical data and public policy. *Psychology of Women Quarterly, 19,* 299–313.

Kahn, P., & Blum, L. (1998, November–December). Not just 9 to 5: The problems of nonstandard working hours. *Working USA,* 50–59.

Kalleberg, A. L., Marsden, P., Knoke, D., & Spaeth, J. L. (Eds.) (1995). *Organizations in America: Analyzing their structures and human resources practices*. Thousand Oaks, CA: Sage.

Kelly, E. (1999). *Maternity leave policies in changing legal environments*. Paper presented at University of Massachusetts, Amherst.

Kelly, E., & Dobbin, F. (1999). Civil rights law at work: Sex discrimination and the rise of maternity leave policies. *American Journal of Sociology, 105,* 455–492.

Knoke, D. (1996). Cui bono? Employee benefit package. In A. Kalleberg, D. Knoke, P. V. Marsden, & J. L. Spaeth (Eds.), *Organizations in America*. Thousand Oaks, CA: Sage.

Lambert, S. J. (1999, March). Lower wage workers and the new realities of work and family. *Annals,* AAPSS, 174–189.

McCarthy, J. D., & Zald, M. D. (1977). Resource mobilization and social movements: A partial theory. *American Journal of Sociology, 82,* 1212–1241.

Milkman, R. (1990). Gender and trade unionism in historical perspective. In L. A. Tilly & P. Gurin (Eds.), *Women, politics, and change*. New York: Russell Sage Foundation.

Mitchell, O. S. (1997). Work and family benefits. In F. Blau & R. Ehrenberg (Eds.), *Gender and family in the workplace* (pp. 269–279). New York: Russell Sage Foundation.

Morris, A. (1984). *The origins of the civil rights movement*. New York: Free Press.

Nussbaum, K. (1998). Women in labor: Always the bridesmaid? In J.-A. Mort (Ed.), *Not Your Father's Union Movement* (pp. 55–68). New York: Verso.

Osterman, P. (1995). Work/family programs and the employment relationship. *Administrative Science Quarterly, 40,* 681–700.

Presser, H. (2000). Non standard work schedules and marital instability. *Journal of Marriage and the Family, 62,* 93–110.

Rossi, A. S., & Rossi, P. H. (1990). *Of human bonding: Parent-child relations across the life course*. New York: A. de Gruyter.

Seyler, D. L., Monroe, P. A., & Garan, J. C. (1995). Balancing work and family: The role of employer-supported child care benefits. *Journal of Family Issues, 17,* 170–193.

Stinchcombe, A. L. (1965). Social structure and organizations. In J. G. March (Ed.), *Handbook of organizations* (pp. 142–193). Chicago: Rand McNally.

Western, B. (1996). *Between class and market: Postwar unionization in the capitalist democracies*. Princeton, NJ: Princeton University Press.

16
The Contradictory Effects of Work and Family on Political Activism

Rebecca E. Klatch

While feminist scholarship in the past 25 years established the intrinsic connection between family and work, little attention has been paid to how work and family intersect with the political world. Other than the literature which focuses on the family as an institution of political socialization of children, few studies focus on how women's and men's commitment to work and/or family affects political commitment or, on the other hand, how commitment to politics affects one's work or family commitments. This essay analyzes these issues, examining the interrelationship between work, family, and political activism. I use the term *work* here to refer to paid labor outside of the home, i.e., jobs or careers. Based on a study of 1960s activists of the left and right, I find contradictory effects of commitments to family and work on sustained commitment to politics over the life course.

Method and Sample

In a comparative study of left- and right-wing activists of the 1960s I conducted life histories with 74 activists from two youth groups of the 1960s: Students for a Democratic Society (SDS), the leading organization of the New Left, and Young Americans for Freedom (YAF), the most prominent organization of youth on the right. Both SDS and YAF were founded in 1960. While SDS was more well-known and visible during the 1960s, YAF was the leading student group on the right and served an important role as a training ground for a whole generation of conservative leaders, many of whom hold positions of political prominence today (Andrew, 1997; Klatch, 1999). In comparing left and right I was interested in the interorganizational similarities and differences as well as the intraorganizational differences within YAF and SDS. For example, within YAF there were crucial differences between traditionalists, those who adhere to a religious and social conservatism, and libertarians, those who believe in the free market and individual liberty. Such differences proved critical to YAF's history (Klatch, 1994; Klatch, 1999). These ideological differences also provided an opening for the eventual convergence of libertarians in YAF and countercultural elements within SDS. One of the surprising findings of this study was the parallels and convergence between libertarians and leftists during the late 1960s as well as the commonalities shared by libertarians and leftists in their adult lives.

The sample of former SDS and YAF activists was selected based on the following criterion: All those chosen were committed activists who had been active for at least two years in SDS and/or YAF, with most involved for many more years.[1] I also wanted to compare women and men; the final sample of activists contains 34 female activists, equally divided between SDS and YAF, and 40 male activists, 19 from SDS and 21 from YAF. Although a serious attempt was made to diversify the sample racially, because both organizations primarily were comprised of white activists, all activists interviewed are white except for three black activists in SDS and one in YAF. Activists were also chosen to get a mix of both leaders and rank-and-file activists. In SDS the sample contains 24 rank-and-file members and 12 who were part of national leadership and/or were at the Port Huron conference, 6 of whom were women (50%); the YAF sample consists of 23 rank-and-file members and 15 members who held national office and/or were at the founding Sharon conference of YAF, 2 of whom were women (13%). However, among the rank-and-file activists, some in the sample were leaders of local chapters. I also chose people who were active in a range of locations across the country.

In addition, the sample was chosen to reflect the ideological differences within each group. YAF activists include 25 traditionalists and 13 members who defined themselves as libertarian, reflecting the approximate proportion of traditionalists and libertarians in the organization. The SDS sample includes five Progressive Labor members or sympathizers, five Weathermen members or sympathizers, and two RYMII (Revolutionary Youth Movement Two) members or sympathizers; the majority of SDS activists were either unaffiliated with any factions during the 1969 splits (12 activists) or were uninvolved in SDS politics by 1969 (12 activists).[2]

In addition to life histories, this study is also based on participant-observation at reunions of 1960s activists of the left and right as well as on archival research of the organizational materials of SDS and YAF including papers, newsletters, pamphlets, correspondence, and other documents.[3]

I trace the political socialization of these individuals across the life course, examining the families they came from and the early influences which led them to politics as well as the complexity of forces which led them to embrace an activist identity. I also trace what happened to them during the 1960s, as leftists and libertarians became radicalized, and follow them from the end of the 1960s through their adult years. This article focuses on what happened to activists during their adult lives. How were their adult lives shaped by the politics and activism of the 1960s? In particular, how did their commitment to paid work and family affect their commitment to politics? In turn, how does commitment to politics affect decisions regarding families and children? How do people with a passion for politics look to the worlds of paid labor and family to express their beliefs and values? And, at the same time, how do work and family commitments impede political commitment?

One of my main findings in comparing leftists, traditionalists, and libertarians is that across the spectrum politics remains central to the identity of these activists over time. Yet as people age they also face new issues of identity which compete with their immersion in politics. In particular, identities as workers, spouses, and parents compete with their identity as activists. Throughout the life course the salience of these competing identities shifts so that at certain times identity with a profession or as a parent competes with, or even supercedes, identity as a political activist. I will discuss first the contradictory effects of work on political commitment and then turn to the contradictory effects of families on political commitment.

The Pull of Occupational Life

One of the main preoccupations for activists during the 1980s and 1990s was finding employment that is meaningful. Having spent many years during their youth consumed with politics, during their adult lives work and the choice of occupation increasingly became central to their definition of identity. But libertarians followed a different path from traditionalists in YAF. Libertarians and leftists remained both geographically and vocationally mobile from the 1970s to the 1990s, spending months or even years wandering between jobs and locations, unclear about their direction. Traditionalists, on the other hand, followed more straightforward paths from politics to their adult work lives.

Many leftists reported a restlessness and uncertainty over the past two decades, taking winding paths to their present occupations. Some activists were still uncertain of their futures at the time of the interview or reported they were living "economically marginal" lives, a comment none of the traditionalists made. Leftists tended to follow experimental and tentative paths in their adult lives. Jack Whalen and Richard Flacks's (1989) follow-up study of radical leftist activists in Santa Barbara found a similar struggle over vocation, a refusal to settle down or focus on material comfort.

Some libertarians also drifted between jobs and locations over the past two decades. In part this wandering is connected with the effects of the counterculture. Unlike traditionalists, who abhorred the counterculture of the 1960s, many libertarians embraced the counterculture in beliefs and lifestyle during the 1960s and continued to be involved in counterinstitutions and alternative lifestyles long past the end of the decade (Klatch, 1994). Like many leftists, some libertarians also were still trying to figure out their futures at the time of the interview or were drifting between jobs and locations. On the whole, though, libertarians have more stable job histories and more settled occupational lives than do SDSers.

In sharp contrast to both libertarians and leftists, however, traditionalists spent none of the past two decades wandering about, uncertain or tentative about their future. Typically, traditionalists moved from one political job to another, following a course that has brought many of them to positions of political prominence today. In fact, Washington is full of ex-YAFers working in think tanks or as political consultants or heading conservative organizations. YAF contacts have been critical in building the network of conservative organizations in Washington today (Klatch, 1999; Andrew, 1997).

When I compared the current occupations of these three groups, I once again found parallels between libertarians and leftists as distinct from traditionalists. Overall, at the time of the interview, both SDSers and libertarians were concentrated in nonprofit organizations, social service agencies, and educational institutions, while traditionalists—particularly traditionalist men—were predominantly in positions with direct political affiliations, such as working in political consulting firms, campaigning, and working on conservative journals. In short, many traditionalists, particularly men, are seated in institutional positions of political power. In contrast, the main base for leftists and libertarians has been colleges, universities, and other educational institutions. Their influence comes mainly through teaching and scholarly research, rather than through traditional political means. These different locations of activists indicate that political ideology has direct effects on choice of occupation.

Meanwhile, over half of traditionalist women became full-time homemakers, a position only one SDS woman and none of the libertarian women chose. Thus, among traditionalists, political beliefs and commitment led to different consequences for women and men in terms of commitment to career and families, a point I will return to later.

In sum, like other follow-up studies of leftist activists (Whalen and Flacks, 1989; Fendrich and Lovoy, 1988; Fendrich and Turner, 1989; Jennings, 1987; McAdam, 1989; Abramowitz and Nassi, 1981), I found that contrary to media stereotypes leftists have not sold out, abandoned their principles, and become preoccupied with making money. Rather, *like activists on the right,* they are employed in jobs that are consistent with their beliefs and values.

Jobs and Careers as an Extension of Politics

As activists chose occupations, they confronted the issue of how to integrate politics into their adult lives. Some people resolved this dilemma by choosing work that embodied their political beliefs. For example, traditionalist YAFer Emmy Lewis now owns a company that specializes in direct marketing, membership development, and fund-raising. Her clients include the Republican National Committee, the Republican Senatorial Committee, and the National Right to Work Committee. She sees her job as a direct expression of her politics: "When I get up before groups and talk about direct mail, I evangelize because it's the most important mass communications tool we conservatives have ever had."[4]

Some libertarians and leftists also have found jobs that directly express their politics. For instance, in 1982 libertarian Sheldon Richman began working as associate editor for *Inquiry,* a libertarian magazine started by people affiliated with the Cato Institute. When *Inquiry* fell apart in 1984, Sheldon spent a year with Citizens for a Sound Economy. In 1985 he began working as public affairs director for the Institute of Humane Studies, an educational organization located at George Mason University, which supports libertarian scholars. At the time of the interview Sheldon was senior editor at IHS, overseeing all of the printed material at IHS, as well as teaching and editing libertarian books. He also writes about foreign policy for *Liberty,* a journal of libertarian thought.[5] On the left, former Weathermen leader Bernardine Dohrn is now director of the Children and Family Justice Center at Northwestern University. She acts as the legal advocate for children and families, researches children's experiences in legal systems, and works to improve Chicago's juvenile court system. She sees her work in juvenile justice as a change in tactics, not substance: "It's a lens to see the whole world, all the issues of justice and equality and peace, all the issues I care about."[6]

While some people have found occupations that embody their politics, others hold jobs completely separate from their politics. These jobs are not a vehicle for the expression of politics, yet even for these people political values continue to shape their work lives. SDSers in particular pointed out the ways in which politics informs their work, discussing how the skills and knowledge they acquired in the movement help them in their professional lives. For example, Lynn Dykstra (a pseudonym), formerly involved in the Weathermen, is a surgeon. She said what she learned about oppression helped her survive a male-dominated system and taught her to speak out about problems that she, as well as others, faces in her work life. Her values also inform her relations with patients, both in terms of spending more time with them and having a broader, more tolerant perspective.[7]

Another SDSer, Derek Barron (a pseudonym), is currently a judge. Although this career prohibits explicit political involvement, Derek sees his work as directly connected to his values and beliefs:

> "My attitude toward change is that I have a responsibility to use the means at my disposal, the resources [and] the contacts that I have, the position that I hold, to bring about change that I feel is worthwhile for those in need. It very often means calling upon a lot of skills that I've had to develop over time . . . that in some ways, important ways, are related to the skills that I developed in the civil rights movement. There's no question that a lot of it is organizing, just no question, but without an explicit ideological agenda."[8]

For Lynn and Derek, as well as for other activists, their political values inform and infuse their work lives. The fundamental experiences of the 1960s provided skills, values, and perspective that help them in their professional careers.

Occupational Life as a Competing Interest

Regardless of their present occupations, the majority of activists continue to be involved—to one degree or another—with politics. For some people this means occasional participation in and/or giving money to organizations that embody their beliefs, while others have sustained a more constant involvement in the political world. Some people are sporadically involved, moving in and out of the political world. Why do people drift in and out of politics? One reason for the decline in time and energy devoted to politics is commitment to jobs and careers. For those people who are not in occupations that are directly political, politics becomes a competing interest. Whereas during their youth time was plentiful and most people had few job or family responsibilities, now the competing interests of both work and family infringes on the time and energy needed to sustain activism.

For some, work has taken on primary importance, surpassing their commitment to politics. Their identity as professionals has replaced their primary identity as political activists. Typically, libertarian YAFer Marilyn Bradley (a pseudonym) is now a top administrator at a liberal arts college. Marilyn works until 7:30 each evening and also serves on boards and educational committees, requiring frequent weekend travel. She says:

"As immersed as I was in politics, I have been that immersed in professional life over the past ten years. . . . My priorities have shifted. . . . I took the same energy . . . [and] ability in leadership and I just plopped it into my profession. . . . I'm not involved politically. I would like to be, but I just don't have the time. I'm burning on all jets right now."[9]

Marilyn's priorities have shifted. Saying she hopes to be politically active again sometime in her life, she doesn't see that happening soon. In addition to her career, she has a young son. Her commitments to work and family fill up her life, leaving little time or energy for politics.

One interesting difference among activists is that SDSers are more likely to be plagued by doubts about whether they are doing the right thing in their current lives than are YAFers. Leftists seem to be less settled and more critical about the conflicting pulls between career and politics, as well as with their current lifestyles. As history professor Michael Kazin puts it, "When we're worrying about how to pay for a new carpet upstairs, I still feel—and I hope I always will feel—"What are we doing? We should be out there doing some kind of homeless work. . . . I should be working more with the labor movement."[10] Michael says he integrates his beliefs into his teaching, but even this does not seem enough; compared with his former life as a full-time activist, he feels he lives too easily. Other leftists express this sense of dis-ease about the direction of their lives, wondering whether and how they are contributing to social change. More so than libertarians or traditionalists, leftists continue to wrestle with the choices they've made, questioning the gap between their youthful days standing outside the mainstream, leading their lives in a critical fashion, versus their adult lives centered on work, family, and more material concerns. Such questions continue to nag at them. As Dorothy Burlage comments:

"Everybody that I know . . . we all say the same thing. . . . We *still* don't feel comfortable that it's all right [to have a career]. . . . It's a feeling of not living as meaningful a life as I did before, of not being as committed to my ideals as I was before, feeling like I have to make a lot of compromises to survive."[11]

For these leftists plagued by doubts, commitment to careers and professional identity conflicts with their core identity as activists.

A minority from both SDS and YAF have withdrawn from politics completely, no longer wanting to put time and energy into that part of their lives. But even among these activists, the majority say they would come "out of retirement" if the right issue or cause came along. A core part of their identity remains tied to activism, dormant in their consciousness but available for future causes. In short, despite the range of involvement, for the majority of people on both the left and right, politics continues to define their adult lives and to pose important questions in their everyday world. Their adult lives are complicated, however, by the pulls of work. Families also beckon activists away from politics.

The Pull of Families

The other main pull away from politics is family. As they've aged, many activists have married, had children, bought homes, and settled down. While the majority of both SDS and YAF activists have married, not surprisingly, traditionalists are much more likely to be married than leftists or libertarians. In my sample, 80% of traditionalists, 58% of SDS activists, and 46% of libertarians were married at the time of the interview. As with their work lives, libertarians and leftists are less likely to conform to conventional norms of adult life than are traditionalists. In other words, there is an association between political beliefs and the likelihood of marriage.

Gender also plays a role in who is likely to marry. Among libertarians and leftists, men are more than twice as likely to be married than are women. While divorce accounts for some of these unmarried women, 25% of libertarian women and 41% of SDS women never married, in contrast to *none* of the traditionalist women. Given that activists were in their 40s and 50s at the time of the interview, these never-married women represent a marked departure from convention. Two of these never-married women, both SDS activists, are lesbians. Most of the remaining women say being single was involuntary, not a conscious choice. Yet this, too, represents a marked departure from traditional norms.[12]

It is not surprising that traditionalists also have more children overall than either libertarians or leftists. Traditionalists had an average of 2.8 children, compared to 1.5 for leftists and 1.2 for libertarians. Further, about one third of traditionalists have four or more children, compared to only two SDS men, one libertarian man, and *none* of the leftist or libertarian women. Again, these statistics are compelling as marked demographic differences associated with varying political beliefs and experiences.

In short, libertarians and leftists have followed different paths from traditionalists not only in terms of careers and mobility but also in terms of lifestyle and families. Both groups—and particularly the women in each of these groups—continue to lead less conventional lives. Final evidence of this difference is the fact that while four SDS activists identify themselves as gay or lesbian, none of the YAF activists do. Richard Flacks (1988) argues that decisions about whether to marry or how to spend one's leisure time are private, individual matters which, when socially patterned, take on public, historical meaning. Given the participation by libertarians and leftists in the counterculture and their consequent differences in lifestyle from traditionalists, these configurations of individual lives represent a renegotiation of the terms and conditions of everyday life. They indicate the impact of political beliefs and commitment on sexuality, marriage, and family relations.

Families as Sustaining Political Activism

Families act in contradictory ways: They sustain commitment to politics as well as pull individuals away from the political world. In terms of supporting activism, the vast majority of activists on both the left and right chose partners with beliefs similar to their own, people who understood and supported their passion for politics. In fact, many activists met their partners through their political activities. YAFer Anne

Edwards, for instance, met her husband, Lee, through a letter to the editor of *New Guard,* YAF's monthly magazine. She says she could "no more marry out of my politics than out of my religion because it's a set of values."[13]

Many activists commented that they could not even imagine being involved with someone who did not share their political views, saying that a marriage of people with opposing views would be difficult. Sheldon Richman, for example, says it would be impossible to marry someone with divergent views. Sheldon's wife is also a libertarian and enjoys politics even more than he does. He says:

> "It would be inconceivable [to marry someone with divergent beliefs] . . . because I had a couple of relationships with non-libertarians and . . . it didn't lead to big blow-ups . . . but it was enough that had it gone on, it probably would have become a problem. I can recall just watching the news and making a comment and the other person totally doesn't understand that comment. Those would be hard conditions to live under. . . . It would be like being in one religion and marrying someone of another religion."[14]

Many other activists also comment that a marriage of people with opposing political views would be hard, adding stresses and strains to married life. SDSer Michael Kazin is married to a woman seven years his junior, who entered high school at the end of the 1960s. Although she didn't share Michael's experiences, she does share his leftist values and beliefs. Michael says:

> "I couldn't imagine . . . having a long-term relationship with somebody who I had major differences with about politics. Because politics is not just politics, it's philosophy. . . . She's a doctor and if [she] believed that national health insurance was a terrible thing . . . I would have a hard time living with someone like that. A hard time living with someone who thinks that black people are complaining too much about racism. . . . Also, if she thought politics was unimportant . . . that would be tough. Relationships begin with sexual attraction, but obviously they don't last 13 years if that's all there is."[15]

Although gay SDSer Aldyn McKean would not expect a man he's involved with to be an activist, Aldyn says he would need to share his political values:

> "It would be difficult for me to have a serious relationship with someone who did not basically support my politics. . . . There's no way that I could ever be involved with someone who was basically conservative and voted for Republicans. There are gay people who are like that, although somehow [he laughs] I don't understand them."[16]

A number of SDS members said that in addition to wanting partners with similar beliefs, they also need their friends to share their political views. In particular, the 1960s serve as a common frame of reference for many leftists. Some feel they cannot be friends with someone who was uninvolved or had opposing views during the 1960s. SDSer Barbara Haber comments:

> "It's hard for me to connect deeply with men who were not involved in the 1960s or who don't have that passion about social change. Most of the men I've been involved with

have been people who were activists. But that's not enough for me. I want them to still care now. . . . All my close friends are political in some way or other. . . . So my life is filled with people who in one way or another are political. We talk politics a lot, and our expectations about relationships come from the 1960s. And we help each other to understand our experiences through that lens."[17]

In this way, partners and friends with shared beliefs and experiences reinforce activists' values, sustaining their involvement in the political world. For many people devoted to politics, shared perspectives and experiences become a basis for *choice of a romantic partner or spouse.* As with choice of occupation, political commitment shapes the expectations and decisions these individuals make regarding whom to marry, live with, or even be friends with. Because activism is a part of their core identity, as they've aged these people continue to fill their lives with other like-minded individuals who share their passion for politics.

Families as Competing Interests

Yet families also pull people away from politics. In particular, having children creates a shift in priorities. Parenthood becomes a competing identity, absorbing time and energy. Both SDS and YAF activists talked about how their commitment to their children has become primary. As SDSer Naomi Schapiro, a lesbian who now has a partner and two daughters, puts it:

> "I'm going to have to be less active certainly until the kids are a little older because I didn't have kids in order to go to meetings all the time. . . . Also, I don't think I have quite as much energy as I did when I was 20. . . . I'm also committed to spending a lot of time with my kids. So it means that instead of writing a leaflet at ten at night, I'm scrubbing the bathroom because there wasn't any time to do it during the day or preparing supper for the next day or else just bed because I'm so tired."[18]

The shortage of time faced by those trying to balance full-time employment with raising children was also mentioned by SDSer Cathy Wilkerson. She says:

> "I sat down actually about a month ago . . . to figure it out. I have seven free hours a week that I can use for something assertive as opposed to just keeping my finger in the dike. . . . That includes reading; it includes everything. So you don't have time to do anything."[19]

It's not that the will to continue activism has abated; rather, at this stage of the life cycle the responsibilities of family and work act as disincentives to political participation.

Having children inhibits activism not only because it limits a person's time for other things but also because being a parent makes an individual more careful, less willing to take risks. As SDSer Bernardine Dohrn says:

> "Having kids throws you into a whole other way of seeing the world that in some ways is much richer and broader and multidimensional and something that you can relate to lots

of people. But it also makes you slow down around taking risks and being able to make a whole set of decisions. . . . You have to come home that night and make dinner."[20]

In addition, many activists found that getting older and having children leads to a more settled life, involving homeownership or stable employment. This, too, acts as a disincentive to political activism. SDSer Michael Kazin says both his career move to Washington to begin a job as a professor, and having children, have taken him away from activism. At this stage of life, his priorities have shifted:

> "You know, having a house and a mortgage—It's banal, but it's true. Those things do have an impact [on political activity]. . . . And so does age. I like to have more than five hours sleep a night. I think more about planning for a few years down the line because . . . I don't have all the time in the world and there's things I want to get ready. And, if I were honest with myself, that's really more important right now than my politics."[21]

Thus, competing responsibilities for jobs, families, and children, combined with a more settled lifestyle, diminish the time and energy needed for the sustained political commitment these activists had in their youth.

While libertarians and leftists discuss this dilemma of finding time for politics amidst the balancing act of work and family, few traditionalists mention it. One reason for this difference is the fact that traditionalists are more likely to be in marriages in which women are full-time homemakers, alleviating the conflict between work and home. Thus, the way marriages are arranged in terms of the division of labor also affects the amount of time and energy available for politics.

Unlike libertarian and leftist women, over half of traditionalist women in this study became full-time homemakers. Once they began having children, these traditionalist women withdrew from both politics and paid employment. While a few of these women work part-time out of their homes, all feel their primary responsibility is to their families. These women don't face a time crunch between jobs, family, and politics. Rather, they have set their families' needs above politics or career. What is particularly fascinating is that several traditionalist women who had been leaders of the "pro-family movement" decided to leave politics behind and dedicate themselves to family. Some of these women say it was a contradiction to live the lifestyle of feminists while calling for traditional roles. Mary Fisk, a traditionalist YAFer, has forfeited politics to devote herself to her children. Now divorced from a former YAF leader, Mary is committed to staying at home with her son and daughter. She says politics is "low down on the list of priorities":

> "[Politics is] not what's important to me. My family's what's important to me, especially now as a single parent. . . . If I have time, I want to spend it around the home with my children. I'm very active in church stuff. It's not really burnout; it's just a shift. I only have so much energy and [politics is] not a burning thing for me anymore.

Like some of the other traditionalist women, Mary says in retrospect she was trying to lead a liberated life that didn't work for her:

> When we were married . . . I had . . . everything the world says you're supposed to have. I had accepted the stereotypes of the feminists. And I felt betrayed. . . . I had the career. I was editor of a legal magazine. . . . I was going to Georgetown for my Ph.D. in philosophy. And I had this wonderfully upwardly mobile husband. But it wasn't enough. So that's when I started saying, 'What do I really want?' I want roots, I want a home, I want a family. That's what was important.

Mary worked until a week before her son was born. It never occurred to her that she would want to stay home with him; she assumed she would be bored to death. She returned to her job five weeks after he was born, but about six months later she realized that the highlight of her day was coming home to her son. She comments, "I was so blinded by the stereotype that I had accepted that this was liberation. So I was growing into my own definition of liberation. Not somebody else's."[22] Mary now works part-time out of her house doing desktop publishing. She's also involved with a group called Mothers at Home, a nonprofit organization that serves as an information source and support group for women who stay at home with their children. While a few of these traditionalist women seem to have retired from politics altogether, others say they will come out of retirement once their children are grown. When Kathy Rothschild married, she quit her job as director of the American Legislative Exchange Council, a conservative organization founded in 1973 to help elected representatives share ideas concerning public policy. Kathy moved to Chicago with her husband and now devotes herself to her two daughters. Kathy admits she misses her job and politics but also knows she is doing what she wants and hopes to return to politics one day.

> It would be untrue if I said I didn't miss politics, but I don't pine for it. I don't wake up every morning thinking, "Gee, I wish I were there." . . . I imagine I will [return to politics]. Once it is in your blood, it is in your blood. [But] my priorities now are my husband and my home and our children. . . . To do it right takes a lot of time.[23]

While traditionalist women are dedicating themselves to caring for their families, their husbands are free to continue their wholehearted dedication to politics. As discussed previously, many traditionalist men are now in occupations with direct political affiliations. Meanwhile, because none of the libertarian women and only one SDS activist are full-time homemakers, they continue to face the conflict of balancing paid work and family responsibilities, leaving little time or energy for political action. In these ways families inhibit activism, as people are torn between the multiple identities in their lives.

Conclusion

For this cohort of political activists, so immersed in politics in their youth, family and paid work have contradictory effects. While both can draw people further into the political world, each may also act to deter involvement. While work can operate as an expression of politics, or even a direct enactment of political beliefs and agendas, occupational life also acts as a competing interest drawing energy and time away from political involvement. Similarly, while families can act to support and enhance political beliefs, sustaining commitment to activism, children in particular act as competing interests, drawing people's time and energy away from immersion in the political world.

Whether they balance the demands of jobs and home or whether they concentrate on their family's needs, activists on both the left and right have less time and energy for politics than they did in the past. In contrast to their youth, when they were immersed in politics day and night, now careers, families, and involvement in schools and churches are competing interests pulling them away from the political world. Although careers and involvement in schools may also have political meaning, few of these former activists define such activities as "political" compared to their full-time dedication to politics during their youth. While their beliefs and values hold true, and few people shift far from the ideals of their youth (Klatch, 1999), for these activists the demands of family and jobs have consequences for sustained commitment to the political world. As activists have aged and found meaningful work, become parents, bought homes, and settled down, activism is no longer the master identity of their youth. At this stage of the life cycle, the responsibilities of work and home absorb the time and energy of many activists in contrast to their youth. While they still may be more politically engaged than the average American citizen, for many activists there is a disjuncture in their level of involvement between their past and present lives.

However, two caveats are in order. First, given the intense commitment to politics these activists had during their youth, it would be impossible for their involvement to have *increased* over time. It is important to recognize that this is a necessarily skewed sample because people were chosen based on their very high level of involvement with politics during their youth. The only possibilities, then, would be for people to either sustain the same level of commitment or to decrease involvement over time. Because of this very select sample, this study represents only one possibility of the effects of paid work and family on political involvement. For other people, political commitment may in fact be *motivated* out of their commitment to family or to work. Indeed, vibrant social movements centering on labor issues, educational issues, or children's rights may awaken political consciousness and provoke other sectors of the population to activism *through their work lives and concern for families*. Analysis of the interrelationship between work, family, and political engagement and such movements would necessarily entail different kinds of studies and would yield variations on political socialization over the life cycle.

Second, it remains to be seen whether for these activists of the 1960s there will be renewed involvement as they age. Once children are grown, and as these activists retire from work, there may be renewed opportunities for engagement with the political world. Given the centrality of politics to their core identity, we may see a resurgence of high levels of activism for this cohort as their time and energy is freed from the realms of paid work and family responsibilities. In this way work and family not only have contradictory effects but may also have shifting effects on political activism over the life course.

Notes

1. I say "and/or" because I was surprised to find a small number who became involved in both SDS and YAF; these were primarily people who initially were involved on the right but who ended up shifting their beliefs to join SDS during the mid- to late 1960s (see Klatch, 1999).

2. The interviews focused on four sets of issues: (1) *Background and upbringing.* This included questions on the demographic backgrounds of activists and their parents, parents' political and religious beliefs, family dynamics, and early political and sex role socialization. (2) *Political involvement and organizational experiences.* Questions focused on how and why individuals became involved, the experiences of men and women in YAF/SDS, and the development of ideology. (3) *Interpretations of key events* of the 1960s, including the 1964 and 1968 elections, the assassinations of John F. Kennedy, Robert Kennedy, and Martin Luther King, the civil rights movement, the Vietnam War, the counterculture, etc. (4) *Post-1960s lives.* Questions focused on changes in lifestyle (occupation, religion, marriage, children, etc.) as well as any shifts in political beliefs during the past 20 years.

3. For a complete discussion of the methodology of this study, see Klatch, 1999.

4. Interview with Emmy Lewis, March 13, 1990.

5. Interview with Sheldon Richman, March 20, 1990.

6. Interview with Bernardine Dohrn, September 12, 1990.

7. Interview with Lynn Dykstra (pseudonym), November 10, 1990.

8. Interview with Derek Barron (pseudonym), June 7, 1991.

9. Interview with Marilyn Bradley (pseudonym), August 15, 1991.

10. Interview with Michael Kazin, July 19, 1989, and May 2, 1991.

11. Interview with Dorothy Burlage, July 23, 1989.

12. Doug McAdam found a similar "marital gap" among women and men who participated in Freedom Summer. See McAdam (1988, pp. 220–223).

13. Interview with Anne Edwards, July 10, 1989.

14. Interview with Sheldon Richman, March 20, 1990.

15. Interview with Michael Kazin, July 19, 1989, and May 2, 1991.

16. Interview with Alydn McKean, November 28, 1989.

17. Interview with Barbara Haber, December 6, 1990.

18. Interview with Naomi Schapiro, October 27, 1990.

19. Interview with Cathy Wilkerson, March 6, 1990.

20. Interview with Bernardine Dohrn, September 12, 1990.

21. Interview with Michael Kazin, May 2, 1991.

22. Interview with Mary Fisk, April 30, 1991.

23. Interview with Kathy Rothschild, September 13, 1990.

References

Abramowitz, S. I., & Nassi, A. J. (1981). Keeping the faith: Psychological correlates of activism persistence into middle adulthood. *Journal of Youth and Adolescence, 10,* 507–523.

Andrew, J. A. (1997). *The other side of the sixties: Young Americans for Freedom and the rise of conservative politics.* New Brunswick, NJ: Rutgers University Press.

Fendrich, J. M., & Lovoy, K. (1988). Back to the future: Adult political behavior of former student activists. *American Sociological Review, 53,* 780–784.

Fendrich, J. M., & Turner, R. W. (1989). The transition from student to adult politics. *Social Forces, 67,* 1049–1057.

Flacks, R. (1988). *Making history: The American left and the American mind*. New York: Columbia University Press.

Jennings, M. K. (1987). Residues of a movement: The aging of the American protest generation. *American Political Science Review, 81,* 367–382.

Klatch, R. (1994). The counterculture, the new left, and the new right. *Qualitative Sociology, 17,* 199–214.

Klatch, R. (1999). *A generation divided: The new left, the new right, and the 1960s*. Berkeley: University of California Press.

McAdam, D. (1988). *Freedom summer*. New York: Oxford University Press.

Whalen, J., & Flacks, R. (1989). *Beyond the barricades: The sixties generation grows up*. Philadelphia: Temple University Press.

Contributors

Ernestine Avila is a graduate student at the University of Southern California and does research on Latina immigrant nannies, the emotional labor associated with their paid work and how motherhood practices and care work are transformed by immigrant women who live and work in the U.S. while their children remain in their countries of origin. Her dissertation, a qualitative study, explores the challenges and issues that Mexican and Central American immigrant transnational mothers and fathers encounter and how they cope.

Christopher Carrington is Assistant Professor of Sociology and Human Sexuality Studies at San Francisco State University. He is the author of *No Place Like Home: Relationships and Family Life among Lesbians and Gay Men* (Chicago: University of Chicago Press, 1999). He is also the author of a forthcoming book about the gay dance and circuit party scene entitled: *Circuit Boys: Into the World of the Gay Dance and Circuit Party Culture*. His research interests include ethnographic methods, family studies, gay/lesbian sexuality and the sociology of deviance and social conformity.

Dan Clawson's current interests focus on the contemporary U.S. labor movement. He teaches sociology at the University of Massachusetts at Amherst and is a member of the Coordinating Committee of Scholars, Artists, and Writers for Social Justice, which strives to build connections between academics and the labor movement. He is the co-author of *Dollars and Votes: How Business Campaign Contributions Subvert Democracy* and the editor of *Required Reading: Sociology's Most Influential Books*.

Marianne Cooper is a doctoral student in sociology at the University of California, Berkeley. Her research on fathers in Silicon Valley grew out of her interest and specialization in sociology of gender, family, and work. Her work was funded by a fellowship from the Cal@Silicon Valley Fellowship which supports graduate students whose work makes contributions to high-tech industry.

Francine M. Deutsch, a Professor of Psychology at Mount Holyoke College, is the author of *Halving it all: How equally shared parenting works* (1999, Harvard University Press), a National Science Foundation sponsored study of the division of domestic labor among dual-earner couples. Her articles on gender and the family have been published in the Journal of Personality and *Social Psychology*, *Psychology of Women Quarterly*, *Sex Roles*, the *Journal of Family Issues*, and *Current Directions in Psychology*. Her most recent research examines the gendered life plans of Chinese college seniors in the People's Republic of China.

Naomi Gerstel, a Professor of Sociology at the University of Massachusetts, Amherst, focuses on gender, carework, and family and work policy. Recent articles address the effect of women's employment on care to family and friends, family policy of unions and the Family and Medical Leave Act, the contextual character of men's caregiving, and the effect of children on the care women and men provide.

Marjorie L. DeVault is Professor of Sociology and a member of the Women's Studies Program at Syracuse University. She received her Ph.D. from Northwestern University and writes on women's work, household life, and qualitative and feminist research methodologies. She is the author of *Feeding the Family: The Social Organization of Caring as Gendered Work* and *Liberating Method: Feminism and Social Research.*

Pierrette Hondagneu-Sotelo is Associate Professor in the Department of Sociology, and in the Program in American Studies and Ethnicity at the University of Southern California. She is author of *Gendered Transitions: Mexican Experiences of Immigration* (University of California Press 1994),and *Domestica: Immigrant Workers Cleaning and Caring in the Shadows of Affluence* (University of California Press 2001).

Rebecca Klatch is Professor of Sociology at University of California-San Diego. She is author of *Women of the New Right* and of *A Generation Divided: The New Left, the New Right, and the 1960s.* She has also written articles on social movements, family politics, and the formation of feminist consciousness.

Demie Kurz is in the Women's Studies and Sociology departments at the University of Pennsylvania. Her primary research is in the area of gender, the family, and carework. Her current research, on families with teenage children, incorporates the perspectives of both parents and children and explores how families negotiate children's progression from dependency to autonomy. Her book on divorce, entitled *For Richer, For Poorer: Mothers Confront Divorce* (Routledge 1995), analyzed the social and economic impact of divorce on a diverse group of families. On the Steering Committee of the Carework Network (a network of researchers, policy makers, and activists concerned with promoting further understanding of carework), Kurz is also co-editing a book, *Gender, Citizenship, and the Work of Caring.*

Annette Lareau is an Associate Professor in the Department of Sociology at Temple University. She is the author of *Home Advantage: Social Class and Parental Intervention in Elementary Education* which won the Willard Waller Award for Distinguished Scholarship. With Jeffrey Shultz, she is editor of *Journeys Through Ethnography: Realistic Accounts of Fieldwork.* At present, she is completing a book which analyzes social class and race differences in children's daily lives.

Andrew S. London is an Associate Professor of Sociology at Kent State University. His ongoing research spans three domains: the impact of welfare reform on women and children; the organization and consequences of informal HIV-related care; and the influence of remarriage on family structure and functioning around the turn of the 20th century. In addition to his work with Ellen Scott on the Project on Devolution and Urban Change and the Next Generation Project in Cleveland, he also works with a team of researchers analyzing data from the HIV Cost and Services Utilization Study, a nationally representative, longitudinal study of persons in care for HIV.

Nancy Myers, R.N., M.Ed., is a doctoral candidate in Medical Sociology at Kent State University. She has extensive experience in the planning and implementation of population-based health programs, as well as health policy development. Her research interests include the ways in which sociologists contribute to the social construction of health/illness, as well as ways to bridge the gap between social science research, health policy, and medical practice.

Margaret K. Nelson is the Hepburn Professor of Women's and Gender Studies and Sociology at Middlebury College. She is the co-author, with Joan Smith, of *Working Hard and Making Do: Survival in Small Town America* (University of California Press, 1999). She is currently working on a book about single mothers.

Stacey Oliker is Associate Professor of Sociology and Urban Studies at the University of Wisconsin-Milwaukee. She is the author of *Caring and Gender* (with Francesca Cancian), *Best Friends and Marriage: Exchange Among Women,* and articles about welfare reform. Currently she is studying networks of support after AFDC.

Mary Pattillo-McCoy is Associate Professor of Sociology and African American Studies, and Faculty Fellow at the Institute for Policy Research at Northwestern University. Her areas of research are race and ethnicity, urban sociology and qualitative methods. She is author of *Black Picket Fences: Privilege and Peril among the Black Middle Class* (University of Chicago, 1999).

Ellen Scott is an assistant professor at the University of Oregon. Her current research focuses on the impact of welfare reform on women and children. With Andrew London, she is a principal investigator on the Cleveland ethnographic component of Manpower Demonstration Research Corporation's Project on Devolution and Urban Change and on the Next Generation project. Her previous research has focused on racial politics in feminist organizations.

Lynet Uttal is an Assistant Professor in the Department of Human Development & Family Studies at the University of Wisconsin, Madison. Trained as a sociologist at the University of California, Santa Cruz (Ph.D., 1993), her research interests include the relationships between employed mothers and childcare providers, how they are sharing childrearing in the new markets of childcare services, and how communities of care form around childcare arrangements. She regularly teaches "Racial Ethnic Families in the U.S." and "Qualitative Research Methods."

Carrie Yodanis is a researcher and lecturer at the University of Fribourg in Switzerland. She received her Ph.D. in Sociology from the University of New Hampshire. She continues to conduct research on families, with a focus on women, work, inequality, and violence.

Robert Zussman is Professor of Sociology at the University of Massachusetts-Amherst. He is the author of *Mechanics of the Middle Class: Work and Politics among American Engineers* and of *Intensive Care: Medical Ethics and the Medical Profession*. He is the editor of *Qualitative Sociology* and one of the editors of *The ASA Rose Series in Sociology*. He is currently working on a study of "autobiographical occasions."